John E. Odegaard

Thank you for being a leader who understands that the language of conscience is not words but the motivation of the heart, and for your part in creating a culture of character for today and tomorrow.

作为一位社区领袖，您深谙道德的理念不仅仅是宣传，更重要的是身体力行。我十分欣赏您对此问题的深刻理解，同时也十分感谢您为当代与未来创造一个具备鲜明特征的文化所做出的贡献。

Gracias por ser un lider que entiende que la lengua de la conciencia es no palabras sino la motivación del corazón, y para su parte en crear una cultura del carácter para hoy y mañana

અંતરમાંથી આવતી અવાજ ફક્ત શબ્દો જ નથી પરંતુ હ્રદયમાંથી આવતી પ્રેરણા છે એવું સમજવા માટે અને આજ અને ભવિષ્યનું ચારિત્ર્યનું ઘડતર કરવા માટે જે ફાળો તમે આપ્યો છે, એવા આગેવાન બનવા માટે આપનો આભાર.

תודה על היותך מנהיג שמבין כי שפת המצפון איננה מילים, אלא הנעה של הלב ועל חלקך ביצירת תרבות האופי של היום ושל מחר.

अंतःकरण से आती आवाज़ केवल शब्द नहीं है, परंतु हृदय से उत्पन्न होती प्रेरणा है। ऐसी बोध शक्ति वाले नेता होने के लिए और, आज और कल के चारित्र्यबंधारण में योगदान के लिए आपका धन्यवाद।

Tieman H. Dippel, Jr.

Thank you for being a leader who understands that the language of conscience is not words but the motivation of the heart, and for your part in creating a culture of character for today and tomorrow.

你为一位领袖而受赞誉，您深谙良知的理念不仅仅是言语，更重要的是身体力行，同时也十分感谢您为当代及未来创造的品德的促进。

Gracias por ser un líder que entiende que la lengua de la conciencia no es palabras sino la motivación del corazón, y por su parte en crear una cultura del carácter para hoy y mañana.

[Hebrew text]

[Hindi text]

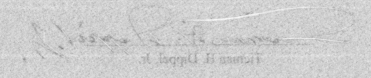

Thomas H. Dippel Jr.

Instilling Values in Transcending Generations

Bringing Harmony To Cultures Through the Power of Conscience

Tieman H. Dippel, Jr.

Book Three of The Language of Conscience Series

Texas Peacemaker Publications, L.L.C.

Published by Texas Peacemaker Publications, L.L.C.
Brenham, Texas

Distributed by BookMasters, Inc., 30 Amberwood Parkway, Ashland, Ohio 44805
(800-537-6727)

Cover design by Tim Snider and Ryan Feasel of BookMasters, Inc.

Library of Congress Cataloging-in-Publication Data

Dippel, Tieman H.
 Instilling values in transcending generations : bringing harmony to cultures through the power of conscience / Tieman H. Dippel, Jr.
   p. cm. -- (The language of conscience series ; bk. 3)
 ISBN-13: 978-0-9721608-4-1
 1. Social ethics. 2. Political ethics. 3. Conscience. I. Title. II. Series.
 HM665.D56 2006
 170--dc22
                 2005035181

Dedication

This book and the Language of Conscience Series are dedicated to:

- ❖ Those who seek a civilization governed by the ethics of morality rather than the rationalization of relativity;
- ❖ Those that recognize the belief that the nature of man should be shaped by the enlightenment of conscience rather than the promotion of convenience;
- ❖ Those that understand that the concept of individual responsibility builds a nation's strength of character rather than concentration on the expansion of entitlements through the concept of victimization;
- ❖ Those who are willing to engage the political correctness of the times to help produce a culture that brings out the best in man because they recognize their obligations of conscience to each other and the benefits of compassion.

They recognize that great acts come from perseverance and patience in building the foundation of a stable society through maintaining its values or, at the very least, a society, which has in place a set of ideas that can compete for positive leadership in times of crisis.

In either scenario, their actions may be unappreciated during their lifetime, but they join an international and generation-transcending "band of brothers" tied together by honor and respect for the obligation of every man to better society. They receive the wisdom of those that preceded them in life. They bestow that knowledge on the next generation, but they also must engage their peers in their era, arguing for sacrifice and the morality of conscience against the great power of convenience. Their God's glory is intelligence, which brings light and truth.

Theirs is often a thankless and controversial task whose reward is years hence when crisis forces actions and choices. But they are the stewards of civilization, the uncommon few, who may speak different languages and develop different cultures but see life with a sense of a warrior's honor and character that provides obligation. If they fail to keep stability and balance in society, the culture eventually deteriorates and the rise in another form is more difficult and often more suspect.

They are the unsung heroes—not just because of what they do, but why they do it.

Contents

Foreword

The world is often filled with commentary, advice, and sensationalism; the challenge for people is to develop a model or framework from which to filter information and sort what's valuable from the waste. Only by doing so can one harness information to make a positive difference. *Instilling Values in Transcending Generations* has developed the concept of Enlightened Conservatism. It follows in the work of Rene' Descartes who thought the complex could be made simpler through reason.

In his book, Dippel takes ideas of the past and demonstrates their relevance for the future. Maslow's Hierarchy of Needs and how it affects human perceptions is balanced equally with Rambam's Eight Levels of Charitable Giving that moves in philanthropy from giving grudgingly to the ultimate concept of giving a man an opportunity in order that he may be independent. It looks to the nature of man and realizes that at any time society can be dominated by a culture of conscience, which is driven by affection and honor, or by convenience, which is often driven by fear and greed.

Dippel believes that the tremendous expanse of technology, education, and communication as energized by market systems will challenge the existing cultural values and economic interests of almost all societies. It is friction between enlightenment and existing cultural value structures that will have great impact upon the stability of all societies. To him the critical issue that determines the balance between these forces rests in the perception of the individual dignity of each member of society. Dippel looks at the three powers that affect the concept of individual dignity. These are the powers of economics, of politics, and of culture. He points out the competitiveness of politics and economics by their very nature and notes that culture, which is the one major binding force beyond economic and political alliances, is the one truly based on common values. To him the preservation of basic concepts like the Golden Rule, the Common Good, and the Rule of Law are the concepts that need to be understood within a culture. He develops the concept of the triangles of Enlightened Conservatism, a method of thought through analysis, trends, and measurements of the forces and powers that interreact within society.

Dippel demonstrates in dramatic fashion that what values shall govern society is increasingly critical. The world has become increasingly multicultural. We have reached a defining moment in determining how societies shall operate in the future. We must choose between individualist and collectivist values or an acceptable combination that is based on individual responsibility and respect for human dignity. He focuses upon the point that the culture gives us law, not law the culture.

His goal, as he did with the Texas Lyceum and many other organizations, is to provide a framework of discussion that gains the respect of all sides because of its sense of honor. This important trend—the nature of our culture and whether it will be peer driven to conscience or convenience— is one dominant theme.

The important theme in the book is the rise of Asia and the tremendous economic, political, and cultural consequences of globalization. To him the significant player is China, although the U.S., India, Brazil, and a combined Europe will have impact. But China's growth rates and the economic relationship with the United States will be one of the most critical factors in the strategic direction of the future.

Whether China and the U. S. come to understand each other in a cooperative fashion or become significantly competitive is one of the great-undecided issues of the present time.

To Dippel, these two ideas converge; the world of the future must find some common values or civilization will disintegrate. Dippel argues for a culture of responsibility. This is the reason that much of his life has been spent in building character-based organizations in Texas. As the son of a famous Texas sheriff and a devout Christian mother, his set of values are consistent but from a different perspective. He looks at religion as based upon free choice; people should serve as examples and not try to force others to adopt their views. But, he looks at justice from a sheriff's perspective. That blend provides an interesting framework for understanding the world.

At the Fund for American Studies we have been educating young leaders since 1967 about the values of freedom, democracy, and free market economies. Our goal has been the preparation of young people for honorable leadership by educating them of the benefits of freedom in both theory and practice. Our efforts in Eastern Europe have shown the validity of the ideas of freedom and personal responsibility. The great question in this next decade is whether a culture conducive to freedom can be developed in countries that have for many years been centrally controlled.

One part of the Fund's work looks very specifically at the concept of obligation to others, which is why we founded the David R. Jones Center for Leadership at Philanthropy. We help prepare young people for roles in the nonprofit sector, while simultaneously developing the core of individual responsibility. Dippel's concept of a culture of service is consistent with our experiences as we have worked around the world. Dippel makes a very interesting analogy to the three great theories of physics that emerged in the last century. The first, Einstein's Theory of Relativity, dealt with the universe and the rules by which the great objects operate. To him that is the overall importance of a peer pressure environment of conscience. There is a tension between conscience and convenience. Conscience generally prevails at lower levels because of the adherence to the Golden Rule and other accepted norms of behavior. But when you reach the areas of concentrated power, convenience dominates. So Dippel again argues, unless you give power to conscience by making it convenient in that the society honors and seeks it, conscience cannot ascend to power.

His analogy to the second great theory, Quantum Mechanics, how small objects such as atoms operate, is a different set of rules from the large objects. Dippel compares it to the interaction of the powers of politics, the media, and the forces of change in existing values. Understanding these rules is critical, and the America/China relationship will become a crystallization of these forces and will have impact on the rest of the world as to global prosperity. The final theory, Chaos Theory, is one less well known but looks at nonlinear circumstances and describes the motions and dynamics in sensitive systems, which are mathematically deterministic but often unpredictable. It shows that what may be perceived as small changes can have big results.

It is clear, as Dippel demonstrates, that China will be a great impact on world politics and the global economy. If you read the international press, the place for discussion of change within China and the ideas considered often come from white papers that are discussed within the Central Party School of the Communist Party, which trains the leadership for its military and its government. President Hu arose from the Central Party School, the Vice President of China is its head, and it is the organization that serves as the ideological think tank of change and models many of the programs considered in China. It is significant that the publication of *The Language of Conscience* has been translated into Chinese by the Press of the Central Party School. It is said to be the first Western book published with the School's insignia. While it is clear there is not an agreement with all that was in the book, it is an extremely positive sign. It is a potential bridge in the areas of ethics, morality, and cultural values. The fact that this is considered a serious work and read by its scholars adds dramatically to the chance that the best of Eastern and Western culture can be assimilated for a more positive future. More significant was that in January of 2006 a collaboration agreement between the School and the Texas Lyceum was signed that provides for an exchange of scholars, journals, and other efforts. The Lyceum, of which Dippel was a principal founder twenty-five years ago, specializes in being a catalyst of a variety of institutions but is dedicated to the principles of integrity, respect, and the Common Good. We feel the Chinese chose very well a base for discussion, and this book develops the framework of that discussion. Without doubt, Eastern and Western scholars will have disagreements on important issues. But on the issue of the need for individual dignity, personal responsibility, and morality, we must reach agreement in order to advance our mutual understanding and build a peaceful and prosperous future. A serious discussion of ideas such as those set out in this book can change paradigms.

Roger Ream
President
The Fund For American Studies

The Heart of the Book without the Nutshell

*You have asked how the new book, **Instilling Values in Transcending Generations**, differs from **The Language of Conscience** to which you contributed. The difference is primarily in its purpose. There is a great story that is circulated on the Internet of an Indian chief training his grandson to be a warrior. One key point the old Chief made was that in every man there are two wolves constantly fighting—a bad wolf that is fed by envy, jealousy, hate, and the worst attributes of men and a good wolf that is fed by honor, integrity, compassion, and the best attributes of men. They fight constantly for a man's soul and destiny. The grandson asked, "But which wolf finally wins?" The Grandfather replied, "The one that you feed the most." **The New Legacy** focused on the importance of family and its value. **The Language of Conscience** taught about the importance of character and morality in shaping individuals and the futures of nations. **Instilling Values in Transcending Generations** talks about the power of morality and the necessity of having a common core of ideas so that catalysts can be formed. The previous two books were centered on feeding the good wolf. This new book is focused on teaching the good wolf how to more effectively fight in a world dominated by the powers of convenience, corruption, and terrorism.*

Tieman H. Dippel, Jr.
To the Integrity Task Force of FIDIC
(The International Association
of Consulting Engineers)
Beijing, China
September 7, 2005

Enlightened Conservatism has been described as a philosophy focused on unifying people through the power of conscience, with instilling character as its executive force. That is a good description, but it is also a synthesis of the lessons of history. Alexis de Tocqueville noted "America is great because it is good. If America ever ceases to be good, it will cease to be great." Character is destiny. Alexsandr Solzhenitsyn perhaps captured it on the individual level when he noted, "The line separating good and evil passes not through states, not between political parties...but right through every human heart." Enlightened Conservatism starts with the heart, hoping, in time, to change or maintain the values of a nation. The power of a culture of values creates the paradigm for economics and politics if it becomes dominant.

> Tieman H. Dippel, Jr.
> *Instilling Values in Transcending Generations*

In understanding the thought process of Enlightened Conservatism, it is essential to understand its goals from a strategic perspective. The best way to explain the logic of that thought process would be to take an example that I have used in many speeches. If I were to ask four people to each take a position, one in the center of each wall of a square, and I stood in the middle of that square room and then held up a mirror, when I ask each to describe what they saw, they would see the same object but one would describe the reflection, another would describe the blank back, and two would describe the relatively indistinct edges. Those four perspectives would represent the knowledge of the object. If I then undertake the process of slowly turning the mirror where each side sees what the others did, it begins to accumulate enough knowledge of the true perspective of the object to allow discussion. That process is the acquisition of knowledge. The next level would be the acquisition of wisdom. It involves using the knowledge to the best and most effective purpose. If each person looked into the mirror, they could perceive the use of its convenience in making certain their appearance was appropriate. Or, at a different level of thought, by looking at themselves they could judge their own sense of personal dignity and whether they lived their lives in such a way that they were happy with what they saw. This brings the question of knowledge and wisdom into a focus. Normally, we attempt to generate great amounts of knowledge to seek wisdom, but quite often when we have too much knowledge, the instinct and common sense of what is important is the true wisdom that can allow us to look at what we want to achieve and the goals that we need and engineer back for the knowledge that helps us achieve it. In Enlightened Conservatism it is wisdom that conscience and character are necessities for a stable and harmonious world, and we must find the knowledge and perspectives to achieve it by a process that turns many mirrors. It is not just an issue for the individual, but is an approach that needs to be taken by nations internally and by efforts between nations globally.

Tieman H. Dippel, Jr.
Instilling Values in Transcending Generations

Cultural Wisdom (or Thoughts) from the Heart

It is important to distinguish between the concepts of equality and excellence. With resources there is always a choice—ten different books in one great library for excellence or one book in ten libraries to give some knowledge to a greater number. Finding the necessary balance in a competitive world is an increasingly critical decision. It is a decision complicated by the confusion of the interrelationship of people and ideas. For people you seek equality of rights and opportunity. For ideas you seek excellence because all ideas are not equal. Some ideas are far more important to destiny than others. Equality of individuals is often a bottom-up process of building consensus. Implementing excellence in ideas often tends to be a top-down process prioritizing the most critical ideas. The great problem in culture is balancing the ideas that combine both. Political correctness and individual rights evolve from equality of people, group obligations, and collective concepts from ideas of common good. A system is often needed to make these balance choices more distinct, and this is why the cultural concept of enlightened conservatism evolved. It is not a system that is designed to tell others what to do beyond focusing on conscience, but to enlighten them as to a broader perspective.

Tieman H. Dippel, Jr.
www.thelanguageofconscience.com

Honor is recognizing responsibility for obligations; ethics is the definition of those obligations. Ethics thus cannot be relative for you to have an effective code or culture of honor.

Tieman H. Dippel, Jr.
www.thelanguageofconscience.com

As technology and materialism begin to overwhelm the environment that instills values in our children, we must strengthen key cultural values to provide balance and stability to society. Even if we teach our children the best of our heritage, an environment dominated by convenience either corrupts them or hinders them. Our obligations to our children include an effort to positively shape the world they will inherit. That requires understanding the strategic choices and acting positively upon them.

Tieman H. Dippel, Jr.
www.thelanguageofconscience.com

The most durable and best cultural bridges are built not just upon the words and actions of men, but also on the honor and wisdom of their ancestors and concern for the future of their children, for wise men understand that the lessons of history are also the strategic forces shaping destiny.

Tieman H. Dippel, Jr.
Central Party School, Beijing, PRC
September 9, 2004

When cultures interact and clash, there must be efforts to blend them. At first it is an appreciation of the concept of multiculturism. Often diversity follows in an effort to have respect for personal dignity given to groups rather than to individuals to whom it has been denied. Then a critical choice occurs—do you attempt to reunify the diverse cultures to common denominators of character and conscience or do you rationalize the problems by the path of relativity of morals and ethics to avoid confrontation? The strength of society hangs on this choice because it defines the level of responsibility and obligation to others and to society as a whole. Civilization is the regulation of our basic instincts, which are stronger than reason unless we have a common obligation. You must unify first on common values to the degree possible. Then you build on common interests in the benefits of a culture of ethics, conscience, and character. All cultures exist with both virtues and vices, but the dominant determines the nature of the culture and the direction of progression of the society. The fact that societies of history have not found virtues to be vices, and vice versa, demonstrates both internal understanding of good versus evil and the operational benefits of character.

Tieman H. Dippel, Jr.
www.thelanguageofconscience.com

Civilizations encounter many threats that may destabilize and destroy them. What often preserves them is not their strength or knowledge. Strength with excess can become brittle; intelligence with excess can become elitist. What is critical is the ability to change and adapt to the threat. This requires a unity that lets them use their strength and knowledge. It is the cultural bond of common values that draws sacrifice for the common good that is a catalyst for change.

Tieman H. Dippel, Jr.
www.thelanguageofconscience.com

This will be the century of cultural friction between the fundamental nature of enduring cultural values with entrenched economics and political interests and the pressure of modernization, which creates a new economic and political elite. It is not so much a conflict between nations but is a conflict within societies and will generate a different paradigm of concerns such as terrorism and corruption. The issue in the Mid East is less between those states and the West as it is the conflict between existing traditional values and change. In time this will be more clearly understood. Our difficulty is that the issues are often framed in this environment at the extremes. The advancement of civilization will depend upon the ability to unify a principled understanding of the common good more than a relativity of toleration. Be it in the United States, Europe, China or the Middle East, the search for a common ground will be the goal. It will not be found in the politics of transactional compromise, but instead on transformational agreements based on principles of honor, character, and the larger common good that become embraced by a diverse enough leadership to create the strength and power for a new paradigm. It will not be just the strength and vision of these leaders as much as the growing weakness of systems that will bring change. It will require people to learn how to think in new terms of values. For if you learn how to think with a complete and organized perspective then what you think is easier because facts and truth quickly overcome hypocrisy and hate. The answer to hate speaks truth not toleration and hypocrisy. The issue is learning how to think, and for kids to want to learn they have to be excited by the importance of wisdom.

Tieman H. Dippel, Jr.
www.thelanguageofconscience.com

(These quotes are continued in a ***Summary - Key Thoughts from the Heart*** on page 299)

良 知 的 独 白

The Language of Conscience

[美 国]Tieman H.Dippel,Jr 著

[美 国] 华孚德研究发展中心（CHARC） 译

[中 国] 肖 虹博士 校译

With Case Studies of Private Sector, Nonprofit Leadership

中共中央党校出版社

Preface

The Quest for Conscience in a Global World

If we take the time to learn more of others' heritage and show respect, even if we differ on issues, we can accomplish far more. *The Language of Conscience* (the Chinese cover is on the opposite page) involved understanding the implications of an issue through thought. It is not a concept of weakness but is the basic strategy of strength that allows you to access whether a battle must be engaged or a solution can be found. *The Language of Conscience* chronicles what I learned from public involvements in life, but it symbolizes certain universal values as well. In my experience, many battles could be avoided and positive results for all achieved if egos and preconceptions subjected themselves to examination. A perfect example is the seven sentences that follow:

Gracias por ser un líder que entiende que la lengua de la conciencia es no palabras sino la motivación del corazón, y para su parte en crear una cultura del carácter para hoy y mañana

અંતરમાંથી આવતી અવાજ ફક્ત શબ્દો જ નથી પરંતુ હૃદયમાંથી આવતી પ્રેરણા છે એવું સમજવા માટે અને આજ અને ભવિષ્યનું ચારિત્ર્યનું ઘડતર કરવા માટે જે ફાળો તમે આપ્યો છે, એવા આગેવાન બનવા માટે આપનો આભાર.

תודה על היותך מנהיג שמבין כי שפת המצפון איננה מילים, אלא הנעה של הלב ועל חלקך ביצירת תרבות האופי של היום ושל מחר.

अंतःकरण से आती आवाज़ केवल शब्द नहीं है, परंतु हृदय से उत्पन्न होती प्रेरणा है। ऐसी बोध शक्ति वाले नेता होने के लिए और, आज और कल के चारित्र्यबंधारण में योगदान के लिए आपका धन्यवाद।

شــــكرا لـــك لأنـــك قائد يعي أن لغة الضمير ليست كلمات ولكنها تحفيز القلوب، ولدورك في بناء ثقافة متميزة للحاضر وللمستقبل.

Thank you for being a leader who understands that the language of conscience is not words but the motivation of the heart, and for your part in creating a culture of character for today and tomorrow.

作为一位社区领袖，您深谙道德的理念不仅仅是宣传，更重要的是身体力行。我十分欣赏您对此问题的深刻理解，同时也十分感谢您为当代与未来创造一个具备鲜明特征的文化所做出的贡献。

These sentences appear all to be different, but in realty say the same thing. Knowing that, one of the foreign sentences is less imposing. The same is true of broader discussions if you feel comfortable with the intent of the other party. But what I have learned is that it becomes very important to address the issue of those values early. There are many preconceived thoughts by different cultures and by different groups within cultures because we have divided ourselves in many ways. The ultimate goal is to look at certain values such as personal dignity that affects the perspective that we have on many of these issues. So before the question is asked, "Whose values should anyone teach?" it becomes important to understand how values are created and how we can create a matrix that lets us do comparisons and adjustments. This book has never been intended to answer ultimate questions, but instead to generate thought as to what are the most critical questions once you consider the complexity of our modern world. But central to any solution is leadership with character that appreciates personal responsibility. How to develop these leaders or "uncommon men" are a big part of any solution because they help set the tone of the culture that instills value in the next generation. Their perspective of life is what makes them special.

Cultural power often is not obvious until it is a significant factor and is "discovered." The difference in cultures can be subtle but significant. At the end of World War II, both the German Army and the Japanese Army were in retreat and finally reached points where the outcome of the war was fairly obvious. Both armies had fought fiercely as the battle reached the homeland, but eventually the Germans began surrendering in the face of the inevitable. The Japanese, with a culture based on intense personal honor, fought to the end or committed suicide in many circumstances. The concept of "face," honor or personal dignity in Eastern cultures is very intense. It is not often fully understood by Western cultures that may be equally dedicated to honor and willing to die for it but do not apply it so personally to their individual perspective. The more individualized, as opposed to collective values of the West, often disguise the intensity of the potential level of commitment. But, as has been seen on numerous occasions, once engaged Western culture unifies. Personal dignity is the key to both, but like conscience's parts of compassion and obligation the triggering point is different. The Germans had fought to the end, their obligation of honor they felt fulfilled. The Japanese, in the same circumstance, had a passion of conscience that made surrender unlikely. As cultures begin to deal with each other, it is critical that such distinctions of intensity be understood. At the Alamo the sense of honor of Travis to die for a common good, is not quite the same as the sense of the honor of Japanese soldiers committing suicide on the captured islands off Japan. Both are types of cultural power and must be appreciated as such. To overlook the power of honor in a culture is to totally misunderstand the culture because you cannot judge the personal dignity component that provides the strength to the society.

The book is based on reality that other people are usually not for or against you, but for themselves. So understanding the common interests of man is critical, but understanding yourself is even more necessary if you wish to analyze others. Personal dignity as a good judgment criteria, one's self-esteem combined with understanding of both reality and opportunity, is a key to that self-development. Hope, ambition, fear, honor, and other characteristics coincide with both individual and societal circumstances. But the concept is one of the ages that was perhaps best described by the Chinese philosopher, Lao-tzu:

> *Knowing others leads to wisdom;*
> *Knowing the self leads to enlightenment.*
> *Mastering others requires force;*
> *Mastering self calls for inner strength.*

This book starts with conscience as opposed to convenience being the driving force of a personal dignity. It is the ultimate base of inner strength of character and personal responsibility from which you gain personal enlightenment. Once you have it and become an uncommon man, you search wisdom to bridge with others. This is the base of a way of thinking, the first division of perspective, conscience versus convenience as a life choice and the balancing force of personal dignity. As a Christian, I respect the concept of free choice as to how one lives life, but also I respect the obligations it entails. Force should not be used to coerce others or there is no free choice, but force is on occasion necessary to guarantee free choice and common good. These concepts are looked at differently by one's perspective, but the truth is the battle may not be as much between us as within us. We partially correct or worsen the problem by what we pass on to our children.

In politics and economics competition dominates the nature of the structure. In culture—as opposed to the concept of "society"—common goals and equality are more the norm. This is why culture must play a critical part in binding society together and is the logical place for the ultimate rules of the society, beyond the law, to be found. This century will be one where bridging cultures, which is an examination of the basic perception on life, is crucial. It allows the flexibility in society to adapt to new and different challenges.

The point I would make in including the following articles is that we will always have differences, in some periods pronounced, but there is a lot of opportunity for bridging. These provide an excellent case study because the macro issue of the next generation will be how the world organizes itself in a time of transition. The two likely superpowers will be the United States and China. Their relationship will shape much of the environment. It is the large top-down issue, the bottom-up issues, and the values in each country that will shape what is allowed in the macro relationships. Perhaps the following Chinese media description gives the best description of how you start an individual effort.

Cooperation Memorandum Signing Ceremony
Between CPS Publishing Department and
Texas Friendship Press House Held in Beijing

In the afternoon of September 9th, Cooperation Memorandum was signed between Publishing Department of China Central Party School (CPS) and Texas Friendship Press House in CPS, Beijing. *The Language of Conscience* (Chinese Version) releasing symposium was held at the same time. Vice Principal of CPS, Wang Weiguang met the guests from the U.S. and extended his congratulations on the cooperation between the two press houses. Mr. Wang hoped the two sides would seize the opportunity to cooperate more closely and make more contribution for Sino-US international Culture Communication. Li Yuanchao as the Director of Publishing Department of CPS and Vivian Lee as the President of Texas Friendship Press House signed the memorandum on behalf of each side.

In recent years, the Publishing Department of CPS lays more press on foreign cooperation and attaches more importance on the development and import of overseas publishing resources, which has developed a relationship with several overseas publishing houses on copyright trade and has begun to import and publish some kinds of excellent foreign social and scientific books. This cooperation between Publishing Department of China Central Party School (CPS) and Texas Friendship Press House is a new tryout for this department to broaden its scope, extend its book category, establish the information and cooperative channels adapting to the market and international trends of the publishing industry. The two sides will develop a broad cooperation in the field of book promotion, sales, and copyright trade.

After the ceremony, *The Language of Conscience* (Chinese Version) releasing symposium was held. Author of the book, Tieman H. Dippel, Jr., came from the US specially to attend the releasing symposium. Experts and scholars from Central Party School, Chinese Social and Science Research Institute, and State Religion Affairs Bureau communicated and had an intensive discussion on views in the book. Scholars of China basically shared common views on conscience, sincerity, ethic of cooperation, and value orientation in the book. They also fully explained related concepts and ideas of Chinese thoughts for American guests.

Chief editor of the publishing department, Li Xiao Bing, and CEO of Omega International Group, Ted Li, along with the directors of related departments attended the ceremony and releasing symposium.

Brief introduction to
The Language of Conscience

Translated from the Chinese publication

In his book *The Language of Conscience*, Tieman H. Dippel, Jr. stresses repeatedly that through the process of education in basic morality and common values, a culture of service can be created gradually among people and that culture has a strong influence in helping bring out the best in man. It is especially important for younger leadership. He also mentions the topic of modern political morality (or political philosophy)—how a leader should use the power he has.

This point is obvious in his book. He believes that a good leader must possess at least a basic moral code and good common values. In other words, a good leader must be a good person first. Of course, good leaders, especially great men and women, need to have not only foresight, but also wisdom that is beyond common people, and, more importantly, they must have loyalty. The key point here is how leaders use their power and for what motive. To be specific, it must be made clear whether they are exercising their power for the common good or for their own interest. This question should be asked to identify whether or not they have the basic moral character that leaders must have. This thought, as the author quoted, "You can be respected for power, but you are admired for your motivation in how you use that power," can serve as an enlightening for us to check the budding of corruption from deep inside the mind.

There is a leading melody throughout the whole book from beginning to end. That is to uplift the level of education, to shape good values in culture, and to stick to the basic morality that helps increase the common good of society thereby awakening the conscience of man. It is significant for enhancing the unity of society, for raising leaders of new generations and for speeding up the development of economy and culture. It is worthwhile for us to pay attention to the way he propagates his concept. He does not use preaching as is commonly done, but touches the hearts of people with facts and thoughts.

In his book, Tieman H Dippel, Jr., refined his own life experiences into many vivid words, significant in meaning and profound in thought apothegms, words that convey wisdom and philosophy of life. Everyone who reads them will be enlightened. Among the apothegms there is a basic concept that the author tries again and again to convey that is far more important than money, wealth and power and that is responsibility, accountability, wisdom, loyalty, and conscience

I sincerely hope that thoughtful readers can thoroughly use the apothegms in the book as food for thought and combine them with your own life experience. I believe, in order to take the thinking and morality of Chinese people to a new historic level, we can benefit by using the book *The Language of Conscience* for reference.

Dr. Song Huichang

Dr. Song's introduction serves as a good representation of the discussions at that seminar. We may not have agreed on some things, but we agreed on the importance of morality, ethics, and honor—and most importantly, the part they play in a stable and harmonious culture.

The next step in bridge building occurred in April of 2005 when the Central Party School sent a delegation to the 25th Anniversary Gala of the Texas Lyceum in response to an invitation from the Lyceum leadership to whom I had delivered a complimentary Chinese version of *The Language of Conscience*. The Texas Lyceum history had played a central part as a case example in that book and had been a topic of discussion at our earlier seminar.

The Texas Lyceum event was rather symbolic of the organization. It is a nonprofit, non-partisan educational research and transmission organization with a perspective of government based on the common good, the preservation of Texas values (especially integrity, individual responsibility, and toleration) and leadership training. The Lyceum had many more similarities with the Central Party School than would first be evident. But the publication of *The Language of Conscience* defined some of the very clear interests, which the seminar had magnified. Politics is nationalist in nature, and economics involves self-interest. But culture is a unique bridging vehicle if you find common value, and it can bridge to other areas once respect is shown and trust gained.

In organizations that teach leaders, you often have a common theme—what my Father called "a warrior's honor." These organizations have strength and victory as the goal, but understand far greater strength of character and dedication can be achieved with honor of purpose and conduct. This was what I loved about the United States Navy and its Judge Advocate General's Corps' philosophy. It was not law but justice that was sought. One of the Chinese who read *The Language of Conscience* told me that from what he saw of my father's values, Dad would have understood the Chinese culture and its critical start with the Duke of Zhou who never took the throne of his young nephew and originated the Mandate of Heaven concept of just purpose prevailing.

Having read more Chinese history now, I realize he was correct. Dad could work with those who disagreed with him if they had the conscience of their position. However, if they were men of convenience then respect and support were often bad strategy because they would turn upon you when inconvenienced. But with a true warrior's honor understanding, in which both sides worked through strength, honor, and common respect, they can solve problems in the creation of new paradigm that men of words alone cannot.

This is how the Central Party School, which is the executive training facility of the leadership of China and perhaps its most significant cultural think tank, matches very well with a similar nongovernmental organization focused on leadership training through cultural values. Power is not either's goal, but influence is a natural byproduct of their action in the development of ideas. I think the School was best described in an October 19, 2005 article in *The New York Times* covering the significant speech Secretary Donald Rumsfeld delivered in China:

> *For Mr. Rumsfeld, the chance to deliver his message to the Central Party School, which serves as the Communist Party's ideological research institute and as the main training program for cadres slated for senior posts, clearly indicating that he wanted these future leaders to hear a senior American official say that China's future remains undetermined and that the course of this Asian giant is in their hands.*

The Secretary's comments further described the U.S./China relationship as "a complex one, with its share of challenges." To me, the best way to build bridges of understanding is to find what you have in common before we focus on our differences. That starts with a showing of interest and respect. For the Lyceum and the School it began with the 25th Anniversary Gala of the Lyceum in April 2005.

The night of the Gala in Texas, the focus was not on the fact that every living Governor and Lieutenant Governor was an honorary host, even though many of them were formally political adversaries. The focus was not on the fact that when the chairpersons of the 25 years stood on the stage they demonstrated transitions in power in the organization between races, gender, political persuasions, and certainly political parties. The organization was not controlled by a distinct group or philosophy, but by the concept of its purpose. The sense of honor of each new leader to fulfill this purpose gave him the selection and gave the entity its core. What stood out that night was the huge diversity of the audience that let very different groups and interests unite not just behind what they had done over 25 years of leadership training and policy development. Not even on how well they had done it with a President of the United States, a United States Senator, numerous Congressmen, the Governor, Attorney General or scores of other leaders in all fields as alumni. But what was key was why they had done it—their motivation for the common good and their willingness to stand for a set of values. It was an idea that was crystallized in an evening.

For my Chinese friends I explained it in the terms of the symbolism of the great Imperial Dragon that represents China. The dragon holds the characteristics of many groups that favored and respected animals, fish, birds, and serpents in the early unification of China. Parts of each are part of the dragon so that each group sees in it a part within the unity. It was the essence of seeking the common good.

Two significant events were barely noted that evening but set in motion very inter-related and significant efforts. The first was a charge to the Lyceum by Lieutenant Governor David Dewhurst of Texas for it to renew its efforts at public policy by undertaking a project to look at the future of the state and its most critical issues over the next 25 years just as it had begun 25 years earlier with the program looking at Texas in the year 2000. That evening over $125,000 was committed by interested individuals to undertake the Commission of 25. The second effort was the delivery of a letter from Dr. Wang Weiguang, the Vice President of the Central Party School, expressing his regret at not being able to attend the event, but inviting the Lyceum leadership to the Central Party School for discussions. In the future 25 years, few issues will be more important than the interaction of China and the United States, particularly with the Chinese growing economic involvement in Canada, Mexico, and Latin America and the joint economic efforts that will impact everyone's standard of living. Understanding the world from a global vision of a competitive world makes it far easier to design "win/win relationships" as opposed to protectionism.

That return visit to China with the presentation of a plaque, took place in the first week of September 2005 as a part of a multifaceted trip. Of significance was also the fact that the Texas Lyceum and the Central Party School both understand the need for operational (organizational) leadership and inspirational (motivational) leadership since they deal with broad leadership in society as a whole rather than more *silo* organizations. These two leadership goals come together in a cultural leadership style that are more like chess than checkers or tic tac toe. The results to be measured in this style flow from a strong system of accountability to a well-designed plan with strategic focus. Both accountability and focus are difficult with what is effectively a political arena with varying views and personal interest defusing the power on which accountability and focus are based and measured. In this realm the peer pressure of culture and the internal demands of teamwork help a leader keep focused inspirationally and obtain results operationally. The proper systems create internal pressures within them.

To create that power of peer pressure (or culture) you need clarity of purpose beyond individual interests and ambitions that can rally support for a common good that rearranges how the always present personal interest is strategized to achieve their goal. So thought and vision blended with logic and character are critical in the process for learning how to prepare them in ever-evolving situations, how to adapt them or what the true concept of leadership training involves. While most leadership envisions a great omnipotent leader, the modern world of complexity and communication makes that less likely. Leadership in partisan terms is divisive and usually brings gridlock. Political correctness, in its usual extreme is focused on individual smaller issues, as are single purpose but emotional issues. They tend to divide rather than unify. If leadership is to build an effective base, it must address more of a group concept and put focus on the common good rather than individual issues. This is like the proverbial "herding cats" in a modern world of individual opinions. But increasingly over the next decade from issues involving security to stability, its value will be recognized and appreciated.

To unify the common good requires strength of vision to keep the focus on track, but also willingness to admit the values of others can perfect a better vision. If consensus is sought, even with a strong cultural force to unify it and keep focus, you must take conflict from the personal level to one of mutual discussion. That requires humility of leadership with strength. The language of conscience style of discussions allows those that may not agree to at least have input, and they may well buy into the plan on the basis of at least having had their say. But the style of those discussions is created by the wisdom and the fairness of the discussion format and the culture of character that builds trust. Trust is the key. Conscience of purpose rather than convenience of power is essential to success. It is never perfect, but it creates leadership catalysts that take both expertise in unifying for the common good and the wisdom of how to think through the process and structure the analysis of problems in a logical unifying approach to a much broader base.

The joint efforts of the Lyceum and the School let each see the best practices of the other in conscience-based leadership while letting the East and West see opposing views to issues in a cultural leadership rather than in a political or economic immediate focus. It also brings a healthy discussion of group concerns versus individual concerns into a structure that is better understood by both. If you would have a bridge built between East and West, then there is no better way than two associations that are catalysts of thought in their respective cultures and inclusive of some of the best and most experienced minds and ideas to look at issues with mutual respect. By not telling each other what to do, but instead by showing through their strength of dedication why they do what they do, there comes understanding and honest discussion not intimidated by the fear that is often involved by protocol or political correctness. Thus the trust and purpose are set by mutual choice and respect and is gained from the choice of the values being sought.

If 20 years from now two babies are born, one in China and one in America and we look to their future, there is little doubt that a world based on the *win/win* concepts of mutual growth provides a better future than nations adopting protectionism or focusing on domination. This agreement was formally signed on a return visit to the School by a Texas Lyceum Delegation on January 6, 2006, which is discussed later in more detail. It is appropriate for discussion as a case study of the importance of perspective and how you look at issues both with more background information and a direct thought process.

Every nation will be building or remaking itself in a competitive world, and the focus for the common good in each country will become its own style of nationalism. But the more nations can develop trust and confidence in each other, the better the standard of living of both babies will be because the global growth will benefit all. The agreement between these two organizations is but an acorn. But it is an acorn with powerful genetics and planted with great care for location where a sense of conscience can nourish it against the many elements that can be destructive. Hopefully, it will grow branches and roots that involve many other groups, so that even greater consensus can be built and an ever greater array of thoughts can be examined, but within the sunlight of conscience. The value of their relationship is not who they are as much as what they both seek for their respective cultures. They are "the dragons of cultural thought" that both seek to unify a much greater society composed of many parts. It is why the plaque carried, focused on a language of conscience that focused on mutual respect and common values as the basis for a bridge.

The return trip included other events to build this bridge as well. Ms. Vivian Lee, who had signed the original Memorandum of Cooperation with the School on the book, is also the President of CHARC, a nonprofit cultural foundation focused on building cultural relationships between China and America. She patterned CHARC on the concepts of the very successful Texas nonprofit organization HARC, Houston Area Research Council, which served as a volunteer administrator of the Lyceum in its early days and was a catalyst of private sector, governmental, and educational institutions in the integration of policy. Due to the influence of Dr. George Kozmetsky and Dr. Skip Porter in the early years, it also appreciated the critical place in economic growth that technology and its commercialization played. This is even more true in the competitiveness of the modern world.

Ms. Lee hosted on CHARC's behalf a dinner at her Lu Yang Compound in Beijing, which formerly was the residence of a prince at the Summer Palace and was later occupied by members of the Foreign Delegation at the time of the Dowager Empress. It focused on a perspective of China–U.S. educational collaboration primarily focusing on cultural exchange. As part of the program, she served a menu of a rare ancient dinner combining two dynasties with period-costumed attendants that set a unique stage. But the guest list was perhaps as unusual as any that had gathered since the diversity of the Foreign Delegation. Four of the senior directors of the Central Party School attended, a delegation of publishers and journalists who were in Beijing for the Beijing Book Fair and headed by the publisher of ForeWord Magazine, Ms. Victoria Sutherland, the officers of the Texas Lyceum including Mr. Walter Tomlinson, Chairman, Mr. Jordan Cowman, President, and Mr. Dougal Cameron, the Vice President, and representatives from FIDIC, (the International Association of Consulting Engineers) led by the Chairman of its Integrity Task Force, Dr. Felipe Ochoa of Mexico. What everyone had in common was an appreciation for the power of ideas in shaping culture for the growth of conscience, morality, and integrity— and in so doing bringing a greater harmony within societies and between them. CHARC had translated *The Language of Conscience*, the Central Party School had published it, ForeWord Magazine had recognized it as a finalist in its Philosophy Book of the Year competition, and the Lyceum and FIDIC were case studies within it along with the Ethics Officer Association of the United States that regretfully was not able to attend.

Mr. Li Yuanchao the Head of the Central Party School Press spoke on the School's hopes to use books on a more international scale to build a better understanding between cultures, and I spoke on the issues that we all had in common followed by perspectives from each of the group leaders.

Three days later we visited with the Central Party School, the Lyceum delivered its plaque, and we also spent a day on two concepts. The first was how to build a relationship that went beyond the book to uniting scholars in thought, exchanging scholars, building networks of interested parties, and the similar expansion stage of implementing a structure with which to continue the development of the common ideas. In the end, a Collaboration Agreement was negotiated between the Central Party School and the leadership of the Texas Lyceum Association that was reduced to a Memorandum of Understanding. This memorandum reiterated the history behind the effort, defined it "whereas the parties each seek to provide a culture of service and responsibility within their respective organizations and society as a whole, and . . . see value in a broadened understanding and perspective on each other's culture, moral, ethical, and business climates, and . . . the parties believe that creating an environment of conscience and ethics is critical to the success of society. In recognition of the increasing significance of relationships between the parties and their desire to collaborate on a mutual program, the parties agreed to several joint initiatives. These included public forums, publication exchanges, joint publication, a bilateral exchange program, and sponsorship of visiting scholars in both directions." It was a solid organizational effort but was clearly based on common goals.

I spent a good part of the day with the second issue of the seminar in which I was joined by part of the Lyceum Delegation and Dr. Felipe Ochoa the Chairman of FIDIC's Task Force on Integrity. I brought letters of regret from several other organizations that due to timing could not make the meeting including the Ethics Officer Association of the United States which also had done a significant amount of work in the fields to be discussed. We talked about an integrity system for fighting corruption and the part that government and the private sector both had to play in not only creating frameworks for integrity, but also developing cultures within corporations through the process. However, this led to probably the key part of the School's presentation. We received its vision of "A Harmonious Society," which gave great insight to where the School envisioned China's ultimate goal to be as a society. It also enumerated many of its problems and the issues it had to address to reach it and how many of these issues were not Chinese alone but global. I compared these with the concept of enlightened conservatism that had been the core of *The Language of Conscience* and much of the base of this new book. It was remarkable how many similarities were found and the core of these two presentations are included later in the discussion of the American and Chinese axis of the next 25 years that will have such impact.

The following day I spoke to the Integrity Task Force of FIDIC. It is the International Organization of Consulting Engineers and was holding its 100th anniversary in Beijing. I quickly learned that the common concepts we had assessed the previous day are not just Chinese and American issues, but they are truly global. All countries have people seeking a common culture of integrity as a basis for a stronger society even though they are often surrounded by a significant number of people that do not focus upon it. Too often the efforts of these groups of conscience are internal organizations and small. There must be a catalyst to unite a very unappreciated demand for substance within the world for a culture more regulated by conscience and integrity. That fact was not lost upon those with whom I spoke.

Two days later I was attending one of the world's premier trade and investment conferences, the 9th CIFIT (China International Fair for Investment and Trade) at Xiamen China, which made me fully understand the part that Asia would play in this century. The speeches all gave a *win/ win* theme to global commerce. But in the private discussions, my point was simple. Transactional economics is not difficult because the economics of self-interest and political nationalism, unless you can define fair balance. *Win/win,* even if true on a global scale, is lost in individual assessments of individual nations. Cultural understanding, concurrent with the economics, not only lessens fear and improves opportunity through more trust but also builds a far more stable world by giving a clear understanding to the importance of the global rule of law to enhance commerce.

You can see the changes that reality is bringing to world financial markets. While many view China as an export-driven, mercantilist economy, I think it simplifies the issue too much. It is really a vendor-financed economy at present because China funds much of American consumption by buying American bonds through its savings. The relationship is much more complex, not just because it affects world pricing through its labor, but also long-term interest rates through its savings. New concepts like the Britton Woods II analysis try to explain this new phenomenon. Only time will allow us to fully understand these forces. But one thing is evident—the United States and China are far more linked economically than most perceive, and they have many mutual interests. Where a mercantilist economy can "beggar its neighbor," a vendor-financed one that takes the neighbor's debt has a different self interest. China is using the world market (principally the U.S. as a the premier consumer) to learn to get market prices, and it will probably continue to do so until it develops an internal consumer-driven market. That might require a doubling of its current per capita GDP and may be a decade down the road. The imbalances the present system creates may not allow a smooth transition, so any number of crisis situations can occur. However, one thing is certain, the more knowledge both sides have of their common interest, the less bad judgments will be made. The more cross-border investment is encouraged, the better imbalances can be automatically adjusted. So these efforts are critical.

Over the last years, I have often been told that I am too much of an optimist and waste my time by trying to bring out the best in people. I am often told that these ideas are from a past century and do not fit in a modern world that is being driven by economics and politics that require more convenience. Perhaps it is true, but for ten days in China, I could not have been shown more courtesy or higher levels of protocol. I was not what was important but a set of ideas that were appreciated for their worth. At the 25th Anniversary of the Lyceum, you saw not a social club, but the dynamics and the power of vision driven by the right issues. As Confucius noted, "Life is really simple, but men insist on making it complicated." The Golden Rule, the common good, and the rule of law require a morality and integrity that should be the core of all men and the basis of all civilization. Rather than being ideas of the past and ineffective in the future, I think on the contrary they are a necessity of civilization and will emerge not only as the vision of the future, but more importantly as its most significant implementing force.

The relationship between China and the United States will be the pivotal driver of the next decade. This will be a transition decade that establishes relationships and balances that will reach far into the future. Will there be two competing superpowers or a symbiotic relationship that creates the environment of the next century? Presently, the two are linked by economics not only in the production of goods and consumption, but also increasingly by financial considerations as China invests heavily in American debt adding critical marginal funding to the American economy. But this will create imbalances. How the risks are monitored and addressed has a great impact on the world's economic growth. To me, the critical issue may well not be the economics or the politics, but the perspective of thought that is driven by the perspective of the people of both nations. They determine the politics and they react to the economics. But their perspective is set not just by the information they hold but also by the sense of the intent of their leadership and the confidence within it. The future challenges are going to require a type of leadership that instills confidence, and comes from a cultural perspective of how they view themselves—a personal dignity and character forged both from history and a concern for their family's future as well as the immediate.

When I am asked my thoughts on China, I describe it as similar to my experience during the Vietnam Era when I was in the Navy. Even though I was a lawyer in the Judge Advocate General's Corps, we were also trained for leadership in fire control and some training in navigation. Perhaps nothing gave me more of an understanding of the complexity of guiding a great ship than the training in the BZ Trainer at Newport, Rhode Island. In a simulated convoy, all of us were in teams to direct a large ship on the screen and keep it in position. You quickly learned that small boats reacted more quickly, that big ones were very complex, and that you had to start movements early with a significant respect for the time, speed, and power of other obstacles. It was easy to crash without careful thought and experience. China is like that great ship. The United States is as well. The media has its stories of individual instances that give many different impressions of each because we focus on the short term in media. But in reality, both countries will have groups that differ internally. The key is where the trend is determined that sets the course for the longer term like that ship. How long are the timeframes allowing decision? How experienced is the Captain for uncharted water? How much power does the ship possess to keep a course? What big obstacles must be anticipated? For the United States, partisanship clouds the answer to many of these questions because it deprives the power to unify behind a decision. Also the financial imbalances are big obstacles, but America has a history of being resilient and unified in a crisis, but what made that resiliency is a dedication to character and values that allowed sacrifice. Its retention of its culture of values is essential.

China is different in that it is much more centrally controlled and uses the benefits of that consolidation of power for growth. It also is in uncharted waters as it broadens its market economy at an uncertain time in the world that is in part cause by its growth and investment decisions. But China is not as opaque or confusing as most would make it. The Communist Party controls the government, the military, and has a great impact on the culture. It understands the power of culture because of its history, and it often uses culture to accomplish its ends. For that reason you need look at the ideological think tank of the Communist Party to see the ideas being generated for consideration of the leadership Captains and the location on the grounds of the Summer Palace where these future leaders are trained. It is called the Central Party School in China, often referred to as the Cadre School abroad. It is their finest minds focused, in part, on how to run that ship in the BZ Trainer. China understands the importance of time and thinks in generations in making moves. It understands obstacles by focusing on fighting corruption as a necessity for building the economic system. And it understands that the long history of culture in China is a tremendous power to unify its people to keep stability during economic turmoil. It also understands the problems China will face with the environment, the necessity of future growth, and the host of problems all large nations have when governments must make choices. The school's research will increasingly become a part of their vision of a "Harmonious Society" that gives insight on how China looks at the future. It may be a trial balloon for discussion, but it is discussion at the highest levels.

China usually does what is in its best interest, as its leadership understands it. So the interaction of East and West is best served by building bridges so that a more complete understanding of implications of mutual actions can be appreciated. That is difficult to do in economics or in politics, but culture is the unifying force. The School has begun to build its bridges thoughtfully and knowledgably on that base. They are focusing on cultural values, morality, and ethics as cultural components that hopefully will form a significant base in their "harmonious society" with the Eastern appreciation of personal dignity and "face." If there is a cleavage point on the diamond of understanding China and in many ways the future world, it will be what is in the concept of a "harmonious society" and how well the leadership of China embraces its core and the world seeks to understand it. As the great Chinese philosopher Lao Tzu noted, "Wisdom is knowing others, enlightenment is knowing self."

To me the future is brighter than many people think. The world will face crisis, but crisis brings a desire for wisdom. And leadership is becoming more prepared and thoughtful than is probably perceived by our reading of the media. Values will be seen to matter because sacrifice toward a solution necessitates a vision of the future and a willingness to care beyond self. The battle of cultures will ultimately be, not between cultures, but within cultures for what visions of the future take hold and what values are chosen. Those cultures with character's determination and dedication have the balance of history on their side. It is not the strongest that survive. It is not the most intelligent. It is the most adaptable, and that requires the cultural ability of unification of common values. The world will always have crises. The problem is that those crises of the future may have more serious disruptions because of the leverage of growth. The individual problems may not be as much of a necessary focus as the method by which we address them cooperatively. How we think about them, and the process we use to solve them, may be more critical to the future than individual problems themselves. The Golden Rule has always been a good beginning until man or government leaves conscience to seek personal convenience.

(Pictures of the previously described events in China are shown on the following pages.)

Texas Lyceum Delegation Visit to the Central Party School
in September of 2005. Tieman H. Dippel, Jr. with
Dr. Wang Weiguang during discussions.

Presentation of Texas Lyceum Plaque to the Central Party School
following the Central Party School Delegation's visit to
the 25th Anniversary Gala of the Texas Lyceum.

ForeWord Magazine Publisher Victoria Sutherland presenting a Philosophy
Book of the Year Finalist Medallion to Mr. Yuanchao Li, Director of CPS
(Central Party School) Publishing for the Chinese Edition, and Ms. Vivian Lee,
President of CHARC, the Editor and Co-Publisher at the Lu Yang Compound
in Beijing, China September during the 2005 visit.

September 2005 Delegation to Ethics and Values Seminar
with Hosts at the Central Party School

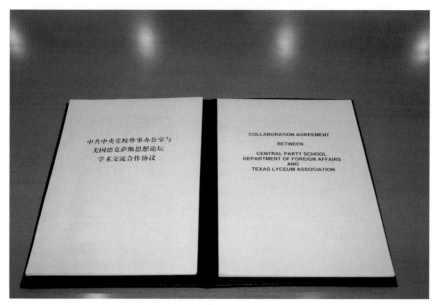

Collaboration Agreement

Signing Ceremony of the Central Party School — Texas Lyceum
Collaboration Agreement January 6, 2006.

Introduction

From Whence Do We Come?

This book has been written much more in a conceptual oriental style than a more Western tradition. It is the way in which a translation can be most accurately conveyed, but it often relies on repetition to help connect various conceptual points. The best explanation would be that the Western languages are based on a common alphabet that uses a structured style of words, sentences, paragraphs, pages, chapters, and books. It is very linear in its approach because of the focus it instills on the process. The Oriental languages tend to be much more graphic and not as structured aimed more at building a concept. They have many more symbols than we have words. While we in the West may talk of a certain paragraph, the difficulty in translation (or communication) may lie not in understanding that paragraph, but in understanding how that paragraph fits within the concept being built. Just as those familiar with a natural language often overlook the "the's" and "of's," and shift focus to key words, someone not as familiar with the language is not so focused. I learned this in Mexico when a friend gave me a long sentence to read quickly and asked me to count the number of "f's." He did the same to a Mexican friend. To my surprise we differed because I had jumped over the "of's" and in my speed looked at the critical words. My friend read them more closely because it was his second language, and he did not focus as quickly as I did. So care needs to be taken that focus is clear, but a little repetition connects concepts. At the same time, the educational systems of the East are more structured in the style of engineering where the West adds more individual thought and imagination, similar to teaching law. So the development of the graphic triangles at the conclusion are an effort to create a vehicle for discussion and thought. The method by which you think affects how you think. There is a natural human desire to be right, and we process much information instinctively. So opening and broadening our minds, from our own perspective, by working with others from different perspectives, is an ultimate goal.

When seeking a title for this book, the choice rested between "Instilling Values" or "Instilling Character." They are similar but character captures a more direct concept and much of the book looks to national character and its development. However as the book moved forward, values became more important because the creation of a value-based culture was the best way to instill conscience to a succession of generations.

We use personal dignity as a key reference to both individual men and men as a society. The perception of personal dignity is in effect a balance between the pull of the humility of conscience and the aggressiveness of power. It is why both East and West have symbols of leadership of a warrior and a scholar combined (at the Confucian Temple in Cofu) or a monk and a knight combined in many Western settings. The enlightenment of bringing together this balance in the right measure requires a disciplined process of thought as to how values are integrated with actions. Thought without action is often without substance. Action without thought is only emotional and often without purpose. Personal dignity requires both of these things as sense of power in the concept of choice and a satisfaction that is given by an enlightened motivation beyond power alone.

Since the interest of a Chinese seminar involved not only on the subjects of conscience, ethics, and the building of a nonprofit culture that helped support these concepts, but also the potential efforts of joint ventures with Western think tanks and universities, as well as other groups, the book was written to provide a common ground for discussion of potential courses. It is expected to be read in the context of *The New Legacy* and *The Language of Conscience* which provide a series of books with the website, www.thelanguageofconscience.com that have attempted to develop the concept of cultural ethics or enlightened conservatism as the more unified thoughts are consolidated.

The ultimate question of cultural ethics is what is taught to the next generation of children. Are they taught to kill and hate and then that will be their future as has partly been the case in the Middle East? Or, will the foundations be laid for an appreciation of toleration and the benefits of conscience in both expanding the economy, since markets work by competition which is destroyed by corruption, and in politics where the assumption of responsibilities through nonprofit organizations remove the burdens on government and bring a sense of individual responsibility giving strength to the society? Children learn at ten years old much of what they are going to carry with them through life. Parents have the responsibility to teach their values to the next generation and will be judged by the values that they convey. How children learn to think and their perspective to evaluate the information they learn is value based.

Similarly, we as a unit of society need to look to how society through its institutions has a culture that rewards conscience and not convenience so that the values we teach our children will neither be a detriment to them nor will they be corrupted. These are issues that will be at the forefront of this century's discussions. The middle of the last century was an ideological one of politics with leaders such as Kennedy, Johnson, Brezhnev, and Mao defining an era that was ideological or political in content. The next era of the '80s saw the results of the second driver of society, economics, as market systems blossomed under the leadership of leaders like Reagan, Thatcher, Deng, and Gorbachev (who had to address the problems of Russia).

As the world has moved from its focus on political systems to economic systems and now is beginning to focus upon cultural systems as the power paradigm shifts, the concept of critical mass becomes the issue. Only when there is the perception of a critical mass forming do you begin to redefine the standard logic of the present. In other words, there is what Malcolm Gladwell defined in *The Tipping Point* as a change in behavior that then will create a new reality. The value and power of culture to help solve these problems and its study for those reasons will increasingly emerge. But the reality of cultural power is that it succeeds when it binds people more closely, not necessarily when it just tolerates differences. In the extreme, that brings about an avoidance of the discussions that might solve problems. Political correctness serves the purpose of awareness of problems, but it is often a token solution that in reality avoids the hard discussions that lead to true understanding. The "tipping point" of this cultural paradigm can go either way. Either it builds a culture of responsibility and character, or it contributes to the demise of personal responsibility. How this issue is explained makes a huge difference. Partisanship is not the ally of such understanding because it works to divide people. Corruption and terrorism are not allies because they work to build relationships on greed or fear. It is a problem that will only be solved over a generation by what values are taught to children. It will not be an immediate change because it requires the education of many. But it will be a growing consciousness that reframes the issues and brings about initial work that will be expanded.

This century is beginning to see the powerful driver of culture set its agenda rather than the drivers of politics and economics. The unsettled circumstances of the Middle East and Islam are a value-based cultural battle of traditionalism versus modernization rather than an ideologically based political or economic concept. China has moved to be a world player in economics with its joining of the World Trade Organization, but at the same time is searching to bring its past cultural values and strengths forward. Christianity is finding rebirth in parts of the West. Europe is debating the levels of tolerations society can accept and remain effective as a group.

For all of the difficulties and negativism found in the world today, there are also some very positive actions that are of significance. The Asian tsunami was symbolic of other natural disasters and the world's response to it was heartening. It is not just that charity and support are given but that the motivation behind it is sincere.

Some Western institutions question whether universities should deal with teaching values rather than just building knowledge by research. But it was a similar set of thoughts on the power of free markets to help the individual that had great impact on the dramatic change that took place between shifting the world from a political environment to an economic one in the 1970s.

Milton and Rose Friedman in their study *Free to Choose* and the dramatic impact of the study of market economics at the University of Chicago had an impact worldwide as the truth of the concepts spread. While it was a crystallization of a trend, it was not unlike Henry George's work of the late 1800s. It helped define the way we think. It is my hope that this book will serve a small part in helping understand the inter-relationships of society and how dealing in ethics alone is like beginning with a game level of tic tac toe. Checkers graduates to understanding that the real issue is the nature of man and how it has to be positive to provide the peer pressure of the culture to give it power. Chess is how the other powers of economics and politics interact with culture to dramatically affect society, and how for this century the power of culture can be used to shape economics and politics for the better. Institutes that teach how to think from a value-based perspective should be developed to seek wisdom and influence in this century. This could give a "tipping point" push at a critical time of choice.

Instilling Family Values
The Core of Value Instillation

*To be ignorant of what occurred before you were born
is to always remain a child.*

*For what is the worth of human life, unless it is woven into the life of
our ancestors by records of history.*
— Marcus Tullius Cicero

*Words and family are at the center of our lives, the foundation of our
dignity as a free people.*
— President Ronald Reagan
1980

*Machiavelli noted that half of life was determined by fate and that the
other half by our actions. If that is so, let us ask God's favor on that half
that we cannot control, but let us be certain to design the half that we do
control to deserve God's favor on the half we cannot.*
— A Dippel Family Philosophy

All cultural values are really a reflection of family values—either
by what is taught, or by what is omitted. The family is the core unit that
shapes the perspective of the next generation. Often by ten years of age,
many impressions are naturally acquired. It is not just what is taught, but
what is perceived. In nature the young must learn quickly to survive, so
they gather much from what their parents' value or fear. If it is material
wealth, then that is important. And if it is a concept of moral values,
then those values become primary. Interestingly, the *dynasty style* of
families in politics, economics, media, culture, and entertainment usually
become dynasties transcending generations because they understand the
importance of family and building it as a unit. By understanding this
heritage, they aggregate and pass forward their predecessor's experience,
values, and wisdom. It is from this heritage that the next generation forms
itself to meet the challenge.

An example could be a generation of great athletes—the genes
obviously matter, but so does the training that the parents provide,
the knowledge of doctors for specialized injuries, and the confidence

and drive that is instilled to achieve family expectations. In political families, it is the way that the image of the family and its values of the past have been promoted that help by symbolizing a concept and developing loyalties. Similarly, it may be the family fundraising Rolodex and networks that give a base.

In economics, it is the relationship with other wealthy families through social and charitable activities and the relationship with institutions. A base of wealth is of great help, but training in acquiring and managing it gives a great benefit to their children. But in all cases, family in the first generation of development or as a dynasty needs an organized approach to teaching family history and its core family values.

If these values are totally mercenary, then you seldom have a strong dynasty because you teach the convenience of personal materialism. The individual, not the group, becomes the focus. Children fight among themselves. Broader values and obligations build family, and a perspective of service to society strengthens both the family and society. One of the books most influential in my life was *Think and Grow Rich* by Napoleon Hill who chronicled the characteristics of success. The path to wealth lies in your character and it develops your mastermind network.

You must focus not only on family financial assets, but intellectual ones as well to fully develop the concept. If you focus on keeping peace in the family and jointly developing the family's finances, it may provide options that are beneficial so common values are not only worthy but are required for business. A combined family's assets are often leveraged much more effectively than just a group of individuals, particularly if they are in an existing business or development that would be dismantled or sold to partition. Another critical point is how the family views itself. Often being a member is judged by blood that often produces an inward and sometimes divisive atmosphere. Asian families more often have an appreciation for blood relationships, but also judge by different degrees of affinity with outsiders. This approach gives additional strength and a growth orientation.

Perhaps the best example of crystallizing family values and relationships come on the rare opportunities when the family can spend a lot of time together on a vacation. You notice the things that are important, not necessarily the sights and history but the growth of the next generation. The Mayans believed that life began anew every 52 years and to a sense it does when you have grandchildren at about that age. When I took our extended family, three children and spouses and three grandchildren on a Caribbean cruise for a week, I realized how much it means in later life to have the chance to have the family together again, and even more as your children realize what you had to do for them as they take care of their own.

We saw a lot of sights, but watching Margaret Grace, our youngest grandchild at eight months, learn to eat solid food in the form of bread crumbs she made on her own for the first time, and her excitement at the experience was more important than the other sights. Watching Clara at a little older than four take an interest in jewelry and at the Cayman Turtle Farm actually hold a turtle rather than run from it was an experience in itself. Wright, at two and one half, who loves monster cartoons and films of his age, took great pleasure in telling his Dad, "Don't worry I got that towel monster and made him go away." (Clara was less happy about the towel rabbit being dismantled, but for Wright it was a real accomplishment of which he was proud.)

The point is that we learn from our children in that they remind us of how we were and how much we have learned in life and often forgotten as to what is truly important. Whether it is travel or a local vacation, the opportunities are the same. We had taken our kids on a series of vacations as they grew up and tried to make it an education not just in geography but also in the realities of life. We showed them poverty not to make them feel guilty or fortunate, but to help them understand the reality of life and why compassion mattered. And to teach them also why good policy mattered and why you have to be involved in society. The policies of a government and the culture of a nation have a great amount to do with the success of the people. Individual responsibility and good government with a vision can turn a difficult situation into a positive one, while all the bounties of nature can often be lost when a nation does not have its character. The one point we taught them to watch was the level of opportunity, which often comes from policy and vision, and the execution toward that opportunity which comes from the character of the people. Travel, not only brings a family together, but also gives a tremendous opportunity to appreciate family values and family vision.

Yes, family vacations and organized discussions build a foundation where all can communicate and develop methods of interaction. Values are implicit since they are handed down. In our family the values were—what you do is important, how well you do it is significant, but why you do it is critical. (Dad's side). Mother's side was more religious—character is what you do when no one is watching (with the admonition that God is always watching). If you know the limits of what you will do morally, then you look to build family security through wealth generation. Dad always noted that three generations are usually involved. One provides the base, the second builds it, and the third either loses it or takes it to the level that they can plan for future generations. The family is then secure because the wealth has hit a critical level. On occasion this can be done with one great event at one time that conveys wealth, but on average it is a disciplined growth. Common family values and vision are a necessity of this trans-generational coordination. Every generation has a new environment to which it must adjust, so it needs to understand the arenas of power and the ultimate goals of the family. Having vacations and getting everyone together annually is often key— a simple inexpensive fishing trip might be more important for building family than an established family's vacation at their private resort. The building family needs capital consolidation where the established family is only judging alternatives. But both need quality time set aside to discuss these issues so all are involved and informed. At these events you are not just providing information, but you are teaching them how to think analytically and also in terms of values and conduct. The things you have acquired or even what you have accomplished are not the most important, but the experience that shaped you and why you have done what you did. My father taught me the importance of a sense of honor, of integrity in choices, of compassion. But he also taught me the necessity of toughness and how to think rather than responding with emotion. These are not in slanderous "blogs" of consciousness on events but coordinated development of a perspective or mindset and how to react to issues and problems. They are the development of the next generation's concept of their *personal dignity* and how they will judge their own satisfaction and success. Dad often pointed out the importance of knowing not only family history and respecting the memory of those before you, but also knowing the history of your society. Cultures and civilizations can be judged on how well they respect the past because it gives an insight to their common unity.

The emergence of ethical wills, which tell your heirs what you want them to know, is important. A regular will tells them what assets you want them to have, but it is incomplete if you do not also convey advice from life's experiences. It can be a letter, a book you wrote or books of others with a note. But it symbolizes the value you place upon wisdom.

Regardless of the level of wealth, a family vision unifies it. Even if the parents cannot leave a great deal of material wealth, leaving their experience and concern for the next generation instills focus and respect. And by the family integration, they better integrate with and change society. It should be noted that society as a whole, its culture, is the blending of these various levels of family values. Strengthen the family values, and you eventually strengthen and shape society's values. There is an appropriate Chinese poem that says that all rivers flow to the sea and mix.

In each family a generation needs to re-energize the importance of heritage. My in-laws have done a great deal of research on their family tree. Their history went to Charlemagne and the Magna Carta. And I had research efforts to fill in the blanks on our family so that a 300-page volume of our children's common heritage would be a document that each child and grandchild could pass down. With modern technology and combined research, a lot can be done for reasonable cost. It gives a sense of being and understanding. Not the pride of who ancestors were, but the understanding of the place each holds in their generation, and their generation is the stair step to all those that follow on that chart. What wisdom will they have? Every family has its own history and values, and they differ. But their history and values are the glue that holds the family together, and they also build the habits and discipline of the youth. They assimilate what is important. They make each of us appreciate that we live in eras of time as each of their ancestors did on the generation chart. Each of them is still a part of us as we will be in future generations that we shape.

Every family has the same background to a large degree, but keeping the family close and in touch is a responsibility of each successive generation.

Each generation knows only what it is taught. Society will be shaped by the way children are shaped by family structure and vision. Single parent families have even more responsibility.

Values have a cost if you hold them dear. Like King David who needed a certain threshing floor, an altar, and a sacrifice to stop a plague in Israel (according to his prophets), you should not accept the easy out such as the owner giving it all to you. King David knew that a sacrifice that cost him nothing had no value. Family commitment and values build character even though they involve risks. Everyone makes choices. The hard choices and the willingness to address them build the discipline and strength to persevere, which is what often matters.

Perhaps one of the most overlooked factors of instilling values in generations is the fact that the process works both ways. While we instill values in our children, children themselves, by the nature of their care, are extremely demanding and require a great deal of sacrifice that has tremendous impact upon the parents' perspective. You can protect children too much. When you sacrifice a great deal for your children in a family relationship, then you care much more about what happens to them even after you have passed.

I think the best way to make this point came to me in an interview that I was doing about the Texas Lyceum. I had talked about it being a character-based organization that trains leadership. The way it trained leadership was not necessarily just coordinating people with others of similar interest or providing speakers that both educated them on transformational leadership. But far more it was the pressure of putting on the events. Effectively, each of us is a lump of coal. If we want to turn into a diamond, we have to have a significant amount of pressure applied by difficult circumstances that sharpen our abilities and take us to different levels of performance. If we do not have effective competition or the will and drive to achieve, we are fairly easily satisfied. Just like a muscle, "the decision muscles" in our character and the willingness to take on pressure have to be exercised and built or they never reach their full potential.

In the interview I was asked which of the events of my varied career had put on the greatest amount of pressure. I could think of a number. I was certainly concerned when I went to the Central Party School to speak with six of China's most notable professors on the concept of the book before their media. They would be asking very thoughtful questions in Chinese on material I had not read in two years. But then reality flashed before me, and I realized that that was nothing compared to the 1986 Brenham Dance performance in which my daughter Beth participated at about the age of 5 or 6. This was the pressure-filled experience that would have even challenged my father's legendary coolness. My wife, Kitty, had been ill and the doctor put her in the hospital for a spinal tap to see if she had meningitis which had several outbreaks nearby. They took a spinal tap, which indicated that she was fine, but she could not get up for 24 hours. That is when she uttered the fateful words, "My goodness. What are we going to do about Beth's dance recital tonight? She is going to be heartbroken." After being convinced that this was a traumatic experience in Beth's young life, I bravely said that I would help. "Don't worry about it," I reassured Kitty. She did not seem that reassured but explained to me that there were only four performances. Beth had to change costumes for each, and it was my responsibility to be sure that she was with the right group at the right time. Kitty said I should get the schedule to see when the dances took place and told me where the costumes were. She could remember only three of the dances, but was sure I would have no problem getting the fourth.

At the time, I mainly wanted to reassure Kitty. And while I had a slight degree of trepidation, I was a veteran of perhaps 30 Brenham Maifests. I was considered a strategist with a variety of degrees, including military training, and how difficult could a dance recital be? Also in the back of my mind I realized that the first rule was to engage a professional whenever you need overwhelming force to solve a project. So, after reassuring Kitty and leaving, I immediately called the perfect expert. My sister Deanna was a veteran of seventeen recitals, a drum major who could keep a band in order, a superintendent of curriculum whose gaze could immediately chill all children into discipline before her, and a Maifest official who had dealt with costumes all her life. She would be able to sense what needed to go where and bring order out of chaos with a nod. Unfortunately, my telephone call revealed that Deanna, at the time I most needed her, was out of town with my mother, the other professional who has even more experience in these matters.

Beth and I arrive early at the place of the recital. And I was immediately lost. This was not an ordinary recital. It was a magnificent production a year in the making that is looked upon as almost military precision. All of the mothers were herding kids and making final adjustments. I have never seen so many children or so many costumes. When I got a schedule I found that there are a number of names of performances but I still did not know the fourth. I am the only father attempting this for all other mothers and kids were in the back changing rooms behind the high school auditorium stage while Beth and I were given a small area behind the curtains. The costumes were significantly difficult since they were not in one part but in several parts. It was like building a Rubik's cube solution, which goes with which having never seen the performances before, and seeing no one else wearing a similar costume.

The next three hours go with painful rapidity as I attempted to find out what type costume fits with which dance. Beth is young and wants to be helpful but senses my panic and is extremely concerned that she is not with all of her friends. I asked what costume goes with the dance, but she doesn't remember the costume. She just remembered the pirouette when you start. And I still did not know the name of the fourth number in which she participates because everyone that is going to get back with me never seems to do so. Finally, I got a program and got through all of it to try and find her name for the fourth performance. Once done, I then had to figure out which costume goes to which event. If there was a time of pressure, this was it. But the benefit was that Beth and I lived through it together. I am sure that she remembers that particular performance as one of her earliest memories.

This story points out that the sacrifices we make for our children not only build character in us but gives us a perspective that pulls us away from our daily lives and points to what is important. Learning to sacrifice is an acquired trait because you only do so when you find something in which you believe. And once you have learned to believe in family and care about them, then it makes it much easier to believe in the values that are going to enhance the future for the next generation. The sacrifice that is needed you may not do for yourself but for others for whom you care. What is learned in family relationships is a bonding of interest and an instilling of values that goes both directions

To show how this affects parents, last Christmas I had a request for two Disney princess dresses from our four-year-old granddaughter Clara. My daughter Meg thought I went overboard when I bought all dresses in the selection as well as all of the accessories. In fact, my friends in the hunting department where I buy guns, ammunition, and fishing supplies were quite curious looking at my basket when I requested they go in the back and find Belle's summer dress if they had any extras. Little will my son-in-law Dathan appreciate as I do the fact of having children learn how to dress in coordinated outfits early in life is an extremely important undertaking.

The heroes of children matter a great deal. Today sports, music, and entertainment stars seem to reach "hero" status in media's marketing efforts. Distinguishing between admiration of ability and credibility of thought becomes harder as even adults seem to lose the distinction. Heroes used to be chosen on why they did things, bravery for example, more than for what they did. Conversations that make this point are critical early in life, so they need focus not just on what people do well, but why they do it. The most important understanding is that morality and character are based in strength, not weakness.

The ultimate goal of many people is to be remembered after their death, to transcend generations. Monuments, businesses, and achievements often aimed at how many people remember your name, attempt this goal. The purpose of life should not be just to leave a legacy of a number of accomplishments, but should instead be to have changed the world so that it is more positive for your having been a part of it. Those require two different mindsets. In one you work to achieve recognition, in the other you work to achieve positive change. One deals more with ego; the other deals more with purpose. But the real "transcending" generation deals with ideas and values and is often focused on family because these guide their further success and are directly taught.

In this arena, one may be less important personally, but the ideas that transcend set the future for one's core ideals. The world may know you or your family, but your ideals define you more than just a name. Look at who is remembered in history, and with them is a positive or negative impression if they were significant. Beyond that, these values are what are instilled in the next generation, as our family has seen as a case study. These are often the same for people in different cultures. I have focused on morality between men as opposed to higher morality and religion. Too often the installation of basic moral values gets trapped in inaction because academic freedom, political correctness or difference of religion becomes the focus. If we start with fundamental values of integrity, family values and relationships, the common good, the Golden Rule, and the rule of law, we have a common bond between even differing cultures that all care for their dignity and children's future.

The essential part of the structure of the culture of responsibility rests with a core of uncommon men and women who provide the leadership to make it function. They are often not the elite, but the much more numerous leaders of the middle class that set the tone of responsibility through their service to society. They build the nonprofit structure of human or social capital in developed economies. What they believe has great impact on children because of their more localized influence. We need to understand them to fully understand the foundation they provide to larger structures. I have used my Father as an example because it shows an era and a culture that was built on what preceded it and affected what followed. If you understand him and his perspective of honor, you understand that basis of these concepts. He never wished to tell another what he had to do or to feel morally superior to any person. He told people what he was going to do and why. He felt sins were of omission as well as commission, so everyone could do better. He was a man who lived his life for others and gave strength to the community. Understanding him gives insight to how to instill values.

Just as important is that in understanding him and his father, it is easier to understand where my thoughts arose, and how and why I convey them to my children. We are all stereotypes to those that do not know us. Our actions and our ideas can be looked upon as mean and ruthless, or instead as honorable and tough depending on our motivation. This longer examination of family values transition thus gives an insight to the core of these thoughts and an example of an uncommon man that must be the base of strength in a culture of service and honor. Many families of various cultures will identify with us and with our ultimate motivations. Dad was a father, a teacher, a role model, and an *uncommon man* because of his dedication not just to family, but also to society. The duality of interest shaped his perspective on both.

People shape perspectives and family values and these become a part of how you think about life. In late 2003, my son Tee decided after the 9/11 tragedy that with the efforts in Iraq taking place, he needed to participate and voluntarily joined the Naval Reserve. A number of people questioned that logic because he had a good job, he was getting married, and it was not perhaps the best of timing to be entering the military. However, a lot of that depends on your perspective. When he was sworn in as an officer, there was a special ceremony on the retired Battleship Texas at the San Jacinto Monument where they fly a flag for the officer, and the Commissioning Reserve officer was kind enough to let us be involved in the ceremony. Since I was a retired Lieutenant Commander from Navy JAG, I was able to give the Oath. Kitty's father who was a veteran of World War II and had fond remembrances of the Battleship Texas covering his landings in North Africa was able to put on Tee's hat. His fiancée and his mother were able to put on his lapel pins. They took down the flag that they had hoisted for him and gave it to him as a remembrance. I gave him for his flag shadowbox the compass that Grandfather Knolle carried in World War I, a worn silver dollar Dad carried through World War II that I mention in more detail in the next section, my National Defense Pin from the Vietnam era, and his Grandfather Wright gave him some memorabilia from his time in World War II. The shadowbox probably would say more with those items about why he decided to do what he did than explanations to people who think such an action was foolish. There are values that give substance because they are instilled within people by the history of the family and the culture. They are not as much learned, as they are an understanding, not different from Confucius' recognition of the obligations that people have within societies.

The Development of Uncommon Men:
A Case Study of "Jackrabbit Dippel"

There are three marks of a superior man: being virtuous,
he is free from anxiety; being wise, he is free from perplexity;
being brave, he is free from fear.
— Confucius

Growing up in Brenham, Texas, I often heard my father called a number of things. Most called him "Dip." A lot called him "Sheriff." Some of the Texas Rangers nicknamed him "The Peacemaker" because of his reputation and very muscular build at six foot three and 240 pounds. So it seemed rather unusual when every now and then an old friend would call him "Jackrabbit."

Dad was born in 1910 in the small town of Brenham, Texas, which was in the center of Washington County, and the heart of Stephen F. Austin's early settlement. Sam Houston had lived nearby, and his wife was buried at Independence to the Northeast. The family of William Barrett Travis of the Alamo had a farm toward Chappell Hill, and his wife was buried in the Masonic Cemetery there. Dad took great interest in the upkeep of that old cemetery out of respect for heritage that was chronicled there. Stephen F. Austin had lived at San Felipe not too distant to the East. And Washington on the Brazos, which was nearby, was where Texas Independence had been declared. It was an area steeped in history, but still relied on agriculture and land as its basic economy. These factors helped shape the culture of the area.

Dad's father, Henry Dippel, had come from Germany in the early 1880s when he was six years old. He was not a large man but worked very diligently and established Brenham Wholesale Grocery. I recently ran across a letter from my Grandfather Henry to a company from whom he bought in California. In 1929 grandfather advocated that Dad and several friends spread their wings after they had "remodeled and rebuilt" a car. They were just out of high school and took off to the West. Since he did business in a number of places with the Wholesale, he had many ties throughout the country and sent letters similar to this one to a number of people along their route.

This letter was symbolic of how the networking of families through business was helpful when they could not visit often and makes a critical point of how relationships were particularly important in those days. The credibility of relationships from people who knew and trusted each other formed a strong network. As people traveled by car, they normally found they knew people along the road and brought a series of letters with them. It was the calling card of youth in that era and had an effect upon them that was dramatic. They felt an obligation to behave and honor the faith placed in them by the giver of the letter. And it also showed the importance of respect and relationships that someone would accept them based on the name and reputation of a man far away. The culture of that day reinforced the necessity for integrity.

Grandfather Henry's pride and joy were two great horses that caught everyone's attention when they were in tandem. He spoke four languages and built up trading relationships going as far as Mexico. He was successful enough to be included in Archie P. McDonald and Ronald L. Spiller's *Notable East Texans* that profiled his contributions to commerce. After an early success, he built a house on a hill on South Market Street that contained great varieties of wood. He got his friends to send them with the packing crates from different parts of the world as he purchased merchandise. Dad said one of his father's great disappointments was a special wood cask he had gotten to age wine that he specially made from a vineyard in an orchard he kept and tended behind the house. He and Dad filled and buried it, as was apparently the custom. Five years later they dug it up only to find a knothole had come out and drained it. His dad told him to remember that he could plan, but fate had its own agenda. His response was to try and order another cask. Dad learned from him the value that a broadened mind search for experiences could bring to life.

Grandfather Henry was a man of ingenuity and strong principles. One of the things that most drove Dad to be a sheriff had been the fact that when he went to school on an occasion in the 1920s other kids told him that his father had better be careful what he said or he would end up tarred and feathered. It was a time of unique political unrest and various informal organizations sympathizing with the Ku Klux Klan movement of that era emerged. It was the time and the political battles where Governor Dan Moody set a tone with Grandfather's apparent support. Dad rushed home and told his Father who noted to him that he was aware of some people's thoughts, but it was easy to be afraid, much harder to have the strength of character to do the right thing for the right reasons. Dad often made that point to us. Conscience is of strength, not of weakness.

In those days there wasn't a great deal of entertainment, but the one thing that mattered was high school athletics, particularly football, played on Friday nights. It was not as developed in those years with leather helmets, and you only had the ability to go to bi-district. But it was the focus that pulled a town together, particularly if you had a really good team. People played both offense and defense, and Dad was both a linebacker and a halfback. He had not developed the size that he did later in life, but he had speed and ability and was extremely difficult to catch in the open field. Brenham won bi-district two years in part because of long kickoff returns that he made for touchdowns. One would have thought that he got the name "Jackrabbit" from that prowess on the football field. But as life would have it, that only added to a "local legend."

Dad used to take all the neighborhood dogs to hunt rabbits at the outskirts of town. There would be all types of dogs in his collection. He taught some of them to hunt and others joined in, but he knew the characteristics of rabbits. Swamp rabbits often use water to evade, cottontails often hide, and jackrabbits run. Many times you could tell the nature of the rabbit by the way the dogs followed him and barked. Dad often went to an area not too far from town out on "Gun and Rod Road." At the time this area was secluded and heavily wooded with several creeks and a swimming hole that was a favorite among the local kids. The road leading to this swimming hole crossed a small bridge.

One day the dogs spotted a jackrabbit. They ran the rabbit hard for about twenty minutes with Dad following. By listening to the dogs' howls, he knew that the rabbit was circling back and figured it to be a jackrabbit. Since jackrabbits usually don't like to swim through water but run, Dad figured the rabbit might go to the bridge and cross there. So he cut across in that direction, arriving just as the rabbit was running across the bridge. At close range he could see that the animal was totally exhausted but the dogs were further back and silent.

The rabbit continued up the road, but rather than shoot it, Dad dropped his gun and gave chase thinking he could catch it without wasting a shell. Just as he was closing in on the rabbit one of the local families happened to be driving down the road in a horse-drawn buggy. Panting, Dad ran right up beside them, grabbed the rabbit by the ears and held it high in the air to demonstrate his success. The family was astounded. Soon the word spread around town that Dad trained for football by running down jackrabbits and surely was the fastest and toughest young man anyone had seen in a long time. Dad often pointed out to me that this was a good example of why one should view acclaim skeptically. It was always far wiser to judge a man by solid evidence and a long track record than by a certain event.

The other nicknames that he got through life were particularly appropriate. Mother and all of his friends always called him "Dip." He learned a great deal from his father. During the depression in the '30s, Dad had gone off to the University of Texas and was playing football until he hurt his knee. But with the Depression the wholesale business was doing poorly, Grandfather Henry had to let many of his people go. Dad had to come back to help and one of the first things that they did together was for him to show Dad how to crack eggs with a spoon with the least damage and how to rip flour sacks so that little damage was done. Dad was very concerned that his father had succumbed to the pressure of the times and asked him why they were damaging good material when times were so difficult. Grandfather Henry told him something that shaped his entire perspective of life. His father told him the men he had been forced to let go came back often looking for work. There was none and they were having a difficult time. If he offered to give them the eggs and flour some would refuse charity, others would accept and lose dignity. Asking them to help by buying damaged goods solved the problem. He noted that personal dignity was the most significant thing that a man could have and that it was important to show respect for it. It was beyond courtesy, but was an obligation to other men by the Golden Rule.

After Grandfather Henry's death, the family sold much of their interest in Brenham Wholesale, and Dad and his brother kept and ran the Dippel Coffee Company. He took care of his mother who preferred to move to a smaller apartment behind the bigger house, and because of its size and appearance, she leased it to the local funeral home. Dad always had the desire in later life to go back and restore the home and bought thousands of bricks over the years for that potential undertaking.

During the era of selling Old Homestead Coffee, he probably completed more "white china" sets than anyone around since he gave them as souvenirs with the coffee. While the coffee had a great reputation, the new effort of keeping it fresh by vacuum packing spelled the end of the Dippel Coffee Company because of the investment required to try and expand it in a fairly tough economic era. During this time, Dad married Mother whom he had dated in high school. Her family had moved to Brenham from nearby Wesley and her father had been a renowned doctor from a family of doctors. Unfortunately, Grandfather Kinch Knolle died when he was forty-two in part, it is believed, from pneumonia and fevers that he suffered in treating many of the epidemics of that era and during service in World War I. He had a compass that he carried through much of World War I that Mother gave Dad that he always treasured. Two years after his death, Mother's mother died of leukemia, and she was left alone at sixteen in charge of raising her two younger brothers. With the family's help she did so and became the administrator of the local hospital. When they were married, Dad spent a lot of time helping her youngest brother "Buddy" who was only three yeas old at his parents' death.

Since he had responsibilities and the Coffee Company was not a great future, he looked at one of the best paying jobs locally during the time just after the Depression, which was being sheriff. He ran, and in a field of eight won outright. He greatly enjoyed not the power of the position, but the respect that it held if you spent your life helping people. He was elected in 1940, and America became involved in World War II in late 1941. Because he had a position that made him ineligible for the draft, he resigned as sheriff and turned it over to his chief deputy and volunteered for the army.

During that time period, he made a number of unique friendships such as future Texas Attorney General, John Ben Shepperd, when they served together in Battle Creek, Michigan. Dad's physical abilities and knowledge of weapons made him a natural instructor in martial arts and for various weapons. So he ended with different postings than many of his local friends. A number of them were in one unit, the 36th Division, which played such a significant part in battles such as Salerno, Anzio, and the Rapido River with tremendous casualties that always had an effect upon the area and added to a high level of patriotism. Dad etched a silver dollar with the date he went into the military and the date he came out, and always carried it as a remembrance. At the time of his death it was in his pocket, and it was incredibly well worn. It was something I kept as probably one of the closest representations of him.

When Dad came back from World War II, he again ran for sheriff and won and served until 1960 when he retired to become a banker. His time as sheriff gave him a unique perspective about life, the different ways that the law functioned and how discipline within society worked. Enforcement was important. But the nature of enforcement, or how discipline was applied in a society, was as significant as the laws themselves because the respect for the law often depended on whether people feared or respected the law. How the law was enforced and the attitude of a sheriff mattered. He could be a policeman that looked for what they did wrong or he could be a peacemaker that they knew would enforce the law, but whose first concern was their wellbeing. His father's lesson on personal dignity set his concept. He was a solid friend if you were honest but a formidable and determined adversary if you were corrupt.

To make extra money during these sheriffing years, Dad had a ranch at Chappell Hill that we called Thunder Ranch where he leased several hundred acres. The Thunder Ranch was an interesting brand because it had the THD of Tieman H. Dippel made with the "TD" and a lightening bolt making the "H." (But also this ranch had the reputation of being a place where it always thundered and almost never rained.) It seldom had good grass, but it had an old farmhouse that Dad filled with hay and some great gullies. Every Saturday I would go out with him while he worked the cattle and take my BB gun to develop my prowess with it. I learned a lot about electric fences the hard way, a bunch more about hornets and yellow jackets, but I actually did kill a couple of mice in that old farm house. At lunch we would go into town to Lesser's Store where we would get a coke, cheese and crackers, and Dad would visit with a number of his friends. Mr. Harry's store was one of the oldest representatives of the National Tailoring Company. And I must say that when I was young both Dad and I had some of the finest fitting suits tailored and measured I have had in my life. It showed that even in small towns there was a lot of civility and quality that could be achieved if you looked.

The great ranching experience I most remember was going to the King Ranch to pick up one of the very earliest young Santa Gertrudis bulls. Dad's cousin, Val Gene Lehmann, had been very active with the wildlife development of the ranch in its early stages and told Dad about the uniqueness of this new breed. Dad had often hunted down in South Texas, bringing back long rattlesnake skins that could be made into belts. So when Val Gene arranged for him to buy a bull, he decided it was worth the investment.

We went down to Falfurrias, Texas, to pick up the bull in a 1953 Chevrolet affectionately called "the rocket" because Dad had souped it up for chases. We had a trailer hitch with a small trailer in back. I was relatively young at the time and all of those bulls and cows looked extremely big and not very friendly. This particular young bull was right off the range, and it took a lot of effort to get him into the smaller trailer, which he shook from one side to the other.

I could tell Dad was a little concerned how the trip back was going to be. After the long drive of six or seven hours to get to Thunder Ranch, he let the bull out which proceeded to chase him rather than running away. I thought that my fun times on the ranch were now ended. As I told Dad, I thought that bull would kill him if he was not careful. And I didn't have any doubt that if I was anywhere out there, he would kill me, and I didn't know why we wanted to keep him. At the time, Dad was throwing out some cottonseed meal to the rest of the cows and the bull had run off to the far extremity watching. Dad made an observation to me that within a month or two the bull would be up at Dad's hands pushing the other cows away in order to get the cottonseed meal. He would find some of it. He would eat it, and he would understand with the rest of the cows what was happening. And he would change his approach to life from one of independence to one of dependence because it was a lot easier. He would watch the herd and adapt to it.

His point was very clear because he felt that individual responsibility is what gave strength and character and that you trade off a great amount of that independence when you start accepting the fact that others provide everything for you. It was a point not lost about individuals or even society, which he felt, was losing much of its core strength.

In the times that Dad was sheriff, he had three experiences where in all likelihood he should have been dead. The first was one where a man drew a gun on him and actually pulled the trigger while Dad grabbed the gun and the pin lodged in the skin between Dad's thumb and first finger. He noted that he had never disarmed anyone so quickly as in that particular situation. Nonetheless, it had an effect on him because from that point where the barrel was aimed, he felt he could have been dead.

The next time was an interesting one with an older gentleman that had taken a shotgun and was shooting at everyone in the neighborhood thinking that they were Indians. He had apparently become deranged with age and a medical condition, and Dad had to find him and disarm him. After talking with the man's wife and understanding he was out back, Dad proceeded very carefully when he suddenly heard a click. There in the cellar door the man was pointing a gun at him. He quickly shouted, "It's me, Tieman Dippel, the Indians are after me. Cover me while I come in." The man, in shock, hesitated but understood enough to let Dad go by. Dad then told him that he could get a shot at the Indian on the left and asked for the gun and took it and took the man out. A second time he reassessed his life.

The third was a car wreck several years before he retired where in a high-speed chase his deputy was driving and he was in the passenger seat after a robbery in Burton, Texas. In the chase their car crashed, and Dad had broken ribs, a broken leg, punctured lung and a variety of other ailments. But, if you looked at the car both he and his deputy were particularly lucky.

He took an approach to life that it could end at any time and you needed both to appreciate life and be prepared.

He learned a lot in his years as sheriff, but probably the thing he emphasized to me the most was the importance of not letting pride or arrogance ever get control of you. He pointed out that it was not only a sin, but was quite frankly, very bad strategy. His prime example of this was one time when he just returned after World War II and got a call that there was a really big man threatening everybody at a local beer joint. He went there and described a man of about three hundred pounds that had been bullying everyone, but was considerably drunk. As Dad described it, this is when the devil gave him the vision of the fame of a great reputation.

He decided that even though the man was big, he was obviously drunk. Dad was not small and had also been training in martial arts in the military so this would be a chance for him to subdue him and get a reputation as being a really tough man that could help him in the future. Well, Dad approached him, told him he was under arrest, and needed to come with him. And, as anticipated, the fellow took a swing at him which Dad ducked, and then Dad hit him with a right cross—the hardest that he had hit any individual in his life. Well, Dad broke his wrist and now had a three-hundred pound fellow chasing after him around the dance floor while he tried to rabbit punch him with his left hand and kick him into submission for about twenty embarrassing minutes.

He claimed his most humiliating experience was the one where he was running down a felon in front of a number of people, caught him, grabbed him, and at the exact same time crashed into a red hornet's nest. The people in the distance could not figure out what was going on as Dad and the felon were swatting everywhere and running in all different directions while he tried to hold on to him. The word around town was that it was the craziest fight people had ever seen, and for a big tough man, Dad sure had trouble with little fellows.

The people in law enforcement that knew him best—other sheriffs and many of the Texas Rangers—called him the "Peacemaker." In part it was because of a reputation for toughness, but it was also for the philosophy of law enforcement in life that he exhibited. He was a scoutmaster even when he did not have kids because he thought that that was how you taught youth and gave back to the community.

When he was sheriff, he would take a number of the younger kids every couple of years and show them around the sheriff's office, explain law enforcement and inevitably take them to the jail. There a lot of times you would find a big man in the cell that would be "the wild man of green mountain" who had just been captured—the most dangerous man they had probably run into in the last twenty years. He would rattle the bars and give terrifying screams. Dad would explain why you would not want to be in jail. He would then hear a call from Walter Schoenemann, the jailer, who would ask him to come down to take a telephone call. Dad would leave and close the door (which locked) behind the boys as they looked across at several cells. Inevitably, the boys would make fun of the wild man, and the longer they were there, the more aggressive some would be. Suddenly, the "wild man" would push on the cell door, and it would open. The kids scrambled as fast as they could to try and get out the back door, which was locked. After a tense minute or so with the "wild man" just looking at them, Dad would open the door from the other side, and the "wild man" would shake their hands. It was an item of great excitement for a young man in Brenham, Texas, but the discussion that often took place after that had an equal effect on shaping lives. Too many youth in that era had no respect for the dignity of others. Dad's point was, "How many of you made fun of him, and how many of you wished you hadn't?" It was the lesson of the Golden Rule that was emphasized in a way the kids never forgot.

Dad always made a clear point to kids—there is a huge difference in toughness and ruthlessness or being mean. Why you did what you did, and the restraints you placed upon yourself defined you. Power is not greatness. It is only a part of the execution of purpose.

Mother and Dad both saw poverty, illness, pettiness and the like as the real sins more than people. Mother saw the world with forgiveness and compassion. Dad's life gave him a different perspective. He understood the necessity of having and using power because evil and convenience would often fill any vacuum. So where Mother never fully understood the use of force, he acknowledged that reality requires it. Strength was a necessity, but there were many approaches to how power could be used and why. Personal dignity, honor, and character had to be both the base of power and the limits upon it.

What mattered to Dad was the community. He didn't look upon himself as a policeman or even a law enforcement officer. He looked upon himself as a peacemaker with a broader duty. It involved honor and an understanding that just throwing people in jail did not solve problems. He took me several times to the Huntsville Prison Rodeo where the inmates performed, and many of the sheriffs would gather as an annual event. He was not one of the most popular sheriffs with the inmates when his name was announced. With Dad's demeanor that seemed very unusual to me because he went through his life trying to make friends and avoid enemies. He explained to me that the people that were there deserved to be there. There were a lot of them, and they were going to be there for a long time. He had a very strong constituency compared to a lot of others. He had a very clear vision of good and evil. He always said he had the Golden Rule down. He was working on forgiveness but never could forget. His biggest failing was "turning the other cheek" particularly where bad intent was concerned. To him, evil was to be opposed.

In Washington County they tried to redeem youth by giving them additional chances and working hard with the parents to build a culture that respected law and order. He had the support of the community shown in the fact that he had an almost unanimous conviction record of anyone he brought to trial in over twenty-years. Perhaps the only one that anyone could remember that he lost was one of his last cases that involved a man that had been indicted for the theft of a little girl's dog. As one of the Rangers told me that case had bugged him more than many others. The little girl's grandparents were from Houston and were not happy with their daughter's marriage. They had finally visited and gave the little girl a very expensive dog as a gift. It was the only thing the little girl had that she truly cared about, and Dad could tell she absolutely loved the dog. It was stolen and Dad was certain he knew who had done it, but it would be very difficult to prove. He took the little girl another puppy, a beagle, but it wasn't quite the same. He had enough evidence to get an indictment. The fellow spent some time in the Washington County Jail, so there was some justice. But he always felt a special obligation to the most vulnerable, they often had the least in life and anything they lost was particularly painful.

Dad's approach to law enforcement was very methodical. He started every action with a handshake, a smile and a positive intent to settle a problem. He didn't allow his officers to be arrogant. They had to be careful where they parked. They didn't give tickets for parking or often for speeding unless it endangered people. The point was that law enforcement ought to be a friend that protected you and helped you. It should be respected, not be something you feared. He wore a gun only on certain occasions, and usually it was to create an effect. As he often said, a handshake and smile are the most powerful weapons, but a gun and a blackjack never hurt the conversation.

In reality he did not like blackjacks. He had been taught how to use them to try and stun criminals when they pulled a knife. One of the first times he had to use one, the blackjack broke and the sand ran down the fellow's back. He would have probably been knifed but for the fact that the fellow thought he was bleeding and became terrified. From that point on Dad carried a very long aluminum flashlight that he used much as a billy club. He was ambidextrous so it became his main weapon of choice, and he put it in whichever hand was most appropriate. It became so synonymous with him that it got the nickname "the light of enlightenment."

One of the more interesting stories one of his deputies told me was how he liked the aluminum because it had the same shock effect as a blackjack, but bent to limit the damage to the person. He had a collection of those that he had bent in various physical encounters that were relatively common in that day.

He was always very graduated in his level of force. He would begin with a sense of dignity and concern, but to the degree necessary, the level of intensity increased. My mother was a devout Christian and believed that you should never have an enemy in the world. Dad was Christian, but his cathedral was the outdoors and nature. And he looked at life shaped through the concept of justice. If you had enemies, they should be ones that should define you because of where you stand. He would always add a bit jokingly to me, it is also good if they are weak, stupid, and hated. There were two or three people in the county that always opposed him in elections, and it was a matter of pride to him. He was independent and would sacrifice to keep it that way.

Dad had a unique way of making a point and sometimes he could make it sharply in almost a joking manner that took off the edge. As sheriff, he spent a lot of time with the County Commissioners' Court, which handled a number of local affairs. At one time, a bureaucrat, I think from Washington, came to explain a new program and how the county was supposed to implement it. He apparently had talked a great deal about how much knowledge there was in Washington as the local officials expressed their frustration at the practical aspect of what they understood needed to be done.

Apparently the bureaucrat continued to explain that they just didn't understand the program properly and did not have all of the background knowledge that had gone into the decisions to create it. Dad apparently smiled and said, "Mister, you have to understand that around here, being that we are a rural area, we learn a lot from animals and the natural laws." The man looked at him with some bewilderment and disdain as he continued, "Here I think birds make the applicable parallel. In this part of the country there is a rare eagle but a lot of big hawks that are really majestic birds that soar when you get the big winds that make the little birds head for cover. You have turkeys that are good birds in many ways, but are among the dumbest birds that ever existed and some say will drown in a rainstorm staring with open mouths at the heavens. Then you have the vultures that eat the carrion that shows the misfortunate of others and live a life based on it. Here, it is not that we don't understand the program, we eliminated the eagle pretty early, we just can't figure out whether it's a turkey or a buzzard, and that does make a difference."

Dad's perspective was that you should live your life in order to convert people. He didn't think you ever had very effective long-term conversions at the point of a gun even though in an immediate instance it might seem that way. Nonetheless, he was a religious man shaped by the experiences of his job. His favorite badge was chipped on one point and people often told him that he ought to get a new one. He noted that it reminded him that men are far from perfect, as was he. And he hoped that his sins were not of commission but were of omission. He realized that smart men make mistakes, as do good men.

A good part of his job was trying to put people on the right path not necessarily put them in jail. He did not feel it his place to provide judgment on men, but to arrange the circumstances so they were enlightened to it. One time after a rather serious encounter where a man attempted to stab him with quite unfortunate results for the perpetrator, he was cynically asked, "How can you say you are a Christian when you do things like that?" Dad supposedly smiled and replied, "As a Christian I am taught to love sinners and to hate sin. My problem was separating the sin of that knife from the sinner, and believe me I was trying to accomplish it as quickly and as effectively as I could. Unfortunately, it just stayed attached too long."

Dad could accept criminals stealing for he understood evil. However, he could never accept or understand a man beating his wife and children or his failure to accept family responsibility. For that reason, he did a great deal to help in those areas of need. He understood the importance of a man's personal dignity and often went out of his way to acknowledge it as a strategy as much as a virtue. He understood that it was personal dignity that often made men fight and often was the spark that excited problems. He used to tell his deputies to take into account the size of a man and his apparent attitude, but in those days to look at his hands. A lot of people used knives or if they did fight, their knuckles would be covered with scars, and you could tell a lot about how experienced they tended to be. He had much more limited concern about a big man with what he called "pretty hands" than he did a smaller man that had the hands that showed he had a fighting attitude. His philosophy was always to avoid a fight if at all possible, but he noted that sometimes that was unavoidable. And in life, principle on some occasions left you no alternative but to stand. If you had to fight a battle you would lose, then the one rule was to make the loss so painful to the other side that they would never want to fight you again. It was not unlike the old Texas attitude of Travis at the Alamo that we shall inflict the most grievous of injuries before we die.

Dad read a lot of history, particularly of the Old West, and his hero was Captain Jack Hayes of the Texas Rangers. Hayes was probably one of the most feared and famous fighters of Texas history and played a significant part not only in the Comanche Wars, but also in the Mexican War itself before he went on to build a fortune in San Francisco. Dad appreciated the fact that his reputation was such that the Comanches had one word in the Indian language that was the name given to him: Man-It-Is-Very-Bad-Luck-To-Get-In-Fight-With-Because-Devil-Help-Him. Dad liked him because he was a man of honor even if the Europeans did shorten the Comanche name to "Devil Jack." Honor and conscience was much the same thing to that breed of law enforcement and were very significant in those times and were remembered. The twenty years he spent being sheriff created an interesting family life. Dad was absolutely fearless where most danger was concerned. But where Mother was involved, he had significant trepidation.

I remember the time that he took Deanna and me to the grocery store. We were driving back and on the police radio they asked him to come help the city police with a man barricaded in the old Santa Fe depot. He went there, told Deanna and me to stay in the car, lock the doors, and stay down. He walked over to find out what was happening, made an assessment, went in, pulled the fellow out, turned him over to a deputy and was in a rather macho mood as a reporter interviewed him for the news. That changed his temperament rather dramatically as we drove home. It wasn't that he minded being lauded on the act of courage. It was the absolute certainty that Mother would hear what he did and understand that the kids were sitting there in the car. Mother and Dad were to a great degree opposites in styles but not values. His characteristics were toughness, integrity, and honor. Hers were a deep Christianity, culture, and a sense of organization of how you made a home. Having murderers come up and surrender to her as occurred on one occasion, or having the kids involved in potential shootouts did not fit in her concept of family organization. Dad feared little, but Mother's discontent was something that always bothered him. She had a gentle, but very firm way of making a point.

In Brenham we have a Junior Maifest where perhaps 600 or more small kids in costumes are introduced over three hours or more. It has been around a hundred years, and attendance used to be almost mandatory if you had kids involved. One of my earliest memories at about four is being dressed as a Gingerbread Man and kicking crickets on the walkway as I came out. Dad would always attend and for several years a deputy would come after about twenty minutes and say, "Sheriff, we have some problem out at the carnival and need your help." Apparently, about the third year as the deputy was coming up, Mom looked up at Dad and said, "You know Dip, its embarrassing how you don't train your people to take responsibility better and learn to handle problems on their own. That could be a problem in an election." The message was clear, Dad was hooked from then on watching Deanna and me evolve through a lot of costumes.

He was not an emotional man and there were perhaps only two times in my life that I ever saw the equivalent of a tear. The first was when we went down to M. D. Anderson Hospital to have a biopsy done on my mother's tumor that thankfully turned out benign, and the second was when I graduated from the Business School at the University of Texas in 1968. For many years they had not had a 4.0 average, and I had been fortunate to achieve one. I received the Delta Sigma Pi Key and at the reception that followed, Dad was congratulated by a number of my professors. And he was very uncharacteristically ill at ease. For a man who was never intimidated by politicians, criminals or anyone else, I felt it might have been because of his pride in me.

He and mother had sacrificed all of their lives so that my sister and I could have an education and provided the best they could for us. For that reason, I studied and was Valedictorian in high school, did well at college and tried to achieve everywhere that would show them appropriate appreciation. Instead when I talked with him, he felt ill at ease with all of the professors and the amount of knowledge that was in that room. He worshiped the importance of education and had read a lot of history. He felt to a degree inferior to the knowledge that they all had and hoped that I was not ashamed of him. In reality, he had more wisdom than the vast majority of them. I think, interestingly, the most unique conversation he had was with my mentor, Dean George Kozmetsky, who had co-founded Teledyne then went to the University of Texas to be Dean of the Business School and later founded the Institute of Constructive Capitalism. He and Dad seemed to hit it off extremely well. I later learned that much of it had to do with their World War II experiences and with what they believed were the most important aspects of life.

In 1960 Dad retired as sheriff, sold the herd of cattle that he had built over the years, and bought a stake in a small bank in Brenham, The Farmers National Bank, upon the president's death. For twelve years until his death in 1972, he served as head of it and helped lead the Industrial Foundation and was involved in many civic activities. A lifetime of smoking that started in World War II took its toll, and emphysema and a heart condition weakened him. I returned at Christmas in 1971 with my wife Kitty from Jacksonville, Florida, where I was a Lieutenant in the Naval Judge Advocate General's Corps. We had a final Christmas that was very important to him, and he and I had one last conversation.

When I wrote *The New Legacy* in 1986, I used this conversation as an introduction because it perhaps defined my life in that it capsulated everything that he taught me over the years. His was a generation that he felt had failed to move America forward, but in reality, history has shown it to be the one with a great amount of strength. I think he and

Mother would be happy to know of the thoughts that live of them rest in the ideas that they expressed during life. My mother would be very surprised to learn that one of the top women professors of the Central Party School focused on the simplicity of her motto—character is what you do when no one is watching. Dad would be surprised at their interest in his law enforcement philosophy. Little issues can be a base for much bigger things because ideas live on.

The problem in our modern time is that everyone tells us what we ought to be and what we need to do to succeed while we are still trying to figure out who we are. Our early years are captivated by "getting ahead" as we perceive it. While our later years, as ambition, energy, and patience fade, are spent on evaluating experience for the wisdom of life's meaning and values. All of us look at life differently from our experiences. But often, as you go through the trunks of memory, you find things that make you realize that you are not so much the product of what the world has created. Rather who you are relates back to family far beyond just parents and their parents. I never knew my Grandfather or Grandmother Knolle except by the love my mother had for them and how their values shaped everything she did and gave a guilt that made her despondent if she ever felt she would have disappointed them. It was passed on to me and from what my children tell me to them and I think in my grandchildren. It is not just habit; it is the culture of who we are. With wisdom, we recognize this is a key part of our personal dignity. It can be cultivated or dulled by society, but it is still there because it is what we ultimately are. When I read the obituaries of my grandparents due to a late in life find, I can identify far more with why I am who I am and life is more satisfying when one's perspective is not who you can be but who you are. The memorials for my parents speak to their hearts.

For Mother it was a project with Hope Ministry that provides Bibles to inmates in part in remembrance of the fact that she used to bake extra cookies for the people that were in jail at Christmas and at Easter. She cared a great deal about people. For Dad it is an award called the Texas Peacemaker Award given by the Sheriffs' Association of Texas that recognizes the importance of not just law enforcement but of being the catalyst that keeps a sense of conscience within a community. Dad may not have had the knowledge of all of the professors in that room that day at the University of Texas, but he had a great degree of wisdom of how knowledge should be used and what was really important in life. At his death he was a satisfied man that only wanted to pass on a set of thoughts that he gave me in this last conversation:

A Father's Last Words

"Now, I don't want you to worry about me. I will get over this as I have survived everything else. But just in case something unexpected should happen to me, I want you to take charge. Don't let the family dwell upon it. Time and life go on. I have been fortunate to be able to live my life as a lion. Two weeks of that is worth a lifetime as a lamb.

"I chose to keep our family in Brenham and Texas, rather than going to other places and trying new opportunities. That might have been more profitable, but Brenham still holds the values that first brought your great grandfather to this state almost 100 years ago. Some of these values will change, but most will remain the same as they have throughout history. It is important to remember that no matter how they try in Congress, they cannot repeal the law of gravity. God's laws and natural laws are the ultimate power in this world. Some people may only discover them after a lifetime, but they do exist. Recognizing them is critical.

"The most important thing I can leave you is a good name, and I think I have done that. Your mother and I have worked and saved a long time to create this beginning for you and your sister. Home has always been the most important part of our lives and should be of yours. We hope we have taught you the importance of your values and passed along our heritage. You have an education that will help you achieve what is really important in life—being a responsible citizen, loving husband, and sensitive father. There may be more to living, but these three areas can make your life deeply satisfying.

"What I feel I will be leaving you is an opportunity—a start from which you can make your own mark. The time that we spend on earth is relatively small in comparison with the great movement of history. All we can do within our life span is to make the world better than it was when we first arrived. All fortunes eventually are dispersed, but the ideas and values that you leave to society can live forever. I hope you and Kitty will have a wonderful family, just as your mother and I had with you and Deanna. Being a good father is your greatest challenge and responsibility. Teach your children the ideas you think are proper. Give them the best values that you can. And teach them how to judge what is best for their lives and nation. We must try to make every generation's character better than the one before it and build a higher standard of living through wise policies.

"Don't underestimate the power and value of ideas, politics, and money. But never let any of these be your God. Learn to acquire and use them, but make absolutely certain that you understand the purposes for which they are being used.

"Lots of things have changed in Texas since I was a young man, and they will continue to change even faster during the next 20 years as your generation assumes leadership. You will need to keep a clear sense of what's important. I remember hearing how my dad came to Texas from Germany. Whenever a family suffered a bad harvest or business disaster, their neighbors helped them out until they were able to get on their feet again. Now it seems that everyone is out for his own piece of the pie regardless of who else starves. There is still charity, but people are sometimes too busy to hear their consciences. Too often even charity itself is commercialized; but if a dime out of each dollar reaches the needy, it is worth our efforts.

"Life is already different from a few years ago. I'm worried about the way politics is changing. People don't know their leaders personally. They don't seem to have the same respect as they did in my day for the ideas that made America strong. Texas can have great impact on our country. But as Texans, we can either mature and bring our ideas to other Americans, or we can create a petty state that will be defeated by partnership. If that happens, we will make little difference.

"I have hope that you and other young people can understand the changes occurring in politics and economics and how they effect you. Then you'll be able to handle them. In the process, You'll turn Texas and America in a more positive direction again.

"Remember to associate with people who care more about whether they go to heaven or hell than whether they become governor of Texas or head of a company. Ambition can be your worst enemy. Often you are not a good leader until you have lost your ambition and come face to face with what is most important in life. Guard against both ambition and pride, or in the long run you will be a loser, perhaps not in appearance, but in reality. You will have to deal with all types of people in life. Some will be genuine and others will not. It will be hard to judge them until you have had experience with them. Do not hesitate to cultivate friendships because that is what makes life enjoyable. However, watch new acquaintances for a while before giving them your trust.

"One certainty in life is that you are not always on top. There are many people who try to avoid the falls by changing philosophies. These are people of convenience. They're often successful in the short term, while they are on earth. But I have always wondered whether they were successful in the sense of eternity. I feel following conscience is a far better guide.

"Remember to judge people on their merit and not by their possessions or jobs. People should be judged by how they use their success rather than by how much they acquire. There is a difference between self-respect and

pride. Just as there will always be differences in abilities and destinies, there always will be economic distinctions. But we have a responsibility to allow people to keep their self-respect. Your grandfather taught this to me early in life when he took me to his wholesale grocery. The Depression made life in Texas very tough, and few people made money. Everyone helped his neighbors and enjoyed closeness and cooperation. Your grandfather and I would slit open sacks of flour and spend what seemed to be a lifetime trying to crack, not break some eggs. I thought this was one of the most foolish things I had ever seen and could not understand why he would ruin good merchandise at a time when everyone was losing money.

"So he sat down with me, and we had a conversation I will always remember. He said his employees had helped him build the business. They had gone through many long years together to make the business a success. They all knew he couldn't keep them on, but my dad felt he had a responsibility to help. Dad said, `If you offer these people money for doing nothing, some of them would not take it because they would lose their self-respect. Those who would accept the money would suffer equally from a loss of inner strength.' So, I watched with admiration as my father offered damaged goods to his former employees in exchange for helping him move the merchandise.

"The older you become, the more you'll recognize the importance of finding a purpose in life. But first you need to learn about reality. Emotion more than thought rules your life when you are a child. Ambition and ego guide your conscience more than responsibility. As your maturity and responsibility develop, you'll think about morality. Your thoughts will reach a deeper level of understanding. You will discover that God gave you freedom of choice in how you live your life. The most important thing you can do is to find a sense of love and oneness with God and other people. I became a better person when I learned the lessons of stewardship and how to deal with others by reading the Bible. In that way, I found my own meaning for life. You will go through a similar process as you question why you were put on this earth.

"The rule of the world is not just to take from life, but to put something back. We all have responsibilities, although sometimes we would like to ignore them, especially the difficult ones. Some men can affect very little, but they still have the responsibility to do what they can in a positive way. I have tried to do that. On occasions I have been right, and on others I've been wrong. When I was wrong, I was able to admit it. At least God knew my motives. That makes the later times of life, like these, a lot more satisfying.

"There are many things you can learn from the Bible. The parable of the talents teaches you that all of us are judged by what we do with our resources. The more ability you are given, the more is expected of you. God has given you a number of abilities. Please don't waste them."

It was hard for me to accept that my father was dying. And three weeks later he passed away at age 61 from heart failure. Nonetheless, to the end he felt that he had lived a successful life and had no regrets or fear of death. At his funeral a great part of the town turned out, and as we shook each hand the common phraseology was that "he was a truly good man." In each case, they often told of something he had done to help them in a time of trouble either as a sheriff, banker or friend and how it had made a significant difference to them. The *Brenham Banner Press* published the following editorial that I think captured the spirit of the time:

Tieman H. Dippel Sr.

Editorial--
Brenham Banner-Press, January 20, 1972

The death of Tieman H. Dippel Sr. has taken from the scene a tower of strength that nourished all that is good in Brenham and Washington County.

During his lifetime of service to the people here he earned the respect and a place of honor in the hearts of all who sought out his wise council in the years allotted him, which was all too short.

He lived by a set of values reflected in the high standards he set for himself and demanded from those with whom he worked. He would settle for nothing less than excellence achieved through integrity in any undertaking in which he was involved.

First and foremost, Mr. Dippel was a family man, who showed his love for his wife, daughter and son, through example and inculcation that leaves a legacy each can look to with pride.

Whether in the field of banking or as sheriff, that covered an illustrious career in each, he dealt with his fellow citizens on a fair and impartial basis enhanced with dignity and unmarred by petty prejudices or rancor of lesser men so prevalent in today's rush to the proverbial pot of gold at the end of the rainbow.

Mr. Dippel never abused the vast powers of his influence - that could reach the highest offices in the state and nation with a phone call -- for personal gain or as an escape from what he held as a sacred duty in the service of his country as seen by his record of service as a 2nd Lt. in the U.S. Army during World War II, and the example passed on to his son, Lt. Tieman (Skipper) Dippel Jr., now serving in the U.S. Navy.

When he made what was practically an overnight transition from Sheriff of Washington County to the presidency of the Farmers National Bank, an old friend cornered him at his new office on his first day at the bank, and after extending congratulations, asked, "Dip," as he was affectionately known, "just what do you know about banking?" "No more than I did about being a sheriff, when you questioned me on my lack of knowledge of that job 20 years ago," Dippel answered with a sincere smile. "You're right, I did," continued his friend, "and if you become just half as good a banker as you were a sheriff, I know my money will always be safe in your bank, so write up a receipt for my money will always be safe in your bank, so write up a receipt for my deposit."

His friend, like the thousands of customers he dealt with, never had reason to fear for their savings or his ability as a banker, for Mr. Dippel accepted the challenge with the same determination based on sound principles that made him one of the most respected sheriffs in Texas and soon he gained for himself the reputation as a progressive builder in the intricate field of finance.

Through his leadership the Farmers National Bank has enjoyed a rapid growth to become one of the soundest financial institutions in the state.

Mr. Dippel understood the meaning of compassion, as evidenced in his dealings with people in all walks of life.

As sheriff he commanded respect for the law without favoritism, but always tempered justice with mercy where warranted that resulted in restoring many an erring citizen to a useful place in the community and brought tranquility to those homes torn asunder by unresolved domestic problems.

In his role as banker, Mr. Dippel set many a family and business back on a sound financial footing, not always with all the collateral to support the loan, but because of his profound faith in people and his keen sense of judging character.

He held titles of leadership and responsibility in many businesses, civic organizations and fraternal orders. And in each, he left a record of achievements that speak for themselves and stand as a tribute to a man who utilized his God-given talents with a dedication that brought happiness to many and made Brenham and Washington County, which he loved so much, a much better place.

In his quiet unassuming way and without fanfare, Tieman H. Dippel gave unselfishly of himself to God, Country and those less fortunate.

It is with profound sorrow and sympathy to his bereaved family as we share the burden of his loss, and in all humility, we can only say, "Farewell" to a great citizen as he rests in that peace of God's eternal promise, to whom we can only offer a prayer of thanks for the short time he was allotted to be among us.

Tieman H. Dippel, Sr.

Dad was one of those uncommon men that made a difference. It is said that fifteen percent of society—now, some estimate only ten percent—are activists and most others flow with the tide. Uncommon men and women structure the culture of society in what they do in their daily lives. While those that achieve governorships and presidencies are remembered more in history, the base beneath them—the strength and the sacrifice within the people that they can call upon to achieve their ends—are really the ones who matter. When we talk of instilling values in the next generation, these are the core people in a community and a society that make a difference. They set the peer pressure of what is expected and what is valued. They are the people that set the tone of the culture, be it one of ethics or be it one of convenience. This was the core of the great generation that fought Hitler in World War II, a willingness to sacrifice for others, and that is what gave the strength to the nation.

If there is a case study to be done, it is to understand the tremendous importance of *having* and *creating*. These uncommon men and women who not only stand in their local communities for the principles that advance civilization and society, also rise through the power structures of economics, politics and culture/media to give substance to a nation. They are the repositories of the culture before them and the ones that must gain the enlightenment to develop their generation further. They are the ones that need to understand the importance of a mountaintop view of what is significant within society and why the common good, the Golden Rule, and a culture of service truly matter. For the combination of all of those values preserve personal dignity and give the opportunity for the next generation. They care about family and so the future matters to them.

This is why the nonprofit institutions as a structure are so critically important. They develop this core of leadership and friendship to common principles, and similarly they hone the leadership skills and ability by building the networks of those that have common interests.

Although it cannot be seen directly in Dad's life, the issue most involved with him was power. He brought change because he understood power and its cousin, influence. Power was the ability to affect specific acts because of position. As sheriff there were many things he could do within his authority, and he made very certain that the way he emphasized power and used it was very clear. To be seen free of corruption was a necessity to build trust. If you could be bought, you could not be trusted. He cautioned his deputies on the abuse of it and the need to enhance power by the support of the community so that the peer pressure gave strength. He did not have a fear of using force, but the process and the purpose mattered. He made an effort to maintain human dignity and solve issues without animosity, while at the same time understanding and making clear the principles that were being enforced with a certain knowledge of the seriousness of consequences.

As a hunter, he understood the nature of predators was to see the weakest in the herd or the straggler who was more defenseless. To him those were the ones society most needed to protect and that required keeping them with the herd, not driving them away. If that was one's perspective it was the polar opposite of an arrogance of power that often slowly builds from the difference people show to police power. How you envision police power has a lot to do not only with how you exercise the power, but also the type of base upon which you build it—loyal support and respect or increased fear and intimidation.

There was no weakness in integrity of purpose and that itself brought about the impact of influence. Power and influence are much like a rock hitting the middle of a clear lake. The power has the ability to make the decision in the impact where the rock hits, but the waves are the influence that move from the exercise of that power. They are what have a significant effect on the culture.

As we will discuss in detail later, when leaders reach positions of the highest power in the strategic drivers of economics, politics or media/culture, then they have a tendency to move toward convenience of personal interest because of the surroundings and the exposure to greed, arrogance, and the hubris of destiny.

At a local level, conscience has a greater opportunity to rule because men can interact with other men more directly. *The only way to get conscience into power is to have the culture—by which men are selected to the high positions—honor conscience over convenience thereby giving the powers that convenience bestows to the holders of conscience.* That is why these uncommon men and women within a society are so important. They are the creators of opinion that help instill the peer pressures and values of what is important and what is valued. Those above must then consider what is measured in other men and who is willing to stand to make a point. What the leaders of governments do often depends on the support or lack of support of the people who are led by these "uncommon men."

True influence, however, comes from an understanding of the purpose of why you do what you do. If your efforts at leadership solely are to benefit you, the people are normally wise enough to discount those points. As Dad often pointed out to me, it is not what you do or even how well you do it, but *why* you do it that matters in the end. If there are not very many uncommon men devoted to a set of principles that matter, then inevitably those uncommon men lose. But in developing them, you set the stage for a new generation through what they teach their families. They influence many of their peers to take on individual responsibility to help serve others and to build a strength within society looking to the future. They then affect the positive attitude and strength of a nation as it moves forward. The future is often determined as a sense of destiny by the strength of a society. There are natural laws that govern the relationship of economics, politics, and culture. They affect each other and interact in many ways that must be understood. Much of the rest of this book will deal with how those relationships can be appropriately categorized and analyzed, but the most important component of the destiny of any society is the strength of the people. The great Chinese philosopher and warrior, Sun-tzu, pointed it out as a critical component of "the Way." The Western strategist Von Clauswitz did the same. The reason is that both recognized that in any battle a plan and a strategy could be drawn. The strategy would lay out in great detail how victory should be achieved. But once the force is engaged, seldom did things go according to the exact plan. Success or failure were then not in the hands of the strategist, but the tacticians—the generals that adapted on the field to the times and provided the leadership that adjusted to the victory. It is not unlike the modern football play of today. In theory each one should work, but that depends largely on the talent of the players and their execution.

That is why the uncommon men and women within a society matter. They are the local leaders that need to understand why things need to be done and the importance of sacrifice as well as having the talents and ability to lead. They are the ones that give strength to society to sacrifice when necessary. That sacrifice generally comes from a unified effort behind principles. Modern times are not that different from the histories of the past. The speed of the times, the impact of entertainment and globalization all put great pressures on the development of the character of these uncommon men and women and on their ability to have a perspective from a mountaintop of what society needs to advance civilization. Their greatest opportunity is to instill their values in the next generation because that is where society is ultimately most affected. But they do that by what they teach, by how they live their lives, and by how they affect the institutions that are a critical part of their existence. The budget of how government spends money is nothing but a contract with the people. So an understanding of government, not just its powers, but its challenges and responsibilities, is equally important. The same is true of the values of culture and of the need for opportunity and education with economics. Small businesses that flourish in an environment where competition is allowed provide the best majority of new jobs and increase in the standard of living that is essential to the future.

But if one thing can be learned from the case study of "Jackrabbit Dippel," it is that almost all men and women in all societies have a number of common goals. They want the best for their children, they want to live a life with personal dignity, and they want the opportunity to have the economic benefits of a high quality of living. But how to achieve those goals has greatly differed in society. Some civilizations achieved it by conquering and taking it from others. This concept might best be described as a pie that is shrinking and so you expand the size of your portion of the pie at someone else's expense. The other approach has been one of significant growth. This has been the key to America that has opened its borders to many people. It has built an economic system based on markets, the rule of law, a sense of ethics that preserved competition, and a culture of service to others that allowed a more limited government that restricted the need for heavy regulation and governmental involvement in the economy. These were keys for the great growth that took place and expanded the pie, so that everyone's individual slice got bigger.

The base of that growth is the principles of many of these uncommon men and women over a series of generations. The problem I foresee in the future is that many of the very principles upon which this growth is based are no longer being appreciated. The case of societies in the past show that abundance distracted from the need for a vision for the future and the necessity often to sacrifice for the next generation. These are concepts that we will review on the broader basis of society, but it should never be forgotten that the people ultimately determine the nature of their government and society by their action or inaction. The ultimate question is whether the culture of these leaders is one that builds a peer pressure of conscience or of convenience. There will never be a great perfection, one way or the other. It is likely to be more a 60/40 split, if that. However, several percentage points win elections in America and what is valued makes a great difference.

Today we see the emergence of Internet "blogs" and chat rooms that emerge as the new media of the young. These are writings of the immediate consciousness; even opinion is often focused on individual issues, usually with emotion. Where will be the framework to coordinate into an organized vision all the "shotgun pellets" that need to be aimed like a rifle at the critical problems of the future? It is not what you think that makes you wise as much as how you think and organize the knowledge given to you in a global world that becomes even more complex. The giants of the Internet and its search components are under pressure to maintain the Internet's integrity. If they stood forward to build a base of thought from the conscience perspective, it would not only greatly serve them but all humanity as well because the Internet will be the most valuable tool of the future to reach the coming generations.

I was gratified that Dr. Kai-Fu Lee, President of Google Greater China and one of Asia's most prominent computer scientists, noted *The Language of Conscience* in his book, *Be Your Personal Best,* supporting my belief that conscience is the base of the information age and critical to its future. The Internet is the ultimate test of knowledge vs. wisdom. We can know a great deal, but how we use the information is the ultimate key. It is not different from the knowledge of nuclear energy that can be used for evil or good. The powers of the Internet need to concentrate upon assuming responsibility for keeping its integrity if it is to reach its ultimate benefit to society.

The powers of the Internet need to concentrate upon assuming responsibility for keeping its integrity if it is to reach its ultimate benefit to society. As the new educational and organizational vehicle, it can learn much from one of the world's oldest organizations, the Knights Templar (The Sovereign Military Order of the Temple of Jerusalem) of the Middle Ages. In a different age, the Knights Templar were the limited few who were the equivalent of today's special forces, professional Knights, but also a combination with being somewhat of a monk. They gave their possessions to the group in their belief in it. They had a code they would not be ransomed, so they expected death on the battlefield. They became bankers and owned great lands and wealth to support the military efforts. They understood economics and much of their system depended upon it. They understood politics and war and were trained strategists and leaders that were the power wedge of victory for others. But what they built upon was a culture of honor and commitment. That is why so many other organizations have studied them and patterned after them. At their best they combined power with noble purpose. At their low points, such as the battle preceding the loss of Jerusalem, their leaders forgot the lessons nobility of purpose teaches. Friday the 13th is remembered as a day of bad luck in part because it was the day the King of France effectively destroyed the power of the Order. How that applies today is simple, you can build a group of uncommon men, you can educate them, and you can make them great in mastery of many things. But it is the sense of honor that binds them together, the sense of purpose for common sacrifice. It takes an overriding goal or vision and a commitment to it that unifies, and it is this power of unity that makes the difference. If the unity is for the convenience of plunder, it has power. But if the unity is for conscience, it has nobility. From a warrior's perspective, you may die in pursuit of the former. But if you die in pursuit of the latter, your life has purpose. So you learn the power of culture, but from the Templars you also learn infrastructure to support the culture. The Knights they had in the field were the best of the best; they led the others at the point and held the line. But the system that supported them was massive and dedicated. It took great cost and technology to put the best in the right place. It is not one great man or even a number of uncommon men, but a great culture that develops an organization. The Internet, to build integrity, needs not a few good men to write well. It needs an infrastructure of conscience that can build the culture of honor that pervades society.

Section I

What Do We Ultimately Seek for our Children?

To be clear in the inception, this is not a book aimed at giving an answer as to exactly what and how you teach children. There are many very focused perceptions. It is instead aimed at the question of why what children learn matters and particularly how they learn to think and form their perspective on life. If there is a failure to address values that need to be instilled in this perspective to create an understanding of man's collective mutual obligation, then weaknesses occur. Otherwise, people remain committed to the perspective of their individualized unit until the strength of the society is drained. Generations ago education became scientific in the sense of Henry Ford's assembly line that broke down actions. Everyone concentrated on improving his or her individual part, but little focus was left on the overall line. Education's silos grew, but the parts do not always fit together well. There is too much focus on teaching rather than what is learned and what is taught.

In a multicultural environment seeking diversity and tolerance you reach a point where the collective common good is secondary to individualized perspective. To find a common ground you cannot tell people what to believe, but try to find a common denominator and an approach to discussion that allows the examination of ideas without immediate rejection. The issue of this century will be the nature of culture as affected by political terrorism and economic corruption. The culture will always have these components, but the issue is whether they define the nature of man's interaction with each other as based on the concept of conscience or the concept of convenience.

The core issue is getting people to understand how important the common good is to them individually and the linking of the interests of the group and the individual. Perhaps the best explanation I could give is the example of a call I had from my daughter who was bringing her children to participate in the traditional Brenham Maifest. As I mentioned before, at this event hundreds of small children in costume are introduced over a relatively long period. An important part of the festival is a set of historic "hobbyhorses" that compose a "Merry-Go-Round" that I rode as a child and probably my parents did as well. Since the hobbyhorses were being shut down, her call was a desperate request to for me to "do something" to solve the problem. I explained to her that although I regretted it, the city had its own issues, and I was sure this was not my problem. Then the clincher came as only Meg can deliver it, "Dad, you do not understand. Wright, your two-year-old grandson will come out in the festival early, and Mom and I have your seat where you can take him out when he is bored. He loves the hobbyhorses, and they are all he can ride. He is going to be very unhappy with you for two hours if they are not running." Suddenly this enlightened me to the joining of the private and public interest. We see the necessity of group effort when it directly affects us, but we are losing an appreciation of our common ties and goals as a group. It is not intentional on our part. It is just that modern life has changed politics, economics, and culture as a driving force and will continue to do so. This creates pockets of thought, not necessarily the unified cultural thought of the past. This is what we must understand and address. We are becoming much more diverse as a society for many reasons, so how do we unify?

Character is how you should unify diversity, and it has definable traits like the Golden Rule. The purpose of this book is to address the power of culture, how it instills values, and how you can integrate diverse cultures by the study of common values. It proceeds in levels of understanding and tools for assistance with thought.

This is a book aimed at getting a broad perspective of the problems more than a carefully defined answer. The reason is that the answers only come after you bring people together in a common language of conscience. Otherwise, people remain committed to the perspective of their individual background.

In September of 2004, two processes that had been several years in the making came to culmination, and perhaps they give the best explanation of why this book has been written. The first was one in which I participated as a part of a group composed of alumni, administrators, and faculty giving recommendations for the future of my university. The panel on which I had worked was one that looked at graduate and professional studies. I had strongly recommended the inclusion of a resolution for an institute on ethics, leadership, and community service that would help tie together the various approaches to ethics. These approaches are often found in silos of education such as the individual professional schools and need outside organizations to inject the reality of experience, such as the nature of actual problems faced ethically. But additionally, I hoped to see a focus on what I called *cultural ethics,* which is the concept of having an understanding of the importance of both ethics and leadership being taught to children at a younger age. It was more oriented in building a structure for society by developing conscience within the nature of man than just teaching specialized concepts or case studies. Granted this instilling values occurs when they are young, but the university teaches the teacher and the parents.

I was amazed in the discussions at how many of my friends from the educational and other sectors looked upon my views with a degree of skepticism and took a different perspective. We moved from the concept of teaching ethics to the discussion of the value of promoting ethics and on to the concept of students *experiencing or discussing ethics* which was more in the style of current university approaches. In other words, from a doctrine that defined right and wrong to more a study of the relativity of ethics in various situations and case studies. When I made the argument of values as a base, the issue was appropriately put forth, "Whose values?" It was explained to me that modern multiculturalism, and the toleration of differences it requires, necessitates issues to be looked at from differing perspectives. Few things are black and white but are really shades of gray. To some, the purpose of a university is to expose students to a variety of ideas and let them take away their individual values. The nature of academic freedom required such. It was noted that many of the things of which I spoke could better be quantified under teaching leadership and citizenship rather than a values argument. There was a contingent that joined with me that felt that the ultimate purpose of a university was to affect the nature of man. Machiavelli and Hobbs thought man inherently evil. Han Fei, the Philosopher of Chinese Legalism, saw human nature as a blank slate to be influenced. Confucius, Christ, Aristotle, and others thought man redeemable with enlightenment. It was always our thought that the universities were one of the primary sources of enlightenment. As for leadership, it is not so much what you do or even how well you do it, as why you do it that defines you. Many people in history have led, but to what purpose? While cultural ethics may be an inflammatory term to some, the instilling of values within children occurs not just by parents but also by the culture in which they are reared. Sensitivity to this point is critical. The values argument ultimately is a clash between individualism and group obligations. Toleration is a valuable and worthy concept, but it has limits. A failure to recognize these limits brings about the very divisions it tries to dissolve because there is a loss of respect that is toleration's weapon. Respect must be given, but it also must be reciprocated to be deserved. Absolute toleration makes all values equal.

The critical point I had difficulty making was that the culture of values gives us the force of law. Discipline in society protects individual rights, and collective power gives the strength. Democracy can exist as a legal form. But without the strength of the culture sustaining it, it is form only. You have to keep balance.

I could not help but think back to the last of the 1960s and the first part of the 1970s. In those same university halls we had the same discussions over the Vietnam War, only phrased differently. The divisions in America today, and the world, rest on differing perspectives of not just the nature of man, but man's obligations to each other. These are totally related concepts, but those relationships are obscured with the complexity of modern times and the lack of candor the political correctness often requires.

The clearest memory of those days was my race for student body president in 1970. I was a law student, a Naval Lieutenant, who was the Conservative candidate in a field that had two other primary contending ideologies—liberalism and radicalism. My opponents presented the perspective that I favored the war and thereby was against peace because I had joined the military. It was implied that I did not understand how the war was wrong because of the divisions it caused, the lives it lost, and the involuntary intrusion it made on the younger generation's freedom. The fact that I agreed with the university establishment only made me its *tool*. In effect, I needed to go back and get educated. I needed to understand how an individual student felt about his loss of the right to decide his life course.

My reply was a little different than they expected. Quite frankly, I had thought a lot about the war. And I was not particularly keen on it because unlike them I was already in the service and possibly headed over there. Some proceeded to tell of the freedoms and virtues of Canada if I became enlightened. To me, the issue was not the war as much as a sense of honor and obligation. Almost everyone is for peace, but the peace that was worth having comes with strength and a willingness to engage at sacrifice. The war began when I was in grade school. I didn't start it and I wished it would end. But the obligation it imposed was what put me in uniform and from my small town I already knew several wounded, one killed, and many lives interrupted. Yes, individualism is important, but it is not peace. And obligations to each other have to be honored if men are to have the personal dignity of freedom. Principles for which you sacrifice do matter. But that dignity requires that we earn it. It is not just granted by fiat if it is to have any meaning. Rights have to be equaled by duties. These were the times of the Great Society as well as Vietnam and part of what was argued was entitlement, victimization, decline of trust in institutions, and a very aggressive approach to individualism.

My approach was acceptance of individual responsibility, support for the collective good, and reformation of institutions. What I observed in the process was the evolution of these fundamental arguments and how they had fragmented our politics then and even now. It was a rare confluence of events that truly shaped the 1960s generation and the "baby boom" it symbolized. Divisions started there that have only sharpened in the intervening years because our situations and our personal experiences shaped our values at the core.

The more I asked other friends about this division of thoughts in other major universities, the more surprised I was at how perhaps the engagement I found was even conservative. The issue finally came down to a fairly simple concept. "Are values to be used in creating obligations, and if so, whose values are used?" From what I understood, the academic approach was much more one of relativity that tended to preserve academic freedom and toleration. The "moralist approach" that recognized "obligational values" were the fundamental rules of morality that ought to be taught to build an ethical society that understood conscience and the importance of people having concerns for, and obligations to each other. This limits individualism. My friends on the other side argue well that they are *moral* in that they fight for compassion. Morality means different things to different people and it is important to make distinctions so that "straw men" do not complicate the argument.

If you go below the surface, you see patterns of thought in localized regions that dominate enough to give them a cultured character. In the "red or Bush states of the last election" I would suggest that there was probably more individual giving to charity in the "red states" per capita than in the "blue states" which were more urban. In the blue states the compassion was more generalized for government to take many of the actions rather than individuals. Recent media coverage of studies analyzing contributions by state from individual tax returns appears to confirm these trends. Texas may have ranked low in state funding of the Arts, but it did not mean we did not fund them. There was simply more of a privatization. There was simply more of a privatization because limited government drives the culture. Texas coordinates the development of giving more than other states through grants. So you end up with a confusing but important distinction. Those who favor individualism, basically social liberalism, often also favor large government collectivist solutions while those that favor individual obligations, or social conservatism, prefer small government solutions and rely instead on the private sector. A step further, those socially liberal, thus want more compassion through government. The social conservatives generally want less government and more individual freedoms and the economic freedom from regulation and taxes that larger government requires. It would seem, like a trigonometry equation, that both groups agreed with individual freedom and both were driven by conscience. The difference, which is significant, has to do with balancing the two parts of conscience, compassion, and obligation. Stability has to come from bringing the right balance and understanding.

The individualist approach often looks at moralists as trying to tell them how to conform and they resent it. The moralists, eliminating more extreme positions, generally say, "No, you are imposing cultural change on me when a child is sued in school for using the word God and profanity is untouched. Or when the military and government cannot support the Boy Scouts, when controversial issues are not just reported but flaunted and culture is deteriorating." Each side uses a perspective, each side is "standing and delivering" by engagement, but few are looking beyond the superficial issues of divisions that are relaying the ultimate cost to our children and way of life. I have to be convinced our children learning profanity rather than courtesy can neither benefit them or society. The same issues are found globally because technology has created complexity that has outrun existing wisdom. We need a new way of thought that goes outside the existing structural approaches to discussion. That requires addressing morality, individual responsibilities, and compassion.

Ethics is the set of rules society adopts to define its appropriate procedures for interaction in regard to obligations between men. It is today narrowly defined within professions and universities, but we would do well to think of it on a societal basis and how it interacts with the basic concepts of morality and relativity. The same arguments go back centuries where the ancient Greeks used the word *deon*, which translated to obligation. Immanuel Kant refined the concept that today we refer to as deontology, which looks at a proper society as one with moral obligations and a concept of duty.

Other Greek philosophers looked at a less strict formulation of society that emerged into the concept of utilitarianism. Its more modern concepts might be Jeremy Benthams' "rule of utility" where whatever brought the greatest happiness to the greatest number defined good or the concept that the rightness of an action should be judged on the value of the consequences of the actions, which was championed by John Stuart Mill. He felt you could thoughtfully estimate the utility of the actions.

Those judging morality from a religious background, tend to view the obligation theory as more appropriate because God has imposed obligations. C.S. Lewis gave many of the best presentations and thoughts. His radio addresses at Churchill's request in World War II and his *Four Lanes* dealt with the fact we have to will ourselves to love our neighbors so it is by necessity of selfless love without ulterior motive. To him, since God gave us free will, evil will exist, but morality was also from God.

Sigmund Freud, took the opposing view, that morality was really a collection of human experiences that set a framework of interaction. Cooperation with one another was not love. He sought an object, often with motive, not selflessness. This fits more closely with modern relativity concepts because habits and structures, if not internal, are changeable.

It also helps to understand the basic difference between the two groups' concepts of individualism. The moralists look at it as individual responsibility and obligation by which their personal dignity is satisfied by affirmative actions being required—a type of activist Confucianism which formed an obligation to others. The relativists look at individual freedom founded on toleration, which values freedom from explicit obligations that control.

The compassion of the two underlying concepts that co-exist often in each of us is quite like the existence of the two critical sets of rules in physics—Einstein's Theory of Relativity that provides the rules for big objects like the universe and quantum mechanics that defines the rules for the smallest objects like atoms. They are not the same, and scientists have for years tried to find a "universal theory" that tied them together so that a great advance could be made in knowledge. New concepts, like the "string theory" of small vibrating objects, are but one of the new approaches. A similar effort seeking the proper balance of obligation, compassion, and tolerance needs to be found to advance wisdom. It has to balance not just culture, but the other power drivers of economics and politics in a rapidly changing and competing world.

So the issue is how to begin to bring a structure to discussion. Something such as the Golden Rule would seem to satisfy both concepts. Quite often, when bringing the extremes together in a circle of thought on occasion, since neither side will sacrifice principle, they find something they agree on that can result in limited action and begin a dialogue we refer to as *the language of conscience.*

The great books of power are not as applicable here. *The Prince* teaches how to keep power, *Rules for Radicals* how to take power. But for a democracy to maintain middle class power or a nation that needs and wants to give more power to the people, we need a concept that builds responsibility within the society to recognize obligations. As nations seek more democratic process, they must understand the concepts and inner-relationships that liberty is not just freedom but individual responsibility. America itself needs to rethink the future it is leaving its children. That was the concept more than ethics alone that was envisioned for the institute I had suggested. This will be the great issue of this century.

There must be a corpus of shared moral obligations for a liberal society to survive time. Toleration in absolute terms would recognize all morality as equal—Christian morality and Nazi morality—so it is obvious choices must be made. This conflict between group and individual rights and obligations becomes critical when these collide. The concept of personal dignity makes it important to understand that certain rights belong primarily to individuals. Those are the obligations of the collective group to preserve. The group's rights are the obligation of the individual to acknowledge and support. This division makes study and separation easier. It also puts great focus on the concept of the personal dignity of man because it is how he views his place in society, the peer pressures of the culture by society, and its fairness. It is the core measurement of the stability of the society.

Part of the difference I found, is that many of my friends had the perspective of coming from an environment of "education" which often, by nature, works with theory in universities. My perspective came from active involvement in economics, politics, and culture, primarily through the equivalent of think tanks, which dealt more directly with reality and the nature of power. Their knowledge comes from books and mine, like a beekeeper, the experience of being stung. The two approaches of education do not mesh easily and someone *outside the box* is looked upon through the perspective of establishment thought and process. This becomes particularly important because the classic liberalism of individual freedom and limited government that Adam Smith championed economically and John Stuart Mill socially is today more like our political conservatism. Interestingly, today's liberalism actually follows a sense of deontological theory of obligation in its efforts of redistribution based on compassion arguments combined with a cultural liberalism of ever-expanded toleration. The issue being, that clear thought needs to be given as to the basics by which we will decide society's issues rather than trusting political correctness and political arguments of division. The stability of future society is at issue. Stability and instability occur by balancing issues or unbalancing through the drivers of power. The games tic tac toe, checkers, and chess are similar in that they have boards of play, but increasingly complex options. The dominant powers of economics and politics have divided groups in ways that often do not fit together logically in a cultural perspective.

It is not that I disagree with many of the concerns my university friends posed. In fact the strategy for checkers might be very accurate for universities, but we are now in chess with a global world, limited resources, and very complex technological interconnections. The people of America may not be driven by these global factors, but the political institutions are. Economics is driven by intense competition with ever increasing size, capital, and technology demands that often lead to greed beyond self-interest. Culture, the third great driver of power is now being brought to the forefront although it is often perceived as a political force. In reality it is a power trying to decide on new rules and balances to offset the excesses of politics and economics. As mentioned, many look to collectivist approaches of government to accomplish functions. Others looked to individual responsibilities and resulting small government. This often brings gridlock. The problem is the balance. If government will not, or in modern times cannot, give support, who does so, and how do you secure more unity allowing action? We have to define how we look at the actual issue with depth because it is an issue of values and obligations within a culture. What are our individual obligations to each other? Such is the age-old argument of the ultimate nature of man.

These concepts of obligation also fit with the perspectives of family values. While commentators often talk of red and blue states and morality as political issues, we miss the fact that the suburbs and many of the areas focused on morality are also focused on family. They are areas where people have chosen to undertake a greater obligation in raising their children and focused their lives on this. The areas are far from unanimous, but puerility sets a cultural tone and peer pressure. Time committed to the children is significant. This is not to say those who work intently to succeed better materially with the purpose of helping their children love them less. But it makes a difference to the perspective of the child and from whom he or she learns values. Individualism often includes material concerns, and dedication of time to family often interferes with that effort. Modern costs make it hard to raise large families so sacrifice is often necessary. This adds a perspective to society because those that focus upon family as a primary obligation look at many of these issues differently. That is the undercurrent that is often missed.

Like my university experience years ago, we would all be well served to take time to learn exactly what we are each saying without evoking trigger reactions. The natural human desire to be right has been placed on a short time fuse in the modern 24/7 world of instant news and commentary. The emergence of web blogs is a perfect example. There are many levels of morality that begin with the Golden Rule and escalate to the highest, and to relativists the more controversial, doctrine of religion. It is easy to make "straw men" of extremes, it is much harder to take the time to find truth and blend issues to come together. However, relativism and the basic morality of joint obligations cannot be easily blended beyond a certain point of courtesy. Good versus evil are broad concepts, conscience versus convenience are more personal ones. Conscience is when you recognize your actions have effects on others and know your obligations (the Golden Rule for example). Convenience is where you look to what is good for yourself as an individual. Collectively, the nation becomes one of character or of increasing self-interest or convenience.

Relativist approaches often can become rationalizations for self-interest. A moralist approach can look at teaching religion or even the higher arguments of morality that attempt to impose other's views. But certain fundamental concepts are basic and are important to the advancement of civilization and the core of society. Many of these were ones that built individual responsibility and centered on concepts such as the Golden Rule, the common good, the importance of a culture of service, a sense of ethics based on responsibility, and similar concepts that affect the nature of man by effectively teaching conscience over convenience. The critical point is that they require a concept of some actions being good or bad, not relative. This has not been just an argument of modern times but has occurred through the ages. To many there is not a new morality but only morality or immorality.

Understanding conscience and its parts is very critical to this discussion and the blending of views while retaining individual principles. Sigmund Freud applied the equivalent of a scientific method and believed that man was influenced by his parents who operated in a society that made up its own moral codes much as it formulated its laws on a relatively random basis. The necessities of the operation of the culture thus created the values of conscience.

Chinese Philosopher Han Fei and the doctrine of legalism also looked at man more as a blank slate to be influenced by rewards and punishments. But other philosophers of the East and West have believed that there was a natural law, or more properly a moral law, resident within each of us. Many in the West perceived it to be given by God and therefore existing before any judgment by scientific method. Immanuel Kant, C.S. Lewis, and many others have defended an inner law directing man. In the East this concept of natural law is found in Taoism and the thoughts of Lao-tzu and Chuang-tzu look upon the Tao, often translated as "the Way," as a basic principle within both man and the Universe. It looks to a natural relationship of all things as being eternal and absolute. Most cultures reflect that inner values have both a natural and environmental component.

For the purpose of discussion, this means you divide conscience into two parts—the ability to know right from wrong naturally (moral law) and how the environment develops the sensitivity and values of conscience (Freud's concept). The arguments often confuse these two parts. Religion is a major part of the concept of capacity. Indeed, in many cases such as Christianity, God gives a choice and how we use our lives determines our destiny. Many religions approach the same issue from different requirements to reach a heaven. But religion is in effect a very refined set of rules applied to a concept of natural existing conscience.

For the sake of analysis, if we look at the environmental component as not being religion, or man's relationship with God, but instead man's relationship to other men and define it as morality, then we discuss the issue of values in a more defined context. Religion is really a refinement of rules of conscience of morality taken to a much higher level in most circumstances. You can then discuss basic morality, and if you defend religion you can make your logical arguments much more simply to plow the ground for later discussion. That lets discussion begin with the morality of man's relation to man, which is critical in an age of terrorism and corruption. Multicultural solutions have to be sought for success. Diversity is necessary to give respect to individuals as a group with an appreciation to make them a part of a solution. However, we then focus on the most critical areas, how to blend them back together once separated into diverse groups. Relativism is convenient because it lets words often replace actions and skim over differences that are often obligations to a broader society. Moralism or an acceptance of responsibilities is harder but is a more sound foundation for progress. The area of engagement must be between those two issues. The environmental component of conscience often has the two parts that can work together or oppose each other. One is compassion for others; the second is obligation to others. Together they build a culture of service and can come in conflict when obligations are not internal responsibilities but created duties by society enforced by political will that bring resentment.

There is an important distinction between relativism and morality or character that is often missed. Relativism often makes judgment on emotion or how one feels about an issue. Morality and character deal more with how one thinks about an issue in terms of comparison to a more defined set of conduct or thought. Achieving consensus is difficult with differing emotions. Consensus comes more out of discussions where thought helps bridge gaps. Even where you bridge emotions, it is often the thought process that accomplishes it. In character you seek a decision on thought and defining principle. In relativism you tend to rationalize positions with emotions related to tolerance. The hard work of effectively bringing people together thus is best served by more thought and less emotion. But, respect, as opposed to toleration is necessary for an honest discussion.

The reason that character, as opposed to relativism, must follow multiculturalism and diversity is to maintain some unity in the culture to allow it the strength to adapt to change. Adaptability to change is more important to survival than strength or intelligence since it allows the society to use both, rather than gridlock it on the most critical of issues. Modern Europe is a case study of the nature of these problems. An example is often made of the difference between a *melting pot* and a *salad bowl.* In one, common values assimilate the groups in core beliefs, in the other there is a combination but core values are separate. Since the strength of the collectivist unity gives the level of power from the culture to the law or individual rights, this matters. The common glue is the common values and common good. People can be integrated into economic or political systems to some extent, but values are the core of beliefs for cultural unity. Europe has a large Muslim population that has different values from other groups as opposed to America where there are also integration problems. But Black and Hispanic minorities share much the same religious and family values. These are distinctions that are important as you try to blend common concepts in cultures—a salad bowl without a melting pot on common principles such as responsibility, rule of law, language proficiency, and morality separates groups. Economic opportunity is the key to stability if people see a future. But if you have no common melting pot of values, the society often is not open to the minorities. Too often today the effort at multiculturalism and diversity does not entail the necessity of pulling diverse groups back together for their benefit from a common good. It is the controversial hard part of the process that is the discussion not of toleration and compassion but common obligation.

Addressing critical issues forthrightly and early is what avoids crisis. Unless you bring out the best of the cultures being blended and unify them, you eventually divide the society and create tension that affects politics and thereby economics through government policy. Cultural diversity is important but can have unintended consequences if the tolerance overcomes the binding values of society as a whole. We celebrate what makes us different as a focus, which is the best of toleration. But there are limits if we do not also focus on what makes us alike and gives us strength. This is why the concept of the common good is so critical a value to go with the individual impact of the Golden Rule. The concept of a culture of service is what binds both because it gives the vehicle that unifies the concern for others personally and in society. It is why education of the population, which includes these concepts, is so important. The strength of a society, collectively, is an understanding of why each benefit from the common good. And the best rule as to what serves the common good is the balance of the Golden Rule. That is itself built into the culture by people working together in a culture of service. Today we have significant funding of our charities and governmental policy to the concept of creating diversity. We need to extend it in the way of Martin Luther King and Ghandi, to move to the next level of character unification for the benefit of all.

It surprised many people that I had appreciation for those holding the other view and disagreeing with me strongly. The reason is that I have much in common with them. The passion they show for compassion is intense as is mine. We have the same goals but disagree on the solution. Oftentimes what cannot be accomplished by political compromise in the middle can be done in part by turning the line into a circle and taking the best of the extremes that may actually be doable. (An example is the uninsured. You can't financially insure them all, but if you targeted only the ones who truly need help and cannot acquire it independently, it might be manageable.) The effort is to frame the process for discussion, and identify the right questions. That is the great benefit of efforts at universities. People of conscience on all sides get to discuss issues with candor and respect. But this requires universities to allow not only differing perspectives, but also outside practical voices. The key realization that is missed is that conservatives generally look at the obligation (personal responsibility) men should show each other. Liberals generally look at compassion men ought to show. While those are revised in some instances, the key point is that you need both. Without obligation there is no common unity, and without compassion there is no enlightenment of civilization. The issue is not one or the other, but it is the balance necessary between them. That is where personal dignity plays a part in how men look at the rules of common good and morality balanced with self-worth and independent thought and values.

I was happy to see positive changes in curriculum evolve from the concerns at the university and took comfort that the effort tried to address the issues. It provided me a very enlightened understanding that not only are our university systems, but also our society is moving far too much to relativity, rationalization, and self-interest because we forget obligations that have to be kept between different people. One person told me that I based much of my thought on Western morality and that that was not necessarily the case in other cultures. I pointed out that the arguments I made on reciprocity of obligation were Confucian and, quite frankly, were more from Eastern culture than Western culture. Since multiculturalism was such a significant argument, I think it is important to put several things in perspective. One of the best examples that occurred at this same time was America's first loss in men's basketball at the last Olympics. Even though the American team was composed of some of the finest professional athletes assembled, they lost to smaller countries to everyone's astonishment. The critics talked about several characteristics that they felt were the cause. One was the fact that American pro basketball, in its effort for entertainment, specialized on individual stars and less on the concept of team play and strategy. Additionally, the international basketball rules were not played the same way in the pro leagues and traveling, palming the ball, and a variety of other rules were much more strictly enforced in the world's rules.

These are not unusual characteristics of modern America where the individual rather than the group is the point of focus. Eastern cultures are somewhat different. They look at the group and usually its protection and internal obligations as opposed to the individual. Family, courtesy, and the honor of face, all enforce those obligations.

What East and West have in common is the need to find a common set of rules by which civilization can advance. In an era of terrorism which uses fear to appeal to the convenience—as opposed to the conscience of societies—a new set of thoughts needs to be developed looking at the obligations of each of us to each other and to civilization as a whole. You begin a society with a set of laws that set the base minimum you owe each other. You carry that one step further with morality that is the Golden Rule of why you feel obligated to do for others beyond that, and finally you have a culture of service or compassion that is what you do because you wish to out of compassion or conscience. The problem is that they fit together in a stable society. You cannot pick and choose for obligation and compassion balance just as responsibility and rights go together.

Obligation can be transferred to the concept of accountability, which plays a significant part in defining the nature of a culture so far as group versus individual approaches are concerned. Partisanship is a clear example, regardless of which party affiliation. The culture changes where people begin to believe the issues are about them and the party as opposed to the nation itself. The issue is not necessarily whether a problem is solved by group efforts or by individual efforts, so much as it is whether it is for the collective good (conscience) or the individual good (often convenience).

To break issues down, it becomes important to find fundamental questions and interests judged from a perspective of longer-term national interest. That is seldom done today because of the culture. For approaches to change a lot of perspectives have to be integrated into new concepts. You quickly learn the truth of the old concept that people are not for you or against you normally, but for themselves as they perceive their interest. We have to create an understanding of what we all gain from honoring obligations, but to honor them you must understand them, to understand them you must discuss them, to discuss them you must gain enough nucleus to be a catalyst so that they become relevant.

It is important to distinguish between the purpose of ideas, and, for example, the books that represent them. Much of the book industry is commercial with entertainment as the key that drives commercial success. Serious books have a smaller audience, but make more impact. The most serious books, those that deal with complicated broad thoughts out of silos, have possibly an even smaller audience in the beginning because they require serious study and understanding. But they can have the greatest long-term impact if they add a new perspective to thought or a different way to proceed. It is not the strength of the idea alone. The weakness of the times in which it originates creates the need for the perspective. The question is how such an idea takes root because its development requires the understanding of not only the concept but also its relevance to the critical issues of the time.

Confucius was a positivist who looked at action. Lao-tzu in his Daoism looked skeptically at actions both as to whether they were always beneficial or often produced unintended consequences. From a combination of the two, the concept of the proper *way* requires a thought process that balances and tests. The issue at hand is the nature of future civilization. We are presently at one of those eras that set a stage for realignment on a great many issues, and outcomes may depend more on the actions of people within nations and cultures than between nations.

Society can be aligned on many perspectives, fear and greed are among the most powerful, but it also can be founded upon honor and obligation to others. Broad strokes of words and an absence of actions are dwarfing these individual decisions. They are in effect words for they are ideas, but only if they are words of commitment do they count. To start to unify these various different perspectives to get a more common division between the nature of men that is more clearly presented, we need to examine a synthesis of many related ideas of history as applied to modern time. We also need to understand our goals and measuring points and create a method of thought that can be expanded and explained by differing perspectives initially. We need to refine a new way of thinking about issues and ourselves. With thought we can gain common ground. Change usually does not occur without crisis, but in crisis all tend to look carefully at the best option of self-interest.

The obligation or accountability of the nation to the individual under this concept is best described as an assurance of personal dignity. Beyond the inalienable rights of human dignity, the best of cultures go further to provide the opportunity for an individual to be all that he can be. But that requires understanding the necessity of policies, which are group related. The economy, for example, can be slowed dramatically by over- regulation for individual benefit. Corruption, when convenience is the approach, eliminates the very competition upon which markets are based. And efforts to assure equal results do not foster the incentives of individual opportunity. Markets provide the greatest benefits, provided they are fair and honest but that requires the support and sensitivity of the individual to the cost/benefit effects. The culture that allows the best markets should also show compassion for those the market treats harshly.

How to decide on the balances that exist between these choices requires not only understanding but also a helpful scorecard to organize thought and relationships. Different answers will come from different societies because their cultures have different balances between the individual and the group. But the purposes for which actions are taken, regardless of the method, can be quite similar and thereby be more globally compatible than might be expected. Justice, not the form of law, is the goal.

Saint Thomas Aquinas consolidated the morality of Christ with the science of Aristotle to give a synthesis of some of the fundamental thought of the West. The thoughts of Confucius were blended with those of Lao-tzu and legalism to make a broad part of the Chinese synthesis. While there are many more cultures, because of economics and political strength, these will prove to be two of the most dominant. In the modern world because of the position of the United States and the People's Republic of China, how they blend will be particularly important. This book is written to reflect the argument for basic morality and character (a culture of ethics) as opposed to the relativity of morality (a culture of flexible ethics). It ultimately rests on conscience over convenience or character, as it is perceived by the individual's personal sense of dignity that embodies both obligation and compassion.

The second event of impact of which I spoke culminated on September 9, 2004, and was a press announcement and ceremony of the publication of *The Language of Conscience* by the Press of the Central Party School of the Communist Party of the People's Republic of China. Those familiar with China understand the unique position of the Communist Party in relation both to the military and to the government. It provides the leadership of all major institutions. The Central Party School is looked upon by many international publications as the heart of the understanding of the direction of the Party and therefore of China. The President of China has emerged from it. The Vice President serves as its head. It models many of the programs of the government and plays a major part in the training of the rising younger leadership of China as well as the executive training of the senior leadership of China. In view of its impact on the future of China and China's growing international power, it could easily be considered one of, if not *the* most significant, international think tank on public policy if impact on global affairs is considered. *The Language of Conscience* was one that its Press placed in bookstores throughout China and, I was told, was the first Western book given the insignia of their Press. Five of their senior philosophers representing not only the School but the major Chinese universities and institutions gave their reviews and opinions and while not advocating some of the book's perspectives, they supported the concepts of conscience, morality, and individual responsibility found in the book that was in part written for character groups in the United States and also for a bridge for the Confucian Museum to the West a few years earlier. It was to be a book to bridge with scholars from the West on ethics, morality, and cultural values. *The Language of Conscience* contained within it much of the moralist as opposed to the relativist approach to ethics within society that we previously discussed.

It would be appropriate to explain my choice of the emblems on its cover and their relation to the creation of a culture of conscience, which is the ultimate issue. Values are instilled not just by what parents teach, but also by the values of the culture in which they exist. The American flag was chosen because of the importance of the rule of law within such a culture. The Declaration of Independence and the American Constitution give a fundamental appreciation of a structure in society that addresses the dignity of man. Within the Constitution itself, it seeks a balance of protection of the collective or government in the body of the document

with the Bill of Rights that follows protecting the individual. Such is
the balance of a system for stability. As noted previously, much of the
instability of today comes from a subliminal conflict of whether problems
can be solved collectively or individually.

Technology and economic growth have made the world complex and
often it requires natural laws such as markets and freedom of operations
to effectively operate, but where are divisions of responsibility to be
found? Politics and economics are now complex drivers. Depending on
culture to give structure in more of a vacuum, the nature of the cultural
values is now the issue. The Washington County Sheriff's badge signifies
discipline within society because even with the rule of law the method of
enforcement is critical to that same dignity. The Texas Peacemaker Award
given by the Texas Sheriffs' Association, in my father's memory, carefully
chronicles the best of those concepts. Particularly in an age of terrorism,
law enforcement succeeds when people support it and respect it rather
than fear it. The pictures of Christ and Confucius symbolize the Golden
Rule of Christ (and the Silver Rule of Confucius) that look at reciprocity,
which is in many ways the foundation of a culture of ethics, which defines
obligation. Aristotle and a symbol used to represent a variety of cultures
look to symbolize the common good and a culture of service. Aristotle
believed in a moral life and understood the concepts of why men must
serve society as a whole and why they must be educated to understand
the importance of laws and their values to them, which is in reality the
common benefit. Without appreciation of the great benefits as well as the
great responsibilities of freedom, it is not destined for true success. It
requires cultural knowledge and cultural ethics to truly thrive.

A number of people have expressed surprise to me at the Chinese
publication of my book by the Central Party School. My background as a
former Naval Lieutenant Commander, free enterprise oriented, Christian,
"military hawk," would seem strangely inconsistent with the image some
hold of China. However, the dissimilarity of backgrounds is a point of
critical importance. A search for conscience and honor bridge discussion
of different backgrounds. There are some things in the world that can unify
people beyond many other competing interests. One of the foremost among
these is the concern of what part they can play to set a better world for their
children, and that requires a very critical cultural understanding of the
nature of the advancement of civilization. China has a 5,000-year history
of such understanding and the patience to see a change mature once the
seed has been planted. At the Confucian Temple in Shandong Province, two
very similar great statues tower over visitors. The only difference is that

one holds a book and the other holds a sword. The Chinese understand from their history that power and knowledge have to be combined. Civilization advances best when wisdom (an appreciation of values) is combined with power be it examples like Marcus Aurelius in the West or the Duke of Zhou in the East. That wisdom cannot just look at the present but now must look at the future global world where different cultures will have power and must coexist. Is it a world of corruption and terrorism where competitive nations beggar their neighbor economically or is it a world of where at least a partial dominance of honor and integrity exist? How does everyone fit into that world? The great Chinese Philosopher Lao-tzu noted that "knowing others is wisdom, knowing self is enlightenment." China is doing both. It is trying to understand the outside world more clearly, but it is also bringing back many of the best aspects of its own culture in the value systems of the ancients. Morality and integrity must supplant corruption. China will become a power that changes the dynamic balance in the world. The issue is how. But the answer will not be in its political and economic power in the effect on others. Ultimately it will be in their cultural power, which is internal because it will determine the strength of the other. Unity or lack thereof is the key.

Much of the press conference was in Chinese and discussion of other books with Tejano Publications LLC, my licensee of the rights to the book. But what I did perceive from all that occurred was a sincerity of interest and a depth of understanding of the discussions that I had seldom seen in the United States. When I went to see the book in Chinese bookstores, I was rather amazed at the Beijing Bookstore which takes up almost an entire block and is six-stories tall. The Philosophy Section on the first floor was huge with a massive crowd equaling the tightest density I had ever seen in any American mall. The Ethics Section of that Philosophy Department in which the book was found was over five feet tall and probably twenty-four feet long. That was incredible to me in comparison to American bookstores. It was very significant that it was not that China did not have knowledge of ethics and cultural background. It is an issue of implementation on a massive cultural scale. My assessment of the Chinese interest looked to the point that under the leadership of their President Deng, they had recognized the necessity of technological innovation to strengthen their economic growth and competitiveness. As their economy grew with technology, it became increasingly clear that some parts of centralized government control do not do well in delivering performance in complex systems. The more complex the system gets the more it needs to be on the automatic pilot of natural market forces. China has accordingly modified its economic system to a blend of free market economics and the existing legacy systems. In doing so it effectively changed the method of production in both theory and reality. This has significant implications. While Karl Marx specialized on economic systems, his mentor Fredrick Engels in the *Preface of the Communist Manifesto* (German Edition of 1883) made what is still a very accurate observation of the relationship of the great powers:

The basic thought underlying the (Communist) Manifest is as follows: The method of production and the organization of social life inevitably arising there from constitutes in every historical epoch the foundation upon which is built the political and intellectual history of that epoch.

As I perceive what he was saying, the method of production (the economics) determines the social structure (the culture), and that is the foundation of the intellectual thought (the politics). These strategic drivers of power, economics, culture, and politics are inevitably bound together and that is the core of the thought and analysis in *The Language of Conscience.* It was a book written in part for character groups in the United States and as a bridge for the Confucian Museum in Shandong Province of China to help interact with groups in the West. It does in large part address these issues from a combination of both Chinese and Western similarities. It focused on enlightened conservatism, which is not a political philosophy as much as a cultural balance between enlightenment (technology, global change) and cultural values (tradition, existing structure). The ongoing friction between these forces determines much of the stability of society.

Of more importance, I think, is that it was a book written from a perspective of what a generation had done in Texas with various character groups and how a set of thoughts and values had been preserved that looked to conscience over convenience. It did not tell anyone in America, in China or in the rest of the world what they should do, but instead primarily described what we had done, and more importantly, why we did it. It was a book that could be used as a handbook by a variety of cultures to decide those parts with which they agreed. And it tried to bring out the best of cultures by having people identify the importance of character, family, and honor as a common tie. It focused on the importance of enhancing personal dignity. It explained the use of the nonprofit system of social capitalism to ease some of the harshness of market economics, especially during transitional phases.

Of the questions that different scholars asked me privately was the issue of whether "my conscience" was religious or philosophical. My point was that I am a servant of Christ, but a friend of Confucius and Lao-tzu. The conscience of thought you develop first is the conscience of man. While religions may teach us the Golden Rule and the necessity of how we show respect for each other, these are relationships of the conscience of morality of how man interacts with man. There is a basic beginning understanding of men's obligations between each other that is based on a fundamental conscience of the very nature of man to make him civilized. Religion is a perfection of that conscience combined with a belief in a hereafter as men may individually choose. It develops the conscience of obligation more affirmatively to a concept based on love of fellow men and respect for a great power that founded nature. As several scholars noted, they did not agree directly with my religion or my intense free market support, but what they did find of great value was the concept of the importance of conscience directing a culture and how those concepts could be of help in building ties for joint discussions in a global world.

To me, the depth of their questions showed the seriousness of thought, but most important, those I met from the School often had PhD's in philosophy. Unlike the business and other leaders I met on trips, they left dinners walking or on bicycles, not in Mercedes and without the trappings of wealth. If what is said of the power of the School is true then China may not be the stereotype that so many scholars characterize through the glasses of past writers and existing structures of thought. Its past culture with its historic power of the dignity of man, "face," and morality is beginning to re-emerge, and, more importantly, its thinkers and leaders look at the global sense of the problems of a global world. They have studied Russia, Europe, and the United States, but they see a different and unique China that can be formed. Some of the key thoughts are reflected later.

I think the more practical aspect of the book is the fact that the Chinese Communist Party has as its premier focus an extremely strong effort to root out corruption within its society. It is recognized as the greatest threat to the country and China's advancement in the long run as market systems mature. While Chinese culture may have interest in the discussion and bridging of intellectual values, the power of morality within an emerging economic giant is absolutely essential. If I learned one thing from my visit at the Central Party School, it is the significant intelligence of those with whom I discussed issues. One of the points made in *The Language of Conscience* is that the cultural structure has a great deal to do with the effectiveness of the economic structure. It is in effect Engels' theory slightly in reverse. Market systems that are necessary as complexity grows are only marginally effective if there is not a moral market. The reason is that markets are driven by competition. And competition only exists to an appropriate degree when you have a market that is free, open, transparent, and honest. If bids are fixed or corruption dominates, free market systems do not work. Much of the Western free enterprise system has been adapted in China, but one of the things not apparent in the beginning was the great impact that this moral component has had. With the numerous recent financial scandals, it is now being more fully appreciated in the East and West. There is a critical relationship that is being understood globally. The future value of assets looks to the scarcity of items, the future values that assets can generate, and to the future environment and the nature of its stability. Market integrity is a key component of all of them.

In the last century, China has suffered the hardships of many wars, adverse economic environments, and internal conflict. Many scholars point to such periods as one where there are informal approaches to taxation and economic relationships. How would a military have to be sustained during revolutions? The nature of central planning in itself has different mechanisms by which success is achieved. When you combine a market system with legacy systems developed through times of difficulty and then place it on a massive scale, it is easy for an environment of corruption to expand dramatically particularly in the modern world where materialism is the focus of success to many in that culture. Even though you may understand the importance of ethics culturally, the forces of nature, size, and the speed of technology can overwhelm any good intentions. Safeguards built for one system may not be appropriate for another. In American football, for example, a defense that is excellent against the run is often weak against the pass. The point is that it is the same problem as America faces greed in a market system, but from a different perspective of origin. It is not the economic system at issue, but how the culture seeks to address it as change removes internal barriers to corruption.

There are basically two ways to address corruption and build ethics. The great Roman Emperor Marcus Aurelius noted them both in his comment that "men should be upright, not be kept upright." To be kept upright you need a strong system of law and enforcement that consistently applies well-known rules fairly. But for men to be upright, which is by far the most significant issue because of the peer pressure it places within a culture, then you must have a culture in which the power of conscience dominates. Conscience works well with individuals. Convenience always dominates in power. *The only way to get conscience into power is to make it convenient to be of conscience and that requires the culture to value conscience.*

Toward that end, I think the Central Party School appreciated that *The Language of Conscience* was written primarily to describe the importance of the creation of that culture. Groups such as the Ethics Officer Association, the Center for Value Based Leadership, and a number of other groups focusing on American governance (and international transparency) supported the book with their endorsements and their contributions of thought. But this ties closely to my observations of relativity and morality as well as the difference between theory and practice. What the Chinese perceived more than my American friends is the relationship between the drivers of power and how they operate through each of us individually as well as through collective institutions.

America has had its own difficult times, and it is increasingly recognizing that if you are to have an ethical corporate climate, its development needs growth or it will naturally deteriorate. I think it is very important that the federal sentencing guidelines have recently changed their wordings on "compliance" to the words "compliance and ethics." They effectively integrated ethics and after analyzing and monitoring incentives to commit misconduct, both positive and negative ones. The addition of ethics is a cultural concept and is quite important. Compliance normally looks to the law, which is generally just a floor even though it is almost constantly changing in modern times. But the law itself is not necessarily a concept of morality but is instead simply a statement of rules. It doesn't address challenging questions in the gray areas, and it often is relatively behind the times in attempting to address the emerging issues. The cultural component of strength of character and integrity normally serves as a peer review in place that is far more significant than the law. You can change the strength of laws and compliance, but with an increasing focus on ethical values you add a far broader structure that can be strengthened over time if you build in the proper incentives. If you have strong controlling issues within an environment such as ethics, integrity, and morality, it sets the operating tone of the environment by influencing the consciousness of the people. The internal structures of auditing, training, and integrity reporting systems to make an easy flow of information and complaints available simply reinforces that environment. You may have an operational reporting system of compliance, but it is only effective if you have an ethical drive to see it used. Just as technology forced centralized planning to add a market component to improve "speed of response." Moral systems have to have the quick response of peer pressure rather than lagging timeframes and ineffective rules.

The significant point is that the cutting edge of most thought in fighting corruption today has gone back to the issue of men's responsibility to do the right thing. In America we have systems that believe we can "lawyer" our way around issues by disclosing. And even if it is in fine print, we have no ethical obligation if we have advised the people. Our auditing systems are primarily used whether or not they complied with certain very specific guidelines, like generally accepted accounting principles. The English accounting systems have always been more of an obligatory one ethically to explain problems and concerns. Increasingly, America is looking at its system as being a bit *relativist* as opposed to being *moralist*. Worldwide scholars are looking for ways to compare these cultural issues in relevant ways that can bring about transparency and integrity because of the tremendous impact of corruption, piracy, and theft of intellectual property. That makes these issues universal ones, but because of America's significant economic position in the world economy and China's position as the most rapidly growing economy, there is no more significant place that fundamental study could more appropriately take place between two systems. Ethics in economics is driving an examination of the place and power of culture that is really the ultimate issue in national strength and international cooperation. The focus on corruption both in America and in China is ultimately about much broader issues. Because all of these issues are related and of growing critical importance, economic and political issues can be discussed more easily.

This brings to point the necessity of understanding the importance of some basic level of standards. "The language of conscience" in the intent of this book is not to tell anyone what they have to do or to fault legacy systems, but instead to provide thought that can be analyzed as the basis of adaptation. As I tried to explain to my friends at American universities, just because you want to put in a fundamental set of values does not mean you are teaching religion or challenging academic freedom. Concepts of integrity, honor, and ethical conscience bring about an understanding of right and wrong. Relativity and toleration may well be very positive intellectual concepts, and I am the first to acknowledge that when you get to questions such as the damage of little white lies in saving someone's feelings, you could certainly discuss relativity in a strong philosophical sense. *But the issue is that relativity is not relative in the serious context of the world's culture at a time of political terrorism and economic corruption.* The strengthening of an understanding of right and wrong and of man's obligation to each other is an absolute necessity. The power of the religions and their morality add and contribute to its understanding. But regardless of what crop is grown in a field (if we look at the higher levels of consciousness of religion as such crops) the plowing of the field and its preparation in the sense of morality is equally important to all. C. S. Lewis talked of spiritual love of God. Sigmund Freud spoke of cultural rules learned from experience. The thoughts of Lewis and Freud come from different origins but the final values are similar. Many are the same morality at a number of levels, and they need to be brought together co-operationally for impact without the different sides arguing the straw men of extremes. How that is done needs to be studied and passed on to the next generation so civilization advances and solves its problems with the greatest good. Those that object to teaching almost any values because it may open the door to other values, miss the point that some values are essential even to their arguments.

The ultimate key is what our children learn not just from their parents. But what the culture instills within them and how they react as a peer pressure to create the environment in which they will live with each other. To discuss those points is the purpose of this book largely in response to many of the questions I had in China. These were issues of concern to them and should be of concern to America because the destiny of nations flows in cycles that are well connected to character. In times that require us to work together we must find the ways to do so. America and China are in all likelihood the centers of thought of the next half century. Europe, Africa, Latin America, and many others will have increasing or decreasing power as demographics and global demands shift. But, English and Chinese will increasingly be the scientific and economic languages on the web because of the power of economics and of commerce. That these two cores of thought of West and East fully understand each other and not historical or political stereotypes of each other makes a great difference in how the future world develops. Will it be in a framework of cooperation on differences in structure of integrity or two separate camps of interests? Realists would argue the second, idealists the first. The perspective you hold will judge the materials that follow, but idealists tend to see them in the most positive of developments. The original collaboration agreement with the Central Party School Press and Tejano Publications LLC, only deals with books. But books are collections of ideas and if ideas are sought, wisdom is gained and exchanged.

I have been asked whether I felt the Chinese translation of *The Language of Conscience* was an accurate one, and I have noted that people I trust assure me so, even though translations of words of the heart are difficult. But I note the respect given the book by keeping its cover in tact when it could have been easily changed. That indicated a positive effort, with significant thought, to build bridges. The West equally will need to show respect in similar ways for Eastern values. The bottom line is the language of conscience does not require you to agree. It requires you speak with truth, act with integrity, and show respect for others' dignity.

The Natural Human Desire to be Right and its Effect on Perspective and Personal Dignity

*And therefore the Philosopher (Aristotle) says in Metaphysics VI
that good and evil, which are objects of the will, are in things,
but truth and error, which are objects of the intellect, are in the mind.*
— St. Thomas Aquinas
Summa Theologica

*Character is that which reveals moral purpose,
exposing the class of things a man chooses or avoids.*
—Aristotle

In developing that core of uncommon people, we must begin with the nature of man and what ultimately drives his perspectives and thereby his actions or inactions. Perhaps the most powerful human emotion is one's desire to be correct in what one thinks and says. Many times it even exceeds self-interest because of the importance to one's ego. This is a critical concept because it has tremendous effect on perspective and how we process information. Each of us can look at a glass as being half empty or half full depending on what our attitude has been previously, and we can take what information exists and process it to confirm our original perspective. It is often referred to as a fairly common psychological phenomenon that is called confirmational bias. You tend to accept or ignore data depending on whether it supports or contradicts your viewpoint. So the perspective by which we look at the information has a great deal to do with how we interpret the analysis and the trends that are to be selected. How we think affects what we believe.

The modern world is greatly complicated by our division into groups. We have always had perspectives based upon historical or geographical relationships, religious backgrounds, ethnic origin or a great variety of different parts of our background that we accentuated because of their importance to us. More importantly, in recent years we have seen the number of groups both expand and be consolidated through the concept of diversity. When individuals could not receive proper recognition, rights or dignity as individuals, they assimilated into groups of various natures, which sought and often received recognition of these rights or dignities through the support of the size of the group. Unfortunately, this can often lead to information being processed from the perspective of that group because of the way the information is presented.

It is much like being in a forest of trees looking at the individual trees. A more significant perspective would be a broader view from a mountaintop that got you above the valley so you might see more clearly the path that needs to be taken. This becomes particularly true when the concept of *victimhood* or victimization is brought forth. In modern times a small industry has emerged in building organizations on *collective victimhood*. Often the concept is to create guilt and seek reform, usually with someone else paying the solution. The significant effectiveness of these organizations in a time that technology has overwhelmed us often has perspectives looking at the information presented from a very narrow judgment of how it supports this more limited concept. It may well be correct as an answer to a specific question. But the broader issue is often whether that is the right question.

The real solution to many of the problems in society is for people to talk with each other, even though they may not agree. Quite often, if you use conscience as the basis of a perspective, you tend to look at concepts such as the Golden Rule, the common good, and from the perspective that also puts you in the other man's shoes. This provides the framework of how you work with others. Normally, if you can begin with that perspective, you have a much better opportunity to communicate with others. You will not necessarily always agree, but you see a greater perspective. And the effort in that environment is more ethical and the discussion is more realistic because it builds a model in all men's minds beyond the limited model in a specific group's mind. That is where progress ultimately takes place.

Perhaps the most significant movement in diversity has been that of the civil rights movement. Its most expressive leader was Dr. Martin Luther King, Jr. The judgment criterion that he often referred to was character. I think character is best defined as the choice of conscience over convenience as implemented by individual responsibility. In his greatest speeches this was one of the most critical points. He believed in the ultimate goodness of men and that one day good would overcome evil.

When he received the Nobel Peace Prize in 1964, he noted, "I believe that what self-centered men have torn down, men other-centered can build up." In his most famous speech, he probably defined this perspective best, "I have a dream that one day this nation will rise up and live out the true meaning of its creed. . . . I have a dream that my four little children will one day live in a nation where they will not be judged by the color of their skin but by the content of their character."

That to me captures the essence of why character and, most importantly, the conscience of men that it represents needs to be the perspective by which information is judged. If you ask a question, "Have minorities been ill treated?" The answer is yes, and the response of logic is blame. But if you ask, "What is the best way in the future to bring true equality with judgment based on character?" Then the answer is the promotion of an environment where that concept rules. How time is spent, and the attitude taken, is critical. Blame may have a part in bringing understanding, but vision as to what you seek is the crucial path to success. This is where the focus must be placed to succeed. If you unify or divide, the question chosen often directs your actions. If we confirm our facts and our acceptance of facts on the basis of that broadened approach, we will find the environment in which we operate far more susceptible to finding common solutions. Pettiness and revenge are not winning strategies nor is hypocrisy. In the short-term they provide emotional gratification, but in the long-term they corrode your leadership abilities. True strength is being for something not against it. Great leaders are transformational not transactional. It is easy to unify on hate and envy, but it is more difficult to unify on principle, honor, and the common dignity of man. This is what great leaders are remembered for and requires the greatest of internal strength and ability and is driven by enlightenment.

Similarly, if we move to the convenience of trying to promote selective interpretations that may satisfy the ego or short-term politics, nothing is contributed to the true advancement of man. Man will never be perfect. He will always be a combination of conscience and convenience pulling him in different directions. But if the culture of the whole is to look to character and acceptance of responsibility for feelings and actions—as opposed to the convenience of a shorter-term benefit or emotion—then we and our children will benefit greatly. The environment fifty years from now will probably be traceable to the seeds of perception of the ten year olds of today. If we pass over emotion to the dedication of values, we change the culture not so much for us as for our children and grandchildren.

Personal dignity, or human dignity as a group, is the ultimate goal or method of measurement. In policy it is prioritization of concept. If we are materialistic and only judge by the level of wealth, then that gives our culture its motivation. An environment of success at any cost drives our motivation. If our motivation is politics, political power is the ultimate goal.

There will always be divisions in some sectors of society. But for society as a whole, if the fundamentals we teach our children are materialistic we will create instability rather than stability because only a few can ultimately be satisfied. The issue here is what fundamental values transcend generations. If good character is the criteria of the dignity of man, then politics and economics will be positively shaped by the culture and provide the most opportunity for the greatest number. A key point that is often forgotten is that respect for one's dignity is in large part *earned* on an individual level. The more ritualistic approaches of protocol and courtesy that in part began with Confucius' concept of establishing and maintaining relationships through respect have waned in society.

Two people who most understood human dignity and its importance to the action or inaction of men and women were Gandhi of India and Dr. Martin Luther King, Jr., who I previously quoted. I think several more thoughts capture this concept best. From Dr. Martin Luther King, Jr.:

> *Moral principles have lost their distinctiveness. For modern man, absolute right and absolute wrong are a matter of what the majority is doing. Right and wrong are relative to likes and dislikes and the customs of a particular community. We have unconsciously applied Einstein's theory of relativity, which properly described the physical universe, to the moral and ethical realm. An individual has not started living until he can rise above the narrow confine of his individualistic concerns to the broader concerns of all humanity.*

And, a key observation of Mahatma Gandhi that parallels Thomas Paine's vision of the power of the culture of society if you refined self-discipline and dignity:

> *Political power means capacity to regulate national life through national representatives. If national life becomes so perfect as to become self-regulated, no representation becomes necessary. There is then a state of enlightened anarchy. In such a state every one is his own ruler.*

> *He rules himself in such a manner that he is never*
> *a hindrance to his neighbor. In the ideal state, therefore,*
> *there is not political power because there is no state.*
> — **Young India**
> November 17, 1921

It has been noted, there will never be such perfection, and there will always be government. But its size, its involvement with daily life, its contract with the people through its budgeted spending, all relies on the character of the people.

Perhaps nowhere is the clash between individualism and collectivism going to be more distinct than the current efforts to move to an "ownership society" in America as contrasted with the New Deal of Franklin Roosevelt. President Lyndon Johnson's Great Society was more an equalization attempt focused in part on compassion. The choice between a very strong safety net of government and private programs versus a more risk, but greater opportunity based, ownership concept is fundamental economic policy in the modern world. It defines changes in society because the nature of their involvement in the economic system affects the perspective of the people and how they make choices. Incentives, open competition, all lead to different economic policies. Government, as it matures through its regulatory structures becomes not only bloated but also a negative force because it calcifies and is structurally difficult to change economically. This often leads to corruption in the form of graft or the more informal types of convenience related influence. These are political policy choices that will affect the culture and the economic system as needs for change clash with the inertia of status quo interests— the friction of the forces of enlightenment and existing legacy structure. It also poses a choice for individualists who favor government action over private economic initiative. You cannot be part free. Systems move you in one way or another over time as more natural laws have their affects. If personal dignity is to have opportunity to achieve all it can, then it will have to accept the risk of failure. The horns of the dilemma are that to protect against all risks you remove much of the opportunity. That is the issue that will be faced. The Chinese culture has long recognized this in that the same symbol represents danger and opportunity. We will face it because of the nature of change. Older systems will be obsolete in a much more competitive world. An example is protectionism. Some talk of curing trade deficits by legislation that requires other parties to buy equally from us. But logically that would be like saying we have to sell equally to the grocery store where we buy food or the dry cleaners or the doctor. The specialization of labor as a concept gives a higher standard of living to all, but it is also a painful equalizer.

The answer is to have a resilient society that always changes to develop more and better products and services rather than consuming its seed corn. That is what is at issue here between the two concepts of risk and opportunity and has to be realized. Democracies have cycles, and you must constantly reaffirm the basic values and re-implement them just as companies must reinvent themselves. That has always been, and I think will be, America's greatest strength. The reason for the change from the New Deal concepts has a great deal to do with changes in the world. Competition has made companies less willing to keep pensions, and so to compete they need lower costs and more flexibility. There are tradeoffs in our standard of living such as environment and compassion that we cannot forfeit, so we must develop more competitive systems and create the incentives that drive these systems. It is interesting that the strongest support for many of these economic initiatives in the form of deductible retirement accounts involve the ability to leave them as a source for family members at death to help give the next generation opportunity, which is a cultural value. This begins to combine the concepts of family, culture, and economics. It defines the issue not as social security or trade deficits, but the real issue of the economic theory that will be the base of our public policy and the foundation of our cultural perspectives. International competition will have great impact on the decision over time, and only looking at longer term impacts and the effect on our children can we fully appreciate the decisions we make today.

This is a book not so much on morality as the power of morality. The concept of power is an important one here. I quote Martin Luther King and Gandhi often in the text because if you give the benefit of doubt through conscience, you often can change the power equation between the parties. If you do more than is required or expected, it can create an obligation on the other side to respond positively or negatively. You sometimes have to take risks to move forward, but as the later chapters indicate, risk must be judged carefully as to consequences.

These concepts can be a bridge. The tolerance necessary for multiculturalism is critical, but it must be remembered that in absolute tolerance all versions of truth are equal, so a balance and structure with morality must be found. With terrorism the political issue of the century and with competition and corruption the economic issues, the redefinition of the world needs to globally focus on developing cultures of integrity.

I have often thought of management consultant Peter Drucker's observation that you achieve the greatest results if you supplant the word "achievement" with the word "contribution." The reason is that it changes the focus to what is really important. The issue of how you think affects your actions in a nutshell.

Section II

What Knowledge and Talent Must We Attain and Use?

Understanding Critical Concepts for the Development of Personal Dignity and Individual Responsibility

There is a flickering spark in each of us which,
if struck at just the right age, will light up the rest of our lives.
— President Ronald Reagan
1982

To know how to grow old is the master-work of wisdom
and one of the most difficult chapters in the great art of living.
— Henri Frederic Amiel

Over thirty years ago when Dad told me that summary of thoughts in his last words to me, I felt I understood exactly what he was saying. But the maturity of going through life brings much of it to clearer perspective. There are two prominent core issues to all that he expressed. The first was good character, which is in effect the choice of man's conscience and concern for others over his own personal convenience as implemented by recognition and acceptance of individual responsibility. The other was the concept of personal dignity. I understood character better then, but did not have a full appreciation for the tremendous importance of personal dignity to the individual, the family, and ultimately the society. Personal dignity is our individual assessment of the success of our level of influence or control over life and thereby how we view the actions of others where we are concerned. It shapes our perspective of how we see the world, and in doing so it sets the stage for our success or failure. If we envy the wealth of others it can either lead us to work harder to achieve the same, or lead us to push efforts to redistribute wealth from them. If we judge our success only by the level of our wealth and what we provide in material goods, we have a hard time feeling successful and we are driven to always acquire more. The cautions of the Chinese philosopher Lao-tzu on the possible evils of competition should be well noted. Maslow's Hierarchy of Needs explains the evolution of undeveloped societies as people move forward from satisfying their basic needs and how the nature of needs change. In societies that are in rapid growth this becomes particularly important.

If personal dignity is significant because it is one of the most controlling forces of how we set our perspective, it is also the criteria by which we judge our own success. Thereby it sets the stage for our vision of where we wish to go and the limits we wish to place upon ourselves morally. This in turn eventually sets family values, and the values of society. It is not a simple concept. All people desire wealth and power. Almost all people desire to be popular and well known, and all wish to have power over that which affects them. However, we must each inter-react with six billion other people on the planet that have similar considerations. All circumstances are different, and it is the natural order of the world that these are settled on a more localized basis by the vagaries of the three great arenas of power—economics, politics, and media/culture through their interactions. But the evolution of personal dignity to a point in each society that gives a level of satisfaction and confidence in life is significant. It is that satisfaction with the level of personal dignity that gives substance to a society and builds the relationship with its government and other entities. For Dad the ultimate goal was a sense of honor that he was respected by others for his integrity and for his actions. He did not have to be rich. He did not have to be politically powerful. He did not even have to be that socially acceptable because he often called things as he saw them. However, he felt that a sense of honor was the core of a man's self-respect and for that reason conscience mattered.

In Chinese history he would have patterned himself after the ancient Duke of Zhou. The Duke preserved the kingdom of Wu for his small nephew in establishing one of the great Chinese Dynasties. He could have at any time taken power, but he was a man that set great value on the integrity of responsibility. He did much to develop the concept of the Mandate of Heaven that justified the assumption of power by a new leadership when the former leadership no longer put prosperity and peace of the people as their primary agenda. Dad's view of government was exactly the same. Thirty years ago he pointed out that partisanship as opposed to the common good would be the quickest way for Texas to lose its unique character and one of the easiest ways for the nation to lose its strength.

If I were to go back and add today to what thirty years have taught me, I would begin with what Dad left as advice and an update on those two very critical issues of conscience and personal dignity. I would explain that the times today with their forms of entertainment, the speed of technology and communication, and globalization require a focus on purpose far more than the past when times moved more slowly and thought was analyzed with the benefit of time that granted wisdom. Today the focus is very much on economics. How do you get rich quickly? There are hundreds of books that supposedly give you the answers.

It is easy to gain the perspective that money is easily made when you see the stories of all of the rich placed in the media. What is not shown, and a banker can tell you, are all of the many endeavors that fail because they are seldom reported as newsworthy. The world is very competitive, and growing more so. People differ in the amount of resources that they have. They differ in levels of education. They differ in talent, intelligence, and, of significant importance, levels of discipline.

As I have often told young people, the secret is to assess yourself, your talents, and most important, your desires and make a realistic assessment of how they might best be strategically used.

This often starts best with a family unit helping each child go one level higher. I have been extremely impressed with the cohesiveness of Asian families and the dedication of their youth to study. I have been similarly impressed with Hispanic families from Latin America that look to explore opportunity to make the next generation positioned for a level of growth. Success may well come with one great burst of opportunity and talent. But more often across the vast spectrum of people that do not have particularly impressive opportunities or talents, it is the result of hard work and dedication and a strategy or vision that makes use of all opportunities and resources available. However, there are critical factors that are often perceived but not understood until you look back at life and have the wisdom and perspective that age gives. These are factors that affect one's perception of their personal dignity and can well affect their success. If understood they contribute to the understanding of the concept of conscience. But of equal importance, they are issues very necessary to a broadened sense of thought. Education is more structured and in "silos" so the knowledge can only be converted to wisdom by understanding the inter-relationship of forces and ideas. This is often lacking in courses as history and the classics have been minimized. There are a variety of things a broadened mind must understand to have the foundation for strategic thought, which affects how you think.

Some of these concepts are divided into two general groups. The first consists of personal characteristics or factors that crystallize a concept that is important to success. The second group is factors of the nature of society as a whole. We will later deal in longer presentations that build an understanding of how relationships operate in response to each other; these are items that are critical building blocks to that understanding. In the later section we make an attempt at being an architect or engineer in assessing and creating a structure.

Here we take an individual concept, say the power of incentive, and understand its use much as a Roman engineer would understand the use of the arch in construction. The addendum on "the triangles" is a tool to help keep all the forces in view, but keep the focus on character and individual responsibility, which are keys to success both personally and for society. Look upon these individual items as going shopping for all the materials to build a house. They are components of the knowledge necessary. Just as a child needs to learn values like courtesy and respect, they need to understand drivers that will allow them to succeed in a very competitive world. They also need to learn what drives the society in which they operate so that it is globally competitive. These are a few critical factors among many that are driving attention to the importance of knowledge and then consolidating it into wisdom and structured habit or public policy. None replace dedication, ambition, focus, and many other key leadership factors. There are simply some that are not always fully developed in thought to be appreciated. In a following section we will tie these concepts together with a set of writings on their inter-relationship and finally provide a finish with the discussion of the triangles, which help structure discussion of relationships. These items are more personalized to be easily understood.

PERSONAL INSIGHTS

Risk

That which is necessary is never a risk.
— Paul De Gandi, Cardinal De Retz
Memoirs

The first item that any person must understand is that success in business and life often involves the toleration of risks. People are very different in their acceptance and judgment of these levels of risks. Many people that have made the greatest fortunes have taken on great risk while others have let the recognition of the risk level prevent their action. Similarly, there are a great number of people that have not recognized risk and have failed for every one that succeeds. So making money or other successes is often not an act of brilliance but may be the result of luck in that the markets prove favorable. In the times of real estate expansion, many people that took what others would consider foolhardy risks were rewarded by immense fortunes because of their positions at the time. Inflation was the primary benefactor. That is not to say that there are not those who are very intelligent in real estate or business and make their money by the knowledge of the situation, but taking on risk is complicated. Poker, for example, is less a game of chance than a management of resources anticipating risk. Life is similar. It is hard to know the future even if you do know trends and have expectations. If you have a family and a concern for your children, is the acceptance of risk that might put them at a disadvantage something that you wish to accept for a potentially higher level of wealth? Or is it felt to be better to take a more guaranteed course that would assure them a lesser but more certain level of economic position? This shapes your perspective of life and your concept of personal dignity.

No one can predict with certainty the future. But beyond using the best information available to assess it, you must not look just at the degree of probability if you are correct, but additionally to the level of consequences if you are wrong. These are equally important considerations that must be in the assessment. In fact consequences may be the most important.

Your perspective when making a decision must also be considered. If you have been successful at the present, you may be overconfident and are at a point of the greatest risk to make a poor assessment. Similarly, when you are at a point of heavy distress, you may not be bold enough to act.

People who are under pressure on a more regular basis develop the "decision muscle" not to panic or over react because of the habits it builds. This is why political campaigns tend to turn "lumps of coal" into diamonds due to constant pressure. As you move to higher levels of competition in any endeavor, you build habits that more easily factor in risk. It is why few people move quickly from low levels to the top unless it is a unique field. Like in sports, each level of competition is harder and faster and this takes time to get experience.

This is a critical part of understanding the triangles of thought we will discuss later. Just as people individually react to this level of risk, a nation has levels it will accept that vary. How to explain the assessment of these risks is critical. You start by understanding its effect on you personally, and you soon realize the importance of a broad perspective of understanding of forces (the triangles) to quantify or identify risks.

Recognizing this difference in your acceptance of risk versus others is a critical step or you may feel disappointed in your efforts. A lot of the knowledge of risk comes from experience or your natural environment. A good example might be understanding the nature of whitewing doves and mourning doves. If you hunt an area in South Texas where they are both found, you see very different characteristics. Whitewings tend to fly higher and straighter, usually in bigger groups and with less fear. Mourning doves weave and duck and tend to fly scared either alone or with a few others. Nature has created differences in peoples' nature that is affected by experience. So learning about yourself is key. Handling risk will require not only knowledge, but also temperament.

If you have inherited wealth or have achieved it by transactions, it plays significantly into your assessment of risks. When you have something to lose and you appreciate how difficult it is to gain, it adds conservatism to your judgment that can both be beneficial or detrimental. To someone with nothing to lose, maximizing return appears a more logical strategy, even at high risk, as opposed to someone who has a lot to lose. The point is simply that the recognition of levels of risk, and the ability and acceptance of them, often has a great deal more to do with economic success than just talent factors. It is often noted in American law school classes that the "A" students are usually hired by the best defense firms and earn high salaries. The "C" students often become the trial lawyers that succeed or fail due to their unique talents or opportune cases and have the shot at greater wealth. Acceptance of risk is a factor that all young people need because it is one of the considerations in making the decision at what point they are satisfied in life and are making conscience judgments. There is always the opportunity to hit a homerun and to hope for it. But most often "chasing rabbits or the brokering of deals" has only a rare success. It takes rare opportunity and usually capital to convert such an opportunity into reality. There are many times that accepting the risk is worth the potential loss because the opportunity is such that it is worthy. But thinking through these consequences before you meet the opportunity and become enamored by it sets a sound base. As Lao-tzu noted, knowing others is wisdom (or here the facts of opportunity) and knowing self is enlightenment. Good risk judgment requires a close assessment of both.

Risks are specific or general. The stock market is an example. An individual stock can have bad performance news and it is impacted directly or the market as a whole is perceived as overvalued and goes down. Much of modern portfolio theory uses the potential changes in individual risks in combinations to lower overall market risk through strategic diversification. Life's risks can in part be handled the same way. Strategic segmentation can keep one single event from having an overwhelming impact.

In finance the concept of diversification, of holding different types of assets that react to circumstances in different ways, is the main way to minimize risk even though it often does not maximize return as a 100% commitment to one excellent asset might. The same concept works in other areas where networks of friends, involvement in different activities, or similar "social capital" investments give you ties for difficult times. Information and knowledge play a critical part in reducing risk. But even more important is the wisdom of perspective that lets you have a matrix to create your personal model of the world. Even though you can work to know yourself, you must have a way to assess external factors. The triangles and analysis later discussed help in creating that personal model regardless of how its focus is changed. The triangles deal with the relationship of the drivers of power in society, which are always relevant to success. They also point out that if you maximize return just on materiality, you risk the loss of the happiness of a more balanced life. Additionally, the more you understand risk, the more you desire more certainty as opposed to luck or relativity because you want more substance for judgment.

Beyond the individual at this level of society, there is a key understanding of risk that is not appreciated. In politics, risk may be the judgment of whether you have accumulated and consolidated enough power to attempt to secure the next level of power. In economics, it may be whether you have appropriately judged the risks in taking a certain product or effort to a certain customer audience and executing the strategy to success. But in culture, you have a different situation. Success or failure, as it is judged, may well be in your internal judgment of success. Do you care what others think about your actions or whether they are correct by your judgment of character? There is a difference in being "something" and being "someone."

This affects society because it impacts what people expect from their leaders. If character is valued, over time it is recognized in people. But doing the right thing is often not easy because it involves sacrifice for the future, which creates current disappointments. Cultural risk is that choice between conscience and convenience. And the goal is to have the peer pressure of the culture understand it and support it so that what people think of you and what you think of yourself is the same. Then stability reigns.

In Eastern cultures this is particularly important because there is a group orientation, which believes that the common goal is more important than any individual benefit. Conscience is much more important than the Western individualized outcome. The cultural issue of risk comes down to whether the honor of the culture is of the heart or is judged ceremonially.

Vision

Knowledge dwells in heads replete with thoughts of other men;
wisdom in minds attentive to their own.
— William Cowper

Vision is anticipating the future and relevant trends that must be prioritized as to their effect. How you perceive and think about things often determines what you think and how accurate or successful your actions will be. What is your perspective? Is it individualized or a part of the success of a group or several groups? There are economics, politics, and cultural groups of which each of us are simultaneously a part. Which dominates our perspective? Enlightenment helps us structure our perspective. Companies used to have to change in character every twenty-five years to evolve. With modern technology that has shortened very dramatically; the same has been true of the careers and talents of individuals. Economically, everyone wishes to find the "next great thing."

In the 1950s and 1960s many people wondered why the children of many of the wealthy went to Midland, Texas. The reason was that many of the well-established families of the East Coast looked to the next great opportunity and that at that point was oil, and Midland, Texas was in the heart of it. In the 1980s technology and centers such as the Silicon Valley, Austin, Texas, and various other areas of development emerged as the new place to be positioned to catch the wave of growth and wealth.

It is critical to recognize how the world is transforming itself at increasing rates due to technology. It challenges the speed that our knowledge can be processed into our operational culture, which has been accumulated historically and in a different context. The computer of today's information revolution is as significant as the farming process of grain was to the agricultural revolution or the steam engine to the industrial revolution. The effects of the computer are just fully being integrated with existing systems, but we have a period of transition culturally as new talents have value and old skills diminish. Chemistry dominated the 1800s, physics the 1900s, biomedicine will probably emerge as this century's masterpiece, but it will bring not only great opportunity as it expands lifespan, but far greater decisions on values within culture as economics looks to division of resources.

The increasing decline of individual traditional cultures may be one of the greatest opportunities and greatest dangers since that relates to success in absorbing and adjusting to change. It takes a new way of thinking combined with an enhanced knowledge base to give wisdom. Economic changes enhance the impact of the transition. Today America is the consumer of last resort, China and Japan, the lenders of last resort. European demographics and structural systems make it a less flexible force, so the great future pressure will be how America and China integrate or disintegrate their economic interests. This will have great consequence for the world's future because of the inter-relationships being transformed. It is the cleavage point on the diamond because it affects the value of the dollar and thereby the fiscal concerns which affect both countries. For that reason, the opportunity and danger signs are both appropriate as the next big thing. The types of knowledge that have value here are different.

You should also look at how you can build your life from foundations of your work—in other words how you build your future based upon your accomplishments. In yesterday's economy, you often stayed with one company or effort and advanced by its systems. However, today you may undertake different careers and employment, so it is important to think how what activities you choose can be packaged or coordinated to advance. Like power that is built in stages of acquisition and then used to advance, the basic power must be preserved as a foundation. Similarly, contacts, social activities, knowledge, and other experiences need to be looked upon as building blocks and more care given in decisions as to how your life is integrated for the future. A good way to look at it is the concept of writing a book in your older years. What did you learn out of life and how did it affect your future?

We have moved through the transition between the industrial revolution and the information age. The value of information was understood and led to the explosion of the "dot.com" era. Its failure was in part the result of people not recognizing then that owning the information was not as important as what you did with it. The future will look more to shared information that helps build economic feasibility. People will have to develop methods of collaboration more than in dividing control. This requires trust and systems based on integrity and knowledge. All the new technology is but a tool to use the information. You do not hire a plumber because he has a wrench but because he knows how the system works and he has the knowledge to make repairs. The same overview of the new fields of knowledge will be sought but with integrity on increasingly invaluable trust.

Similarly, as we look at the world today, globalization is going to change dramatically the way the next twenty-years are shaped. Fast developing service centers in India, manufacturing centers in China, and natural resources in South America and Africa will become areas of growth. They will be the new frontiers, but the question of how people within those nations and people abroad can jointly have increasing growth together depends a great deal on how societies begin to interact to provide opportunities for trust that expands trade. Large companies with massive resources can do deals of size because there is a cost justification. How individuals or smaller companies can similarly benefit will depend greatly on how networks of friendships and organizations of common interest can be developed to enhance trade. Even now the maquiladoras of Mexico that have been hurt by the lower cost Chinese competition are finding ways to work with Chinese companies in order to further specialize labor and distribution for evermore effective strategies. The great new era will be international in opportunities, but the ones most successful will be those that build the most effective networks that provide them market intelligence, dependable relationships for trade, and a vision of the products needed.

In America the great opportunity will be the provision of services and products for a growing middle class in China that is becoming increasingly wealthy. As it reaches the basic needs, it will move logically from desiring wealth, to desiring the trappings of wealth, which involve travel, cultural works, and the highest levels of education and healthcare. Just as healthcare will be one of the greatest domestic opportunities in the United States because of an aging population, the global opportunities will be necessary to rebalance the transfers of wealth occurring in the world today. It will not be easy because the local businessmen in developing companies like China are very competent and at home in their own market. But for China to advance beyond a mercantilist style economy, it will have to realize its growing impact on the world. While it will trade with the West, it will increasingly play a major role in economic impact in Asia beginning to rely more on that as a driver of its economy. That has implications for the world as a whole as a new trading area consolidates and competes. The battle over free trade and protectionism will resurface, but the ultimate answer for any nation is probably like the answer I was given when I inquired about losing hair. I was told a certain number fell out every day. That was not the problem. With age the number coming in was less and that was the problem to address. Countries have to concentrate on building their competitiveness, which often involves sacrifice and is not politically popular. The developed countries of the world have pension systems, tax systems, regulations, and a different structure than developing nations. Both have to understand the implications of their actions and develop systems to communicate the implications of actions to each other.

International competition and trade are going to cause major dislocations. In America the youth should worry about the competitiveness of our economy if we do not address the unfunded entitlements, deficits, and tax structure that are a legacy from a former environment. Much rhetoric can be placed on the unfairness of international competition and the loss of American jobs. The problem is that American companies go to offshore platforms like China and Mexico to survive European and other competition. It results in lower costs to consumers and higher living standard, until you are a nation that has not adapted enough to remain competitive. The young people in China, India, Eastern Europe, and Latin America will be able to compete for the high paying jobs far easier than before. They intend to be the best to have that quality of life. America's answer for its own, and the world's sake, needs to be a resurgence of adaptability and policies of growth. Because of the dollar as the reserve currency, we are late in addressing many of these issues because the world has loaned us their money so they could build the infrastructure of jobs to provide goods. Shortly, they will want the goods for their own rising middle class. What we can develop and sell to them will be one of the next "big things." But that takes engineers, innovators, and businessmen. They are the heroes of many of the young thinkers of the rest of the world. Our American focus is on entertainment. In a competitive world, balance will lower the living standards of the uncompetitive. That is an unfortunate consequence, but you cannot address the problem foolishly or you only make it worse. Thought and sacrifice, not emotion, must guide your strategy or you will consume your children's and grandchildren's seed corn.

The way this affects the "vision" of each individual is that these big issues will cloud media, and sensationalism does not give clear perspectives. Trends are more accurate in some areas such as demographics, but can be misleading in areas where the trend is so good many others get into the business and will make it fall. Reading a variety of thoughtful and diverse magazines, newsletters, and newspapers are a necessity. But this has to be built on a framework or model in your own mind. The triangles we will discuss later give ideas of the type of issues and level of understanding that help create that model. It has to be international for some of the reasons we have just discussed. Each individual has a separate perspective and position, but he needs to build his own mental model of the future as he prioritizes it. Too often individuals plan the future by trusting luck rather than thought.

You also must recognize that change is constant. Problems and answers are constantly evolving, so some approach such as the triangles must be fluid in part to the physical changes but rigid in part to the cultural values that give discipline. Life is a journey neding a comprehensive map and a moral compass.

Talents and Limits

Talent does you no good unless it's recognized by someone else.
— Robert Half

The third issue is to recognize the limits of your abilities and the opportunities that they may give you. A mathematics genius might have only been able to be a mathematics teacher at a smaller salary at the turn of the twentieth century. At the turn of the twenty-first century he might make a half million dollars a year as a software engineer. Different talents have different rewards in different eras. Today rock stars, athletes, and financial professionals as well as trial lawyers do particularly well. That is how American society sets it values because their talents are very unique in specialized arenas. With today's media it is easy to feel you know the people covered and you understand their path to success. But you must realize how few make the top one percent and adjust your concepts or risks and vision to your personal situations.

In football, think how many start in grade school, how fewer play in high school, how many fewer in college, and very few as professionals. Even if they earn large salaries, it is because the system screens talent. You need to know where your talent level reaches a bar and then how to maximize your strengths and reduce weaknesses.

My father, for example, was a great athlete, but despite expectations, I was both slow and highly breakable. It took me a broken wrist, a cracked rib, and a broken foot over three years of high school football attempts to learn the very important concept of recognizing abilities and also recognizing limits. Each of us has talents that can be enhanced. Whether they are sufficient enough to put us in the top one percent of our field is another question that brings up the issue of limits. Ambition is often a necessity to achieve success. But it is important that this ambition be put in the most strategic venues and that proper assessment of opportunities is made. Not everyone can be President. Not everyone can be the richest man. And even when there are levels of leadership in professions, it is important to rank your abilities and target the stretch opportunities without building in failure. The importance of understanding talent levels and limits is that it also helps shape your perspective of life. It makes you appreciate those items that are most important to you which may be family, friends, and participation in society. Many of our uncommon men and women are people that do have significant talents, but have decided to apply them at a local level where they feel they can make a much more significant difference.

This also leads to the question of how you can amplify your talents by joining the right combination of other talents with yours. In a complex world with many people, it is seldom the individual that brings success. Rather it is the support team. Our media focus on entertainment and personalities obscures that point. Just as in sports, competition brings the need for strategy. A great player without a support team can be the focus of the defense, which can eliminate his opportunities. Choosing the right talents with which to join requires not just a combination of talents but also a chemistry that allows them to be better as a group. That requires an attitude of concern for others and the group as well as self. Those you choose will define your success. Fate determines much of your life. But you control your choice of friends, the place you choose to ultimately live, and the environment you create with your talents. Fate deals the cards in your hand, but how you play them is up to you. Life is a journey over time, so there can be more than one hand dealt, and talent can always rise. An environment of economic opportunity simply deals more hands to play.

The Significance of Time

Nine–tenths of wisdom consists of being wise in time.
— Theodore Roosevelt

The fourth item that requires better understanding is the significance of time not only its solid use in your individual life so that it is not wasted but appreciation of it and the tremendous power that exists within its control. How you spend your time defines your values and often your success.

In economics everyone is familiar with the graph of compounded interest where a dollar invested in youth at a certain multiple produces a far greater leveraged effect as you reach maturity. Similarly, time changes perspectives dramatically. As I look back at my youth, I remember going to a friend's house to see a six-inch television screen in black and white that was one of the first in town. I marveled at it as the newest creation in my world. Today, I ponder Blackberrys and cell phones, GPS navigation, and the Internet. Fifty years have made a dramatic change. It is this change that later in the triangles we consider to be enlightenment because technology has made information far more accessible. This saves time physically and requires time mentally.

In the longer scope of time, only from a perspective of age can you look back and see how those changes have affected politics. Lyndon Johnson used a helicopter for the first time in campaigning for Senator in Texas, which gave him notoriety. When you think back to his era and the social and political changes that occurred in the '60s worldwide, you appreciate the fact that change is very constant and that many of the things you worry about today will be totally irrelevant several years hence while others will remain critically important.

In youth, all issues matter because you want to gain knowledge. You look to those older than you out of respect for the wisdom that they may have. But oftentimes they may not have thought as wisely of the change that is constantly taking place. When you become older, you look back at your life and wonder if your time has been well spent. Did you choose to be well known, did you choose to be wealthy, and did you choose to focus on the things most important to you in life personally? Quite often with age you realize with the complexity of the world you can make few of the changes that you felt you would evoke for the world in your youth, but that does not mean that it is not worthwhile to look back on having tried. An impossible dream may not succeed, but it may have positive effects. The key point to remember is that when you are dead, when all men are dead, what is remembered about them is what really matters. What contributions have they made in society? Being wealthy may be the goal that you perceive in life. But it can often be accomplished while at the same time storing a number of memories and activities that with age you will look upon more favorably for differences you have actually achieved in your brief time on earth.

How you choose to spend your time is what truly defines you. It is your most precious and limited asset. Is it spent with family, in business for the family's benefit or on personal favorites? Each has a different consequence, so evaluating time and values together is necessary.

The organization of time is essential for productive endeavors, and a thoughtful use of it lets it balance with the values you desire.

The pressure of time, not just upon you but society, has to be fully appreciated. We now look for short summaries of events, decisions, and news rather than deeper understanding. And we must find new ways to categorize the information we do receive so that it is most beneficial and more easily prioritized and understood.

We must understand that in financial pressures, time is a critical component because the fiscal situation normally gets better (time is then an ally) or is deteriorating (time is then an enemy). This builds in pressure and usually difficulty. It both shapes peoples' attitudes as the pressure intensifies, and it drives action. Just because one personally is not pressured, does not mean security because of the impacts on society as a whole.

Time must be seen as a power to force action or allow its delay, the consequences of which are calculated in risk.

Patience is nothing more than an extension of these concepts. In the West, a business plan is coupled with an annual budget and a generalized longer-term strategic plan of perhaps three to five years. In Asia, particularly China, our five-year long-term plan is their short term. Their long-term perspective can involve generations, and this perspective has built a natural appreciation of dedication. This difference in the appreciation of patience will be brought into focus as globalization unites the two approaches and requires adjustment. In the West, patience, as opposed to a management approach focused on quick action and effectiveness, can seem to be procrastination and delay. But the Chinese approach to issues, such as economic development, is a slower escalating momentum with stability as a goal. Recognizing what issues best fall into the different management styles becomes key to a global business. That requires understanding not just the issue, but also the larger vision of which it is a part. Time is both short term and long term in perspective and dimension.

This is significant because Eastern culture looks to the collective good more than the individual's interest. So decision processes are slower as consensus is built, but speed is gained with the momentum of the group acting together when they start. Time is treated differently in different cultures and has to be appreciated as such.

Leadership

Many people fear nothing more terribly than to take a position which stands out sharply and clearly from the prevailing opinion. The tendency of most is to adopt a view that is so ambiguous that it will include everything and so popular that it will include everybody. Not a few men who cherish lofty and noble ideals hide them under a bushel for fear of being called different.
— Dr. Martin Luther King, Jr.

The fifth concept is one of leadership because it is necessary to set you apart from peers if you choose to have an impact. The reasons for leadership can fall in many categories. Ambition and self-interest are certainly several. Desire to complete a cause may be another. Often these and other reasons may be combined. We will talk of leadership in many of the later sections, particularly as it relates to the uncommon men and women that build the structure of a society. While it is important to note that as a characteristic it is developable in the tactics of organization, it is much more a matter of the heart and mind in its purpose. The great leaders are those that have a commitment beyond themselves and that simply espouse the ideals which others seek to achieve. Attaining leadership in any field gives you a special position and a special responsibility.

You have to think differently when you become a leader. Understanding leadership requires the concept that you move from an individualist to a collectivist method of thought. When I first entered Officer Indoctrination School in the Navy, one of the instructors started out by saying that officers have defensive weapons not offensive ones because their job is to coordinate their men, not just be an individual example of bravery. Their success is no longer judged on these individual accomplishments, but those of meeting the challenges given to their command. Leadership requires recognizing a different mindset and preparing for it mentally. It requires top down thinking focused on goals.

Once you have changed your mindset to the necessity to think of leadership of the group in a unit success measurement and accepted the burden of responsibility, it is helpful to remember an African tradition about how to lead. A simple but very appropriate symbol was the icon or walking stick many tribal leaders held that had an egg at the top. The symbolism for a leader was simple, press too hard and the egg crushes, press too lightly and it falls and breaks. Measured thought and discipline is the key to true leadership. Atilla the Hun focused on two key points in his leadership when he had masses of people to organize, one was discipline the other was morale; they have to fit in combination and are the basic components of the leadership pressure. There are many sophistications of leadership for modern times, but fundamentals always matter.

One of the unique often-overlooked concepts of leadership in modern times was the ancient Greek concept of stoicism. Stoicism centers in part on dignity with a perspective that you control whether or not you are a victim. Perhaps the stoic philosopher most on point was Epictetus who taught the importance of strong character which leads to courage. He looked to the creation of an inner invulnerability where you realized you might not always be in control, and therefore anticipated the worst while mentally preparing for it. Ultimate courage is knowing the inner self and being ready in mind to accept negative outcomes. Otherwise, the fear of the outcome prevents the effort and often leads to failure. To rely on wishful thinking is bad planning, just as relying on negative thought is defeatist. A leader mindset has to be strategic, not emotional.

In the final analysis, leadership is taking responsibility. It is acting boldly when risks are approximately equal so that decisions are not foolish but are made quickly and effectively. There is an old military saying that fits with business—it is easier to get forgiveness than permission. So when the balance is close, it is probably best, on average, to act. Systems that fail are often characterized by paperwork and bureaucracy that indicates everyone wishes to cover risk and not be bold in accepting both the risk and the attached responsibility. That is why great care must be given in legal systems that victimization is not the controlling concept, but justice with a view to what should be the level of responsibility taken. It is the individual initiative and acceptance of personal responsibility of the "uncommon men" that add the character and strength to a society. While individuals show leadership, it is the system or environment that does much to shape it. Over time it strengthens or weakens the willingness to take responsibility by rewarding or punishing it.

Leadership occurs in each of these arenas of power and is often the most sought after subject in Speakers Bureaus or nonfiction books. It can be transactional or transformational, in other words, improvements in individual style or a reorientation of thought on a large scale.

When I am asked how I distinguish between transactional and transformational leadership, I have always felt that a quotation from Peter Drucker, perhaps the father of conceptual management, states it best, "Management is doing things right, leadership is doing the right things." Drucker understood the importance of people in any endeavor. They were not important just for their talents, but also for what I call their personal dignity. Beyond what his writings teach in accomplishing goals in business and life, he is worthy of study. Throughout his life he had faith in the social sector of society, the nonprofit culture of service that is the goal of the leadership representing the grown man's compassion to others beyond moral obligation.

There is nothing more beneficial to leadership growth than reading a vast array of biographies not just to broaden the mind but also to develop thought by gaining insight to others. Peter Drucker was not only a broad thinker, but also a man with a focus on life. One of his ways of making a point was to return to the question a teacher had posed to him in youth, "What will you be remembered for?" He kept that focus in life. He based his work on the experience of the actual marketplace rather than detailed academic theory. And due to that, I feel never got the support or credit he deserved from academia. His is but one example of how a biography can help organize a leader's thought.

True leadership is knowing one's ultimate purpose and values and remembering to do the right thing, even when success pulls you to other more convenient avenues. Organizing transactions can be measured in efficiency, but helping change the world requires caring what the world of the future will be. What also is clear is that original thought from the real world is critical as an ingredient to change, but it is often not quickly accepted by vested interests. The two forces that conflict are often enlightment in education and technological change vs. the existing structural interests and culture. A leader will be on different sides depending on the issue. Sometimes change is necessary. Sometimes it is rash. Values need to be preserved. But in some situations with more knowledge, they have to change. There is no right answer. Change, by its nature, constantly changes the paradigm, but judgment criteria can be constant. There is only the need for a process of thought to think through the issue (efficiency) and the need to have a vision of what world you seek (leadership). That is the purpose of the triangles we shall discuss later.

This involves the key point of how you keep a position of leadership in changing political environments and remain true to principle. Politics is a rugged business. Churchill, Thatcher, and many others are good examples of principled leaders that fell to changing times. Leadership comes not out of gratitude for past service as much as interest in gaining or keeping power. So transactional and shorter term strategies are necessary. Understanding Machiavelli and Chinese "Legalism" help, but the best leaders find ways to adopt those compromises in such a way as to stay consistent with the overreaching principles. They may have to take a step back, but they do not go in other directions. This consistency in the long run builds confidence in others who look upon hypocrisy as a tell tale sign of future problems. People have a style that shows their inner confidence or their inner insecurity. Courtesy told Dad a lot. How you think about compromise tells the same thing. You must do your best to fit the short term into the long term, and the transactional into the concept of the transformational. You will be surprised if you think about how on most occasions you can adopt a position mover consistent with what you believe by redefining the issue. It also builds others' confidence in a leader because they learn his judgment is analytical not emotional, and most realize the long-term best odds are from thought.

And later sections have essays that deal with this in more depth because of its importance. I have always felt style of leadership was the key to success. These styles are often encapsulated in a comparison to insects—the butterfly, the fly, the hornet, and the honeybee. Butterflies fly and look pretty but seldom have real power because they are deemed fragile. Flies have their own interests and affect things through their eggs that produce maggots. Hornets intimidate and use their power to get their way. Honeybees are my favorite. They make something useful from the world and their own individual talents. They also have a stinger and work as a group if their creation is threatened. The butterfly, hornet, and fly are largely transactional. The honeybee can be transformational in its approach and creation.

If you want to put conscience into culture, leadership is the core of success. You must have a strategy for a battle, but once it begins, all things change. Success comes from the ability of the leaders in the field to adjust tactics, keep their composure under stress, and provide the confidence for "the way." In the later triangles it is the critical component of politics for purposes of discussion but fits with all the powers including economics and culture.

Networking

Not until we are lost, in other words, not until we have lost the world, do we begin to find ourselves, and realize where we are and the infinite extent of our relations.
— Henry David Thoreau

The sixth area, particularly critical to the development of understanding and vital to the development of the uncommon men and women upon which we are focused, is networking or the building of alliances. It is well established that success in life, particularly as you are a younger person going up the ladder of achievement, rests both in what you know and who you know. Today you need to know many in different sectors of knowledge and influence. Life is such that relationships and the alliances that you make throughout life are critically important. They leverage and magnify your power and influence. This is perhaps the most significant reason why understanding the difference between choosing conscience or convenience as a mode of operation and perspective for life is so important for young people wanting to succeed. You do not know the closeness of your friendships and relationships until they are ultimately tested. Many people look to potential success in an election to run or undertake an effort of leadership and are highly disappointed with how few of their friends actually committed effort for them. When people look to promotions, when they look for favors, when they have business difficulties and need the help and assistance of others in a time of stress, they learn the quality of their friendships. One reason for taking on leadership positions when young is to learn how dependable people can be and how incorrect first impressions often are. These particular efforts help screen people of dedication. Your talents have to be amplified by your friendships not drained by them.

As I mentioned earlier, there is an old saying that people are generally not for you or against you, but are for themselves. Your success in life may often depend upon how well you can expand that small group of people that are for you and minimize the people that are against you. This is where the concept of conscience as a purpose matters greatly. A man of convenience operates primarily for his own interest and is greatly affected by greed and fear. A man of conscience is normally driven by a concern for others and builds relationships through love and principle. The networks that you thus create in life have the strength of your commitment because that is the foundation upon which all relationships are based. As Confucius taught, it is these obligations between people that define much of society and the strength in which those obligations are perceived are thus quite important.

A man of convenience that is willing to lie has fewer restraints than a man of honor who tries to operate within ethics. On an individual basis the man of convenience can often succeed. However, when you add in the building of alliances and networks, the dimensions tend to change. A man who is only interested in himself can build alliances that accomplish his end, but they seldom have great strength and durability when they are tested. They may succeed because all face peril and have common interest. But once success is achieved, often your allies are either controlling you or plotting to replace you. If the common goal is based on ideas, a different perspective evolves. A man whose relationships are built on common principle can normally count on the dedication of others. While these are often not absolute approaches to life and combinations always exist, it is the reason that the nonprofit structure is so beneficial to the creation of the uncommon men that build networks based on principle. It is through their common effort with others that they meet the people that serve as their core base of relationships and where they build the more personal ties. Be it in politics, economics or culture, there are networks of friendships that tie people together and help people up the ladder of success. The culture of an institution or a society can make it far more difficult on men of honor, as Machiavelli pointed out, if they are surrounded by men solely ruled by convenience. So the building of a network of friends of conscience also requires the building and preservation of a culture that is conducive to it, but even without that culture the quality of relationships that are built and one's willingness to sacrifice for another are significantly different. Your network of relationships are your foundation if all else fails, so it must be built thoughtfully. The power concept of going the extra mile to shift the balance of power in the circumstance is often key. The best of allies recognizes the dependability and often responds affirmatively because they are seeking the same type ally of substance and character. You need to find people that have a similar moral compass and use it.

Measurement

We judge ourselves by what we feel capable of doing, while others judge us by what we have already done.
— Henry Wadsworth Longfellow

One of the critical areas of success is building in a system of the measurement of success in a variety of areas of life. I am always amazed as a banker with many customers' lack of interest in financial statements. They look at them as a nuisance to be prepared out of necessity, when in reality they ought to be one of the prime management tools by which people judge their options and their strategies. Anything that is observed or measured tends to be valued, and therefore it gets a great degree more attention. The other great benefit of measurement is that it forces you to sit down and determine the criteria that are most important to you so that you have a valid method of rating your performance. This pressure on focus is extremely beneficial. As we will later see in the triangles, you need to judge the success of actions by specific perspectives to know better how to improve performance. Every individual knows their capabilities, and those that succeed best will almost constantly measure their level of performance and seek ways for improvement. It becomes a part of personality and a habit that is extremely valuable. This concept is covered in more detail later, but conceptually is vital to success in all endeavors.

Privatization is the method of using measurement to set strategy and tactics. The critical issue of success is addressing the items that can make the greatest difference in a timely fashion.

One of the greatest problems we face in measurement of our public policy issues is that you cannot easily measure debt, which is heavily used in policy if it is not explicit or on the books. Too many unfounded liabilities off balance sheet items, proforma reports, give inaccuracies of size and impact. The same is often true in corporate strategies, but not to the degree of the public sector. Measurement requires an accurate system to be in place to be relevant.

The Laws of Nature

Nature never breaks her own laws.
— Leonardo da Vinci

The eighth concept, and one of the most critical, lies in the modern under appreciation of the laws of nature. As we live in an increasingly short-term society of twenty-four hour news and bullet stories, surrounded by advertising, sensationalism, and commercial sales, it is very easy to lose perspective. The technology stock craze at the turn of the century is simply an example of the manias that inevitably pass through history. People become captivated with the vision of opportunity that they see presented and often do not look as effectively at the situation. As noted in Section I, it is much like the analogy of walking through the trees in the forest in a valley and focusing on the easiest immediate path where the simplest method to traverse a larger forest might be to climb a mountain and see a much broader horizon and which immediate path below would best serve you. Natural laws react with time, and you should never lose sight of them through short-term imbalances. They tend to return extremes to the mean.

A good example of one of the most important laws of nature is that of scarcity because it sets the value of products, the labor of men, commodities, and almost all else. The scarcer a commodity is (and this concept includes strong demand for it as a part of scarcity) the higher the value that is placed upon it in a competitive market. The question is often whether the high price and value given to that scarcity can increase the amount of production so that the supply and demand is altered. Or whether it is truly one of a kind where the level of demand may well be the popularity of the product. Oil is a perfect example in my home state of Texas. When it is scarce, its price rises dramatically, but that generally stirs additional production and conservation worldwide that has a tendency to lower it. So the question in any circumstance lies in an appreciation of the relationship of existing scarcity to future value. The future earnings stream of a company sets value the same way because higher earning companies over the long haul are scarce.

Another example can be found in the stock market. I believe it was Benjamin Graham, one of the true visionaries of value investing, that looked upon the stock market as being in the short term a voting machine on the popularity of stocks, but in the long term a weighing machine that gave them value based on performance. The perspective of time that we discussed before is critically important because time often brings reality.

An example of how to position more appropriately for the effort of natural laws is found in how many people buy stocks for their IRAs or other retirement accounts. Oftentimes a broker will call with information about a stock that has done extremely well the previous year, and someone will buy it. The next year the same thing occurs, each time the person hopes that he gets a very good stock that performs well in the future. It is an approach very similar to the shotgun blast of pellets that I often use as an analogy. There are many small items that are not connected with a lot of noise. The alternative portfolio is one that takes a different concept. It looks at what goals the individual wants to reach by financial planning. It doesn't look at the individual stocks at the beginning, but looks instead at what needs to be accomplished. What are the levels of income at retirement? What are other concerns within the family? What rate of return do you have to have to meet the needs that you have detailed for a later point in life? While that can never be exact, the generalized effort gives you an idea of where you are in the future. It is top down planning rather than a bottom up approach. In making this type of analysis you get an idea of how much you will need to save and what rates of return you will have to have on the potential savings that you can muster. You use the retirement account in concert with all of your other investments to see that you have diversification and balance.

So you look at a global picture of your needs, a diversity of what assets you have to meet those needs, how you can organize them, and the levels of risk it will take in order to meet your final goals. The point is simply that the rate of return you get on most investments has a fairly close relationship to the amount of risk undertaken. You may be able to choose less risky investments that have more of a certainty of performance because you may not have to have as high a rate of return. A well-planned diversified portfolio normally withstands the vagaries of markets and time more than individual stocks coupled together that have no real relationship or balance and were picked because of performance at one stage in their career. That high performance at one time may be in a certain market that because of the very nature of the market may reverse. While it is possible to beat the averages with a few well-chosen picks, normally diversity provides benefit. The natural law that this addresses is that time brings reality, and you must plan for reality not short-term perceptions of reality. This requires a different way of thinking. It doesn't mean you don't seek all of the information in the same ways you have, but your perspective of how you put it together is much broader and more strategic. This is true both for individuals and for nations, and the reason that the governance of a nation matters is the significant effect over time on our individual situations.

So if we are to do effective personal planning, we need to understand much more of the relationships of economics, politics, and culture because they effect our planning dramatically. This is more true in an internationalized world. The rule of law makes a huge difference in allowing some security that allows investments of a longer term. It makes dramatic differences in the methods of financing that are available. The ethics within a society tells a lot about how much you can trust its markets. Is it a case where any investment you buy is inherently weakened by all of the benefits taken by those who sell it to you promotionally? Or is there a reputation of a company that is so strong with a product that it produces that you trust it and thereby give it a competitive benefit? Is the culture of service such that you are involved with people with whom you trust that you can do a smaller level of individual projects that fit unique niches in the markets with significant returns and where you can control your own destiny? Quite often it is difficult to find friends whom you can trust in partnerships and that level of trust only comes after knowing and working with people in circumstances over time.

These are only some examples and symbols of what I call the power of natural law. The powers of nature and the working of the world may be set aside temporarily, but time eventually brings water to the same level. Parachutes may slow descent but they recognize gravity and do fall. Even though we have looked in the case studies at concepts of the individual such as the importance of personal dignity and a perspective of thought, much of what the following portion of the book looks to develop is how the broader range of society, the powers of economics, politics, and culture (which are often shaped by the government) have an impact on personal life.

Much of America's strength is in the people of the middle class that own their own homes because of policy approaches taken in the last century. Owning something has done much to shape popular opinion of economics.

Just as when the Roman army was professionalized by Marius, the soldiers in large part came from lower classes with their loyalty purchased by the promise of a piece of land probably in a conquered territory. This was a method of politics, but it changed the perspective because of man's natural self-interest that is fundamental natural law. But, you must remember you can incentivize both good and bad policy, and great care must be given to envision ultimate consequences.

The future sections all talk of relationships between the powers of economics, politics, and culture. There are in effect natural laws being described because they control the balance in the relationships.

Understand the Power of Incentives

We are more easily persuaded, in general, by the reasons
we ourselves discover than by those which are given us by others.
                                                    — Blaine Pascal

The next issue that needs to be understood is the incredible power that incentives have both in public policy and in individual activities to bring change. It is far easier to guide a society or individual action by building in an incentive that adds to the personal benefit of the individual involved. That is a lesson that has been learned from the ending of the Cold War and the advancement of many Western principles that have transitioned countries from socialist to market/socialist or to market economies. The reason is that oftentimes governments try to force people to take actions through regulations in a variety of areas. Normally these end in controls that impact investment and the desire of people that take actions that enhance growth. Many of the problems of France, Germany, Italy, and even India come from the stagnation that a lack of incentives provides.

Vehicles such as tax cuts, economic reforms, and freer labor markets are important, but an ordered process in public policy that emphasizes incentives first, then secondarily the creation of private institutions to accomplish goals, private or nonprofit institutions to created impact goals, and a resort to regulation as a third option is nearly always beneficial. The power of incentives plays a great part in making the individual understand that his actions do make a difference. It is that under-appreciated aspect of market economics because it opens the vision to a considerable number of other issues. Governments often use tax policy not just for revenue, but also to reward or punish certain behaviors as an incentive that leaves a legacy of tax policy that may be inappropriate for modern competitiveness. These types of tools have to be understood in creating balanced public policies because they do work, but often have unintended consequences.

When I speak of incentives in public policy, it is important to go beyond the concept of economic incentives, which normally are the vehicle of implementation. Too often we focus on economic competition and self-interest viewed only in economic terms. Individuals, government, and the community that shape policy through its implementation all need to be focused on the ultimate goal. The war on poverty, which focused on monetary solutions primarily, had side effects of social breakdown and demonstrated the need for incentives that built character and responsibility as well. The concept of personal dignity is highly visible here because people want happiness, self-respect, and a purpose for being. Formation of character and the acceptance of responsibility contribute to this process. So incentives must look beyond economic concerns to the creation of an economic-supported but character-based strategy. The lessons of The Great Society programs would be worthy of more study as they are compared to the current theories of "The Ownership Society." Incentives need to be long-term to have effect, and their full impact appreciated and monitored. A changing premise produces nothing but waste or an economic boondoggle as many tax incentives with their structured economic interest only reach limited beneficiaries. A critical point is also that incentives only work if people understand them and think them significant enough to affect behavior.

Controlling Emotions of Personal Dignity

He who gains a victory over other men is strong, but
he who gains victory over himself is all powerful.
— Lao-tzu

I will not be concerned at other men's not knowing me,
I will be concerned at my own want of ability.
— Confucius

As Dad always told me, life is too short for petty battles. Save your capital for the big ones where something worthwhile can be done. Each of us have had occasions where we wish we had not taken certain actions in a quick emotional response but had waited in time until the emotion of the moment had passed. My mother used to tell me to wait three days before I wrote an angry letter. In a modern world with time constraints and mechanical answering machines where you never talk to a person, the anger component has increased considerably. Each of us feels more of a need to respond often to demand attention simply to be recognized in a more mechanical world. If you add to this the discrimination that often takes place on race, sex, religion, and a host of other issues, while combining it with the advantages that some have economically over others to affect processes, each individual has an ongoing mental fight to preserve their self-confidence and relevance against what is often perceived as a very difficult and threatening world.

Personal dignity is an issue of respect with each of us having expectations of what is satisfactory in the level of our treatment by others. In an angry world, any slight becomes significantly escalated in our measurement. The problem is that every action begets a reaction, and oftentimes we only escalate the issue by our actions and complicated solutions. Thus, it becomes extremely important to be able to judge issues thoughtfully and intelligently at the inception of the slight. The first issue is whether it is personal or whether it is one of principle. The two are different. My father used to point out that if it was a personal issue, you could judge it differently. He looked at where the slight began and the intent. Some people were foolish enough to not know when they insulted, and he forgave them. Others were intentionally trying to create ill will. And if he knew their purpose and could handle it with dignity, nothing irritated them more and served justice better than making them look small and petty by how an issue is handled. He often cautioned about having a personal dignity that bordered on arrogance. It was not just that it had the weakness of false pride, but it was a very poor strategy. Because if ever you were wrong or the future placed you in a weakened position, you had substantially alienated people that would have an incentive to make you remember your previous actions. There is an old saying that says to treat with kindness those you pass going up the ladder of life because on many occasions you may well pass them going back down.

One of the things that is most lacking in a modern world is the courtesy that used to be much more prevalent. Confucius looked upon the necessity of keeping relationships in place and providing a protocol for solving problems based upon the maintenance of a respect for the relationship which often embodied itself in series of courtesies that showed respect. You can disagree with people, but how you disagree with them makes a great difference as to how solutions can be found. You will meet a man at a middle ground who you respect out of conscience far more quickly than you may meet a man for whom you have no respect whatsoever even if you are closer in principles. Personal chemistry makes a large difference in relationships. It is part of the natural human desire to be correct and the impact that it has in processing information. Each person's sense of personal dignity in part reflects the nature of that process and predisposes how we view actions.

Nations are no more than compilations of this approach to personal or national dignity. Few people in the West understand the importance of an apology, even a general one in the sense that is found in Asian countries. In the West there is more of a legalistic system of right and wrong by which information is processed. The degree of duty sets much of the stage of what we think is appropriate. The sense of face or honor of Asia is different in its code, and ritual has a much greater importance. As we talk of personal dignity throughout the following discussions, it is important that we each refine our sense of obligation to others and their obligations to us. There is much in life that we can ignore and would do so to our benefit. Just as there are smaller issues upon which we may need to stand even though they may be unpopular and in doing so may affect the opinions of others toward us, thereby affecting our personal dignity. But as you build a culture or an environment, this is one of the most critical issues to fully understand. Emotions and reason both have a place in our actions. Understanding how to recognize their impacts is the basis of a sound strategy of action. One's opponents often recognize such a failure as a weakness to seize.

On a larger scale, the sense of individual dignity is the balance on a scale of the friction between the forces of change and existing cultural structure. The Medici family, for whom Machiavelli wrote *The Prince,* always understood that the people by their action or inaction determined the government. Is the loss of hope that depressed personal dignity such that revolution takes place in the face of strong control or is there a rising sense of hope and personal dignity even in difficult circumstances that gain stability for time? In modern democratic elections this sense of personal dignity usually influences the choice because you vote primarily on satisfaction or dissatisfaction.

Understanding Criticism

It takes a lifetime to build a reputation, and seconds to destroy it.
— An old axiom of truth

To understand the power of the *concept of face* or the *concept of honor* we need to understand the ultimate test to it, which is criticism.

Few people want to be criticized for what they believe or for the actions they take. But you have to realize early in life that criticism is often really an indication that you are having impact. If you are doing nothing of substance, few people care to oppose you. Rather than fear criticism, the proper reaction is to evaluate it. If it is correct and you are wrong, then obviously retreat. But if you agree with your position, then press on because you probably have an advantage and are having success. This is a critical part of leadership. Criticism is also often instructive because it brings focus and thought to your actions, and reduces the influence of hubris and arrogance. How it is received and how it is given are issues, not criticism itself, which are part of a learning and teaching process of improvement.

The evaluation of the position has to take into account the cost of offending others by considering the importance of your point. How you argue from the first opposition is also critical. If you consider the dignity of the other side and use strength with diplomacy (the iron fist in the velvet glove of Napoleon's characterization), you leave less bitterness. Controversy is an important situation when you have a concept of conscience, which requires both strength and consideration because we are trying to maintain a level of personal dignity yet accomplish an end. If people perceive you speak for personal benefit, they have one predisposition—if they feel it is from principle, then another. That emphasizes the importance of reputation. But reputations also give flexibility in response.

My father's approach was the graduated escalation of argument, ever reasoned, constantly evaluated, but with a certainty for principle. The creation of that image in others' minds is key. If you have shown your approach to be disciplined with reasoned strength, others will test you far less and you have less controversy. Too often when you try too hard on the other approach of conceding too much, the opposing side sees a weakness and pushes for more. The habit you create in handling controversy has much to do with how much you are seen. It is a delicate balance. Dad would look at courtesy, as a sign of strength not weakness, so he made sure that his gradual disciplined escalation of engagement was perceived from the outset. "A handshake is the best, but wearing a gun helps."

My father also taught me to separate personal feelings from the principles involved and to place my arguments accordingly. To him, enemies were not individuals per se, but conditions like pettiness, greed, poverty, disease or crime. He believed in forgiving the sinner but hating the sin. It is not to be misunderstood that he didn't jail criminals or engage and oppose others on principle. He simply tried not to make it personal unless the other person pushed the issue to that point.

He tried not to tell anyone what to do but to lead by example and explained what he did or was going to do and why. He believed in forgiveness, but not in forgetting because past experiences always determined future strategies as a base of information. To dwell on vengeance or a bruised ego was a detriment to future success. Change and adjustment to future challenges requires optimism, not negativisim or fear. He knew that giving into petty criticism affected attitude and that thick skin is important.

Rather than try to appease both sides of an issue (the neutral *Prince* by Machiavelli's description who pleased no one), he would try to focus on the core of an issue and build a consensus from the logic and morality of an argument. A modern example is the controversy on the value of the United Nations on an issue. Some people would defend it as of great value, while others would say it was of no consequence. To Dad, it would not have been whether they gave a blessing to something as an institution, but as to the logic of why they did. Was it political payback or self-interest or a true moral judgment of the right thing for the right reason? More often than not, this logical approach will bring criticism because it favors neither side's beginning concepts and thereby not their natural desire to be correct. However, it helps build a decision process that ultimately unifies if you have the strength to withstand the criticism.

He cared greatly that he did the right thing, but you separate that from public reputation. You can care so much about the vanity of how you are perceived that it can chill your efforts to accomplish good. The place you go to find the people to convert to conscience may be in the jails more than the churches. You have to take some risks with reputation to do good. Your concern has to focus on not being used by others improperly, but you need to engage beyond total safety. Many organizations that profess values will do little to help others even in good efforts if it does not benefit them or has any risk. Their commitment can thus be judged as much by what they omit as by what they do. Their reputations suffer accordingly among those that carry forth. The issue is as much one of strength as strategy. If your reputation is strong enough that people do not question your motivation, you have the chance to change the balance of power in the equation. But the true key to strength is to lose the concern of self, to become part of what you believe. Others perceive it, and it changes the equation of your own talent level because you have added a new dimension of power.

Change and Character are Destiny

It is not the strongest species that survive, nor the most intelligent,
but the ones most responsive to change.
— Sir Charles Darwin

For the United States, problems really fall into short, intermediate, and long range problems that need to be addressed and are not well calculable. The short-term problems are the imbalances in the economy and its deficits and higher leverage. The intermediate term is the dominance of the dollar because, as Britain and other world leaders have experienced, loss of the dominance of the world currency brings a substantial set of problems resulting in a significant impact on the standard of living. The longer-term issues are Social Security, Medicare, and other governmental problems that may not be sustainable to the expectations of the population and will create instability where crises cause them to be addressed. The leveling of a world by technology will affect many existing structures with economic pressure—Europe's social system, American private pensions, healthcare options, and numerous international imbalances that are growing. For all of the predictions on both sides, the reality is that the world is very uncertain. Terrorism could have an impact. The emergence or stalling of the economies of Europe and Asia can play a big part. The policies of fiscal responsibility adopted, or not adopted, do much to slow or speed up the impacts in either positive or negative directions. Both perceptions of the future and the reality of natural law work out over time. If politics is to allow positive solutions, it will take a unity that partisanship does not allow until crisis comes (when options are very limited), so common good values in the culture must overcome partisan needs. The debt and deficit imbalances will have impact, but America is still the dominant world power, and that is a major factor beyond just economics in the fate of the dollar. It is still a huge part of the world economy, so change may not be as quick as might be perceived if natural forces play a more dominant role above perception.

China's rapid growth is significant, but its GDP is more similar to California than the entire United States. High growth rates on a small base are different from lower growth rates on a large base. America's military and homeland defense spending probably equals the amount spent by the rest of the world, particularly if you view it from a technological advantage viewpoint. You must always begin analysis with where you are and the rate of change in the perspective of time and size. The issue will be how the imbalances created by the new growth paradigm of Asia and the slow growth of Europe interplay with the American economy. America is still the financial center of the world due to its markets, and major negative impacts on America will resonate hard on world growth. America still has the culture of investment and is discussing the concept of an ownership society that would work to build a culture of saving and fiscal focus. The point is not that America is headed in a positive or negative direction as much as the point is that it is a society at a critical juncture of its history. It has to begin to make tough choices with the time and treasure it has, and to do that it needs a unity of vision on what is the common good and how it benefits all far more than is perceived.

The great Chinese philosopher, Sun-tzu emphasized that victory goes to those who *plan effectively* and *change decisively*. There is a balance that must be achieved between enlightenment (technology, advancing knowledge) and the existing status quo represented by cultural values (historical truth) and existing economics and political structure. This balance is what wisdom defines. Character is the core of values and helps preserve the best of these traditions through acceptance of responsibility. Change is a necessity because without it the default position is the status quo, which may or may not be favorable over a long-term trend. The balance between these two forces involves many other factors, including politics and economics, which are both drivers of change and supporters of existing relationships. Change occurs by design or by default. If by default, it is usually through the pressure of crisis as a trend is no longer sustainable. The governmental and private retirement systems in a number of countries that were funded on worker contributions are good examples. They were based on a concept of an ever-expanding population to fund a smaller retirement group. But changing demographics—with less workers, higher life expectancies, and higher medical costs—puts great pressure on the sustainability of the program, not to mention the moral question of burdening the next generation. Economics will eventually force action, but much more severely than if actions were addressed early so expectations could be adjusted. As we look at the decline of nations in the next section in a historical perspective, this search for the wisdom to balance change with character becomes more obvious. Change usually is accomplished when people are willing to sacrifice for something they believe, such as a better life for their children. It is the concept of individual responsibility. Enlightened conservatism is the search for not only this wisdom, but also a method to educate so that the people can see the vision of why sacrifice and change may be necessary for the common good and through it, themselves.

The purpose of education is for society to be able to understand the choices before it. To camouflage logic with political correctness or economic greed, only brings gridlock and default solutions. In all likelihood, in modern politics many nations will follow the standard cycle of historical democracies that are chronicled in the next chapter. But to bring the best from the cycle at the earliest stages, you need to have the support of the change that individual responsibility brings and the strong values an appreciation of character preserves. Both rest on conscience, which is the core of the triangles. The wisdom of balance can be measured by an individual's sense of personal dignity. He may not be happy with change and the loss of values that adversely impacted him economically. But did he feel the process was fair enough that it may have disappointed him but did not offend? That requires a level of understanding or of trust in leaders that is extremely difficult to achieve in a modern world and usually only occurs in crisis where anything is a better alternative. But a great amount can be done earlier in these cycles if there is a language of conscience that lets opposing sides agree on basics that must be done to ease future problems. Having a strategy in place as a scenario plan when the problem does emerge is the best way to see thoughtful logic implanted rather than emotional solutions in chaos. A more level and competitive world will negatively affect significant numbers, but many natural forces cannot be stopped. What can be done is recognition of the choices that limit the damage rather than enhance it over time.

INSIGHTS INTO SOCIETY'S INSTITUTIONS

Institutions alone fix the destinies of nations.
— Napoleon Bonaparte

Society is nothing more than a competition of the values of its members affected by their level of commitment for change. Personal dignity is a part of their satisfaction, but it may or may not have a strong component of obligation to others. In many cases, Maslow's Hierarchy of Needs is a good guide to levels of development. But the problem faced is that the competitiveness and economic sophistication of the society have a great deal to do with the success of its members. Argentina at the start of the last century had immense opportunity to be a great economy, but faltered on public policy. In the mid 1700s China produced almost a third of the world's GNP, but in the mid 1800s Western manufacturing output began to climb with technology and eclipsed the East well in the last century.

This is rapidly changing and no nation or group of nations has been able to maintain weaker competitive positions against strengthening competitors unless they adjust and enhance their own competitiveness. Systems as well as individuals lead to success, and this involves government as the collective voice of the people. It also involves the institutions and process that affect it. Whether you have gridlock or adapt to change depends on how it is perceived—a creation of the media. How power works, and whether it is influenced by the common good or the political correctness of interest groups, must be understood.

Unlike the personal approaches we just discussed, these are operating concerns of the culture. The culture is affected by economics and politics, so we need to understand the tools of both.

One of the primary tools of the modern world is the use of institutions. In past history, you began with a political organization, units of tribes that became principalities, which became nations. But just as technology has impacted the processes of humanity, various types of groupings have been formed to specialize and carry forth the power of groups. Institutions have been involved in many ways depending on the culture and the purpose for which they were formed. But the very nature of institutions themselves always has to be understood. Some of the finest strategists in modern times from Napoleon to Dwight Eisenhower have commented on the military industrial complex revealing an insight that is often overlooked—the tremendous pressures exerted by institutions or combinations thereof.

Each of us is one of six billion people on the earth. We focus our perspective from where we stand and how we see life, which has a great deal to do with where fate places us. Yet if we go into a modern airport and look at the variety of people or if we go to a great city and realize the tremendous amount of wealth and investment in any particular building, we only begin to perceive that we alone accomplish very little unless we are able to unify through the vehicle of institutions. Institutions are not necessarily the culture or society. They have different interests that change over time because of the leadership and how they are affected by outside forces. If they are formed in the economic world for economic purposes, they are shaped by competition. If they are formed in the political world by power and the stability of the people or if they are formed in the cultural world, often the nonprofit and nongovernmental creations are shaped by the shifting cultures of the times.

Thus it is quite important to understand that what drives the institution is often historic because how they are created often has a great deal to do with how they function. There are any number of institutions whose time has passed, but they remain because of the structure put in place and the inertia lacking to bring about change. It is why bureaucracies are incredibly strong in most institutions and the culture is often one of maintenance. Leadership and culture are critical issues within any institution. Change seldom takes place from the bottom up. It normally has to be driven from the top down by the very nature of power and the inertia of bureaucracy. It takes transformational leadership of strategic understanding of where you need to go and being able to convey that clearly and thoughtfully to those below. To be effective it has to include not just what needs to be done, but why it needs to be done, and of equal importance, why that is beneficial to the individual. If their interests are aligned with the organization, this becomes a necessity of education.

To further this concept, it becomes important to understand shaping the culture of the institution. What is on paper in its rules and guidelines may be entirely different from the operational approaches that are taken. The very nature of how the organization operates can be fairly easily determined by simply talking to some of the lower and mid-level individuals to find how they are told to react to issues such as corruption, questions or ethical issues. Even if there is not corruption, the unwillingness to bring an issue forward means that higher leadership does not see it early. In many developing societies where you have had more centralized planning as a step beyond individualism, this becomes an increasingly important issue as you move to free markets to maintain competitiveness at higher levels.

The culture of the institution is effective in many ways. How is the institution's leadership selected, by concern for merit and the purpose of the institution or through favoritism or cronyism? One approach gives pride; the other breeds contempt that eventually can be a self-defeating prophecy as morale drops. The best talents are lost or not gained, and there is a failure to care about purpose. Government is often the area of most affected service as so much leadership is by appointment. Boards and commissions are often led by directors or volunteers working with professional executives—whether by appointments or for vision and merit or as rewards for support. This says a great deal about the future directions of an institution even with the normal inertia. It sets the tone of the organization and that sets the ultimate level of contempt or honor with which the culture of the institution is perceived.

In the later sections of the book, we talk about institutions such as universities. We also talk about the culture of markets, such as stock exchanges, that must rely on integrity to function appropriately with transparency in a competitive environment. Since the institution is the tool by which society unifies and projects its power in a variety of fields, it needs to be understood carefully from the set of ideas that drive it, from the culture within it that shows a dedication to those ideas, and its adaptability to the changing environment that surrounds it both in its arena and globally. Too many institutions lose their beginning drive and only exist for the benefit of those within. They are the butterflies of organizations as compared to the honeybees. Other organizations have significant talent in their intelligence and their abilities, but they lose their desire to engage. And just as we noted with the talent of individuals, it can be great. But desire trumps talent oftentimes in competitive environments.

Change within institutions is particularly difficult because you oftentimes have to change the culture in order to bring the full force of operational efficiency and focus. Thus many of the concepts that we talk about later in the triangles become increasingly important. Within any organization, you have the existing bureaucracy and cultural structure with vested interest. You also have the pressures of change that often are addressed by changing leadership. How you bring those forces together within institutions is critically important. As far as society as a whole, the creation of institutions at certain stages becomes absolutely essential. In societies that have been centrally planned and move to free market economics, you automatically have the creation of a number of imbalances that may help the standard of living of the people as a whole but very directly negatively impact individuals. This is where nonprofit institutions can often be of the greatest help in reducing part of the blow and reducing part of the burden upon the government. In America these institutions developed with the model of the market system.

It is important to remember that the question is not whether or not you need a system. In economics free markets provide a system of their own that is natural in nature. In politics not only in government but also in nearly all socialized functions, civilization requires a method by which people compromise and work together by a common set of rules. Those basic organizational efforts, toward a certain end, constitute what would be called institutions. Government is perhaps the most significant of them because it sets many of the rules for the others. The issue is not whether or not you need a government. The discussions are the nature of that government and how involved it should be with the other institutions. What often happens is that when a government is inefficient the focus is one of disappointment with the government, and criticism is directed at the government itself. The important thing to remember is that you must have some form of government. It is the structure and culture of the government that is at issue. In thinking about the issue in this way, whether it be a corporation, a government or an additional social body, you change the concept from whether or not the body is needed, which is the first question, to the issue of what it needs to accomplish, its ultimate goal. From that point the institution can be analyzed much more effectively. The world effectively works through and is processed by systems. They may be efficient or inefficient, but they are in effect the method by which much is accomplished. The culture within these systems is what gives them strength and to a great degree determines their effectiveness. The structures may be like the skeleton of the body, but the culture is the system of muscle. The circulation system that feeds it could well be looked upon as being the set of values that are within the culture because they often affect much of the muscle.

As is noted in later presentations, Adam Smith is remembered for his economics in *The Wealth of Nations,* but much of his life was spent discussing *The Theory of Moral Sentiments,* which looked to the importance of issues such as conscience. Later sections of the book talk of nonprofit institutions that helped create a culture of conscience by their impact. The world of the future will be much more level and much more competitive, and the concept of an institution's integrity will exist in the image of its brand. Does it have quality? Does it stand behind its product? If you look at modern American balance sheets, this is one of the issues most protected and of greatest single consequence. It will be something of magnitude in growing countries like China and India because reputation and face are appreciated and will begin to be placed in economic terms. So institutions are no more than vehicles that have many of the same considerations as individuals, just on a more coordinated and larger scale. The later sections of the individualized essays, which talk of more focus on leadership, on culture transformation, and on the creation of institutions to fit specific needs in vacuums created by change, are far more detailed. The critical point upon which to focus is that while we act individually, we affect only certain limited changes. When we are consolidated, significant change is affected. But this consolidation generally takes place through the vehicle of existing institutions that act or do not act. It is in understanding these institutions and how change can be brought positively to them that we have the greatest impact both for leadership and for a positive enhancement of society.

There are several distinctions that are often important in judging leadership. There is a difference between fear and caution. Caution is particularly necessary in picking the right battles for the ultimate chance of success. Fear is a significant negative because usually leaders win by being aggressive. It is important to establish within your own mind whether hesitation fits into either category. It is also important to judge leaders by the lasting effect they leave on an organization. Oftentimes leadership is characterized by bold individual effort. This is particularly true when you have an "outsider" take over an organization. The question in such a case is to view the outsider's leadership by the lasting impressions it has on the structure of the organization, its philosophy, and its strength. The leader's individual style and strength is something quite separate from his leadership of the organization itself and how well he has guided it. Personality leadership is more transitory unless it focuses on becoming transformational to the organization. Is the leader's legacy an image, a reformed institution or both?

It is also important to understand that maintaining a rigidity to change is not necessarily bad, and criticism has to be very carefully analyzed in its implications. Quite often change needs to be slowed so that society can accept it, and in some cases, change violates the very principles that most help society. A typical example has been the independence of the Federal Reserve System in the United States. That fact that it has not been more governmentally controlled and subject to politics has been an extremely positive enhancement and foundation of the American economic system. To look at other countries and the problems that they have had with currency inflations makes it extremely clear why there should be dramatic opposition to any change in independence. The same issues are true with courts. Quite often the issue is that you may have interpretive judges that go beyond the law in either direction. The problem is not the court system but the judges that reflect the politics of the culture. Institutional fundamentals must be the base of any consideration before change.

Institutions are thus one of the primary vehicles for impacting and directing power within society, and closely tied to them are their perceptions of their importance, image, and substance. Just like a brand, how institutions are perceived does a great deal to enhance or diminish their power. The perception of power is often power itself.

Media and Its Relation to Culture

The medium is the message because it is the medium that shapes and controls the scale and form of human association and action.
— Marshall McLuhan, *Understanding Media: The Extension of Man*

Many consider media to be the third area of power with politics and economics. However, I think culture is a far more appropriate and broader description of that context of power. Entertainment, historical cultural values, religious beliefs, and a variety of other forces that develop and compose culture have tremendous impact upon it. That is particularly true as we move forward in a modern world. Media will increasingly reflect culture because of the economic considerations involved. When there are only a few broadcast networks, the media had a tremendous effect on culture. But with the narrowcast of the modern age and people receiving information in a variety of sources that are increasingly specialized, the economics of the media business make it less dominant and more responsive. The recent explosion of blogging is an example of this significant change.

Nonetheless, it becomes increasingly important to understand how the media or the distribution and creation of these ideas affect perspectives including personal dignity. In the West, the media serves a very important aspect of the culture by having a "watchdog position" on what occurs in politics, economics, and the rest of culture. Its attitude is often one of skepticism and to a degree sensationalism. It looks for what is abnormal rather than pointing out what is normal because that is what the audience desires. There is a media example often used: 100,000 men go to a bar in New York City and one is killed—the headline is "Man Killed in Bar" not "99,999 Men Successfully Return Home from Bars."

Thus, it is important to understand that good stories and positive issues that do make it into the media are often short stories. The discussion of events with deep thought is limited to a few magazines and documentaries. Even the top best selling nonfiction books are read by a very small percentage of the population (but often the "uncommon men" of change). To instill character involves the necessity of balancing the perspectives of coverage beyond exposing evil to also having a conscious effort to look at promoting good. People react to publicity. If even a small portion of time was given to spotlight those that did positive things, it serves as an incentive for others.

You can have the finest ideas and goals in the world, but if no one knows of them, you will have limited success. A good idea poorly marketed is not usually as effective as a bad one heavily promoted. However, if you expect to eventually gain support for the ideas because of excellence, you must build a substantial foundation for them so that they can withstand scrutiny and gain interest.

Media can be promotional as in advertising or editorial as in influence. The two are very different in concept. One is aimed at convenience, the other at credibility, so you must choose your approach to fit your ultimate strategy.

The commercialization of media as a result of the change from a few broadcast networks to many narrowcast sources of information, including the modern day blogs, cable, and web news, has had an effect on the nature of the news media. In the past there was more civilized discussion of the critical issues of the day and perspective being given. Today, the media itself plays a significant part in polarization because there is more alignment of views within it, and the natural human desire to be right draws society to the different polarizing points. These parts of the media themselves become the focus of attack, which shows them to be more a part of the process than an outside observer.

But the significant problem is not necessarily partisanship because the new media *watchdogs* will focus upon any significant abuse. The greatest problem lies in what I would call an *adversarial culture.* The media increasingly seeks controversy in a battle for higher ratings because of the nature of our popular culture. Every reporter wants to be the next one to break a "Watergate" and takes a view of skepticism to authority. This in itself has a tendency to undermine the past concepts of traditional leadership, as we have understood them and makes transformational leadership even more difficult. Many shows become parodies or are dominated by hostility between the parties as they represent their respective sides. It is significant as a form of political entertainment and satire, but it is a particularly costly approach for the people as a whole. Most of the parties are representative of their particular points of view, which are often more on the extreme. And there is little discourse that allows the opportunity to build a center point of view that would allow positive solutions through compromise. If all things are viewed negatively, there is little optimism and more good and positive efforts are not only under-reported, but oftentimes viewed with skepticism. Because of the futility, there is a mood created that limits the efforts of people trying to do good. The news media increasingly will have to recognize its responsibilities in a culture. Incentives work, so more positive examples and less sensationalism have an impact. Personality traits, survivor hardships, and cutthroat business competitions entertain, but do they educate society to a more comprehensive common understanding of our problems.

However, in truth, the media effectively panders to the culture that supports it economically. If the media is to change, the most effective way for that to occur is for people to support the more positive efforts that are seen both aggressively and affirmatively, and we need to react positively. What we value as a people has impact on those with commercial intent. If all we desire are shows orientated to "gotcha" or feuding personalities, we create no need for more substance. In effect, the need for more substance exists, but different information groups that are more private are filling it. The problem that this creates is that we do not have the same impact on the culture as a whole. Just like raising your children with values may impart those values to them, when they have to compete in the broader society their success or failure may be determined by the way it operates. If they go into an environment that is corrupt, they fail because of their values or are corrupted by the environment. Within media we need to create a more positive orientation to the traditional systems of providing information and insight more than the accentuation of conflict. Institutions play an important part here. Today many are viewed with skepticism. If we can become involved and impart an internal ethical culture, you help create a base for support. I think the search engines of the Internet may eventually provide a force that is positive in these efforts.

It is also important to understand how media creates values by its marketing, which has more impact in America than the level of excellence of a product or thought. But American media is changing from a media elite that could shape both content and presentation and thereby control opinion. The decline first began in the big city newspapers, then the dominant magazines, and now the television networks. People get the majority of information from television, followed by radio, then the Internet, with magazines and newspapers less important than in the past. The "Bloggers" of today are a perfect example of how mass media has begun to give way to niche areas. More reporters and "media stars" do not come from time tested staircases of training, but are brought in from politics and "news-entertainment." The culture and the values of the modern day newsrooms may yet be shaped by the competition of new players who, in the whole debate, may see the necessity of bringing focus and credibility, which is the lifeblood of media, more easily than before.

Most important of all is that there is little of a "wisdom framework" built for our younger generations. In the past, youth activities were efforts like the Boy Scouts, and entertainment was in part self-evolved. Successive generations have had much more entertainment that is more exciting than the family efforts of the past but does help build a structure or framework of wisdom that grows with us through life. Our perceptions are formed but not as fully as in the era of a slower life and times. Entertainment and media are today intertwined, and this adds confusion to youth trying to establish a system of internal values.

One of the major problems to which many lament is the entertainment industry and how it affects the culture and moral values by often seeking the most basic denominator. But if these efforts were not profitable, there would not be the same effect. For years I have supported the cultural arts because they were a base for cultural values. But in reality violence and sex do far better in selling than high culture. Fictional novels far outsell pensive philosophy. If you look at ratings of television and cable programs, even conservative geographic areas of morality watch the most provocative shows. The law of nature appears to be that we, as a culture, move toward the lowest denominator rather than the best culture has to present. But cycles often bring change.

Much of *The Language of Conscience* is devoted to understanding the importance of creativity. If you learn to create and appreciate creation, it is difficult to destroy. We have few today that help transmit and interpret the higher values of experiencing life and even less that try to synthesize it to lead in an elevated direction. But many are sensing the vacuum that this lack of substance creates. Much of American civilization traces to Europe, but we now have the culture of instant gratification and materialism.

Asia is assimilating many Western ideas, but its concerns and appreciation of quality, originals not reproductions, may be counter influences to these trends as economics makes their interests relevant.

Today the more base nature of man that seeks what is different apparently is magnified by the profit motive and technology of mass marketing to create an even more sensational cycle. To lament what effect this has on morality, the more strategic effort would be to create an *antidote* for the problem. Make people, particularly youth, separate what is fiction and entertainment more clearly by focusing on programming that gives a broader perspective of life and how it fits together with values. You often cannot fight the equivalent of a disease directly; you create a vaccine that limits its effect. It is easier to administer to those that want it, and demand for it can be more easily marketed. It is the same type course colleges ought to refine. All youth, all adults, want more knowledge and more wisdom to some degree. They seek a clear way to think and gain accurate perspective of a more complex and quickly changing world often for the purpose of better understanding themselves and therefore their place in it. To replace ideas—you have to have other ideas and creating a competitive, marketable concept that appeals to interest will at least raise the common denominator to a degree because if successful the profit motive forces its momentum. The key is the type of programming; it cannot be rhetoric but convey wisdom.

In the same way, the presentation of news or choice of stories can be adjusted. The logical way to accomplish much of this is to cover legislation and issues as they arise in more detail, not take a more historical approach of discussing them after the fact. This reports on what came out of the process but little on the discussions that went in. Here is where balance is critical. We get pundits, adversarial think tanks, and sensational media giving the extremes of positions in the process. We get the sensationalism of the "pork barrel" special interest sections. What we seldom get is the logical stories of how balance is being sought and how the process is actually functioning. When are "reductions" really just lessened increases and vice versa? What is the true context of the debate? If we seek this level of concern, free enterprise usually answers positively. The media affects the culture greatly by how it informs. Trust is a key component of how information is accepted. One great challenge we face as a nation is changing our level of demand. If the media covers the process, the process will be better because of the supervision. If we have little interest in the depth and the balance sought, the quality of the process suffers. Unfortunately, we usually only demand this level of reporting in crisis when much is at stake.

The Intricacies of Power

The cause of all these evils was the desire for power
which greed and ambition inspire.
— Thucydides

It is important to understand that power has certain characteristics that often need to be addressed. Power is generally built by being accumulated and then used to reach the next level of accumulation and use. Power, that becomes unused unless the certainty of its use and competence remains, can tend to atrophy. Also when power is not used for some purpose, it often leaves a vacuum that leads to corruption.

Power forces others to do your will. Influence persuades others to shape their decision. When you are concerned with personal dignity, influence allows it where power may diminish it. Convenience often uses power because it is effective and easy. Conscience usually involves influence because it must work upon the inner values of others.

Power also has corresponding liabilities. To a great extent the holding of great power also produces a much higher level of liability. A typical example is a governor. He has the ability to appoint people to a commission, but for every one person appointed he will disappoint another twenty. If he has the power to create results, then any results that are not created or any negatives occurring are also attributed to him. Having power, as opposed to influence that can affect power, often has a more direct responsibility to make decisions even when decisions would prefer not to be made. Of the many great books of power, Machiavelli's *The Prince* probably best tells how those in power can maintain it. Saul Alinsky's *Rules for Radicals* probably best tells how those without power can consider attaining it. Sun-tzu and Von Clausewitz probably best give the Eastern and Western approaches of how to choose to pick battles that give the intelligence of strategy within the maintenance of power. *The Language of Conscience* was aimed more at assimilating the thoughts in all of these arenas into an approach for the power of morality and how to best bring about successful change through moral power. The success of any one type of power at a particular time depends much on the culture and environment in which it exists and probably had significant impact on the concepts when they were written.

The thoughts of Machiavelli are not that different from China's concept of legalism or in some ways from the Eastern *The Science of the Thick and the Black.* All focus on the nature of reality. Oftentimes the things we want in men, conflict with the most efficient methods of the moment, which produce the results we desire. For example, we prefer gentle persuasion, but force is often more effective in the short term. Understanding power is critical to its successful execution. Influence which is not the directness of power but instead the ability to attempt to shape events, is slightly different. The best example of the distinction that I could make is a rock entering a pond. The power hits with force and causes impact when the rock hits. However, the waves have effects in many different directions. Influence can build far greater effect with time because of the power of ideas. These shape the culture in which power operates. While most look to power as being the ultimate goal, it is important to look at the factors that can shape the culture in which power is exercised, because those ultimately determine who holds power and under what concepts. That is why culture becomes so critical. It is the ultimate power but is shaped by a variety of influences. One type of power may win a campaign or war, but it may be ineffective in the peace that follows because the perspective changes.

Power can be both metaphysical (ideas such as social, economics, or political rank) or physical (military, legislative control, actual power to affect outcome). Metaphysical power is normally judged in *influence* and physical power in *power.* Power itself can be defined at these levels with military power being the best way to create an example.

There would be: Class I – Nuclear Power, Class II – Overwhelming Military Force, Class III – Localized Guerrilla Warfare and Insurgency.

Just because you have nuclear power or even military domain, it may not help you in Class III. The U.S. and a few other nations have Class I, but its use is extremely limited because of the devastation and retribution both physically and morally. The U.S. is very dominant in Class II Power because of its technological superiority in weapons, training, information systems, and command and control coordination.

But, as the United States learned in Vietnam and Iraq, Russia learned in Afghanistan, and other examples have shown, localized control is a very different and complex power because it has a great deal to do with local culture, personal dignity, historical conditions, and similar factors. To succeed with Class III Power you must win the hearts and minds of the people and that is not easy to do in such situations. Only if you can make the guerrilla's relationship with people like a fish out of water can you succeed. This requires people to understand what is in their best interest and also to plan from the beginning to address personal dignity issues. Of all items, personal dignity perception affects the stability of the society. As I noted previously, most people are not for or against you, but are for themselves. And it is their action or inaction that determines your eventual success.

The simplest point is that power itself is often in a reverse ratio to its ability to use it. If it is Class I, it is less available. Too much power may offend or bring fear which loses support. Class II is more useful—vetoing bills, for example, legislatively, but Class III is really a chess level issue of the influence of ideas. The point is simply to appreciate the power of ideals and culture and their effect on ultimate success. You can pick your battles carefully, but a global world will increasingly require Class III strategy. Sun-tzu noted its importance centuries ago, but we lose perspective with our admiration of modern technology.

When you use power you may also be at your most vulnerable point if you have not planned. As Napoleon well understood, you are most vulnerable when a major advance is stalled. Defensive tactics are as important as offensive ones because you reduce some risks. Lao-tzu taught that you should look at each affirmative act for its unintended consequence.

It is the combination of the power of "the way" or dedication to a just cause with the warriors knowledge and preparation that succeeds. An example would be the rebellion against the Romans in 60 AD by the British tribes under Queen Boudica. They easily attracted a massive force that resented the Roman oppression and sought freedom. The Romans needed to win to preserve power but were greatly outnumbered. Finally, Boudica's forces met the retreating Romans at a place the Romans had strategically chosen. In an early use of technology the Romans were not only well armored but also strategically prepared. They fought in unison with absolute knowledge of what they needed to do for they were professionals. They defeated a far greater force with immense enthusiasm and dedication, and probably a more just cause in view of the incidents that incited the Britons. They rotated men to the front line in a timely order so that each man when weary was replaced. Thin shields pushed blows upward so they could stab with small swords in the unison of a line. Their pincer movements trapped the Britons where they could not fight well when compressed. The significance is simply this: technology and strategy have always given an advantage that is the reality of power. Attila later defeated the Romans because he lived among them and understood how to fight them. For power to be with honor and for the common good, you must develop the strength and knowledge to compete. Often this takes time, but warriors trained in honor are different from those who succeed by brutality. They gain a loyalty of purpose from those that follow them. Leadership has consequences, so you must not only inspire but also know the strategy by which you can win.

Of importance to a leader also is whether he wishes to be popular in the current times or respected by history. Often the use of power for good purposes causes sacrifice on the part of the people that reduces current popularity. Pushing problems to the future helps currently but ultimately lowers image and reputation. Wisdom is found in building support for the current sacrifice where people sacrifice not for the leader, but for the future of their children. The cultural power allows you to create a goal in the people's vision where they are desirous of the sacrifice and their personal dignity more than that the leader, requires it. Another example of cultural power to establish a political environment is the concept previously discussed of "going the extra mile." At one point a rule existed that required the Jewish community to carry the bags of others for a mile. By carrying it an extra mile, it created guilt and changed the power equation with people of honor that recognized obligation and injustice and thereby shifted focus. Most political and economic power is based on less obvious cultural issues that shape their underlying structure of support.

You have certain amounts of power capital. Like the game of poker, it is a management of resources, beyond just luck, that determines success. We will cover the concept of power in detail in later sections, from its ability to corrupt to its naturally shifting base with time, but one point must always be remembered when power is sought. C. S. Lewis in *The Abolition of Man* captured it best:

Give up your soul, get power in return. But once our souls, that is, ourselves, have been given up, the power thus conferred will not belong to us. We shall in fact be the slaves and puppets of that to which we have given our souls.

The Importance of the Common Good

To withdraw ourselves from the law of the strong, we have found
ourselves obliged to submit to justice. Justice or might,
we must choose between these two masters.
— Luc de Vauvenargues

Power is thus might or right in many cases. The power of right is often encompassed in the concept of the common good. It is the balance of the individual and collective pressures within society.

Personal dignity often depends on the environment that controls us. Freedom and liberty are not exactly the same as concepts. We all want as much freedom as possible, but we have obligations to one another, so there must be restraints. That is where law comes in formally and the Golden Rule philosophically. In the East the importance of the group is significant while in the West the rights of the individual are emphasized. With terrorism these individual rights are being compromised, and with the economic conversion to markets, the group concepts of the East will change as individual rights to property and other protections emerge. But the critical point is that each of us has a vested interest in establishing and preserving a clear understanding of what is in the common good. As we divide into different groups over issues, we lose its appreciation. That common good that binds us together can be ignored and weakened. It has to remain in focus. When we talk of a strong national character that gives the country its inner strength, this concept of togetherness in sacrifice for the common good is the core of what we speak. It is too easily forgotten in partisanship and politics and is therefore a critical part of our later discussion and approach. We have discussed previously that it is the common unity that defends the individual right. The law does not make the culture. The culture creates and maintains the law. Whether the culture is for the common goal or that of a select elite tells all about the society.

The creation of a culture of any type requires a common understanding and support or it will not dominate oppressing ideas. The common good is the often-undefined influence, which binds a culture together, so it has to be the force of discussion in most cultural issues.

The Language of Conscience is not the Language
of Political Correctness

Life is really simple, but men insist on making it complicated.
— Confucius

One of the problems in modern America is how we have begun to phrase the debate both in generalities and a concept of social justice or *victimization*. A strong society should be based on individual responsibility, an appreciation for personal dignity, an appreciation for the common good, and a clear thoughtful discussion of critical issues rather than an emotional one. The media likes a good story, and many universities warp discussions calling it academic freedom. We have to learn to separate logical and emotional argument. When Dad was sheriff, he looked at problems with what his generation called "hobos." If he could help them, he did. If he could not, he understood that some people chose this lifestyle. He would not have been as sympathetic to the "plight of the homeless" for those that rejected opportunities to help themselves. A free system should offer help and opportunity, but it cannot guarantee it will be taken. No matter how much you educate, some people choose not to accept what others desire for them. It is their choice, and it is a free society.

The issue of whether charity is needed, which is an obligation of society and should be done with preservation of dignity, is different when people have the ability to change their actions. The issue of the uninsured in healthcare is no different. Many of the "uninsured" either could be covered by government programs if they bothered to apply or are young people who feel invulnerable and do not do so. There most certainly are cases where charity is needed. The latter are the ones we need to address as a society rather than impose economic burdens on the system that eventually affects all of us. I have served on the Board of Covenant House in Houston and helped form the Caring for Children Foundation in Texas. I feel charity is an obligation of a free society, and government must help those that cannot help themselves. But there is a great difference in using broad arguments that are all inclusive because they can hurt the poor and those that need help. By making programs so expensive that there is not an opportunity for passage, political correctness often defeats conscience. Beyond that, you often promote the very behavior that is destructive by subsidizing it. Issues are often demagogued and not discussed, and this is amplified by partisanship.

Two phrases often come in the debate. One is a broad granting of "rights." They used to be defined in the Bill of Rights somewhat narrowly as reservations from the power of government. Today, they are used as obligations of society that government must answer because people are *victims*. We are being taught to think in a new way that weakens our society just as similar directions weakened Athens and Rome. Great democracies fall from within, often without realizing declining strength.

The mantra of progressive education today is "self esteem," but that, as we will note, is quite different from the concept of personal dignity. In the first, you are using words and treatment to help cover weaknesses, but they do not address reality. In the second, as the way we use it in *The Language of Conscience*, it is reality that we address first and try to recognize weaknesses and improve them. The direction of democracy depends on the strength of the people and their true understanding of the issues. You do not build up strength to sacrifice for change if you are lulled into contentment. Excellence wins, not mediocrity.

Morality and Economics are in all Issues

He who will not economize will have to agonize.
— Confucius

In the analysis of almost any issue, you find both economic considerations and moral considerations. Politics is the approach and result of balancing them. Often one dominates significantly more than the other, but they both tend to be present. Morality is often represented by compassion, and economics is significantly shaped by the concept of obligation or self-interest in the arguments between the two. Where both are involved the essence of the arguments is redistribution from the *haves* to the *have nots*. In some cases this may be necessary when people cannot care for themselves. But when the transfer is not the equivalent of charity but economic redistribution for political purpose, you may destroy the incentives that underpin the economic systems. The issue is often between economics and compassion with passion pushing each argument. Here the solution or way may not lie in the middle through compromise, but in bringing the extremes together in a circle as opposed to a straight line. The reason is that on some issues they are so passionate they might actually compromise for part of what they wish. The center is often so political there is little room for compromise and may be the ineffective choice of a water bottle with tepid water rather than an icepack or a hot water bottle.

Some issues, such as healthcare, bring conflict between economics and morality far more clearly into focus. Others, such as taxes are far more subtle. Tax systems that are aimed, in reality, to redistribute income tend to attempt to favor a moral component of more equality. But they may in reality reach extremes that have the opposite economic impact because marginal rates become so high that incentives for self-interest are diminished. These are never easy questions and can be argued from many different directions.

However, the recognition that both are present to some degree in issues, sets the ability to analyze the true impact of judgments. Simply put a "T" and list economic interests on one side and morality interests on the other. Generally the economic interests of a few may, because of their financial interests (and thereby lobbyists), overcome the policy concerns since the common good usually is spread so broadly that the individual gets so little direct benefit it is not worth much effort.

Significance of Starting Trends

There is no education in the second kick of the mule.
— The Honorable Sam Rayburn,
Former Speaker of U.S. House of
Representatives
(D Texas)

The merit of a man is if he plants a tree
knowing he will never sit in its shade.
— An old Texas adage

Everyone looks at the present as a snapshot of where we are and where we stand economically, culturally or politically. It becomes increasingly important in policy terms, to think of starting trends that take place over time. If a trend is started in the proper direction, it gains momentum and leverage with time. Just as homeownership began slowly in the United States over a century, people having something of value changed their perspective to government, to life, and to each other. In undeveloped nations we often expect far too much in immediate transition. In Russia market systems are difficult to institute when the immediate past system has been one where people did not understand the concept of profit. Time and gradual education of their own self-interests assists most trends. But it is important to monitor them and to measure them for the rates of growth and how the rates of growth of positive trends can be enhanced. A step in a direction begins an effort and is far less difficult than a complete change.

The Grand Canyon in the western United States is a national wonder because of what nature carved in stone. It is also a good example of a trend involving some of the previous issues. The water had power, it was incentivized to take the easiest route, it magnified its effect with time, etc. Trends are combinations of factors that have to be individually understood to determine if they will continue or reverse.

Trends can be part of "Super Trends" which can affect them. While we discuss them in more detail in later sections, one purpose of the triangles in the context we shall discuss is to look at potentially intersecting trends. This plays a major part in our assessment of risk, both in probability and ultimate danger to us. Cultural trends that move toward corruption may have significant impact on political or economic trends that might appear differently on their own. Super trends like technological growth or demographics are relatively more certain than current economic ones or environmental ones.

Indexes provide a combination of different trends and are often the "canary in the mineshaft" that reflect changes upon which attention should be focused. Time is a significant issue, both how long a direction has been in place, and understanding how long it will continue. We become accustomed to the status quo and have an inward assumption things will continue as they always have. It is in the good times that the seeds of bad policy are planted that change trends because we are not focused.

For example, in the discussion of the triangles, trends may be the best way to see the importance of generational accounting when taxes and spending are out of balance and the resulting debt is really a postponed tax on future generations. There is a difference between a snapshot and a videocassette that carries the story forward. To find solutions, you have to begin with understanding the progression not just the present. It may take time and patience for change, but small movements make the difference over time. The concept of Chaos Theory emphasizes this point, which we will review in depth later. In American Social Security and Medicare the projections are overwhelmingly negative when demographics and healthcare escalations are projected. Yet changing the cost of living approaches, adding several years to retirement, and a few other adjustments early make very significant differences to Social Security because of their effect on the trend. As this Sam Rayburn quote notes, "You need to get the issue right the first time and when you see a problem correct it." This was the philosophy of America in Congress that put the country first. Today partisanship gridlocks discussion and will do so until there is a popular demand for substance or a crisis.

The Power of Growth

A rising tide floats all boats.
— An old adage

We talked previously about the importance of growing the pie outwardly so that everyone's slice is bigger rather than placing ourselves in the position of having to re-divide individual pieces of a non-growing pie as people concentrate on taking from each other. Growth has very unique aspects because it allows you to handle many internal problems. If your expense ratios are high in a business, but you are able to maintain them at a lesser growth rate than your revenues, time is to your benefit because the growth shrinks the impact of the fixed expenses. Deficits may be particularly high at one stage while implications such as tax cuts are enacted. But if they are such that they generate growth in the long term then oftentimes the higher growth rates, with time, solve the problem naturally. This is the reason that the economics within the system are critically important.

As we talk of culture and morality, we must look at them in combination with the system of economics, not as being two separate factors. Market economics operate best in a moral system without corruption because it depends on competition. Markets will operate to some levels under other systems, but will lose out competitively when certain levels of parity are reached. The importance of growth in solving problems can never be minimized and has to be as critical a component in decisions as building a moral fairness into the process. If you grow you can share it with others so pressure is minimized.

Growth or opportunity, if it is defined as such, makes a huge impact on stability. Ideology may be secondary to frustration at lack of opportunity. Personal dignity comes into play when people feel their standard of living is not increasing. The lack of momentum is perceived more than the current living standard itself. This growth in living standards brings harmony to society since people feel improvement. Even if they are comparatively well placed, the focus is more to see how others are doing and that often leads to disharmony. Growing the pie rather than dividing it creates a far different political situation. This, however, leads to the trade off between growth and social and environmental problems that are a natural consequence. Finding a balance is essential, but growth tends to produce a society quite different from stagnation or decline. Policies make a huge difference economically, and this is the way economics shapes culture (or social policy) and politics. Growth or lack thereof is a strategic driver.

The forces we discussed previously play a part. China, America, and Europe will all have different growth rates or trends. China's much higher growth rate, with time has startling impacts because of the compounding effect. The more time that evolves the less dependent it will be on world markets as it develops its internal markets. It understands and appreciates growth and has patience. This will gradually change balances of influence globally because large economics spend ever more on military, oil, development, and domestic programs even if they keep the same budget percentages. China, and other developing nations are targeting policies for growth. The economic base is smaller, but the momentum affects peoples' attitudes.

America as a mature consuming economy has not adequately addressed these issues. Much of its growth in recent years has been derived from debt which is not quality, but limits growth. The trends of growth are the most important, and the United States has had unique trends because of the dominance of the dollar on the world reserve currency. It will likely not be displaced soon because of the unique depth of American financial markets, but trends show concerns that need to be addressed early in America, concentrating on growth-oriented policies to make America more competitive and reinforce the desirability of the dollar well into the future. The rest of the world needs to realize that if the United States retreats from being an engine of world growth it is damaging to all. The U.S. has been the consumer of last resort and Japan and China the financiers by buying American debt. At some point, natural forces change this equation and growth will then be harder for all. How well the world learns to work together to expand the pie or is opposed to focusing on dividing it, will determine everyone's standard of living. Protectionism is the first step at dividing rather than growing.

The Power of the Environment

It is foolish to plant an acorn of a great oak in a desert or in rock. The nature of the tree is established within the acorn, but its growth and its development is shaped by all around it. It isn't just the seed, but it is instead the rain, the soil, the sun, and the weather that become a part of it. Ideas, like seeds, must be placed in the proper environment."
— Old Texas observation

Every action has a reaction. A good example has to be the creation of an environment where being good is expected through strong positive cultural values. It is not unlike the comparison of a chamber of commerce working on recruitment and on economic development. They are very different in concept and effort. In recruitment you go after a company individually and try to recruit it to move to a town. Economic development changes the town. It makes sure you have good education, fair laws and enforcement, low taxes, and strong culture, so that companies want to come there. Practicing ethics is a lot like recruitment, it works on specific instances more often than being oriented to changing the culture or creating the environment. The cultural environment that instills ethics is the policing mechanism that helps enforce it by peer pressure so nations and the individuals within them need to have a broader perspective of what might be their self-interest. *The Language of Conscience* was written to discuss these issues in more detail.

The critical issue is to recognize that environments can be changed if knowledge and perception change. That itself will have effect on future impact. One of the best examples has been the history of the tobacco industry over the last century. During World War II soldiers took up smoking to relieve tension, and it became a broadened social behavior when they returned. Early articles noted possible problems, then more public education with documentary evidence. Then emerged the non-smokers' rights movement on secondhand smoke coupled with economic burdens such as raising the price through taxes and litigation that shaped advertising and economics. The point is, much of this did not originate from the individual alone, but the cultural and economic surroundings of which he was a part. It played a big part in changing his behavior. That is why understanding policy and education does matter, particularly in understanding the inter-relationship of interests and forces. This is an area covered in much more detail in the section on the triangles.

The Impact of Taxation

Some taxes will produce these effects in a much greater degree than others; but the great evil of taxation is to be found, not so much in any selection of its objects, as in the general amount of its effects taken collectively.
— David Ricardo, On the Principles
of Political Economy and Taxation

No item has more effect on growth than taxes unless regulation is highly aggressive. It helps set the environment of policy consideration, even if indirectly. There are no taxes that have not had a tendency to lessen the power to accumulate. All taxes must either fall on capital or revenue. Both on an individual level and a national level, an understanding of the impact of taxes is critical. The budget of government is its contract with the people—it says how the money will be spent by delineating the programs and the amount of support. But for money to be spent, it has to be taken from someone else. This can either be by taxation or its equivalent or by running a deficit and borrowing the funds. In the latter case it is a transferal of the obligation to a later generation and just a delayed taxation equivalent.

The nature of taxes can have a great impact on growth, so even if you do not have to pay them directly you lose in opportunity cost. One of the stories told by economists is of the barber whose window was broken. The barber had to have the glass replaced. So at first it appeared the negative event helped someone generate money. However the barber, who had planned on purchasing a new suit, only had money for a shirt because he had to pay for the glass. Yet the man selling the suit never realized the indirect cost.

Like the Eastern concept of Daoism with its skepticism, you must always look to the unintended consequences. Taxes are eventually passed along to others, so just because politics arranges that you are not taxed directly, you should never assume it does not affect you. You should take interest in the broader aspects of the system.

The same concept is true on benefits given in the budget. A provision may benefit one industry greatly, but cost only pennies to each individual. So the lobbyists for the industry are intense, and the general public has little interest. However, multiply that by many industries and projects and the tax costs are huge. The danger to the system is occasionally a few sharks in huge programs, but mostly it is the nibbling of thousands of minnows. The impact of taxation is clear in incentives and thereby growth. In Shakespeare's time they taxed windows so people closed them in. In America's "Golden Age" even the rich used furniture rather than closets, which were taxed as rooms. Taxes are a weapon of government both to raise revenues and for social policy. Most people do not think of them in those terms because they are often hidden. Reduction of taxes normally encourages incentive and growth, but this requires a sound policy analysis. Tax cuts aiding growth is not the same as tax cuts paying for themselves. They may or may not, but the structure for recovery of the cost matters.

Using Good for the Greater Good versus Using Good for Evil

Men of principle are always bold, but those who are
bold are not always men of principle.
— Confucius

One of the great problems of attempting to do good with a passion is that it increases the vulnerability to those attempting to misuse it. In the modern world credibility is a valuable commodity and, like power, it is increased with positive use. The ability to work with others to bring positive efforts to the front of a larger group is often critical to success and funding. There are concerns at both the personal level and the ideological level that need to be understood and recognized. First, we should look at a personal level.

In America, unlike most of the world, the issue is often not quality but the level of advertising. We are bombarded by tremendous amounts of information and opportunity. So if you want to create a greater good, you often need to take risks in working with other groups to expand or leverage projects and information. The problem is that those that want credibility for their own, often financial, purposes will attempt to attach to credibility and use it for their benefit. In many cases the person with credibility is not even aware of it. Groups for good purposes have many join them with the assumed purpose of supporting the efforts of the group. There will inevitably be a few with other intentions. Often these problems are insignificant, and they drop out because they really did not intend to work. But at other times their intent is to use the credibility of the group or individual to personally benefit. If they are unethical, it reflects back on the group or person. It often can tarnish interest in the group and cause heartache to the person who was trying to do good.

There is no sure way to prevent this nature of problem. The best people at "cons" are truly professional and can be the hardest to detect. But you can have sensitivity to the problem and skepticism until people prove themselves. If it is a joint venture, check the Better Business Bureau and references just as you would a business deal. You do not want fear to prevent your using credibility to expand what you believe. But you want to know you have done the best you can to prevent any misuse of your trust.

This is even more important in charities or public efforts than in many other personal efforts. It is impossible to discern the inner intent of men, even the Pope cannot do so. But you must be sensitive to watch even those that want to help, for you presume intentions are of conscience while the greatest purveyors of convenience see good intents as opportunities. Vigilance can save embarrassment. However, if you do the best you can and people change or disappoint you, you will hopefully still be judged on the intent of your effort.

The second area of concern is the revolutionary power of ideas. A few years ago I was in Mexico City and retained a driver to take me to the Museum of the Interventions where I had understood the original flag of the Alamo was kept. I had a Mexican friend with whom I had worked before his death to see if a tour of the flag to Texas would be possible. He felt if I could find an equivalent flag, such as one of the San Patricio Battalion who Mexicans respected, it might be a base of discussion.

On the way the driver suggested that I see Leon Trotsky's home and Amnesty Museum and Frieda Khalo's house. Having seen many times the Diego Rivera murals on the Federal Building at the Zocolo and understanding the part Diego Rivera and his wife Frieda played in getting Mexico to accept Trotsky as he fled Russia and Stalin, I was curious. Trotsky's career was unique in that he was filled with a revolutionary mentality that propelled it. He was one with a utopian faith willing to tolerate great loss of life to achieve it. What impressed me about the house he stayed in was not the bullet holes through the room where the first assassin missed, but the collection of books in the small library and the picture of the group of revolutionaries and their fate often at the hands of Stalin as he consolidated power. Frieda Khalo's house showed the relationship in the 1930s and 1940s of how ideas like Marxism swept between continents—pictures of Mao were on the wall and of Russia—in part by leaders of culture. The Diego Rivera paintings show the cultural power within politics, which affects economics. Revolutions often start for utopian ideals, but the nature of power is such that ideals can be lost easily in individual power struggles or over time.

I had understood the Russian revolution better after seeing the palaces of St. Petersburg and realizing the poverty of the peasants, and why the location of the great Summer Palace is not now in a town named for the Czars, but named for one of their great Russian great writers. The power of good and evil moves back and forth as the culture responds to conscience or convenience.

The values you choose determine if there is a cause for revolutionary ideas or not. Personal dignity and economic fairness do much to set the stage. The principles of power require balance that needs to be sought by a system of law and of honor. Much of these thoughts go toward the understanding of how you preserve a desire for utopia with a recognition of reality. Great ideas can be misused over time as convenience shapes them.

Although I did not find it, the Alamo flag symbolized it best. The men that chose to die there did so for time and principle while their leaders did not rush to their defense, even though they wished to do so. They stayed at Washington on the Brazos to write their Declaration of Independence and Constitution to define the future and culture of the nation for which they fought. It is now an old flag, but it symbolizes a great deal.

Men say the modern revolution is terrorism and that it may be the organizational conflict upon which the future world is organized. I feel it is more basic than that. Terrorism is only addressed when a system of common obligations of men and nations create a framework of common effort and growth, that will be at the heart of a much greater discussion of whether society is organized on a platform of conscience or convenience.

Differentiating Between Structural Culture and Cultural Values

Great men are they who see that spiritual is stronger
than any material force, that thoughts rule the world.
— Ralph Waldo Emerson
Progress of Culture

As we talk of cultural values or bringing the best ideas of the past forward, it becomes increasingly important to understand that cultural values are formed over very long periods of time. Over this period of time structures have been put into place that may not be relevant in a modern world and quite frankly, may pull from the true understanding of cultural values. Too often in the academic arena, scholars look for patterns or approaches to thought to explain the differences between cultures or within cultures. They create stereotypes that are then promulgated to other thinkers who read their work. Oftentimes entire cultures are looked upon through glasses of past thought that distort reality. The experts defining a culture from abroad have probably never been within the culture to fully understand it. It is very helpful on occasion to not look through text filled with footnotes of how you got to a perspective, but to look instead originally, at exactly what the circumstances are today and what approaches may better define the reality of the situation. Quite often what might have been cultural characteristics in an economy and set of politics may be entirely different in a fairly quick evolution through modern technology.

One of the best examples might be the fact that Confucius was in effect a very original thinker. Yet in the East over hundreds of years, his thought was structured to much more repetition. Jesus Christ would have had the same skepticism when His teachings were structured by the church to condone the sale of indulgences.

The primary point being that a set of ideas usually originates as a set of values. But as time goes forth, and the political and even economic processes review those values, they are shaped oftentimes by the political leaders, the intellectuals, and even the economic structure of the time in ways that benefit them more. They may be changed only slightly with a new approach, and it may be done with an innocence of believing it is correct and more appropriate. But often the structure of the culture can separate itself from the values if great care is not given to look to the original meanings. It often may be a little bit at a time taking a concept down a very different path, or it may be dramatic. The point is that the people are relatively familiar with the culture, as it exists in that structure and thus they often accept the structure as much as they accept any values. Changing the structure may also be more difficult than recognizing the values because there may well be established economic and political interests that benefit greatly from the status quo. Making this distinction is one of the critical points within the use of the triangles that we discuss later. It is not the current structure upon which we focus, but the current values. Integrating cultures is quite different than just defining their values. The structure often has joint considerations with the politics and economic sections. The best example of this concept that I often use within the books is a simple story of a woman who bought a pot roast, and cut off one-third of it cooking two-thirds. Since they never seemed to have enough meat for the family, the husband asked why she did that and then serves the other third as leftovers the next day. She noted that was what her mother had done and that is how she learned to cook a pot roast, and they ought to ask her why the next time they visited. They did so and her mother said, "Well, I learned it that way from my mother. We will have to ask your Grandmother the next time we go there." When they asked the grandmother she said, "It's very simple, I have a small pot and only two-thirds of the pot roast will fit in it so I cannot cook the entire roast at one time." If we look upon the pot roast as values and we look upon the pot as structure, we see that changes in the values can occur because of structure and often some of the best values and best approaches are wasted. The secret when we look at cultural values is that we should look at the "whole pot roast" not necessarily how we historically have treated it.

The Catalyst of Crisis - Demography

Demography is destiny . . .
— Often used axiom

What changes structure is crisis because it demands change and a modern case study would be certain current trends. As we look at the world globally, no two issues will be more important over the next quarter century than the changing age and population demographics throughout the world. The reason rests not only in work force productivity and changes that affect economics, but also more importantly on public pension and health funds. In some countries population growth is receding where others are only staying even by immigration, which has become a significant issue in its own right culturally. This is particularly true in Europe where immigration is testing its former focus on tolerance. In Africa the Aids epidemic is a far greater threat to the continent than is appreciated by much of the rest of the world. Aids is also having an impact mainly in the younger working populations of Asia. Generally in many countries like China and the United States you have an aging population, which in itself normally means increasing healthcare concerns and costs. Europe has even more significant problems in these areas because of limited internal population growth and highly structured social programs. Population trends have direct impact on economic growth. While many of the world's geographic boundaries of states may remain in fifty years, the economic power of these states will change dramatically.

America is a good individual example. The average lifespan is growing, so the need and costs for healthcare funding normally increase with age because of additional needs and added years to the average age of a group may boost its healthcare estimate significantly. The working population of the United States has not continued to expand broadly as originally envisioned where new workers would fund many government entitlements. Social Security may be a trust fund, but it does not actually save the money from contributions in the normal corporate sense, but effectively relies on the promise to tax the next generation of workers to pay current benefits. This theory does not work well with current demographic projections nor does Medicare.

Yet healthcare and retirement are critical circumstances for stability in society. These crises will reach a point that they have to be addressed because they are simply too large to ignore any further. Almost all parties have not wished to talk of the sacrifice necessary to make change, but changes that could be made presently such as increasing the age of retirement, changing the COLAs (Cost of Living Adjustment) and the ways they are calculated and limiting the high levels of entitlement envisioned could dramatically change trends over time. The likelihood of that being addressed in the current partisan politics, however, is not positive until a crisis of confidence emerges or is perceived. At that point there are difficult solutions. Government may no longer be able to pick up much of the difference because fiscal deficits and international trade deficits and debt will increasingly limit its freedom and flexibility unless they are addressed. Since the level of spending will in all likelihood not be reduced, the level of taxes either have to be brought to the level of balance or debt simply moves the taxation from this generation to the next generation. One suggestion that will emerge in discussion will be that there should be a means test to determine that those who are not in need should not receive the benefits. This is the type of catalytic discussion that affects the direction of a nation in the cycles of nations.

One group of people have saved all of their lives responsibly in order to make certain that they had proper benefits in their retirement and were not a burden to their children, as well as having a higher quality of life. Others have not saved, or perhaps have not had the opportunity to save. When the allocation of resources takes place what issues of balance will try to be achieved? Do you take the benefits from those who have worked and shown individual responsibility to provide the benefits to those who have not? Is this a fair approach? Do you cut the benefits of all and thereby put many into poverty where they have counted on the government to provide the protection? Do you increase the taxes on the current generation that had gotten no benefit and will receive relatively little? We return to our balance between compassion and obligation as defined by promoting individual responsibility. There will in all likelihood be the use of all three approaches because of the very significant impact that will have to be addressed when the issue is finally confronted. The politician at that moment will look back and lament what could have been done far earlier. In reality we as a society are at fault. Few of our media find it worthy to discuss, few of our political leaders, even recognizing the problem, have addressed it aggressively, and we as a people assume that because it has never been a problem before it will never be a problem in the future. Healthcare and retirement are social issues as much as economic issues. They have a morality context involved in them. The evolution of an increasing technology and quality of healthcare add very high levels of costs. You possibly could have the same healthcare for the price that it was in the year 2000. But five years of advancement add to the cost because of the high cost of developments over that period. Tort reform, changes in pharmaceutical advertising, policies limiting consolidated purchasing, and a host of other changes also have an impact. The truth is, health costs go up with an aging population. While these are catalytic circumstances in America over the next quarter century, they are also catalytic circumstances in much of the rest of the world, and they will test governments as to how to find the proper balance. The earlier solutions are taken before times of crisis, the more flexible and the more intelligent they can be. Debt limits freedom of action so its use is not necessarily a solution beyond the immediate.

But even then changes in economics have a large impact. The Greenspan Commission on Social Security, which adjusted the system several decades ago, certainly knew and studied the baby boom generation's demographics. The things changing the accuracy of their projections were growth rates and income disparity. That should demonstrate that social security, which is the most visible example, is but a symbol. With the globalization of the world, the competitiveness will shrink margins and opportunities so aging populations have to be viewed with levels of economic growth. A vibrant economy solves problems; a structural semi-stagnant one tends to amplify them. This affects not just government expenditures but private pensions and savings. Social security can be "saved" one way or another. Medicaid is a much bigger challenge, but the economic pressure of demographics that is being described as a "leveled world" is an entirely different matter. The policy we need to be discussing is not an argument over dividing the pie but growing it—not economic income division that stops incentives, but growth incentives to offset the problems. Competitiveness economically is a part of these discussions.

The point is that crisis drives change from inertia, which is normally in place. How quickly a crisis is recognized depends on the perspective of the people which often results from the education they receive and how willing they are culturally to sacrifice for the next generation.

Personal Dignity Versus Personal Ability

Talents are best nurtured in solitude;
character is best formed in the stormy billows of the world.
— Johann Wolfganag von Goethe

In the education of American children you have two trends that are accentuating. One is the more elite private school focus on competition. The students' focus becomes competing to surpass their peers to such a degree that what they focus upon is competing almost beyond learning. An example is that in Texas the top ten-percent of classes can automatically be accepted at the best public universities. That makes taking easy classes strategic and focused on beating out others. Lao-tzu's warnings on the problems of competition are very appropriate here.

In the opposite approach, the formalized educational community puts a less competitive more cooperational tone forth. It seeks often to remove competition by making everyone winners and focusing on self-esteem.

Everybody is special, so no one is special. Everyone gets an award. But this approach often leaves the young unprepared for a difficult world of global competition and sets not just a cooperative framework, but also an individualist mindset that others owe success to you as well as respect. The concept limits gifted students and to me leads to mediocrity.

It becomes important to separate a required respect for personal dignity, which is more a respect for the individual as a fellow being with rights to whom you owe an obligation, as opposed to personal abilities, which are different in each of us. We can guarantee equality of opportunity if we try which personal dignity would require, but we cannot guarantee equality of result, which often depends on ability. Natural law is the issue here and reality triumphs.

In the eighth grade I went out for football but had few of Dad's traits since I was small and not that fast. The person on the other side of the line was seventy-five pounds bigger, faster, and a lot meaner—beyond toughness. He had been held back a year or so academically, and football was his thing. He flattened me every time no matter how hard I tried. Now that hurt my ego regarding my prowess in football. But since that was his job and it was competition, it should not have affected my concept of personal dignity unless he did it for meanness. This is a distinction often lost in the play of words of modern educational thought.

An appreciation of personal dignity is not served well by over intense competition that teaches winning above character or by a lack of competition where no character is built by learning from defeats and thereby building strength and perspective of how hard you have to work to succeed. That is the great benefit of sports. We again have begun to operate on extremes when balance is a necessary choice. This sets the stage upon which the younger generation will look at the world. Are they to perceive themselves victims, must they win at any cost or does old-fashioned sportsmanship of how you play the game help people gain respect for each other on the basis of its values alone? Compassion says to build self-esteem and individualism into our children. Self-esteem is important, but how it is taught is critical. Obligation tells us to teach them the realities of life so they can succeed. Balance is a critically overlooked issue.

A good example is that self-esteem is a mental concept not unlike the physical concept of the body's immune system. If you are totally protected from a germ, your body has no immunity to it with a disastrous result if you are exposed. You build a natural immunity from exposure although you try to keep it from being dramatic.

The broader aspect of personal dignity, as compared to personal ability, involves the opportunity that society provides. If you work and develop ability but have no way to succeed because there are no jobs and no opportunity to use it, then personal dignity suffers. The controversy over the Danish cartoons in the Muslim world, the riots in France, the unrest in Holland, were not just about differences in culture. But they also involved a frustration where people viewed their personal dignity as offended by even slight impositions. That increased sensitivity is an impact of economic forces. If you have jobs that you could lose in the future, your impression of your personal dignity is different. High growth countries like China and India have a different mindset. India has a large Muslim population but the reaction was different than in areas of frustration where modern communication allow people to now see what they do not have and realize how limited their future can be. Rural China will be similar in perspective if opportunity is not provided. Personal dignity needs personal ability and drive, but it needs the opportunity that growth provides, which is often in political policy. As the later triangles demonstrate you cannot separate these issues, they are interconnected. If corruption limits political and economic success, it eventually erupts in the frustration of a lowered personal dignity. Corruption often limits opportunity by giving opportunity for reasons other than the fairness of merit.

Balancing Compassion with Obligation

In Asia, the concept of "the Way" between opposites is paralleled in the West by a variety of concepts bringing balance. Just as water seeks its level, weather adjusts climate differentiations; nature has its own way of bringing balance even in society. There are relationships between most forces. If economics produces materialism, it can lead to its own weaknesses. Civilization can go in cycles in positive and negative directions, as later sections will demonstrate.

As we discussed above with self-esteem versus reality choices, the most difficult balance is often compassion with obligation, which are both a part of conscience. Poverty, ignorance, illness, and other burdens are naturally adversaries to be fought by conscience, compassion, and caring for others. The difficulty is that this can often only be accomplished by taking resources from others through taxes, redistribution rules, monetary feats, (which lead to generational inequity) or other hidden means. The bottom line to be asked is what obligation does society have in regard to taking from others. Do we balance Social Security deficits by taking or reducing the benefits of those that are wealthier? Compassion says help those in need, but obligation says it is wrong to burden those who have worked and saved exhibiting the personal responsibility we seek. If you do tax them and ruin the incentive to save, what of future actions? How does that affect the long-term strength of the nation? How we think about issues, our national perspective, shapes those answers and says a great deal about us as a generation.

It is easy to create *rights,* but if they require redistribution from others economically, as opposed to civil rights and dignity, it is a complex issue that is seldom discussed in these thoughtful as opposed to emotional forms. There is no question that the wealthy need to pay more because they have more assets protected by government and get more benefit on many services. It is the redistribution issue that is key. Normally this is not based on assets being taxed but on income. And income taxation often is not heaviest on the wealthy that structure and plan their assets to avoid taxation. But the hardest workers, often in personal small businesses are the ones who generate most of the jobs that provide the opportunity. You may show compassion taking from them and giving to others. But Rambam's Eight Levels of Charity make it clear that the finest charity is giving opportunity to others, the least is giving with discontent, and indirectly that is what you have here. Emotion should not rule these issues, but thought should.

The triangles presented later help make this point; the forces of nature eventually balance out bad policy by crisis. Good policy looks to the soundness of current decisions with appreciation to the fact that economics and politics either uphold the "Golden Rule" in looking at obligations or the society fits into the numerous observations that follow showing you cannot help the poor by destroying the rich.

In a time we must be internationally competitive to maintain our own and our children's standard of living, short-term emotional solutions can do great damage. The personal dignity of a man is in part dependent on his right to equitably see the benefits of his labor and follow his family values and obligations to his children. He should have the right, obligation, and compassion to help others, but if he is forced to do so eventually he resents it and it affects his feelings of personal power or dignity. *Compassion should be instilled in the culture not forced upon it or the strength of the culture suffers because compassion at the individual level recedes.* Private charity is so much more beneficial than public governmental charity. It keeps strength in the culture, and the people receiving it are strengthened not just by the resources but the spirit of the gift. People tend to "pass on" what is done for them. Courtesy is contagious. But if so much is taken by government for their purposes, individuals feel they have done their part. Government is seldom as effective as the marketplace of human compassion.

These previous sections are some among the many building blocks of focus and understanding. Receiving them gives a mindset for the following sections as well as a database. The next section focuses upon the character aspect of nation-building and the cycles of nations. Short-term, the emotion of compassion, redistribution of income, victimization, and excessive individualism may seem appropriate to certain circumstances. But the super trend that keeps "longer term" stability is not as obvious, yet is critically important. If the next generation is not versed in the proper values, strength begins to ebb from the people through disinterest and power soon flows from them.

Again, how we learn to think and the method of thought we instill in our children, determines what we think about issues because it determines how we process the information. We can develop a top-down "mountain top view" that looks largely to analytical thought or we can choose a more emotional, bottom-up view. The secret is to have both where they blend together. The question is whether the "uncommon men" that make a difference in society can find the means and the desire. They set the culture by leadership, and they will determine whether a society stays stable and competitive in a fast changing world. A review of history is the place for them to start. From history we appreciate that the group defines its values and thereby grants the protection of the individual rights as part of the common good, which is created by the power and force of common obligation. As this force weakens, so weakens the common good and the destiny of the group.

Section III

What Wisdom Does History Grant Us?

Perceiving Civilization through History /
China and Its Future Impact as a Case Study

Those who are victorious plan effectively and change decisively.
They are like a great river that maintains its course
but adjusts its flow. . . . They have form but are formless.
They are skilled in both planning and adapting and
need not fear the results of a thousand battles;
for they win in advance, defeating those who have already lost.
— Sun-tzu
Chinese Warrior, Philosopher

This book is a synthesis of certain historical ideals applied to modern times as a new century confronts the world with dramatic choices. It focuses less on the political and economic systems of the last century and more on the cultural value systems that will ultimately define success in both. The modern world operates with incredible speed that favors knowledge and emotion, which help form our habits. But to seek wisdom and substance for sound choice requires a discipline of thought. That is best gained by developing a system that organizes thoughts into related compartments and then relates the compartments to each other. Although fate determines a significant part of life, the strength of ideas can exert great power on the future.

A different perspective is required in the reality of a global world. The following quotations set the basis of the synthesis presented as enlightened conservatism that looks to the development of ethical cultures to bring out the best in people. It explains the power of morality to set the foundation for the common good by securing personal dignity through the Golden Rule. The battle for the future culture of the world will be waged in the terms of character of the individual and of society. It is a battle not between good and evil as much as it is an individual battle of conscience versus convenience implemented by individual responsibility.

The character of the individual forms the character of the nation. If the character of the nation is left in a vacuum, entertainment and convenience shape the values taught to the next generation. To be a defender of conscience, you must not only teach your own children, but you must work to affect the culture in which they will live. Otherwise, they will be corrupted by a culture of convenience and unsuccessful if they honor your teachings. Integrating diverse culture on this basis of common character is a challenge, but finding the common character traits of different cultures is the starting point.

Each of us sees the world physically from where we stand and mentally from a perspective that is shaped by our past history, geography, and values that we term to be our cultural roots. That view is enlightened by our opportunities and our education and is tempered by our experiences. This perspective helps shape the basic nature of man that is within each of us. There has been debate through the ages over whether man was inherently evil or if he could be redeemed, developing his conscience and spirit into being good. In a modern world, the speed of technology, the pressures of economics, political, and media/cultural concerns give little opportunity to enlighten perspectives. That in itself shapes the culture of the future since we pass on only those values we cherish.

As we divide ourselves into groups, we have many mini-cultures that lose the benefits of the perspective of the whole, the common good. We forget that power is the driving force throughout society, and power operates on rules of its own. How a person is treated by others does much to set the standard of how he treats others.

The core thought of this perspective of civilization is: Conscience works best at the individual level—convenience dominates at the higher levels of power due to self-interests, ambition, competition, and related forces. Only by making conscience convenient can it reach power and dominate. That requires a culture that values conscience through character development and individual responsibility and passes these values on to the children. Civilization must not only transcend generations, but also constantly be improved and strengthened or it automatically decays. But to be effective, all of the strategic power drivers of economics, politics, and media/culture must be coordinated and understood.

Morality ultimately drives the best market systems because it enhances the greatest level of competition. The strongest moral culture operates through nonprofit institutions and peer pressure to make private solutions to charitable need and the social capitalism that limits the requirement of governments and courts. The smallness of government limits regulation that allows the greatest benefits of the economic system. All of these come from a perspective of conscience that is being unappreciated in modern times. It is cultural power if described properly.

There are two points in history that have fascinated me because of their effect on resulting political structure through their cultural impact as applied to those events with religious base.

One was the rule of the Chinese Duke of Zhou who set the standard for honor in defending the throne of his small nephew, who he easily could have usurped, and the origination of the "Mandate of Heaven." It set a base for Chinese culture.

In the West, it was probably the Golden Age of Athens around the 5th century B.C.—the age of the great philosophers and of Pericles. This era began democratic thought and gave great weight to the rule of law and to the power of virtue. From it modern Western culture and perceptions evolved.

Honor and virtue were clearer in simpler times. Today we must concentrate harder to bring them to focus, but the lessons of history help.

The following quotations are those that contain many of the thoughts synthesized into the analysis within, including the following on the need for the clarity of a strategy to achieve noble goals. They are presented here, and on occasion repeated, to emphasize that history returns to a theme that character determines the destiny of a society, and personal dignity is the key criteria of judging its strength of sacrifice. Accepting responsibility is the driver of character. In modern times it has been looked upon as a duty that is expected of us by society, but in the proper understanding, particularly of culture and history, it is a voluntary act that responds freely to the needs of society. That is the true strength of character that sustains nations. Ponder the quotations individually for they build the conceptual model. Focus upon the fact that conscience or responsibility is not a weakness of societies of history, but their strength. The political correctness and entertainment of today often minimize this critical point. When people ask "whose values" do I wish taught, I always say fundamental values of conscience, the Golden Rule, the common good—the values referred to in these quotations. The Rule of Law is essential, but a tyranny of law or bureaucracy that punishes those willing to take individual responsibility is detrimental. It is significant to note the people remembered in history for positive achievement had very similar perceptions of the critical items of life. The purpose of the quotations here and in this form is to open one's mind to similarities of the thoughts of great men of history that are seldom in focus today. Note the importance of The Golden Rule and that it is the anti-hypocrisy standard if it is the method of thought. Keep in mind that when decisions are made, people do not know the outcomes. Mary Kay Ash, founder of one of the most successful United States companies in the 20th century, founded her company May Kay Inc. based upon the Golden Rule. She believed that the Golden Rule was the basis for business and was rewarded in her faith with incredible results. Her foresight was acknowledged in the United States in an academic survey of business historians who voted her as the Greatest Female Entrepreneur in American History. History usually judges the results, so a knowledge of history that analyzes those results helps make thoughtful decisions.

Each quotation has a key thought, which once perceived will help prepare a foundation for linkages later in the text. As we noted, the laws of nature can often be seen in history. There is a concept in thermodynamics referred to as the rule of entropy that suggests that the natural order is for things to proceed backwards to a state of disorder. So society has to take actions to adapt, improve, and move forward. When their interest is lost, recession often begins. These are observations that will help us ask the right questions before we seek answers.

> *The more perfect civilization is, the less occasion it has for government, because the more it does regulate its own affairs, and govern itself . . . all the great laws of society are laws of nature.*
> — Thomas Paine
> The Rights of Man, 1792

> *The central conservative truth is that it is culture, not politics that determines the success of a society. The central liberal truth is that politics can change a culture and save it from itself.*
> — Daniel Patrick Moynihan
> Former Senator (D)
> from New York

> *This is the seal of the absolute and sublime destiny of man – that he knows what is good and what is evil; that his destiny is his very ability to will either good or evil.*
> — George Wilhelm Friedrich Hegel
> The Philosophy of History

*When the people of the world all know beauty as beauty, there
arises the recognition of ugliness. When they all know good as
good, there arises the recognition of evil.*
— Lao-tzu
The Way of Lao-tzu I

*He who wishes to secure the good of others
has already secured his own.*
— Confucius

*This is the noble Eightfold way: Namely right view,
right intention, right speech, right action, self livelihood,
right effort, right mindfulness, right concentration.
This monks, is a Middle Path, of which the Taghagata
(the Buddha) has gained enlightenment, which provides
insight and knowledge, and tends to calm,
to higher knowledge, enlightenment, Nirvana.*
— Buddha (Siddhartha Butama)
The Sermon at Benares

*Wealth and children are the adornment of this present life:
but good works, which are lasting are better in the sight
of thy Lord as to recompense, and better as to hope.*
— The Koran
(18:46)

*Always treat others as you would like them to treat you. This is
the teaching of the laws of Moses in a nutshell.*
— Jesus Christ
The Sermon on the Mount
(Matthew 7:12)
Living Bible Paraphrase by Tyndale

*Those who can give up essential liberty to purchase a little
temporary safety deserve neither liberty nor safety.*
— Benjamin Franklin

The people's good is the highest law.
— Marcus Tullius Cicero
De Legibus, III

I do not understand how someone can elevate himself by
suppressing or denigrating another.
— Gandhi

I fully subscribe to the judgment of those writers
who maintain that of all the differences between man
and the lower animals, the moral sense of conscience
is by far the most important . . . It is the most noble
of all of the attributes of man.
— Charles (Robert) Darwin
The Descent of Man 1871
Chapter 4

The next four quotations look not to the individual, but to society as a whole. They talk of the natural law of civilization and the realities that affect them. The Durants studied history, as did Sir Alex Tyler. Edward Gibbon in his studies made a key observation in his *Decline and Fall of the Roman Empire* (1776-1788) that helps set the stage for the following observations, he noted:

All that is human must retrograde if it does not advance.

The issue today, as we are a global world, is how civilization advances on what principals in the age of terrorism and corruption. Civilization goes through epochs of time where the culture enhances personal dignity and opportunity, and then these are pulled back by other forces. There is an over-riding operational philosophy to any culture. Its core values determine how all else functions to a degree. Do the people put a priority on love for their children and obligations to each other or do hate, envy, and vengeance dominate thought. All the other issues are the realism of bottom-up existence; the top down perspective sets the tone for how they are assembled. The bottom-up events happen naturally from self interest and emotion. The top-down has to be developed and maintained. The key points the rest of this book will make are the benefits that a growing economy with personal dignity can provide. Again, it is like the example of the pie that grows larger on the edge, so each person's slice grows in size with the pie. When the pie does not grow, it is the nature of man to take from his neighbor to increase his slice. Society diminishes as people squabble and fight among themselves. Confucius made the same observations of the decline of China for a failure to recognize obligations. The great empire built by the Muslims, in large part on the unification due to the Koran, disintegrated as the internal parts begin taking from each other and, as some scholars noted, forgot what gave them power. As Gibbon noted of Rome, he saw four causes—the injuries of time and nature, the attacks of the Barbarians and Christians, the use and abuse of the materials, and the domestic quarrels of the Romans. It is important to connect the significance of character to each of these progressions of society over time. Conscience, the positive part of character, has many parts but two key drivers. As we discussed, they are compassion for others and obligation to others. When actions combine the two positively, the greatest charity and peer pressure for a culture of service exist. When compassion moves to "victimization" and economic redistribution beyond true need occurs, obligation within the society to allow men the right to their work is impacted. "Incentives" are changed, responsibility shifts from the individual to government or other entities. The values instilled need to be personalized to be truly effective in shaping the culture.

Two nations will play a great role in this half century by their direction—the United States by how it maintains strength of its society and culture and China, which will choose its modern path for the future. The civilizations of the past have had many factors affecting them—war, climate, demographics, and a host of others. But the key is how the governing system reacts to the threat. Is the response wise and unified or is there division and words in the place of action? The culture of the people ultimately determines that response and their own destiny because leaders' actions are impacted by the level of support of the people. They can excite, but the level of character determines the degree of sacrifice given.

Sun-tzu and Charles Darwin both noted the critical issue of survival was adaptability beyond even strength and knowledge. The power to handle change effectively is an issue of cultural unity and common values; it allows you to utilize your strength and knowledge without gridlock. Free market economics that, if properly implemented, gives the best growth that improves the standard of living of the people as a whole, rests on society. That requires a special type of culture with both the freedoms to fail and achieve and the personal dignity rights that make people strive for personal gain. But it must be balanced by acceptance of responsibility and education of the benefit for the common good. I remember a quotation that I think is attributed to President Dwight Eisenhower that describes the situation best: *"Freedom is but the opportunity for self-discipline."* When any culture loses that understanding, it begins to fail and any culture seeking freedom must begin with it as a fundamental building block. Integrity, the core of self-discipline, is the blood and muscle of true freedom because it is the true heart of personal dignity, which gives character and recognizes both the need for compassion and obligation to others. These observations trace its impact in stages as it grows or deteriorates.

> *A great civilization is not conquered from without until it has destroyed itself from within. The essential cause of Rome's decline lay in her people, her morals, her class struggle, her failing trade, her bureaucratic desperatism, her stifling taxes, her consuming wars . . .*
> — Will and Ariel Durant
> Caesar and Christ (1944) Page 665

The average of the world's greatest civilizations has been about 200 years. The nations have progressed through the following sequence.

> *From Bondage to Spiritual Faith*
> *From Spiritual Faith to Great Courage*
> *From Courage to Liberty*
> *From Liberty to Abundance*
> *From Abundance to Selfishness*
> *From Selfishness to Complacency*
> *From Complacency to Apathy*
> *From Apathy to Dependence*
> *From Dependence back to Bondage*
> — Sir Alex Fraser Tyler
> Scottish Historian,
> circa 1787 On Athens

> *Politics without principle*
> *Wealth without work*
> *Commerce without morality*
> *Pleasure without conscience*
> *Science without humanity*
> *Work without sacrifice*
> *Education without character*
> — Gandhi on
> Society's Seven Deadly Sins

You cannot bring about prosperity by discouraging thrift.
You cannot strengthen the weak by weakening the strong.
You cannot help the wage earner by pulling down the wage
payer. You cannot further the brotherhood of man
by encouraging class hatred. You cannot help the poor
by destroying the rich. You cannot establish sound security
on borrowed money. You cannot keep out of trouble by spending
more than you earn. You cannot build character and courage
by taking away a man's initiative and independence.
You cannot help men permanently by doing for them
what they could and should do for themselves."
— Attributed to Abraham Lincoln

History teaches that wars begin when governments
believe the price of aggression is cheap.
— President Ronald Reagan

The line separating good and evil passes not through states,
nor between political parties… but right through
every human heart.
— Alexsandr Solzhenitsyn

The core issue of all of these quotations is to me, the decline of the strength of society's character and thereby weakness in response to threats. Character is the individual responsibility. It is a major part of how we seek our own personal dignity. But when you look at how that combines on a national scale, leadership owes a responsibility to keep an historical perspective within the nation. Too, often, we forget history, and it weakens both our national strategy and our cumulative individual responsibility.

All history is a study of cycles of civilizations with external and internal factors affecting their destiny. Marcus Tullius Cicero, one of the Rome's visionary leaders, made an observation that fits the concepts of many countries today,

The budget should be balanced, the Treasury should be refilled,
public debt should be reduced, the arrogance of officialdom
should be tempered and controlled, and the assistance to foreign
lands should be curtailed lest Rome become bankrupt. People
must again learn to work, instead of living on public assistance."
— Marcus Tullius Cicero

It is very difficult to make quick changes to any Ship of State, so politics is seldom successful in the short term with sacrifice. The better strategy is to change the trend so that time is your friend rather than your enemy. For this purpose, education is your greatest tool, but it is a special type of education that creates citizenship and willingness to sacrifice through understanding historical perspective and the value of individual responsibility. If a leader can manage the finances of the nation in such a way as to maintain and create opportunity, then the individual responsibility usually brings the creativity to succeed economically, and the citizenship that allows it comes from the values of the individual responsibility. Patience is necessary for true change, but setting on a proper trend, is the focus of what must be done.

The problem is not in recognizing decline, but how to change its direction. Politics makes change difficult, particularly without patience. The Ship of State representing any nation is large and hard to guide, so education is the only real rudder. But it is the education of the values of individual responsibility and historical perspective that are really the key. Visionary leaders that want to move beyond rhetoric, need to focus on being a patient catalyst that puts this trend in place. Time is either your enemy or your friend in this effort, if you can make a directional change time corrects the problems. But if the decline continues, it is the enemy. The key point is that patience and education are your best tools, if the education is focused on the things that build citizenship and the leadership has thoughtfully designed the expenditures of government money to build the opportunity that the individual responsibility requires to make it productive.

The ultimate goal is to train the next generation, and how you think about educating them is important. There is a significant link between responsibility and good and evil. Parents try to teach values because they want what they consider good kids rather than bad ones. But conscience over convenience is character morally, and besides this instruction the child learns or does not learn responsibility. It is putting character into action that makes him responsible or irresponsible and makes his actions effective or of no consequence. *The instilling of values thus has two related parts: one is educating conscience. The other is teaching the acceptance of responsibility or leadership. This is what builds the uncommon men and women, the free thinkers who understand sacrifice, and who are willing to stand above the crowd to explain why sacrifice is necessary for a stronger future. They become the examples that others follow.*

Today World War II is increasingly lost in the memories of time. There is an assumption by many Americans that victory was inevitable. Like most hindsight, history is simplified. World War II started long before American entry when the Japanese invaded Manchuria. America did not prepare for the war, had stood down much of its military and procurement, and lost much of its Navy at Pearl Harbor. Hitler's rush to engage Russia assumed Britain was finished and was a fatal flaw. Had he focused on Britain and denied the United States and its allies a staging platform, and had the Russians not put up an incredible and costly defense, World War II might have been different. Perspective of why wars are fought matter. Military engagement should be the last option, but there are reasons to analyze conflicts and see what they mean in a futurist effect. It is not just having the national character to respond. It is responding in a timely manner. Had the world objected to Japan's invasion of Manchuria a decade before World War II, how would history have played out? Would Hitler have been so bold with Poland? You are defined not just by the things for which you live but also by the principles for which you are willing to die. Wars are brutal and won by the most committed. History gives perspective to sacrifice. Decline can begin when this perspective is lost and national character is secondary to personal concern.

There are other symptoms that arise from decline. Just as Confucius looked to the decline in China in the era of the Warring States as being a decline in the honoring of the obligations of relationships, today in society both global and modern, it is the core choice between conscience and concerns and obligations to others and convenience, which is concerned only with self. Good character and conscience are predominant when people take individual responsibility. This is developed by leadership and a structure within society that is often nonprofit and shapes the ultimate culture.

Super Power and Rising Superpower:
Cooperation or Cold War

A number of years ago former Secretary of State and Treasury Secretary James Baker III gave a speech in Brenham. As several of us visited after the speech, he was asked about the critical factors in the world's future. He focused on the American-Chinese relationship. The breadth of his experience and the quality of focus, as well as that of Dean George Kozmetsky, have made me appreciate the true significance of this relationship and its magnitude. I would suggest reading a great opinion piece that Secretary Baker wrote, "Let's not go looking for a 'Cold War' with Beijing: There are Ideas for Mutual Interest To Pursue with China" (Houston Chronicle, Wednesday April 19,2006, Outlook, p. B9). With an excellent set of thoughts, he sets the stage by noting America's unique supplementary position of power at this time, China's rise, and then capsulates the thought of the future:

Taken together, these two phenomena have prompted some observers on both sides of the Pacific to predict an inevitable conflict as Beijing's ambitions collide with Washington's pre-eminence. We should reject any such analysis. First, predictions of conflict can become self-fulfilling prophecies.... Second, such an analysis seriously underestimates the broad areas where Chinese and American interests converge.

His logic continues with a final observation that Washington and Beijing can learn to manage differences if they build a strong consultative mechanism. I thought of significance was his noting the importance of confidence-building measures such as military coordination and "exchange of scientists, scholars, and students." Such initiatives *"are a critical supplement to traditional diplomacy"*. He is correct that our understanding each other is the base of success.

How China evolves in the next quarter century will do much to impact the rest of the world, which will be forced to react to the change. China's culture has been for thousands of years its great strength that let it convert invaders to its vision of civilization. It is the way for China to address its challenging future now that it has shifted its economic system to a method of production in market economics. As Engels noted in the *Communist Manifesto*, the method of production (economics) necessitates the organization of the social life (culture) that inevitably rises from it and that affects the intellectual and political foundations (politics). As market focuses grow, society naturally will change and politics will change. Although foreigners will advise and try to write China's future, it is a nation of independence and strong cultural heritage that it is reviving. Its challenge will be to find a vision and use its patience to push in that direction. It is a society built on closeness and obligations of family, which is critical to its core. How China and America interact will have a great impact on the world as it will exist. India, Russia, and Europe will certainly have a part, but there is reason to look at these two. They are the main examples of a mature nation of abundance and a rapidly developing nation seeking abundance. The way they interact will determine if the competition is such that they oppose or coordinate with each other's interests. They are linked whether they wish it or not. The issue will be the nature of relationships.

India also will play a part, but its path is different. Its use of English makes it the logical place for service industries. Its diverse political groups and democratic system will make its evolution different. It will have more of a zigzag pattern of development as policies are politically compromised in the growth arena. China is impacted by a culture of the group and a half-century of central direction. It takes time to get consensus but then unifies to get support to move forward. This makes it easier to compete on a short-term basis but more difficult to find methods to bring involvement in the mass decisions. Only corruption makes this more difficult in any society because it further attacks the credibility with society. It creates a disorder or lack of fairness that attaches the basics of individual dignity and leads to disorder. Disorder itself or lack of stability demoralizes the people and sets the stage for breakdown and crime.

So rapidly growing nations must plan early to build in safeguards not only to corruption but also the acceptance of responsibility by the mass population. This is a cultural trait that is critical. Not only China, but many developing nations, will face a point where the technology change that impacted economics and required market systems for adjustment will move to a further level through communication and globalization to similarly impact politics. Russia was an example of this impact on economics and politics at the same time causing great instability and corruption. China has been very different, as it has moved in stages. But eventually the natural law question will be whether it moves through its ancient powerful culture of respect for dignity to build responsibility and more gradual popular involvement in the process or whether it faces the "wall of crisis" where forces build until you move to one or another extreme. America faces some of the same potential "wall of crisis" issues with its partisan deadlocks. But these are issues over time, and the answer rests in how the children learn to think and how family and society instill values.

America has dominant military might and is the world's largest economy. Its critical impact in the world is not appreciated unless you view a map of the world scaled to economic size. America might be 30% depending on how it is calculated, and other countries shrink in economic size. China has less than one half its GDP. This is why the dollar remains stronger than many would expect. America is a nation with great strengths, but the future holds great questions because of its trends. Debt has been excessive in the last decade. Gandhi's warning of "commerce without morality" has become more real with the corporate ethical behavior. America's abundance is leading to selfishness and apathy as we become more partisan and demanding on government and the courts. America's strength has been the confidence that has made it the premier place in the world to invest for safety and opportunity because it was the leader in knowledge and technology. It prided itself on innovation. But today I think we are losing much of that technological edge to Asia. The terrorism concerns have added to the problem by making foreign visas difficult. The best foreign students used to come here to study and often stayed giving us a huge competitive advantage.

When I travel to China and talk of education, I am amazed at the respect and interest in education because they see it as so critical to the future. Our American business leaders are treated like rock stars, and people wish to be like them. In America we have begun to take education for granted taking our focus from it to some extent because of the politics of our educational system. America has the choice to work to preserve the principles that built it and unify to remain competitive (grow the pie) or divide and argue (division of the pie). It is not just our edge in technology that is fading. It is also the strength of national character, which has always unified the country. America will remain strong as long as it has the confidence of the world. Once that is lost, much changes. The dollar is the symbol of that to a large degree. And character is the base that prioritizes all other factors and determines how the society should run. America has been helped by much of the rest of the world's weakness. Europe's slow growth and structural systems, Japan's deflation, the developing world's health, corruption, and financial problems have cushioned how high our performance had to be these last few years. The dollar has maintained its position less on strength than the lack of a viable substitute.

The People's Republic of China has the opposite problem. While America needs to retain its character values and competitiveness, China needs to build and evolve theirs to match the new market economy. China has its own strengths and weaknesses. Its growth rate is so strong it will gain in military and economic power automatically relative to the rest of the world. As the manufacturing capital of the new century, it has one benefit that other work centers such as India do not. It directs the purchasing of huge cash flows for raw materials that supply an influence of its own. Its size is a benefit because of the leverage it provides, but it is also a problem because of that same leverage. While the press views it as a rising power, we must remember that Argentina had the same image at the beginning of the last century and never reached its promise because of internal problems that led to bad policies. India, Brazil, and Russia will also press for leadership roles. You look at China emerging not just because of trade with the United States and the West, but primarily as the economic engine that indirectly unifies Asia. Its greatest problem to success is the corruption with its system, which is endemic of many emerging countries that have emerged from a history of feudalism usually tied to a military history. Often to support the military, resources were allocated from the population and along with that early orientation systems evolved that expanded. So you may well have contrasts in some of the cultural values and the methods of doing business. The issue is that markets are only as good as competition, and if the markets have corruption, few bid and the markets are ineffective. Strong financial systems require the confidence of integrity. You cannot ultimately build a great economy without a strong and deep financial system, which requires the trust integrity and transparency provide. This type economy is a necessity for key growth to rapidly build a middle class to maintain stability, which is China's other major problem. If you respect the laws of nature and history, they speak strongly on the reality of these points. Many feel that the corruption issue will be China's strategic weakness, but I see it as a problem they have acknowledged and are seeking to address. The Chinese interest in using their strong historic culture to address this issue is one of the few ways there could be success because it creates a different environment, but it also takes time and dedication. The Central Party School's interest in anti-corruption, corporate and governmental culture of integrity issues went far beyond publishing *The Language of Conscience* to interest in seminars and relationships with many of the front-line organizations facing these issues daily and understanding reality as opposed to theory. This is a cultural issue, which has economic components but is best solved by culture. Great nations define themselves by their character, and the historical culture of China will let them appreciate that point. Confucius and Aristotle had ethical obligations as core points.

As time passes, relationships between these two drivers of the world economy will face significant tension, as both perceive the other's strength and their own weaknesses. This will be enhanced by much of the rest of the world that out of perceived weakness and the same need for national dignity will try to position accordingly.

China could become, as many fear, the polar opposite super power to America similar to Russia in the Cold War. But it should be remembered how much international growth expanded when the walls came down and economic principles allowed the expansion of markets to enhance them. There will be many pressures in a volatile world by those that work their niche at power. Economic competition, nationalism, the vision of their leaders for a place in history, and many other factors can dominate the media and the national mind. In every country there are men of conscience and convenience. There is no culture that does not have its divisions.

As Lord Palmerston pointed out, "Nations have no permanent allies, only permanent interests." So the best way for America, China, and the rest of the world to position to their best interests lies in the development of a strong national character of individual responsibility, conscience, and a belief in personal dignity that builds the nation. It automatically aligns you, even in pressures, with those of like belief.

While many look at Chinese labor and the American trade deficit as great problems, they overlook the other side of the current situation in the reinvestment of these Chinese profits and savings in American bonds that has a significant impact on interest rates. Many new theories have come forth to explain the "conundrum" of long-term interest rates not maintaining the term premium over short-term rates. While that varies and will, as always, change has brought focus with such presentations and concepts as Bretton Woods II that focuses on the impact of not just Chinese labor but Chinese investment on the world economy and currencies. These are complex relationships, and most economists have erred because models have new factors. While in a sense China is a mercantilist economy in production, it is also a "vendor financier" economy that is financing a lot of its purchases through the macro purchase of bonds. That links the Chinese and American economies far more than people realize. It is also a case to argue that the Chinese do not wish to "beggar a neighbor" with mercantilism if they own much of the neighbor's debt.

This is a new paradigm that means that "unsustainable deficits" may be longer lasting because China must put millions more to work each year for stability domestically, but the trade deficit imbalances will grow. Just like the oil crisis of the 1970s we must find ways to recycle and balance out flow of funds or we all face many problems. China and America are linked because of this level of trade and dependence. But they are the growth engines of the world, and the entire world will suffer if they decline. The American consumer will always keep spending. The worry is the depth of his pocketbook, particularly if he can no longer take equity from real estate. China has used America to learn pricing once it converted to markets, but it has been so successful that it has changed the world dynamics with deflationary labor and fund flows. The future is uncertain and dangerous, but everyone is in it together. A critical part of the solution lies in allowing Chinese investment in the United States to recycle dollars similarly to the times of oil crises. If this is not done, you have a growing problem as the baby boomers retire and need to sell assets. With possibly less younger people to buy but with Asia having a surplus of cash for savings, it is a logical mutual benefit. But this process is not easy. It is much simpler for a complex American company to go to China than a Chinese company to come to the United States with our legal and securities system. This is an area that needs early support because of the learning curve.

China will have an increasing part to play in fighting terrorism simply because it intends to be a modern power. The friction between modernism and fundamentalism will be a driving factor in the future. China's systems rely heavily on growth as a philosophy. While it is moving to focus more on the social concerns, its technological drive will necessitate that the social concerns will not alter its drive toward modernization. More than its political and military might, its greatest weapon can be its intellectual contribution to civilization by helping focus thought, in depth, on the fact that growth is not a zero sum game but can create a better life for all. The basics of the frustration that leads to terrorism is that "we cannot be wealthy if they have the money." It is a belief that some are poor because others are rich. The only way to change an idea is to enter with a new one. China understands the concept of win/win structuring. The key is controlling self-interest to levels where success can be implemented.

It is important to note that China is building a middle class that is the key to its future. The middle class is expanding and has the personal interests to push the values of personal responsibility we favor. America's strength is in its middle class, but this group is under pressure and may well shrink in the future unless America brings back its competitiveness of old. This concept of a middle class, and its natural values and self-interests in a market economy will bind the two nations in ultimate interests.

No issue is so likely to divide the two nations as protectionism and the related nationalism it provokes. This will be the cleavage point on the diamond that can be the world's future of growth through cooperation. It is the ultimate combination of economics and politics but is in reality a philosophical cultural issue of how you think, how decisive you are in your actions, and how educated your population has been to responsibility.

The friction between China (and other exporting countries) and the United States will become intense as limits are reached economically due to trade deficits. This may not come as quickly as many predict because the current situation benefits many. The problems of immigration and outsourcing make the economics problem a political one.

If you take the simplified media version of the problem, Chinese trade is taking jobs. You can think simply of the appearance and reality of the deficits. Some people wish to put sanctions to limit trade or retain jobs at home.

A more intelligent way to think requires an understanding that our standard of living is not just between two nations. It is more like our personal checking account. We give money to grocers, to the dry cleaners, and to the government in taxes. We do not have an equal balance of trade of what we produce with them. The question is how much money we add to our bank account and where do we make our money, not so much when and where we spend it. We make our trade money from our specialty talents—in America that has been aided by technology from heavy capital investment in jobs that let us have higher wages and a higher standard of living. Yes you need fair trade without abuse, but many times the abuse is just intense competition.

Competition makes you change and get better. Perhaps the best example was a statistic that Richard W. Fisher, President of the Federal Reserve Bank of Dallas, gave me when we were discussing the issue one evening. He was a trade negotiator that helped open relations with China in 1979. From the time he left Dallas in 1997 to go to Washington, prices for goods not subject to foreign competition have risen: college tuition and fees up 53%, cable and satellite television up 41%, dental services up 38%, and prescription drugs and medical supplies up 37%. But prices of goods subject to foreign competition have fallen over the same period by 86% for computers and peripherals, 68% for video equipment, 36% for toys, 20% for women's outerwear, and 17% for men's shirts and sweaters.

The point is competition and free trade has been key to our increasing standard of living. There is an old saying that people do not work for money, but for what money will buy. Protectionism may mean more money, but usually less goods can be bought with the money because prices rise due to less competition. As I pointed out many years ago in *The New Legacy,* I can buy a foreign belt with cheap labor for a dollar or I can pay $15 for an American to make it at our wage rates. How much I can buy with my limited amounts of money is thus impacted. This is why the specialization of labor increases the standard of living and is why both President Bush and President Clinton favored it. Free trade is a plus for the American economy as a whole, but it can be devastating to the components of the economy most affected.

It is important to understand that trade or outsourcing, which is the issue driving the current levels, redistributes income in the domestic economy. For example, a "widget" is made in the U.S. at $20. It is taken to China with a factory and made at $2 with cheap labor. If brought back, either the consumers get an $18 reduction or more likely a smaller one and the company management and shareholders keep a portion. Many of the companies in China, Mexico, Eastern Europe, and Southeast Asia are owned by foreigners as competitive production engines. If American companies do not outsource, they can become victims of European or other competitors as they try to sell in a globalized world.

The best way to think of this leveling is in sports. In college football and baseball you tried to have great players every year. The rules let a few big schools keep all the talent. They stacked up on good pitchers, halfbacks, etc. So the level of competition, unless with other great teams, was limited. But the rules were altered. The effort for parity with everyone having the same limited number of scholarships, no financial incentives, and the economic interest of professional sports taking players changed that. Now, recruiting talent is critical, but managing that talent effectively is equally critical.

In the economic parallel, capital like talent was invested in only a few countries because of the stability, legal structures, and markets. Now the confidence factors have changed and spread investment. But also the cost structure of mature economies has added burden. Tort law costs, mandates and legacy costs of pensions and healthcare, as well as higher wage levels have changed economic analysis. Businesses are now often multinational, so the economic analysts put money where it is best treated by regulation, taxes, and fundamentals. You manage this environment not by bribing companies to come or stay or by threatening them, but by creating the best economic environment so they will come making thoughtful long-term policies rather than reacting for short-term benefit.

The issue at the heart of the problem is the loss of jobs and the lowering of pay as this leveling takes place. That is what pressures the middle class.

Globalization is very similar to technology in creating what economist Joseph Schumpeter described fifty years ago as the "force of creative destruction." There is havoc in job markets and industries as the new replaces the old, but normally the economy emerges as more efficient and competitive. In globalization this spurs not only more competition but more specialization. For competitive nations this leads to higher standards of living and job growth but that requires the nation to remain highly competitive both in public policy and in economic drive.

China, for example, has a huge trade surplus with the United States, but imports much from the rest of the world. It is important to understand that trade deficits often begin at home by over consumption and lack of saving as core causes. Other countries can make such excesses easier, but the problem starts domestically. It is why a country must stay at the cutting edge in technology, education, culture, and governmental policies if it wants to generate jobs to replace those it lost by "creative destruction."

The best analogy I can use is to compare the jobs to hair. At a younger age I started losing quite a bit of hair, which got my attention. The advice I was given changed my perspective. I was told that you always lose some hair. The issue was not the loss, but the failure to grow new hair. That is the issue with jobs. For Americans to keep their consumption and protect the competitiveness of their companies, jobs will automatically be lost or filled by immigrants. How many new jobs are we creating at higher levels of income? How conducive is our tax policy to taking risks? How much does our legal and tort system affect risk? Do your employees realize the necessity of competitiveness or feel entitlement? Is our government using sound approaches to turn tides as Margaret Thatcher did in Britain and Tony Blair continued with his "Third Way"? Reagan made critical changes to reposition the U.S. Australia, and New Zealand have shown that policies can help make you competitive. But most of all, what do we teach our children to prepare them for this world? How good is the education on which their future rests, and do the values necessary get instilled? Do we instill a work ethic?

The figures, which are used to show the China trade imbalance, make it look as though China is the problem. But a lot of that trade and jobs came at the expense of Mexico and other low-cost nations that had already taken the jobs. China simply was more competitive and leveled them. However, the current trade figures show the deficit more directly with an appearance of the issue being China, not the concept of job loss through competitive attrition.

These jobs will be lost. Our job is to create a culture that is creative, competitive, and unified to a greater standard of living. This is where, when the talent is more equal, the coach's ability to develop talent and create "team" matters. That starts with your perspective and how you think. A team effort is one requiring conscience for sacrifice not convenience for only personal interest. It is why corrupt systems will be leveled by that over time as well. But also, gridlock and poor competitive policies limit the growth in higher paying jobs and new discoveries. Trade has winners and losers automatically, and the concern is how to show oportunities for the losses or you have instability. The key is that you provide opportunity and growth not subsidy as Europe often tries.

As our bank account analogy showed, the future may be more how we make additional money rather than how we cut costs. We have high fixed expenses, lowered margins with leveling, and the need for a unified effort for joint success. The triangle we discuss later tries to show the relationships to build such a creative culture to generate jobs, but this requires a dedicated will to do so. America's future depends not on factors from without nearly as much as the factors within. They cumulatively are our national character, our national will, and our national perspective. How we think will determine how we will react to the challenges or even if we will react. My concern is that American competitiveness will be hurt by our hesitation to encourage the best minds in the world to come for education and stay and that we will foolishly impede foreign investment. Both knowledge and capital create the environment necessary for success any time.

As with the United States and China, it is important to put in context the comparison of the two critical players. This is easily distorted by individual items in the media and fear on both sides. So understanding how the nations fit together is critical.

One of the best examples comes from the Dallas Federal Reserve Bank President, Richard Fisher, who, as I mentioned, gave me a copy of his remarks before the Center of American and International Law on June 14, 2004. (For more detail, these remarks are posted on the Federal Reserve Bank of Dallas website, www.dallasfed.org.) With his permission, I think this is an excellent summary:

> Since 1978, China's economy has grown at an average rate of 9.3 percent and grew at a reported 9.5 percent last year. So we know from the statistics, however imperfect they may be, that Deng laid the foundation for a pretty sturdy expressway. China's rapid growth has been unrelenting. I have been asked today to predict how long the fast growth will last. Possibly, China can grow this fast another two or three decades or perhaps just a decade, if not less. Certainly, though, it can't do so indefinitely.
>
> The answer to how long depends on several factors. Will China continue to reform its economy? Can its leaders maintain political cohesion while they do so? Can China deal with its emerging pollution and infrastructure constraints? There are a myriad of issues the Chinese must deal with, none of them easy.
>
> As you contemplate them, you might start by putting China's economy in context. One can paint two starkly different pictures of China right now, the Big China view and the Little China view.
>
> The Big China view centers on China's manpower and prowess in manufacturing, and it uses purchasing-power-parity adjusted dollars to embolden its case, a convention adopted by economists to adjust

for local purchasing power, which has its utility but may or may not be a useful tool in measuring comparative geopolitical power.

Here are some statistics to support the Big China view:

- America has a labor force of 147 million; China's is 761 million—five times as large.
- China's factories produced just 200 room air conditioners in 1978; today they produce 48 million. Back then, they turned out just 11 billion meters of cloth; last year, 35.4 billion meters (over 3 times as much).
- Chinese households have a rapidly increasing abundance of appliances and electronic products—refrigerators, TVs, DVDs, cell phones, etc.—at ownership rates not far below those in this country.
- They have 28.3 million broadband users and 98.8 million Internet users, according to their Ministry of Information and Industry.
- There are 28 billion square feet of floor space under construction in China, compared with just 5 billion in the U.S. Five of the world's largest shopping centers are now located in China.
- The U.S. manufacturing sector produced goods worth $1.5 trillion in 2004. China produced $3.4 trillion, adjusted for purchasing power parity.
- And the grand statistic of them all: On a purchasing-power-parity adjusted basis, economists put China's gross domestic product at $7 trillion, compared with our $12 trillion—making it already 60 percent of our size.

That's the Big China view.

The Little China view has many more statistics in its support:

- U.S. productivity in agriculture is 33 times that of China; productivity in U.S. industry is five times that of China.
- The U.S. has 19,497 airports; China, just 126.
- We have 150,000 miles of petroleum pipelines; they have less than 10,000.
- We have 481 cars per 1,000 people; they have seven.
- We have much higher levels of education and technology.

I could go on and on with statistics to show where China comes up short. But here are two good summary statistics: On a straight U.S. dollar basis (not adjusted for purchasing power parity), their economy is roughly the size of California's. China's GDP per person is just $1,300, compared with our nearly $40,000. That's just 1/30 of our per capita GDP.

I personally think we overstate the current prowess of China by emphasizing the Big China view. But from either perspective, China has room to grow. To do so, they will have to deal with infrastructure and other problems, which present significant challenges.

The various parts of any and all economies are constrained somewhat to grow in proportion to one another—not in totally rigid ratios, but not in completely flexible ones either.

The article is an excellent one and I recommend it in its entirety. The second point is one made later in the book. China understands this situation completely and plans accordingly.

To me, the issue will be how China brings about cultural change to absorb the impact of its economic change. Ratcheting up the levels of infrastructure will cause significant environmental changes as well as instability. The financial implications are even more significant with the trade and financial balances at stake. Understanding the accurate perspectives and finding mechanisms to address problems is critical.

What can help this process in our generation is the building of an understanding of these factors as a cultural bridge between nations that is in place to bring out the best within all of us. I am often told that is naive in modern times. But on the contrary there is great power in new ideas, in a world stagnant of new thought. This would be the job of universities, but they often deal in theory. In the United States many universities value research and look at values as a possible infringement on academic freedom and ethics courses as consuming time better used for higher-level knowledge. This structures thought as does universities' bureaucracies and ideological groupings. Only if ideas become prominent because of their influence do they get serious study. The more likely evolution of new ideas are think thanks that specialize in public policy and deal with the reality of the world and the realities of power. Too often these are committed to only one side of an issue, so their effects occur slowly. The universities are critical additions to enhance these concepts. But the ultimate framework or matrix of analysis has to be at a location of significant power and respect with the universities, as well as one that has potential international impact if it is to draw knowledge from abroad by partnering in thought with a variety of nations. At this day and time one of the few places such an endeavor to advance civilization culturally and build bridges might well be China's Central Party School of the Communist Party because of its public policy infrastructure, its ties to its greatest universities, and China's emerging power in the world. If understood, it has a rare opportunity to advance ideas on civilization's values on an interesting stage in the next decade. Its success would be determined by the quality of thought that emerged.

How that is done involves the process of developing a perspective and drawing a matrix of the factors involved that can then be broken down by other universities with specialties that can build relationships worldwide. If the study is of the nature of the benefit to the individual that a culture of conscience provides, it sets a stage for the understanding of a new culture.

That leads us to perceive the necessity of developing a modern Rosetta Stone to understand how civilizations can work with each other while optimizing the growth and opportunity within their individual societies. The modern world does much to divide and bring out the worst in us. It takes great effort to find the systems that can unite and bring out the best in us.

But the ultimate issue is one of cultural ethics, what values will transcend to the next generation of children worldwide? Their future is ultimately in our hands culturally, economically, and politically. It is not just that we must train our children in our values. We must have economic and political systems that are compatible with the culture system.

Such is in our capacity, but values must be developed, understood, and promoted. They will only succeed if they embody *the language of conscience* that lets people of differing perspectives come together with a concept of integrity to work toward common ends. This language allows differing views to speak with respect, not shout with disapproval, as is the case of much of our American media today.

The perceived realities of politics, economics, nationalism, and cultural divide, that reach the level of not just resentment but hatred, seem to make an effort to unite and bring out the best in people both naive and futile. All power seems to oppose any solution. But power is ultimately the tool of ideas. Minorities of the elite govern majorities of followers in the way society is normally structured. These minorities of leadership seldom operate with security of position. People do matter, and while they are seldom well informed on most subjects with the complexity of modern times, they have the wisdom and intuition to know the big issues and the reality of who cares for them. Ideas crystallize those intentions. So power has its own metamorphous of evolution to adjust to new times, and that is where the competition between ideas plays a great role.

In the mid-twentieth century, ideological politics dominated in the Cold War—Kennedy, Johnson, Khrushchev, Brezhnev, Mao, and the concept of markets versus central planning were competing ideas. Due to the technical evolution of the world, the second driver of power—economics—became the focus with Reagan, Thatcher, Deng and Gorbachev in the '70s and '80s. Now we have political privatization into markets, but they are made ineffective by corruption, lack of transparency, and bureaucracy. You must have self-interests in markets, but competition can be effectively destroyed by the corruption of its excess, greed. You must have the basis of moral and just rule of law. But it can be turned into the tyranny of law if it is carried to an extreme where individual responsibility and the Golden Rule are replaced by *victimization,* and people avoid taking individual responsibility because of fear of legal action. The second tyranny of law is its unequal enforcement.

There are three drivers of society—politics, economics, and media/culture. Most issues can find a home in one of the three. They affect each other as is the nature of power. But for the early portion of this century the power of culture will arise with undue influence as we look at our problems. Within our societies, the structures of the past are crumbling in the face of technology, communication, travel, globalization of economics, and the end of the Cold War relationships. The competitive leveling of the world is the driving force.

Knowledge is growing quickly driving politics and economics. But wisdom, a characteristic of thought rather than emotion, is being lost in the search for relief in entertainment and summary news opinions. Yet each of us knows that the future, regardless of the nation, is ultimately judged by what we teach our children. Their perspectives and their values ultimately change society to a path that advances civilization to embody conscience, respect, and individual dignity and to show that man is not inherently evil but redeemable.

Each of us in our search for fulfillment has our own concept of our personal dignity that may be offended by others' arrogance or our own pride and envy. Our happiness in life depends on the standards we set for ourselves and not on what others think of us. We need to judge how well we succeed by what it has cost us, so we can work from enlightenment. Once we understand ourselves, our influence is magnified by our confidence. Adam Smith, whose *Wealth of Nations* explained markets, captured the key concept, "To feel much for others and little for ourselves, to restrain our selfishness, and exercise our benevolent affections, constitutes the perfection of human nature." When we have confidence, we can lead. True leadership is taking responsibility and making decisions deliberately.

A good start to refining such nature is to realize what helped change the last cycle of ideas to focus on the importance of market economics. You need a crystallization of a new paradigm to bring attention to it. The writings of Henry George helped focus economic policy in the late 1800s. Similarly, Milton and Rose Friedman produced books and a television series, *Free to Choose*, which showed the values of competition in a market economy to each individual and their individual interests. As stated before, the reality of life is that people are seldom for or against you. They are simply for themselves and their interests, *as they perceive them*. The power of ideas lies in their ability to shape these perceptions. Thereby political perspective has economic consequences. Ideas have to start somewhere, even inconsequentially, to be developed into concepts. In the West there is the parable that from a small acorn a great tree grows. In the East the idea is that every journey begins with a small step in a chosen direction. The key lies in choosing the most critical approach to analyzing cultural solutions. With the structure of politics and economics, you have interests much like a diamond that can be struck with great force to no effect unless the blow lands on a cleavage point that can split it. Often it takes the chaos of crisis to provide the light. The secondary problem is that it must be the right cleavage point or it is ineffective. To take the concepts we have discussed and relate them is helpful. Case studies of comparisons are helpful in doing this.

Enlightened Conservatism and The Harmonious Society

In September of 2005 during my visit to the Central Party School for the seminar on Integrity, we were also presented the concept of a "Harmonious Society." This was a vision of the issues that must be addressed for Chinese society in the future and how many of them fit together. Simultaneously, I presented a summary of this book adapted to the issues that they had suggested as an agenda for the meeting. It is quite interesting how in the discussions that we noted how many of the concepts of enlightened conservatism, which is a Western-based, morality-oriented approach to solving issues, have in common with the School's concept and approach of a "Harmonious Society." Both deal with economics, politics, and culture as being integral parts that have to be coordinated. The comparisons of thought are an excellent case study of how the comparisons in the triangles can be used to attempt to create win/win situations that bring better understanding. But that requires understanding the historic background involved.

The Chinese presentations were of significant interest to me because they are two concepts that are particularly important as China moves forward domestically and internationally. One concept is the "Harmonious Society," which is the vision that the leadership has within China of what critical problems must be addressed, of how to address many of the domestic problems, and how to create a unique Chinese model. The other concept is what is often referred to as a "Peaceful Rise—China's New Road To Development." While it has much to do with the "Harmonious Society," I perceive it also to be a very important concept internationally. "Peaceful Rise" perhaps more defines China's interaction with the global society as it implements its concepts of a "Harmonious Society" and for that reason both are particularly significant concepts to be understood. Both concepts are very logical for the short term. The question in many minds rests with the longer term as China grows in size and influence. No one knows the future and much of it will be determined by events and actions by various parties, but these concepts are a very significant base to affect the world's future. While there is always suspicion between competing interests, there is much more trust that people will do what is in their best interest. You only learn how they view their best interest and how you can interact for your best interest by discussion and understanding. These concepts talk of economics and politics, but their base is a cultural one in the appreciation of the needs of stability required by such huge numbers of people. To understand the future of China you have to begin understanding these concepts and then projecting how success or failure will influence policy. What emerges is that the world has a lot at stake with China's future and the more people understand how they can develop "win–win" scenarios or work jointly on problems the better we will be, and most importantly our children will be.

There are a great many books written on China, and each of these books comes from an individualized perspective of how the author sees the country. In times of transition, as the world faces today with globalization, these perspectives differ greatly. It is no different in America than comparing books of a devout Democrat and a devout Republican. You would have two entirely different perspectives of what was good and bad about the world. In times of transition individual actions and individual perspectives often become the focus because they are more easily explained or deemed more media worthy. This is true in all countries, and it is very difficult to assess the true direction that is actually a culmination of all of these individual actions. Statistics and trends tend to represent them over time when you deal with economics, but when you deal with social issues that are in a rapidly changing environment affected by many factors, these considerations are not easy to perceive in the present. The many books that look at China, and many that look at the United States, are in effect written from the bottom up in analysis in that they are based on the individual perspective of a certain person in a certain place. It is very difficult to have a top down perspective in the United States because while you have significant pronouncements, top down directives, and positions by the leaders of both political parties, it is really the people that tend to sway one direction or another and eventually seek out the most compelling arguments. In the United States the most successful political leaders are those that understand the perspectives, or as I often used the term before, the personal dignity of the individual and how he sees his position in life.

Two people that have always amazed me at their ability to grasp these trends and directions were Texas friends of different generations. Horace Busby was a friend of my father and one of the close advisors to Lyndon B. Johnson throughout his political career. I had the opportunity to get to know him in the later years of his life, and he gave me a number of insights to my father that I never perceived. It is why the concept of having a variety of leaders that are uncommon men became particularly important to me. There is a group of leaders spread out among many different beliefs of politics that do make a dramatic difference because of the respect that generally is held for their opinion and for the reasons for which they undertake efforts. After I had written *The New Legacy,* a foreign Consul General one time visited me in Brenham and asked me to give my thoughts as to how to correctly understand Americans. I sent him to Horace, and he and Bus had a six-hour conversation. I received a thank you note from the Consul General that said it had been the most interesting conversation he had probably ever held because it put into focus for him the importance of understanding history, of understanding culture and values, and of understanding the key points that ultimately make a difference in whether a man is satisfied with his state in life or is determined to make a change. These were the concepts I often call his perception of personal dignity. In modern times, Karl Rove, the advisor to President George W. Bush, has the same traits of understanding history, appreciating cultural values and the effect they have upon people, and understanding what makes change. While the two were from different perspectives, the focus was on the people with history as a perspective and understanding their value systems as a driving force.

For America, the time of transition to a new much more competitive world is going to test a number of the past perspectives of America. It will inevitably take a re-emergence and competitiveness that is only gained with sacrifice to keep the high standard of living that America has enjoyed as the advantage of capital investment that has benefited America moves partially to other countries. Nonetheless, America has time to reinvent itself and tremendous resources with which to do so because of the highly developed economy that exists. The growth rates of many other countries are far higher than America, but the large base that is the American advantage remains. Our development and competitiveness is a management system that is very hard to duplicate quickly. Our financial infrastructure is a key, but its weakness is a potential failure of credibility in the form of weakening morality. Sarbanes Oxley addressed rules, but culture is the key issue. The question is how intelligently America uses its resources and does not squander them in materialism at the cost of the next generations. That will be an increasingly important issue for the people themselves to decide as politicians argue differing perspectives.

In China the situation is dramatically different. There is a much more centralized set of perspectives potentially setting direction for the country. The same issues of personal dignity matter because they are the key to stability. But the cultural aspects of China make it very different from Russia, Europe or the United States. The Communist Party has far more ability to position the direction of the country because of its centralization, and to a great extent, it is much easier to anticipate where the Party envisions China's best interest. Unlike the thousand books written on the potential future of China, the most knowledgeable place to go, to seek knowledge, and read books would be the Central Party School of the Communist Party because as the ideological think tank of China as well as the training institute of its leadership, it is unique. The Central Party School is the place that ideas are tested and to a great extent the concepts of the leadership of China are put into practice. It is the highest school of learning directly under the Central Committee of the Communist Party and charged with the task of training senior and medium ranking officials, as well as cultivating theoretical talents. It has been the place in China for the study and the dissemination of Marxism, Mao Zedong Thought, Deng Xiaoping Theory, and the thought of *Three Represents*. This has been the history of thought of China that has been evolving over the last half century. It is the place where the vision of the new China will emerge from a top down perspective, and, because of the nature of power in China, it is thus the most important place to view China's future perspectives.

This is why understanding the more domestic concepts of the "Harmonious Society" and how they relate with the more international concepts of "Peaceful Rise—China's Approach To Development" become increasingly important. It is also why the Memorandum of Cooperation with the Texas Lyceum is unique and potentially significant. While the School has the ability to venture with almost anyone internationally, it had done so only sparingly in the past, and I am often asked the question of why they would choose an organization like the Texas Lyceum.

The point that I have often made is that I learned very early in life from my father that you don't speak for other people, and you don't try to tell other people what to do. You simply do what you think best, and you define other people by what their actions have been with you. From that perspective, I think the choice of the Lyceum, which was in part based on the earlier publication by the School of *The Language of Conscience,* relates very much to these two concepts. The Harmonious Society, and the Peaceful Rise of China are critical concepts. How to compare them appropriately to Western thought from a cultural perspective rather than a political or economical one is important and in doing so, an environment that allows for a much more thoughtful discussion and depth of analysis through interaction is critical.

The Lyceum is not an organization with great wealth or structure. It is in effect only a culmination of ideas that begin with a concept of the organization being a catalyst for the common good, the preservation of values, integrity, and the training of leadership for thoughtful public policy on those goals. But even more important, I think has been the style in which it has tried to accomplish its efforts. From the inception, the Lyceum has tried to focus on serious thought by the method by which it analyzed issues and the way that the method helped bring consensus.

As I expressed at the signing of the Agreement in Beijing on January 6, 2006, what is most important is how both sides go about being a catalyst for thought. Because of the importance of the School and the uniqueness of the Lyceum, there will be a great number of suppositions as to what the agreement means and why it was entered. Toward that end, I think there are two thoughts that really convey the attitudes I perceived from both groups. Writer Henry David Thoreau probably captured the Lyceum's perspective better than anything else when he noted many years ago that "rather than love, than money, than fame, give me truth." And in a similar Eastern perspective, the Chinese philosopher of the second century BC, Chuang-tzu noted, "he who pursues fame at the risk of losing his self is not a scholar." The seriousness and sincerity of trying to find methods by which East and West can understand each other permeated the ceremony far more than the unique engraved signatory pens, the formalized documents or the celebratory toasts. Common goals and respect for wisdom can unite diverse cultures.

I think the five-year agreement will be unique in that the first year could basically be considered one of information, preparation, and introduction. The second will be a much more appropriate one of consolidation, focus, and prioritization. Like many projects, it can be compared to building a house. An approach to building the house could be to put all of the building materials on the site, which in this case involves distributing books, journal articles, and related materials both directions. So there will be a better understanding not only of the concepts of the "Harmonious Society" and the "Peaceful Rise," but also a better understanding of American perspectives. Many of these issues will be discussed and negotiated between governments. They are the prerogative of governments, but what can never be lost to those that understand how the decisions of governments are made is that people and how they perceive issues set the political and nationalistic stage upon which decisions ultimately are made. So the education of the people in how these issues fit together and what is the true common good becomes increasingly important, even though the populations are massive and the ability for all to understand is limited. Enough information is available in a modern world, if well presented, that those leaders that do care at a localized level, even when they are from all different perspectives, can become informed. The uncommon men and women who want to make a difference can learn, will learn, and will often make the final decisions. What is important is the quality of thought that goes into explaining the options available and how they are perceived. Trust is based upon understanding others as we have noted. Even when trust is not possible to some, a greater security may also rest in understanding how others perceive their common interests because of the understanding that most often they will pursue their common interests.

If the first step is thus to take this information and make it available through literature and networking with various organizations and universities in a catalytic way, then the next stage is finding the contractor to facilitate the construction. That operational expertise is what will need to be developed between the Texas Lyceum and the Central Party School. The third and most critical aspect of the entire project would rest in what I would call the architectural drawings. The materials can be made available, the contractor has the ability to put it together, but what exactly do the parties intend to build? That structure is ultimately why the combination of these two institutions is so unique.

Traditionally, the Lyceum has also structured discussions with other organizations playing key roles and the Lyceum serving mainly as a catalyst through conferences. In all likelihood the six points of the Collaboration Agreement will each form a nucleus for discussion and involvement. For example, the journals might be spearheaded by one or more university presses that would invite interested universities, think tanks, and individuals to participate in the effort. Similar development might occur in China. Another example, would be the exchange of scholars which probably would be held in a similar matter with one university or think tank undertaking the responsibilities for coordination and involving a significant number of other institutions. That would allow a broad representation of those seriously interested to help build a much more complex structure that could be expanded. In all likelihood the Lyceum will eventually forward the project to a foundation created to move the effort forward after a number of parties have become familiar with the effort and the groups involved in both countries. The thought processes and areas of interest will then be more visible and levels of interest can be appropriately judged. It is a method to get to know each other that may be slow and deliberate, but it is structured for broad inclusion. The Lyceum and its nonprofit structure and its value oriented system simply help define the over arching value concepts.

Many people wondered exactly why the Central Party School published *The Language of Conscience.* My impression has been, and certainly reaffirmed, is its interest in looking at how values, ethics, and morality can be used not only to fight corruption but also to bring out the best of an incredibly powerful past Chinese culture. Just as in economics, there are vehicles from the Western approaches that can do much in the transition of China from a more centralized economy to a more market-based one that fits the new technological age. However, China cannot be like the United States. Some of the most significant parts of "Peaceful Rise" and the "Harmonious Society" note the differences that China faces because of its massive population. It should be logical to the West that China cannot have the same per capita GNP as the United States without there being a massive change in the allocation of world resources, which would create significant problems in itself. So China's evolution is going to be different than Russia, than Europe, than the United States. It is going to be much more designed, with thought, to the problems that China faces. For that reason it becomes increasingly important for the West to focus not upon all the individualized impressions of China, but where the leadership of China has focused its priorities. Only then can you begin to see the conflicts or the methods by which the future will evolve. One of the most interesting things that I have discussed with the Chinese has been my belief in the culture of service or compassion that involves the very significant use of nonprofit institutions. This has been one of the ways that the West softens the impact of market capitalism, and it is also a way that can be of great benefit to the Chinese as they try to modernize and decentralize many of their organizations. Without question this will be an area where they can learn a great deal from the West as to vehicles that can keep some of the similarities of the existing system and make transition easier without the problems that Russia faced in the creation of oligarchs.

America and China will both need to understand the significant cross-impacts they have not only through different labor prices, but investment of dollars in each other's economy in different ways. These have significant implications to both sides that are not fully appreciated. Oftentimes the groups that meet and discuss these issues are those that are in silos of individualized government bureaucracies. The benefit of the Central Party School is that it has a top down vision of all that occurs and how the various points of interest interconnect with each other. It is an institution that builds on consensus, but also builds on thought processes. Here you have a unique situation, which returns to our earlier observation of individualist and collectivist thought. America is individualist not unlike a facilitator going around a room asking opinions to get all involved writing them on a sheet of paper. It operates bottom up from the people, and its difficulty is how to prioritize and organize all the independent thoughts into a common plan to execute. But the input from all, through voting, gives stability. Thought in the sense of central planning is top down from a set view but has to also execute by getting buy in from all below. It takes a unique approach to combine both, and it requires a cultural perspective that unites. People are equal but ideas are not. People must move to equity in their ultimate satisfaction of personal dignity, but ideas must move to excellence so the most important ones are the focus. That requires a system of respect and thought that must be a common ground.

The great question then becomes what type of architectural drawing do you create that allows the discussion of these issues at their most thoughtful level. Much of this type of discussion was begun by the Lyceum twenty-five years ago. It started with the concept that you have to decide whether you are dedicated to conscience or convenience. The common good is not the same as personal interest unless you bring them into Harmony. Thus, you need to begin with conscience over convenience as your core belief from the perspective of thought, and once that is done you build immediately to the concepts of individual responsibility implemented by character. If those are the fundamentals from which you set your perspective of thought, you will end up getting very different answers than if you start from different perspectives. That is the perspective of *The Language of Conscience* when it was written which reflected the original criteria of the Texas Lyceum.

If you take the concept of the triangles of "Enlightened Conservatism," they fit very smoothly in addressing the discussion of these issues and those in the "Harmonious Society" and in "Peaceful Rise." The "Harmonious Society" looks to bring balance and stability within China. It is an effort to balance the forces of change with the current structure. The problems that China faces are very similar to the United States, and the solutions are in many ways the same. Personally, I think that China will evolve over time to include many of the perspectives that we have as Americans, but I also see America changing from many of those perspectives that were our past culture unless we focus on their preservation. To make these points, there is nothing better than a case study comparison.

Taking the examples of the triangles of "Enlightened Conservatism," the "Harmonious Society" of the group balances the forces of change and inertia in China. The balance from the concept of "Enlightened Conservatism" is the concept of personal dignity. It is in effect an individualization of the same concepts and stability. How satisfied people are with the fairness of a society determines the actions they take in that regard. With modern telecommunications and communications China will develop its own set of broad-based uncommon men and women and more and more the "Harmonious Society" will require many of these concepts of the common good being explained thoughtfully and put into centralized policy for consensus and "buy in."

So the central portion of the triangle where conscience, character, and individual responsibility are sought is similar in most societies. It is the cultural glue of successful societies, while the balancing of stability in the "Harmonious Society" fits closely with the concepts of personal dignity. The concept of the "Peaceful Rise—China's New Road To Development" is very closely tied to the next set of powers within the triangles. It deals with economics, politics, and culture. These three issues emerge in the "Harmonious Society," but how China will deal with the rest of the world involves each of them in the concept of "Peaceful Rise." To use the triangles to analyze the most critical issues for the exchange of scholars or programs, you inevitably need to look at the critical frictions that emerge because they are the places that understandings are most needed. In the area of economics the issue of the greatest friction will be protectionism and currency, union arguments that often fit that focus on the cost in American jobs and the standard of living, of lower price foreign labor, and investment. These are significant political issues and the very close vote in the House of Representatives on CAFTA shows that in the United States it will be an issue that will be significantly debated and of great consequence. The growing impact of Chinese investments in the United States through its purchase of bonds is an issue that needs to be understood carefully because the American and Chinese economies are becoming much more entwined than is fully appreciated and a better understanding of their joint common interests needs to be a priority not just of individual governmental institutions, but also broad-based policy makers that understand the significant threat of the implications of the two economies separating. Applying generational accounting shows the importance of a joint market as the baby boom generation retires and has assets that are reduced for increased cash flow. The supply and demand of assets and purchases, the better the market maintains value.

This is a time not unlike the end of the 19th century when protectionism and taxes were heavily debated and the works of Henry George with his books such as *Progress and Poverty* and his pamphlets generated great amounts of thought that ultimately affected policy because the common good was better understood. It is a time that academia, government, and the people as a whole need to realize that in this point of transition their future and that of their children will depend very much on the choices made because the choices lead down very different paths. For America, protectionism might be a short-term crutch and comfort, but it has never been an ultimate solution. More importantly, it is not just an avoidance of protectionism, but a regeneration of competitiveness and a resurgence of creativity that create higher-level jobs that are an absolute necessity and will require America to reinvent many of its existing systems, particularly in education. The sophistication and competitiveness of modern business systems moves jobs and resources. You must concentrate on improving your systems so they remain superior rather than show decline. The worry is not just jobs lost, but foreign minds that used to be drawn to America and remain that added the high level intelligence to the system. The modern trend of their remaining at home or returning home after education is as much a long-term threat as job loss because the two are related. You must consistently replace jobs lost with better ones and that requires an increasingly competitive system. The market system rewards and punishes competitiveness. These results are felt on individualized levels and are reflected in politics from a bottom up approach based on their perspective of their position and its change. Whether America rebuilds its systems at higher levels or simply consumes its great advantages depends on the character of the people and its leadership. History shows every great nation is challenged. It is how it reacts to the challenge that determines its destiny. As the previous section demonstrated, the national character determines the result.

In the issue of politics the most significant issue will be national defense. China's significant rise in economic growth will allow it ever-increasing dollars for military purposes. It may not reach parity with the United States for decades, but America will be increasingly pressed to cut defense spending due to the fact that its domestic programs will require ever-larger amounts of money. Whether there is the threat militarily to the United States from China's rise may be less the focus than the perception created as China invests in technology to create a unique counterparty to American military power. The military assessments for both countries could well escalate as China will naturally wish to control its Asian sphere of influence and American interests are potentially endangered by that expansion of power. This will create a significant political question of allocation of resources and the relationships between countries will impact the allocation in both countries. Arguments need to be put forth that can keep credibility between the nations. Perhaps the best example of how difficult some of these arguments often are rests in the question that I have to answer to the Chinese. As a former Lieutenant Commander in the Navy on active duty during Vietnam, I have been one of the staunchest defenders of American military power. I was a supporter of Ronald Reagan's belief that strength brings peace because of all that my father taught me. But my father taught me that you have strength for defensive purposes not necessarily offensive purposes. He taught me to be a Christian that believed God gave you free choice. And that meant you did not tell other people what they had to do, you only tried to set an example of what you did and explain why you did it. As he also noted, the problem with that philosophy is that you had to oppose evil early on occasion to limit its damage. That takes serious and careful thought, with balance to all consequences.

For many years I have been on the board of one of the major Washington think tanks that has opposed terrorism and believed in American military strength through support of military power and funding. That being said, all of my writings and all of the principles in which I believe have a core of the Golden Rule, do unto others as you would have them do unto you or as Confucius put forth, do not do to others that which you do not wish done to you. That makes it very difficult for me to argue to the Chinese that they do not have the right to build a military for defense after the last 200 years in which they have felt the impact of conquerors and invaders. This will be one of the most difficult issues but needs to be discussed. One man's defense system is another man's potential offensive weapon.

America has options to maintain its perception of security other than increasing arms as deemed necessary. However, history provides significant advice that while such concern about the external environment is significant, ultimately destinies depend on how well you focus upon your own domestic competitiveness and expansion. American's greatest security lies in its internal strength, which provides the base of military, economic, and all other strengths. Both China and the United States can let politics define them or let their own values define them. Politics will give us greater danger to our children. You cannot build trust if you are hypocritical. But if you do not have trust, you cannot assume risk to national security. It is a quandary that requires all sides to seek a solution because the resources need to be spent on economic growth. A better understanding of how people think could make a great deal of difference in the perceived threat people carry in the future. In America you have two groups that heavily support national defense. One of them includes people similar to me that believe it is the necessity of a nation to keep its values to have that strength for defense, and another group that often fits into what President Eisenhower called the "military industrialist complex" that normally needs a potential adversary in order to fund the parts of the budget that are their revenue. These are two often combined in support of military funding but in effect are separate groups as to the use of power. China, and indeed almost all countries, have similar groups and perspectives. Perhaps one of the best approaches would be for the militaries of each to interact on the common good of jointly defining what they deem to be a warrior's code and honor. Similar values and similar perspectives of China and the United States over the next 20 years could substantially impact how many of these issues are viewed. It is a potentially controversial issue, but the solution to it could allow both much more allocation of funds to needed economic reform and social needs.

The third great issue on the discussions would be culture and perhaps the most significant part of culture is America and China understanding they have a great number of things in common. The greatest difficulty at present is the perception in the United States that China is not value oriented because of many of the writings of American media that give the perception that China looks poorly upon Christianity and other religions.

While I have seen many books that take differing perspectives on this from an individualized basis, I can only note that my impressions of the present China do not necessarily fit with some of the historical perspectives. China celebrates every religious holiday including having Merry Christmas throughout the country as it has become much more commercialized. In fact I saw more "Merry Christmas" in China than I did in the United States where we have gone to Happy Holidays. I do not think the Chinese perceive the importance the West places on the concept of freedom of religion. Just as the West does not understand how the East looks upon courtesy and issues such as apologies. Religions can be perceived as a threat because they are belief systems, but they are of great benefit if those belief systems are value-oriented and the nation is seeking to head in that direction. When religion becomes political and becomes more of a political force, the perceptions of it change. The bottom line issue is values. Are the philosophic principles of the Golden Rule, the common good, humanity to others, and conscience being implemented? The only point that I can make is that when the School published *The Language of Conscience,* they had the option of changing the cover on which I had Christ, Aristotle, and Confucius who are the purveyors of conscience, but they maintained it. So I think the discussions in these areas will do a great amount of good to find that there are significant common grounds that may not be perceived due to many of the more sensational books and writings that often occur in the United States for a variety of purposes. The understanding of Western nonprofit philosophy and methods will help shape a more common individualized concept of compassion, and the focus on moral values being placed in Chinese schools will be significant. Morality precedes a better understanding of the values religion provides.

As noted, when the triangles are better understood the core values are set in the center, the "Harmonious Society" fits with the concept of personal dignity. The "Peaceful Rise" fits with three great concepts of interaction of economics, politics, and culture. The methods by which we need to analyze and see true positions fit with measurement and prioritization, analysis, and trends that help give perspective. The final set, the three elements of common cultures are worthy of study because they define the ultimate goals of how people view themselves and how a society wishes to operate. They can operate on the basis of very simple law that defines enforced rules, they can strengthen the culture beyond that law with morality and the Golden Rule and have that socially enforced by the power of the culture.

And they can choose ultimately to have what I feel is the best of cultures, that of compassion, where you do for others through service not expecting them to do anything for you because it is your concept of personal dignity to do so and that is how you elevate yourself.

One of the best ways that you can judge men is to see what they do for others and how they treat them when the others do not have the power to help them. It tells you the values at their core. These were the cultures that the Central Party School asked me to define.

In the context of those triangles I would suggest that I think it becomes very significant to understand why thought process matters in this endeavor. And to that end, I have included the introductory comments that I presented in September to the Central Party School that gave my impressions of why this type of thought was important in judging and building cultures. I then would like to include a summary of thoughts that come from three very different presentations. The first from a book that I would strongly recommend to anyone wanting to understand China entitled *Peaceful Rise—China's New Road To Development* published by the Central Party School Publishing House, CPC, and written by Mr. Zheng Bijian. Mr. Zheng brings a unique background to the authorship of his work. He was born in 1932 and educated at the Graduate School of the People's University of China. While he currently serves as Chairman of the China Reform and Open Forum, Dean of the Graduate School of the prestigious Chinese Academy of Humanity Science, Chairman of the Academic Affairs Committee of the Central Party School, and a Senior Advisor to the China International Strategic Study Association, his past work as Executive Vice President of the Central Party School of China and as Executive Vice President of the China Academy of Social Science give him a lifetime of perspective of China from its most critical intellectual think tanks and executive training vehicles. He has not only studied issues but has played a part in their conceptual development. So his thoughts reflect not just academic discipline, but practical experience as well.

Mr. Zheng has been one of the foremost scholars in the development of this thought. The second is a summary of the presentation on the "Harmonious Society" translation that was given to me at my request at the signing of the agreement with the Texas Lyceum. It was presented as the core concept for discussion at our seminar on ethics and is essential in helping grasp why culture is so important in China. It shows how the significance of the group and the individual fit together and how the School and the Communist Party think of these issues, bringing their unique concept of socialism forward. The third is comments from a book by Dr. Wang Weiguang, the Vice President of the Central Party School that helps coordinate the thought. The books should be available in America shortly and give a far more detailed and appropriate understanding of these concepts from a top down approach within China. To understand China they are the books that perhaps give the most direct insight to how the Chinese scholars view their future and view their options. Some of the key thoughts are as follows:

Understanding China's Peaceful Rise

The following selected and abridged comments are taken with the permission of the Central Party School, Publishing House, CPC, from *Peaceful Rise—China's New Road To Development* by Mr. Zheng Bijian (ISBN 7-5035-3347-1). Excerpted comments from different sections are consolidated as shown by . . . to allow an appropriate summary. While sections have been quoted exactly, some numerical distinctions such as second or third may not have a preceding "first" since the key points of various speeches were consolidated without repetition in order that the full breadth of the concept could be encapsulated.

From the Speech to the Bo'ao Forum for Asia for 2003

However, we are soberly aware that the current stage of well off society in China is incomprehensible, quite unbalanced and of a low level. There is still a long way to go before China can free itself of underdevelopment. China remains a developing country and one facing a host of developmental problems of immense proportions. . . .

There are two simple mathematical equations. One is multiplication; and the other is division. The multiplication is one no matter how small and negotiable an economic or social development problem seems to be, once multiplied by 1.3 billion, it becomes a big, or even a mega problem.

The division one is no matter how abundant China's financial and material resources are, once divided by 1.3 billion, the per capita level will be extremely low. . . .

This new strategic path is China's peaceful rise through independently building socialism with Chinese characteristics while participating in rather than detaching from economic globalization.

About this path, first I would like to emphasize that to take part in economic globalization instead of detaching from it in itself represents a major strategic choice of historic proportions.

As a large developing country with a population of over one billion, China cannot afford to and should not think of relying on the international community. Its only choice is to depend on its own strength. That is to say it is to fully and consciously depend on its own institutional innovation, tapping the growing domestic demand and market, translating its hefty household savings into investment, improving the timbre of its citizens, and addressing its resource shortage and environmental problems through advancement of science and technology. . . .

Third, I would like to stress that China's path is not only a path striving for rise, but also a path of adhering to peace and never seeking hegemony.

The experience of major powers heading for hegemony in contemporary history has once and again testified to the fact that the rise of a major power often results in drastic change in international configuration and world order and even triggers a world war. An important reason behind this is that if a major power followed the path of aggressive war and external expansion, such a path is doomed to failure.

In today's world, how can we follow such a totally erroneous path that is injurious to all, China included? China's only choice is to strive for rise, more importantly, strive for a peaceful rise. That is to say, we have to work for a peaceful international environment for the sake of our development and, at the same time, safeguard world peace through our development. In this respect, there are three most important strategic principles: First, we must unswervingly advance economic and political reforms centering on the promotion of socialist market economy and socialist democracy to insure institutional guarantee for our peaceful rise. Second, we must boldly draw on the fruits of human civilization while fostering the Chinese civilization to insure cultural support for China's peaceful rise. Third, we must carefully balance the interest of different sectors, securing a coordinated development between urban and rural areas, between different regions, between society and the economy, and between man and nature, to create a social environment for China's peaceful rise.

**From the Presentation: China's Development and
Her New Path to a Peaceful Rise,
30th Edition of "Intelligence 2004 on the World,
on Europe, on Italy"**

China's path to a peaceful rise that we talk about refers to China's path toward socialist modernization. It will span seventy years from the end of the 1970s, when the well-known Third Plenary Session of the 11th Central Committee of the Communist Party of China adopted the policy of reform and opening up. . . .

That is to say, we have been marching on this path for 25 years and another 45 years are ahead of us before China will rise as a basically modernized and medium level developed country. Third . . . an extremely important condition for China to acquire resources through peaceful means is an opening up to the rest of the world, namely to integrate itself into instead of detaching from economic globalization. As we open up, we also carry out all-around reforms and practice market economy at home. . . .

Fifth . . . as far as development is concerned, China has three big challenges. The first challenge is that of natural resources. Currently, China's exploitable per capita oil and natural gas reserves, per capita water resources, and per capita arable land are well below the world average. The second challenge is the environment. Serious environmental pollution, wasteful use of resources and low recycling rate are bottlenecks for sustainable economic development. The third challenge is the lack of coordination between economic and social development. These three major challenges amidst fast growth mean that China is facing both a golden period of development and a period of big challenge. . . .

Seventh, in striving for a peaceful international environment, in particular with regard to issues related to the international order and regimes, China turns its back on the old practices since the modern times of emerging powers breaking the existing international systems through wars and seeking hegemony through bloc confrontation. In short, China does not seek hegemony or predominance, nor will it tow the line of others. It advocates a new road toward a new international political and economic order through reforming and democratizing international relations. China maintains world peace for its own development, which in turn reinforces world peace. China is a constructive force, not a destructive one for peace and stability.

Eighth . . . "by a peaceful rise I am referring to peaceful development" which is one of the important Chinese characteristics that define China's socialism. China has made history in two aspects: first, as an emerging major country, China has transcended the old path of industrialization characterized by rivalry for resources and bloody wars and chosen to rise peacefully through sustainable development. This is unprecedented. Second, China has transcended the cold war mentality that rejects peaceful development and cooperation on the grounds of differences in social systems and ideologies. China is rising peacefully and building up socialism with Chinese characteristics independently through brave reforms and opening up, in other words, by economically integrating into the world, not self imposed isolation. This again is unprecedented.

China's Peaceful Role and The New Role of Asia
Keynote Speech at Bo'ao International Roundtable
(April 22, 2005)

We want to make our meeting an academic exchange for seeking consensus and wisdom, not a political meeting, still less a war of words. We say we seek consensus and wisdom because the peaceful rise of a country with 1.3–1.5 billion people requires more knowledge and experience than we posses now. So we need to learn from international experience and other human civilizations.

These three big challenges in the first half of the 21st century can, in my opinion, turn into three ways of transcendence, or three strategies, when the Chinese government formulates solutions: . . . The first big strategy is to transcend the old-style road of industrialization and continue on the road of the new-style industrialization. . . . The second big strategy is to transcend the traditional development approach that big powers took in modern history and the cold-war mentality marked by ideology, and to continue participating in economic globalization. . . . The third big strategy is to transcend outdated social management modes and continue to build a harmonious socialist society. . . .

Currently, government functions in China are gradually being transformed, and the mechanisms are being built to facilitate movement of people, rationally regulate interests, provide stable social security, and defuse crises with efficiency. Also, the level of scientific governance, democratic governance, and the rule of law are being enhanced and a harmonious society is gradually taking shape.

The three strategies for China during the first half of the 21st century can be summed up as maintaining peace and harmony—external peace and internal harmony. The two are linked with each other and compliment each other. The goal is to lead the 1.3–1.5 billion Chinese people in their arduous endeavor to build a better life and to make more contributions to humanity in response to risks and challenges and through win-win cooperation with other countries.

China's New Road of Peaceful Rise and
the China-U.S. Relations Speech
of the Brookings Institution
(June 15, 2005)

In my view, both now and in the future, China-U.S. relations have great opportunities and a broad horizon for parallel development. The first opportunity for China-U.S. relations comes from a high degree of convergence of national interest and mutual needs in the age of globalization.

The second opportunity for China-U.S. relations comes from the new security concept of "major – country cooperation" in response to increased non-traditional security threats.

The third opportunity for China-U.S. relations comes from their interests in settling regional hotspots and their joint efforts in maintaining international order.

The fourth opportunity for China-U.S. relations comes from the co-existence and interaction of our two civilizations. Globalization, in our view, is not a time of "clashes of civilizations." Rather it is a time of intercultural exchanges and intercivilization harmony. China-U.S. exchanges and cooperation and cultural resources and cultural industries have already become an important part of an emerging Chinese cultural market. A thorough understanding of the Chinese culture has increasingly become a crucial condition for the United States to live harmoniously with China. . . .

Tenth, I would also like to point out that we cannot just wait passively for opportunities to come to our doorsteps. We should roll up our sleeves to create them. Not long ago, a former American official said the following to me: "If China and the United States can work in closer cooperation, then the 21st century will be a great century. But if the relationship moves back, the 21st century will be a very bad one for the two countries and the world." I cannot agree with him more. It takes two hands to make a clap, so fresh headway in China-U.S. relations calls for common efforts by both governments. Let me suggest to my American friends here, when you look at China's rise and the China-U.S. relations, you may perhaps need to rise above three things: the first is the cold war thinking, which is along the ideological lines that decides one's position according to social systems. When one subscribes to such thinking, he is very likely to make a strategic misjudgment about the Chinese-style socialism and the Chinese Communist Party. The second is the sense of cultural superiority that uses one's own values as the yardstick of right and wrong. Today's world, after all, is already in a brand new age with multiple civilizations living side-by-side and different cultures interacting productively. The third thing that one should rise above is the traditional theory that the emerging power is bound to challenge the existing dominant power because it cannot explain China's peaceful rise and the rising China being a staunch force for world peace.

I think the writings of Mr. Zheng Bijian are particularly significant in the points being noted because they give a perspective from the highest level of a scholar looking at the highest of levels of government. But even though these are among the most thoughtful comments I have read on international relations with China, one of the driving forces will inevitably be the factor of how successfully the Chinese leadership is able to build a harmonious society to keep the stability and allow for such a "Peaceful Rise."

Domestically, China's leadership appreciates the fact that values are a cornerstone of their future. President Hu Jintao presented a moral code that was reemphasized in his March 2006 speech to China's ruling body. It is consistent with their concerns involving fighting corruption and lessening the income disparity within the country, particularly in the rural versus urban inequalities and frictions. Basically, his message was a set of guidelines:

Love, do not harm the motherland.
Serve, do not disserve the people.
Uphold science, do not be unenlightened.
Work hard.
Be unified and help each other, do not take advantage of others.
Be honest and trustworthy, not seeking profit at the
expense of your values.
Be disciplined and law abiding rather than chaotic and lawless.
Know plain living and hard struggle, do not wallow in luxuries
and pleasures.

This is perhaps the core of the "Harmonious Society" and not dissimilar to the comments of Abraham Lincoln noted earlier that form the core of Enlightened Conservatism. But the question is not so much whether it is the correct vision, but how can it be implemented in an environment dominated by powerful economic forces and political change. While there was some criticism that these thoughts were of an earlier age of simplicity, what we have seen, and what I think the comments that follow demonstrate is that President Hu's comments are very much futuristic. They are visionary as to the ultimate problems that all societies will face. Defining them well is the critical issue to solving them.

I had not read "Peaceful Rise" or heard President Hu's comments in September of 2005 when I was presented the following speech at the discussion on "Ethics and the Harmonious Society" at the School. The thought closely parallels his observations and the importance he gives to intercultural exchanges and inter-civilization harmony. The purpose of our discussions at the School were aimed at the methods to best build a bridge to accomplish these goals and this required understanding both cultures and goals of the cultures. So from the international perspective of "Peaceful Rise," it may be worthwhile to discuss the "Harmonious Society" as a case study of the possible harmonizing by common values then move to the triangles of Enlightened Conservatism as the process of convergence. Why the three concepts fit together is probably best expressed by an old Chinese proverb that combines conscience and compassion, which to me are the light and truth of the soul to nations and the world:

> *If there is light in the soul,*
> *There will be beauty in the person,*
> *If there is beauty in the person,*
> *There will be harmony in the house,*
> *If there is harmony in the house,*
> *There will be order in the nation,*
> *If there is order in the nation,*
> *There will be peace in the world.*

The following is the presentation by Dr. Jia Jianfang, Professor at the Social Development Institute of the Party School of the CPS Central Committee. I have included it in full because it gives not only the perspective of the discussion that set the stage for the Lyceum Collaboration but also does a superb job of helping understand the importance of Harmony in Chinese culture. This serves as the domestic underpinning of the concept of Peaceful Rise and gives a great insight to why morality and income balance are so key to Chinese strategy. Many in the West focus on individual items in judging China, but China is far more complex. The issue to understanding it is in our understanding of the method by which the conceptual thought of organization of the parts develops. The Harmonious Society is that organizing principal that pulls the rest into order. It is stability. The Chinese recognize that unity is the ultimate power. It is in reality "the Way" of Sun-tzu. It deals with obligations and looks to a new socialism with Chinese characteristics realizing that China is in primary stage for this process. The presentation is important not just for what it says, but also how it helps understand the process of thought. It emphasizes the equality of people, but it understands the driving force. The similarity to my presentation that I gave that day is remarkable. The same three types of power, the focus on human dignity, the unification of society on conscience, and the power of culture stand out beyond differences in economic and political theory. Neither group of presenters at the seminar had seen the other's presentation. They had only seen the areas of common discussion desired. Her speech has been updated to recent events for possible use in other presentations.

Ethical Values for China to Build a Harmonious Society
Presented by Jia Jianfang
Professor of Social Development Institute of the
Party School of the CPC Central Committee

Social harmony is a long-established ideal of humankind in pursuit of a better society. In a sense, the history of human society is one for all people to pursue a society with harmony. Western countries have rich thoughts for building a harmonious society, among which Karl Marx and Frederick Engel's doctrine for social harmony is a highlighted representative. Nevertheless, Chinese traditional culture has also witnessed various doctrines on social harmony that are profound, deep-rooted and have a far-reaching influence. In the process of building socialism with Chinese characteristics, the Communist Party of China (CPC) and the Chinese government clearly put forth the blueprint for building a harmonious socialist society. On the one hand, this ideal is a continuation of past doctrines in human history and carries forward ancient Chinese sages' ideas about social harmony. On the other hand, it not only symbolizes an essential requirement for building a new socialist society that has been expounded by Marxists in the past, but it also reflects a real demand for China's present economic and social development. Building a harmonious socialist society is of great significance both to the goal of comprehensive, coordinated, and sustainable development of the economy, society, and humanity in China, as well as to all Chinese people and the CPC's governance.

Social harmony can be described as a state in which each subsystem and different factors among the whole social system are interdependent, coordinated, harmonized and interactive. A harmonious socialist society, which China is pursuing now is featured with a focus on six areas: democracy and the rule of law, equity and justness, honesty and care for others, social vitality, stability and order, and harmony between man and nature. The concept consists of three aspects as follows.

Firstly, it stresses a harmony among people or interpersonal harmony, which calls for a harmony in three aspects: a harmony among individuals, between individuals and a public group, and among different social groups. The basis and precondition for a harmony of interpersonal relations is a harmony of an individual itself, which is physically and mentally healthy, i.e., a healthy body, a peaceful mind, a sound personality full of vigor and spirit, a rich emotion, etc. A harmony among individuals refers to a state of harmony among family members and neighbors, as well as between the individual and others in society. A harmony among different social groups aims at a state of harmony among different social strata, interest groups, ethnic groups, and between public servants and citizens, etc. An individual is a mix of his social relations, as well as a subject for every society. Interpersonal harmony is a key and core to social harmony. To harmonize interpersonal relations is an essential task for building a harmonious socialist society. Now China is trying to foster every citizen with virtues such as self-respect, self-dependence, self-improvement and self-love, and advocating mutual respect, equality and mutual benefit, honesty and friendship, mutual help, and brotherly harmony among people. When advocating harmony of interpersonal relations, Chinese uphold a principle that is equality for every individual, mutual benefit among people and a harmony without uniformity.

Secondly, it focuses on a harmony between individual and community (or society), which refers to an interactive, inter-adaptable and mutually promotive state between individual and social organizations or institutions. In other words, economy, politics, ideology, and culture are all institutionalized and orderly. Every individual's rights and interests are protected by law, and the society should provide individuals with more equal conditions and opportunities for their survival and development. Every individual must abide by laws, institutions, regulations and ethic norms, and must undertake his due responsibility and duties. Every individual should perform his own functions, work according to his own ability, do his duty and play his proper role. The whole society is stable and orderly, and in which every person is safe and sound, various social relations are harmonized, and each citizen has a high spirit and peaceful mood and can enjoy a happy life. At present, in order to achieve a harmonious state in society, a lot of efforts are to be made as follows. Expand China's economy to make the "cake" larger to be enjoyed by a larger population. Appropriately adjust income distribution to narrow the gap between the rich and the poor and give greater priority to social equity. Prosper in social undertakings to meet the people's diverse and increasing demands. Make every effort to expand employment. Make innovation in government management to ensure social security and effective performance. Strengthen law enforcement and upgrade social morals to maintain social order and security. Invigorate social elements to carry out a sustainable development.

Thirdly, it emphasizes a harmony between man and nature, i.e., co-existence between humankind and environment. Nature provides surviving surroundings and materials for man's survival and development. In terms of environment, human beings must value natural laws, properly utilize natural resources, and cherish environment. Because China is undergoing industrialization and urbanization, the pattern of economic growth with high investment, excessive waste of energy, and serious pollution has not been changed. The pressure from resources, environment degradation, and a large population becomes more serious, which is a bottleneck for further economic growth. So China pays particular attention to energy and resource conservation and environmental protection and has laid out tasks, policies, and measures for building a resource-conserving society and developing a circular economy.

In sum, a harmony among individuals, between the individual and community, between man and nature, among man, society and nature is a dynamic social state. To achieve a whole harmony is our ultimate goal and a long-term aim. This state can only be obtained on the basis of reality in today's China just as a beautiful flower can only be grown on suitable land. China's aim at building a harmonious socialist society can only be achieved based on its reality of economy, politics, and culture. So improving democracy and rule by law is an important guarantee for China to build a harmonious society. Economically, advanced material and technological bases and an improved modern economic system is a basic necessity for building a harmonious society. So it is imperative for us to uplift our productivity and enrich our material wealth. Meanwhile, it is necessary to gradually improve the basic economic system, with public ownership playing a dominant role and diverse forms of ownership developing side by side. It is also necessary to keep improving the system under which distribution according to work is dominant and a variety of modes of distribution coexist. Then combine distribution according to work with distribution according to production factors (such as labor, capital, technology, managerial expertise), and go on improving the socialist market economy system and macroeconomic control. A national scientific and popular culture geared to the needs of modernization of the world and of the future with Marxism as our guidelines is the soul for building a harmonious society. The CPC and Chinese government will continue to arm people with scientific theory, provide them with correct media guidance, imbue them with lofty ideals, and inspire them with excellent works of literature and art, to guide people in fostering a common ideal for socialism with Chinese characteristics, correct world outlook, views on life and values and to unceasingly upgrade the ideological and ethical standards, as well as the scientific and cultural qualities of the entire people. Notable progress has been registered in socialist economy, politics and culture, and Chinese characteristics, which have created favorable and basic conditions for building a harmonious society. However, China is still in a primary stage of socialism. With the rapid change and development in all aspects, the conditions and advantages for building a harmonious society will be better and better, so Chinese society will become more and more harmonious. China will take a long way to build a new harmonious society.

From the above discussion, cultural progress is an important component for building a harmonious society in China. Ethical values in cultural progress play a particularly important role in building a harmonious society because they can provide a common ideal, ethic norms, strong motivation, intellectual support, and a stable and orderly social environment for building a harmonious society.

Building a harmonious society calls for upgrading people's humanity, quality, and ideological and ethical standards. In other words, it demands to cherish man's value and safeguard his dignity. It also calls for reshaping a citizen's character, sentiments, spirit, and mind. It is necessary to enhance the cohesion of our society by means of ethical values. Other countries in the world have piled up many successful experiences and lessons in this respect. E.g., Singapore attached great importance to values construction based on ethical education on its citizens. This step helped Singapore become a good example of harmonious community.

China is an origin and example of oriental ethics. Since 1949 China carried forward the fine national traditions to promote socialist spiritual civilization and cultural progress so as to greatly upgrade Chinese ethical, scientific, and cultural standards. In the course of reform and opening-up and modernization, the values of Chinese people have been substantially transformed. Among them, the positive ones have created favorable conditions for building a harmonious society, while there also are some negative ones. Generally speaking, before reform and opening to the outside world, China was a comparatively enclosed and stable society in which people's ideas were pure, intact, and uniform, and in a slow change. The past Chinese values were dangerously distorted in the period of "Grand Cultural Revolution"(1966-1976). Since 1978, people tend to follow values that are more diverse-directed, positive, and pragmatic. If we examine the changes in people's values from such three pair relations as between individuals and society, between individual and collective, between personal interest and public interest, three features are highlighted as follows. First, subject consciousness has been strengthened. Second, the awareness of material interest has been emphasized. Third, values direction has been diversified. Great changes have also taken place in ethical values and social morals. Among them there are some positive sides just as people's ethical values more suited to social progress and their own lives. Both virtues and interest are emphasized and people follow a more civilized, rational, and healthy life style.

At the same time, some negative elements in people's ethical values come into being. It is so-called moral degeneration. It is evident that people are in more pursuit of material wealth and dishonesty. Some people forsake their humanity, dignity, and conscience for personal gains. Fetishism and dishonesty can easily be found in all social fields and all walks of life. In political life, some public servants are after money by use of their power, and some boost and exaggerate their performance in reports. Such conduct leads to corruption in government administration and harms the social morals. In the economic field, some companies and businessmen harm others to benefit themselves and care solely for profit. Some companies and businessmen smuggle or produce and sell fake commodities. In the cultural field in the past, the intellectuals were only concerned about man and life's value and ultimate human care. But now some intellectuals are more concerned about real profit, they seek quick success and instant benefits. Profit-seeking mentality, even cheating or unhealthy tricking ways have spread into social life and individual conduct. In order to pursue money or personal gain, some people attain their ends by hook or by crook such as stealing, robbery, prostitution, drug abuse, and defraud. For the sake of personal gain, some people destroy natural vegetation at the cost of polluting environment, deforest and overly explore natural resources, kill rare animals and drain off waste water, gases, and materials at random.

In building a harmonious society, it is necessary to create a harmony in terms of the individual, interpersonal relations, various social relations, and the relationship between man and nature. Therefore, in 2004 the Central Committee of the CPC issued "The Outline of the Plan for Upgrading the Ethical Standards of the Entire People" within which lay emphasis on guiding the whole people in fostering a common ideal for socialism with Chinese characteristics, correct world outlook, views on life and values advocating such basic ethical norms as patriotism, abiding by laws, good virtues, honesty, solidarity, friendliness, diligence, dependence, and devotion to one's work. The Chinese government tries to upgrade a citizen's morals to promote an all-round development of man and aims at cultivating citizens from generation to generation who have lofty ideals, moral integrity, a better education, and a good sense of discipline. In March 2006, Hu Jintao, the general secretary of the CPC Central Committee, clearly pointed that "socialist concept of honor and disgrace" should be promoted to the cadres, masses, and especially young people. Detailing the "advanced socialist culture," President Hu gave a list of do's and don'ts: Love, do not harm the motherland. Serve, don't disserve the people. Uphold science, don't be ignorant and unenlightened. Work hard, don't be lazy and hate work. Be united and help each other; don't gain benefits at the expense of others. Be honest and trustworthy, not profit-mongering at the expense of your values. Be disciplined and law-abiding instead of chaotic and lawless. Know plain living and hard struggle; do not wallow in luxuries and pleasures.

Chinese ethical thoughts enjoy a long-standing and well-established history. To shape present ethics, it is necessary to carry forward the fine Chinese traditional virtues that have been universally accepted during several thousand years' history, to keep up the fine tradition that has been formed in the long revolution and construction by our party leading its people to willingly draw on some successful experiences and advanced culture which every country has made. The progress of citizen's ethical education should represent fine traditions but also take on the characteristics of the times, which are full vigor and vitality.

Chinese civilization and other civilizations co-exist in the world. Therefore, it is necessary for China to draw on the cultural outcomes, which have been produced by other civilizations. Mr. Tieman H. Dippel, Jr., a wise man in Texas, the U.S., wrote a book, *The Language of Conscience*, which gives me a lot and arouses me to think over some in-depth questions. He argued that in terms of social ethics and values, there is some common sense which is basic ethical value based on the fruits of all humankind civilizations. As a bind to maintain the world unity, these basic ethical values and norms are an important bridge through which different countries and peoples can communicate among themselves. He pointed out that cultural ethics will be a key word in the future, especially in the context of increasing world population pressure. Although religious beliefs differ, the ideal ethical norms in different communities resemble, and they are common standards for our mutual understanding and cooperation. He summed up his own life experiences in the book where a lot of exciting and provoking life mottos can be found. He pointed out a basic idea that man's responsibility, obligation, wisdom, loyalty, and conscience are more important than money, material wealth, and power. He believes that the issue of credibility is inevitable in the era of the Internet. That is why it is a crucial matter. The second period of the information era will be an era of wisdom. Wisdom includes not only knowledge but also experience and credibility. It is necessary to begin with fostering citizen's basic ethical values so as to upgrade credibility of the whole society. He stressed that improving education and shaping sound cultural values is conducive to expand public interests so as to awake the public conscience. He attached great importance to cultivate the new generation of leaders' moral quality. He thought that a good leader, at least must have some basic ethical standards and common values shared by the public. In other words, a good leader at first should be a good man. Of course, the so-called good leaders, especially those great men, should have not only far sight but also wisdom that is not shared by common men. At the same time they must be loyal. The key is how leaders exercise their powers, especially what they exercise powers for. To a further extent, do they exercise their powers for public interest or for their personal gains? This question can judge whether a leader is qualified with some basic virtues. Mr. Dippel quoted a saying that "you are respected because of your powers, but you are admired because of your good motivation when using those powers." Mr. Dippel's ideas are like Chinese ideas from the ancient time to now. Of course, there are a lot of human civilizations that we should learn in shaping our own ethical values. But from Mr. Dippel's *The Language of Conscience*, we can see the importance and possibilities of mutual exchange between different civilizations.

In shaping Chinese ethical values, except for the resources of ethics and guidelines, the more important thing is to find an effective way that is suitable to shape the ethical values of all strata and groups in the future. To the end we have been making efforts.

Introductory Comments of Tieman H. Dippel, Jr.
Presented at the Seminar on
Developing Leadership for a Culture of Service and Integrity
At the Central Party School
Beijing, China
September 6, 2005

My Friends,

Our group today comes from different countries and different cultures, but we have in common the goal that we discussed almost a year ago today—finding cultural bridges based on morality, ethics, and common cultural values. Your suggestion has been that we focus our seminar today on conscience and integrity and review the global trends not just in these areas, but the critical areas of conscience, education, and leadership creation—or more importantly, the creation of catalysts of these areas. You suggested focus on a program for understanding the issues strategically in order that program implementation for such a catalyst to build conscience and value-based leadership can be leveraged. To judge the success of the policy, you have to look at measurement, the creation of standards, and how to enhance the public awareness. These are logical and strategic approaches at a critical time. I would suggest that conscience is best analyzed as a cultural issue, rather than an economic or political one. Ethics is a cultural power. I have taken your suggestions and put them in the context of our past discussion, the work that I have done this past year and the organizations that accompany me, to build a model of discussion not just on these issues, but how East and West can address them together. What you measure is what you value, and what you value is enhanced by measurement. So the culture we value and measure helps us in the end to structure our discussion and thought. A year ago the Party School was kind enough to announce its publication of my book, *The Language of Conscience*. In the interim the Party School sent a delegation to watch and understand the Texas Lyceum through its 25th Anniversary Celebration. As an organization devoted not only to leadership, but also to the stewardship of the values of Texas, the Lyceum has through that period helped advance public policy for the common good and has served as a cultural bridge to allow the training of leaders of very different persuasions. It has included both Democrats and Republicans, conservatives and liberals, and also leaders of social, economic, ethnic, and racial groups. The Lyceum was the core case study in *The Language of Conscience.* Another case study was the work of the Integrity Task Force of FIDIC, the International Organization of Consulting Engineers, which highlighted their efforts to promote global integrity within commerce. They join us today for our discussions.

An additional group, the Ethics Officer Association, which represents many of the Fortune 500 ethics officers, was unfortunately not able to join us because of a rescheduling of a meeting from Singapore to London, but they expressed their gratitude in being included in an effort that seeks a common goal of a global culture of ethics.

In the past year, I have taken many of the suggestions and observations that were made at the presentation here a year ago. I have looked more closely at the aspects of Chinese history that were suggested to me, and I have tried to apply the challenges that I see in America and globally to outline a thoughtful discussion of how to approach a very complicated and difficult subject.

Much of this background and research is contained in a new book, *Instilling Values in Transcending Generations: Bringing Harmony to Cultures Through the Power of Conscience* that was presented conceptually to your Press as its potential first publisher at the event Saturday evening hosting many of our friends from the Beijing Book Festival.

I think to begin our discussions, what would be helpful would be a summary in graphic form of the method of analysis and thought that we might consider using to compare cultures for these common goals. From a perspective of conscience we need to understand the world presently or as you aptly described "Global Trends."

One of the thoughts predominant through much of Europe and the West is multiculturalism and the concept of diversity by which individuals that are not able to achieve rights on their own band together to have common rights and values appreciated. Multiculturalism in the West takes the position that cultures should be equally valued and toleration very fully extended. These are the old cultural values that exist and are very strong because they are heritage taught to children. On the other side technology and commercialization have made a global world that pulls everyone closer together. But here you have a conflict that change, which results from technology and economic globalization, promotes the increasing division into cultures with differing values within societies. Rather than blending people together, the cultural values put them into smaller groups. This will become one of the challenging issues for all nations, and I would propose that culture is critical because it is the blending power. In economics we have self-interest. In politics we have nationalism. So it is only in common cultural appreciation of values that we are able to build the bridges that allow us to more smoothly navigate the frictions of the other two great powers of economics and politics. The critical need is how to blend those supporting cultures. We require common perspective if we are to meet a common goal.

To come to a common perspective, we must find a method of thought that allows us a common ground. We should not tell each other what to believe. But we need to show respect for each other's beliefs, and we need to be able to compare cultures and the values within cultures to bring out the best in each of us. That is the nature of the advancement of civilization, the secret by which the Chinese culture was able to overcome all invaders over thousands of years of history. It is simply more difficult in modern times because we face challenges of speed in change that have never before been understood. Therefore, I suggest that we begin with the concept of Rene' Descartes, the French thinker many consider the father of modern philosophy. He used the equivalent of a scientific method as he thought through the use of reason. He conceptualized ideas and believed that there were two kinds of true ideas. These ideas were clear ideas that could be distinguished from others and distinct ideas that had parts that could be distinguished from each other. The purpose of a philosopher was to analyze these complex ideas and translate them into simple ones. He distinguished between the ideas of the mind and ideas that came from worldly experience that he felt could not be as clearly defined. In my earlier books I used the term enlightened conservatism to reflect these concepts as they apply to strategic forces and driving powers. In enlightenment we look to change as driven by technology and globalization in friction with the conservatism of existing economic structure and values. Enlightenment is not a political term as much as it is a cultural term that focuses directly on stability within a culture.

The world has operated in cycles of politics (the '50s and '60s with Kennedy/Johnson, Kruschev/Brezhnev, and Chairman Mao) that evolved into the era of the power of economics (Presidents Reagan, Thatcher, Gorbachev, and Chairman Deng). This change from politics to economics came because technology made economics move so quickly that the individualized decisions of markets were very necessary. Understanding the power of markets was helped greatly by Milton Friedman's work, *Free to Choose,* and the thoughts presented by many universities—the University of Chicago was particularly important. We are now at the transition of that era of economics where the power of culture is beginning to emerge significantly as we see the concept of corruption and its cousin, political terrorism, emerge on a global scale. The next quarter century will be increasingly dominated by the frictions within societies created by enlightenment or change against existing structure or cultural values. The individual person's collective concept of his level of personal dignity will balance that stability within each society. How he perceives his life, and the method by which he values his life, will determine whether that society, be it in the East or in the West, has stability.

One of the best observers of power was Niccolo Machiavelli in his works including *The Prince*. When I was in Florence years ago, I looked to buying books that could explain to me how Machiavelli wrote *The Prince*. He did so to incur favor with the Medici family that dominated the power of Florence for hundreds of years and had jailed Machiavelli. Much of the source of their power apparently was an observation by one of the founders of the dynasty that the people by their action or their inaction determined the course of the events of the powerful. So the concept of personal dignity, which is within each individual of each culture, will have an increasing amount to do with not only how stable cultures are, but also how they interact with other cultures. While many feel there will be a future battle of cultures, in reality it will ultimately be a cultural battle between the conscience of integrity and honor and the convenience of self-interest and personal benefit. The interaction of cultures is dependent upon the nature of the culture. Lao-tzu said wisdom is knowing others, but enlightenment is knowing self. That is why enlightened conservatism begins with a choice of values.

Multiculturalism has been a way that these different values were maintained, but they are now becoming frictions within societies because they are used in political divisions often to bring gridlock. While multiculturalism and diversity have great value, the question is how you pull the separate cultures back together once they have been divided by different values. This rests in the concept of character. Martin Luther King, Jr., and Gandhi gave significant examples of how you unify people from different cultures based on what they value. Character and morality are values that all cultures ought to have. They should be the bridge and the training blocks of leadership. Absolute toleration would make the values of Hitler or Stalin equal to the values of Jefferson and Lincoln. Basic values such as the common good, the Golden Rule, and the rule of law are necessary for the dignity of man. They may be defined differently in different cultures but developing them, explaining them, and putting them in place is what gives stability not only to individual cultures but also to nations, and eventually to a global world. The culture gives you the law, not the law the culture.

Also the values that are taught to children matter directly as generations mature. So looking at how they are taught and what values they perceive sets the stage for their future. How you think is what you think, and it is a critical point that requires not ideology but value-based thought.

For our discussions today, I would like to suggest your consideration of why these particular concepts that I included in *The Language of Conscience* fit well into a matrix that was designed largely in conjunction with discussions that all of us have had in the past.

A Discussion of the Triangles of Enlightened Conservatism

Some have called these triangles the Rosetta Stone of Cultures because they deal with comparisons of forces, powers, and influences combined with analytics and measurement of cultures. They not only look to the basic rules of law as established by the culture, but the obligations of conscience that go beyond those basic rules (the Golden Rule) and eventually move to the compassion of conscience beyond obligation. The economic system often determines a significant amount of how the society operates, which in turn determines the intellectual basis or political methods of government.

Within the triangles, the first decision needs to automatically be one of character and honor. Each individual, and cumulatively the society, has a choice to make between conscience and convenience. That is an ongoing friction within each person and within the society. There is no perfection, and the very nature of self interest in economics and the ambition of politics in all fields push toward convenience. The cultural values, or the ethics of the society, are a power in their own right because they determine whether an individual stands alone through his convenience or unifies and has the support of others toward a common end. Conscience and convenience both have tools of power, but set the stage on an individual basis between the type of friends you will have, the environment in which you will work, and your assessment of your level of personal dignity.

Beyond those frictions you have the friction of enlightenment against established cultural structure or values that reflect entrenched economics and political interests. Enlightenment is often in the form of technology, education, and opportunity, which are normally good. Enlightenment can also be the provision of new approaches of convenience that simply enhance opportunities for convenience. All that is new is not necessarily positive.

The existing cultural structure normally involves not only the cultural values established over long periods of time, but also the entrenched structural economics and politics that have created them. The values represent much of the wisdom gained in the past, but enlightenment can also contain both positive and negative elements that may be a hindrance to adaptability and critical change. These two frictions are balanced within society by the concept of personal dignity of the individual. This includes not only his self interest, his natural human desire to be correct in his perspectives, but most importantly how he views his life and its purpose. How important to him is family? How important is honor? And, most importantly of all, by what method does he judge his level of dignity? Whether he values character above materialism has a tremendous effect on how he looks at the rest of the world and how stable the society that includes him will be. And as I mentioned earlier, how men think often determines what men think. Peter Drucker did much to define modern management by emphasizing the importance of "knowledge workers." He based his observations not on physical structures or from a command and control philosophy but instead on providing insight to morale and incentive. Modern management is competitive, so focus on the workers perspective is critical to success. The same is true of society as a whole as technology challenges existing structure. While man is perhaps one million years old, we have only had civilization perhaps 7,000 to 8,000 years. But in the last 250 years of the Industrial Revolution we have moved at great speeds that will accelerate knowledge and pressures. We need the wisdom to handle the knowledge.

The next series of triangles are the three great powers, which impact this personal dignity. Economics is a driving force because of the very nature of life and an individual's self-interest. Politics determines much of his environment by implementing the rules of the society. It includes all rules from the military to the judiciary to the enforcement of discipline within societies. And culture, which is often put forth by the media and thereby a major component of it, is a power in its own right. Each of these powers interacts and is different within various societies because they balance out other forces. When vacuums are created, they are filled and for each action there is normally a reaction. Understanding each of these is particularly important in understanding the other.

The next level of triangles to a great extent takes three methods of approach to viewing the problem philosophically. The first is analysis that is understood in depth that breaks the ideas into simpler parts. The next issue has to be trends because demographics and recognition of future impact are absolutely essential. The final issue, measurement, tells you what you value and helps prioritize levels of importance for knowledge and action.

For public policy, generational analysis and the impact on future decisions is extremely important to be considered currently. In the East, patience is considered a virtue and changes are looked at in terms of generations. In the West, that is not the case. More immediate focus is given to the short-term. There are benefits and detriments to both approaches, and they need to be understood in the consideration of policy.

The final set of triangles is measurement criteria I would suggest for societies based upon a concept of conscience and the three cultures that can measure it. The first is a culture entitled "Discipline Within Society." It is in effect the concept of the rule of law. Law does not make the culture, but the culture inevitably, by its codification, makes the law. So the quality of the law, and how it is enforced as the rule of law, is a beginning component by which you judge economics, politics, and culture and understand the impacts of change in both directions. It is the least of obligations owed by men to each other. These are the basic rules of the culture and society as they are put forth by the acceptance of the collective levels of personal dignity.

The next culture to be evaluated is the "Culture of Ethics" within the society. The Golden Rule emphasizes that you should do unto others, as you would have them do unto you. The basic codification of law is the minimal level by which we should operate. The moral obligations of conscience—to do more for others because we expect more from others—defines this culture. It is a culture of obligation from conscience and an obligation to society as a whole by one's practice of courtesy, toleration, honor, integrity, and actions.

The final culture is a "Culture of Service," which is often judged by the nonprofit structural development of a society. In nonprofit institutions people collectively come together to help others and give to them through philanthropy. Recognition beyond obligation of the compassion component of conscience drives people to do more than mere obligation, and in doing so, use the power of culture to bring reciprocity out of a sense of honor. This culture of service has to be developed. It is an individual choice, not an obligation to another. This is the highest level of giving, and the greatest reward is the enlightenment and enhancement of one's personal dignity. When it is most strengthened, it affects the economics within the triangles because there is less need for government to help or to settle differences. It defines the nature of the cultural values because it builds a peer pressure to assist others and to accept responsibility. It changes the nature of the politics because the culture increasingly values conscience and judges leadership upon the morality and integrity of the leaders.

The "Culture of Service" (or of Compassion) bridges the triangles to the higher level of conscience of religions, and addresses how each man sees his perspective of a Creator of nature and existence. The great religions focus on compassion for the poor, the weak, and the helpless. In Christianity, for example, Christ notes in Mark 9:35 "If anyone desires to be first, he must be last of all, and servant of all." Much of his philosophy is that you will be judged by how you treated others in need—did you feed them and did you clothe them? It is true for men or nations. It is the essence of the compassions beyond morality's obligations that become the concept of broad love. Islam has great focus on the poor, as do the basics of most religious philosophies that simply refine this basic concept of compassion. To me it was written best by Rambam, a Jewish philosopher and doctor, who was a physician and friend of Saladin. His Eight Levels of Charity held that the least of charity was that which was given with lack of sincerity and more in obligation. The highest was giving opportunity sincerely to another. In the East there is a similar thought in the concept that teaching a man to fish is better than simply giving him a fish. That is why the "Culture of Ethics," or moral obligations between men through the Golden Rule, moves to a higher level of understanding in a culture of service from compassion. It moves higher because a man's internal search for his individual dignity and his realization that it comes most from the strength of looking beyond self to the desire to help others through his free will.

In understanding this highest culture you also validate the other components of the triangles. To reach the culture you must encourage individual responsibility and conscience. Once the culture is achieved it then helps maintain political order and stability as well as aid growth of commerce. In economics free markets require that integrity exist for their best performance by competition. This gives the ultimate opportunity to achieve in the tradition of Rambam and is necessary for the ultimate personal dignity. Because of the nature of the world, there will never be perfection and the parts will always have frictions, but the power of culture and ideas that are its force help seek harmony and balance. The more that is done by each generation to move the world to the appreciation of this conscience, the more it will be attained. Some may do it in the name of religion, others in the name of philosophy, and others because it is not only right but the source of great power. But each, in his own way, sees harmony in society through the lens of conscience as opposed to convenience and will ultimately realize that beyond obligation to the group of fellow men, compassion is the ultimate goal. However, it also is seen that you can never lose sight of the fact that obligation and the nature of the power of the building blocks of society are critical to the creation and maintenance of this culture of service and compassion. It does not arise as a Utopia on its own, but requires that we shape the building blocks that are the support of its pyramid.

Such is the logic and purpose of the triangles. They help you see your ultimate goal of compassion, but also help you understand that compassion does not exist alone but is a final product of forces. You must both engineer back from the goal, and at the same time build back from the bottom. The goal of the triangles is to give a perspective from the top down as well as the bottom up so policies and logic can be coordinated.

In *Instilling Values in Transcending Generations*, I am trying to take many of these ideas and define them from the perspective of different civilizations. The book includes the quotations of many leaders of China and of the Western world throughout history to show the power of culture in both the East and West to affect civilization.

The judgment of the importance of each of these different component parts may differ, depending upon the reader or the thinker, even getting different final conclusions. But what this set of triangles graphically does is to give a set of groupings of the forces and powers of natural law for discussion purposes. Thus we can organize thought, and by doing so, whether we seek organizations with specialties in these areas or books to discuss them, we keep our perspective as to how parts fit together. This is a rifle to which the specialty of organization is needed, an effective bullet as opposed to a shotgun blast where there are many pellets in many directions producing mainly noise in the perspective of the long term. We keep an effective focus as we develop and specialize thoughts adding other organizations.

The seminar today is one that deals with cultures of service and ethics and how you build leadership in those areas. Leadership is the expertise of the Texas Lyceum. Similarly the Central Party School is the major leadership training organization at many levels for China. Both understand the power of culture.

It is important today, for all of us to learn from each other so that we better understand how our two cultures (and with Dr. Ochoa's inclusion and the International Consulting Engineers, other cultures such as Latin and South America) view many of these component parts. It is my hope that these triangles assist us in the depth of our thought since the differences in language always impose burdens. It is but a simple way to consolidate a great amount of information. The reality of life is that forces and powers shape destinies. The truth of life is that ideas ultimately are the source of those forces and powers. The most critical observation of those ideas is that they both shape and are shaped by the culture that decides how they are valued in life. The ultimate observation is the beginning one of Descartes that there is a difference between the clear thoughts of the mind and the more complex concepts of reality. The integrity, honor, and morality we seek are concepts of the mind. The forces, powers, and influences with which we must work are the realties. This is the best combination that I could find of blending the two. But in doing so, as I think you will find in *Instilling Values in Transcending Generations,* there is much that our cultures have in common on which values can be built. And most important of all, we are attempting to develop a language of conscience by which it can be discussed.

You have asked for suggestions as the next step where we can work together. I think it is in the formation of a catalytic set of thoughts that we all better define and eventually the creation of centers of such thought within each culture. Enlightenment is knowing ourselves, and this process lets us discover how to bring out the best in ourselves, and attract those who feel similarly. Courses in such a perspective of ethics should be developed, not the contained, technical ones now taught, but ones that show the power of morality and its value to civilization. There could be no greater catalyst than this School, which has so much influence on China, and China will so impact the world in the future. All of us are insignificant in the scope of time, but great ideas, carried forth by great cultures, are the destiny and salvation of mankind. If today we can but plant a seed to be developed, it should be in the fact that how you think determines what you think. And the future of the world needs thought to be from conscience. But the reality of the world requires us to place that conscience with the support of the concepts of power because of its morality. That requires an educational approach that shows its value, but also can unify its many supporters to a common concept. Let our next step be the joint development of that concept.

The Triangles of Enlightened Conservatism
A Philosophy of Unification Through Conscience

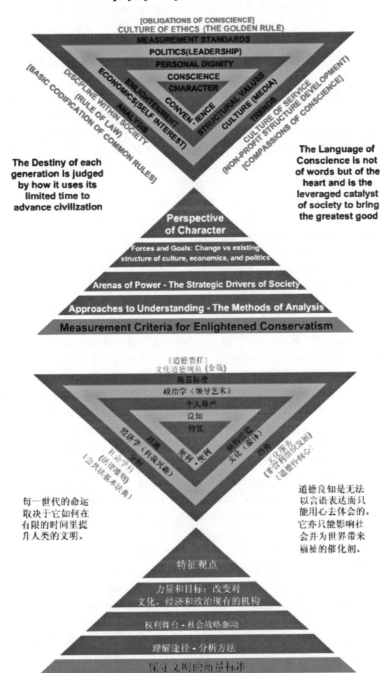

[OBLIGATIONS OF CONSCIENCE]
CULTURE OF ETHICS (THE GOLDEN RULE)
MEASUREMENT STANDARDS
POLITICS(LEADERSHIP)
PERSONAL DIGNITY
CONSCIENCE
CHARACTER

ENLIGHTENMENT
ECONOMICS(SELF INTEREST)
ANALYSIS
DISCIPLINE WITHIN SOCIETY
(RULE OF LAW)
[BASIC CODIFICATION OF COMMON RULES]

CONVEN · IENCE
STRUCTURAL VALUES
CULTURE (MEDIA)
TRENDS
CULTURE OF SERVICE
(NON-PROFIT STRUCTURE DEVELOPMENT)
[COMPASSIONS OF CONSCIENCE]

The Destiny of each generation is judged by how it uses its limited time to advance civilization

The Language of Conscience is not of words but of the heart and is the leveraged catalyst of society to bring the greatest good

Perspective of Character

Forces and Goals: Change vs existing structure of culture, economics, and politics

Arenas of Power - The Strategic Drivers of Society

Approaches to Understanding - The Methods of Analysis

Measurement Criteria for Enlightened Conservatism

〔道德责任〕
文化道德现值 (金箴)
衡量标准
政治学（领导艺术）
个人尊产
良知
特征

经济学（自我发展）
分析
社会学科
〔法律准则〕
（公共法签表法典）

便利 · 规利
结构价值
文化（媒体）
趋势
文明服务
〔非营利组织发展〕
（道德特别心）

每一世代的命运
取决于它如何在
有限的时间里提
升人类的文明。

道德良知是无法
以言语表达而只
能用心去体会的，
它亦只能影响社
会并为世界带来
福祉的催化剂。

特征观点

力量和目标：改变对
文化，经济和政治现有的机构

权利舞台 - 社会战略驱动

理解途径 - 分析方法

保守 文明的衡量标准

The Importance of Dialectic Thought

After the symposium I had a much better idea of the Goals of China internationally and domestically in the Harmonious Society, but that fit only the first part of Enlightened Conservatism. The second part was defining how people thought. The method by which you think often determines your result, and that is the essence of philosophy. Enlightened Conservatism is a philosophy of unifying people through the power and wisdom of conscience and character. Also the creation of that character gives strength to nations throughout history. It was noted by Alexis de Tocqueville in a century past when his observation on America captured it best: "America is great because she is good. If America ever ceases to be good, America will cease to be great."

There is a reason nations try to unify—it is power. The ultimate question is the base of values upon which they seek to unify and, equally important, how they implement it in their culture.

My next question to our Chinese hosts involved this issue because if the Lyceum Collaboration would be successful, knowing how each thought mattered greatly to success and the structure of the discussion, particularly if you were a catalyst bringing other organizations to participate.

In the early years of the Lyceum, one of the people who helped was Robert Lawrence Kuhn. Robert has been a friend over the years but has spent a great amount of time in China. He wrote a book analyzing the leadership of China (*The Man Who Changed China: The Life and Legacy of Jiang Zemin*). Dean George Kozmetsky was a close mutual friend of both of us who pushed our focus toward China's importance. When we visited after the Dean's death, Robert made a point to me of the great importance of communicating properly between the two cultures and why it was necessary. In *Business Week*, April 24, 2006, p. 33, he wrote an article "A Problem of Perception" that perhaps best explained the short version of what he conveyed back then. I would recommend reading it in full, but with his permission I would like to convey the essence:

> Why do China and America have such difficulty communicating? . . .
> The majority of American senators and congressmen were schooled
> as lawyers. But each of China's senior leaders—all nine members of
> the Politburo's Standing Committee—were trained as an engineer...
> Perhaps the difficulties between China and the U.S. lies less with
> dissimilar languages, cultures, and histories, and more with the
> divergent ways of thinking between lawyers and engineers.

He gave a great example of when the U.S. plane accidentally bombed the Chinese embassy in Belgrade, Yugoslavia in 1999. The Chinese government bused students from college campuses across Beijing to the U.S. Embassy in protest. American leadership looked at it as their promoting nationalism. A legal style deduction, but in reality the engineers realized a march through the city would grow huge and become unmanageable so they used strategy to contain the situation.

I was reminded of the Chinese leadership being schooled in engineering at the symposium by my friend Dr. Felipe Ochoa of Mexico, the Chairman of FIDIC's Task Force on Integrity, who joined us at the symposium and to whom I was speaking the following day.

I had requested an English version of the presentation Professor Jia just made, but also asked my friend Dr. Wang Weiguang, a Ph.D. in Philosophy, if he could help guide me in understanding the Chinese method of thought since they were examining how I presented an approach from Western thought in Enlightened Conservatism. Dr. Wang is very unique. He is Vice President of the Central Party School and one of its foremost leaders who also serves as a supervisor for doctoral students. One of his books dealt with this very issue examining a scientific outlook for a balanced socioeconomic development. So his thoughts were important because they looked to how leaders were being taught to solve problems and accomplish the goals.

More importantly conversations with him made me better understand why he and the School had an interest in *The Language of Conscience* and have a better appreciation that they researched the world for thoughts and had their own approach similar to the triangles for pulling concepts together. He focused not just on issues, but how the issues interacted and needed to be prioritized.

This thought process evolved from Karl Marx's dialectical materialism. Dialectic thought is a method of discovering or clarifying truth through the consideration of opposites that are debated. It started with Heraclitus and evolved through the Greek philosophers. But understanding the theory is far from understanding how the Chinese leadership is being taught to think at the School. At first, I thought enlightened conservatism might be an opposite for comparison since it is market based in economics in that it looks at equality of opportunity not result, is democracy based in social policy, and is culturally based in conscience and character. Western perceptions of Communism are based primarily on Russian Stalinism and the Cold War. It is important to remember the base of Russian Communism was in the workers, but in Chinese Communism it was in the farmer.

These are different cultures. China's recent creation of a socialist market system brought forth the more evolutionary aspects of Marx's dialectic, and the change in the method of production requires a change in cultural and political perspectives. Too often the West uses its own terms, such as a legalistic–human rights, where a similar concept that might give even more rights, human dignity, would be better understood culturally and less threatening.

What I learned was that *The Language of Conscience* was not just selected for the ethics of how to fight corruption, but also because it was a comparison of methods to ultimately reach more similar ends than I had ever imagined. So the collaboration needed to start with understanding the School's modern dialectic approach. Dr. Wang had appreciated the higher levels of the coordination of the three powers—economics, politics, and culture. He had gotten it from Marx; I had learned it from Texas Governor and U.S. Treasury Secretary John Connally. I asked him for a contribution based on his book so we could understand the thought process that was the base of the education of the Chinese leadership. When we formed the Texas Lyceum, our thought process was dialectic in that we first got research institutions and universities to help us analyze the critical issues to find where fact was common ground. Then we looked at the most critical strategic drivers and brought in the best experts with opposing views on the questionable areas. For example, in the early 1980s interest rates were negatively affecting the economy. Rising inflation from oil prices was a key issue. So the Lyceum focused on the price of oil as compared to alternative fuels, which would set a top limit on price competitively. Opposing experts debated the best option after perhaps 80% of the facts were researched and stipulated. The Lyceum method of debating opposing views fits in with the School's methodology.

He prepared for me the following article that was published in February of 2004 after making slight revisions in wording and title. I have included it in its entirety because each part, like the repetition in this book, is giving more detailed thought. It is remarkable to me, how many similar goals are in common, whether they can be reached is another question in a world of corruption and terrorism. But a dialogue, and the fully understood common interests you have, helps everyone. We will disagree on many interests, but moving to morality, seeking thought over emotion, analyzing the three areas of power, and envisioning the culture you need to keep stability and dignity seem to have common ties between Enlightened Conservatism and what with these goals might better be called Enlightened Socialism, which is how I would refer to the evolution of modern Communism in the modern economic world. I am a Jeffersonian / Adam Smith Reaganite; Dr. Wang is modern Marxist. By perception we should be polar opposites, but it is remarkable the number of common agreements as compared to disagreements. A great difference is time because China may see these goals but take generations to achieve them. But theory is only a set of ideals, implementation is the necessity, and as the Chinese study Western individuality, the West can learn from collective obligations.

Dr. Weiguang was born in Shandong Provence in 1950. He is a Vice President of the Central Party School of CPC. He is a member of the Legislation Committee of the National People's Congress Council, Vice Director of the National Association of Marxism Philosophical History Research, and Director of the Deng Xiaoping Theory Research Division. Also he is a Representative of the 16th National Congress of the Communist Party of China and a Representative of the 10th Congress of the National People's Congress Council.

However, the reason I felt his work particularly important is that he has long engaged in the study of the most important theory and practical issues for China when he led projects for the National Philosophy and Science Fund. His studies have focused on the issue of interest theory and internal conflict among people, a similar focus to our studies of Enlightened Conservatism or a philosophy for unifying people through conscience. He has published more than twenty academic works that have had significant impact in scholarly circles. When I first saw his list of published works and remembered my own, it was interesting how closely the problems of East and West parallel on strategic driving issues. As I mentioned earlier, he has spent his life studying philosophical evolution from Marxism; I have spent mine from Jefferson/Lincoln/Adam Smith grounding. But we both understand the power of culture; the necessity of conscience and ethics, and that ultimately the issue is the unification of people so that constructive actions can be taken.

The style of the Texas Lyceum dialectic of debating opposites in my writings was very similar to those of his organizations. He has worked with the translation of many Western works on ideologies and understands history. But most important of all, he understands that to communicate effectively, you have to understand how the other person thinks, both his perspective and what drives his method of thought. Because of his background as a scholar on unification, and the fact that he plays such a significant role in the education of doctoral students at the Central Party School, I asked him to allow me to summarize his key book on scientific thought, which gives a Chinese perspective to compare with our Western perceptions and thought process. He provided me with the following summary article, which in the first part details the critical issues facing China and in the second part the perspective of thought given to their solution.

Again this article was first published in February 2004, with only slight revisions this time in wording and the title. With Dr. Wang's permission:

A Scientific Outlook

A Scientific Outlook on Development for an Overall, Balanced Socioeconomic Development

Wang Weiguang

Presented here for your reference are some of my personal observations about coordinating economic and social development in China today.

First, current striking economic and social disparities call for pursuing a scientific outlook on development to ensure an all-round, well-coordinated growth.

Since launching the reform and opening-up program, China has won worldwide attention with a rapid growth of productivity, remarkable economic benefits, flourishing social undertakings, and new heights for overall national strength and people's livelihood—all thanks to the Party's consistent focus on economic development as the central task and adherence to solving problems cropping up in advancement through economic growth. In the 25 years from 1979 to 2003, China's GDP had grown by an average of 9.4 percent annually, winning even a 9.1 growth rate last year despite a disastrous SARS outbreak. China's GDP climbed from 362.41 billion yuan in 1978 to 11.664 trillion yuan ($1.41 trillion)in 2003, breaking the 11 trillion benchmark, with per capita GDP exceeding U.S.$1000.

An excellent situation requires a cool-headed calm., crying out for closer attention to current difficulties, problems and contradictions in our economic and social development. We should not lose sight of the fact that dichotomy in the form of social progress and the comprehensive development of man lagging behind rapid economic growth showcases an urgent issue in our country, with the case even more acute in the rural areas. A 2003 UN Development Agency data report indicated that compared with its fast economic progress, China ranks 104 in the world in terms of social development or at a lower-middle status. That explains the urgency of tackling this disharmony.

— Imbalance between economic growth and progress of social undertakings. This stands out as a striking issue in our country. Indeed great strides have been made on the whole through mounting inputs into science, education, culture, and public health, since reform and opening-up began. Yet things are not so rosy in some areas, where no corresponding systems in public education, sci-tech innovation, public health, cultural undertakings, social assistance, security, and crisis management have yet to be established, even with some staggering laggards. Here are some examples:

✧ Education. Since science and technology constitute the primary productive force and talented people represent important resources, education is of vital importance to turn China's 1.3 billion people into an advantage in human resources. Yet current conditions are worrisome with inadequate popularization of education, low cultural level of workforce, a big gap in education levels between different regions, urban and rural levels, where much leaves to be desired.

✧ Culture. Things are not much better in this respect. The progress of cultural undertaking fails to keep pace with rising needs of the people for a richer cultural life in keeping with the rapid growth of the national economy and improved living standards. Moreover, compared with advanced countries, China's relatively backward cultural strength and competitiveness make it unfavorable for the country in the current worldwide fierce competition in comprehensive national strength that includes economic, scientific, educational, national defense, and even cultural fields. In addition to enhanced economic clout, much-elevated cultural competitiveness is also indispensable.

✧ Health. The unexpected SARS outbreak in 2003 exposed deficiencies in our public health system. Some localities have long failed to allocate sufficient funds for medical care, environmental protection, health insurance, food and medicine supervision, public health, and infectious disease prevention. Meanwhile, a health and medical care system has yet to be in place to suit the market economy, with low capacity for treating emergency public health hazards and even poorer health and medical aid conditions in rural areas. Such problems in social undertakings have greatly increased the social cost for economic growth, thereby affecting and constraining the comprehensive development of society and man.

✧ Relative imbalance between economic progress and fair distribution. Growing income discrepancy represents a major issue in China's current socioeconomic dichotomy. Social progress requires integration of maximum economic/wealth growth with fair distribution. The basic condition for ensuring social stability demands harmonization of economic growth and social fairness/ justice. On one hand, social stability also hinges to a certain extent on appropriate social differentiation that in turn depends on reasonable distribution. Since reform and opening-up, on the one hand, part of the people and regions have become rich, thereby widening the wealth gap and breaking up the original egalitarian practice of "everyone eating from the same communal pot" and thus mobilizing people's work enthusiasm. On the other hand, however, a new problem sprang up, with the income gap ever widening among social members. The case is strikingly obvious in the ever-fluctuating income gap between urban and rural residents from 2.47:1 in 1978, to 1.7:1 in 1984, then to 2.61:1 in 1994, still then to 2.47:1 in 1997 or a little narrower, next then to 3.11:1 in 2002 and finally to 3.24:1 in 2003. If rural expenses on welfare and production cost and price estimates in kind were taken into consideration, the real gap might even hit five or six times. Central to this issue are the difficulties involved in raising the low income of farmers. From 1997 to 2003, national per capita net rural income increase had not exceeded 5% annually for successive seven years, with the peak rise at 4.8% for 2004 and the lowest at 2.1%, or half of the corresponding figure for city residents. The widening income gap also manifests itself among urban and rural dwellers themselves, people living in different regions or engaged in different jobs.

Phenomena closely related to such widening income discrepancy sprang up in the form of wealth polarization, social psychological imbalance among some people, and a glaring problem of social unfairness. Two time-honored international data systems exist for

gauging social polarization. The one is the Gini Co-efficient and
the other the five-graded survey. A Gini coefficient between 0.3
and 0.4 represent a medium extent of inequality, a fairly reasonable
warning line for income differential. A National Statistics Bureau
estimate thus records the rising urban-rural income gap in China
with the Gini coefficient at 0.341 for 1988, 0.343 for 1990,
0.389 for 1995, 0.397 for 1999 and 0.417 for 2000.

If measured in the five-grade method, then in the estimate of some
Chinese experts, things run something like this. Family income for
the poorest 1/5 of the households account for only 4.27% of the
total national income, the lesser poor 1/5, 9.12%; the middle-
income 1/5, 14.35%; the less rich 1/5, 21.13 ; and the richest
1/5, 50.13%. Such data offer you a rough idea of the current
widening social polarization in urban and rural China.

■   A high-income social stratum has surfaced as a result of the
    rising poverty issue reflected in a segment of rural/urban poor.
    In 2000, the wealth gap between the 10% highest income and
    10% lowest income households was 5.02 times (the figure
    being 3.09 times in 1998), while the corresponding ratio
    in the rural areas was 6.5 times (the figure being 4.8 also in
    1998). Another National Statistics Bureau estimate shows
    that about 3.7 million urban households or some 12 million
    people live in relative poverty with a per capita annual income
    of 1059 yuan or 54.7% below the per capita national average.
    The breakdown of urban poor indicates a large proportion of
    old people, without any source of income, disabled persons,
    retired or laid-off workers, especially those in loss-making
    enterprises. Rural poor population now amounts to nearly 30
    million people, making up 3.8% of the rural total. If those
    with an annual income below 825 yuan are included, then the
    figure will exceed 90 million people.

■   The problem of social justice stands out with widening overall
    social polarization centered on income discrepancy against
    the backdrop of an overall rise in income and living standards.
    Differences between city and countryside, workers and farmers,
    between regions, groups, and industries are reflected in terms of
    per capita GDP income, material and cultural life, education and

people's educational quality, concentrated mostly in regional and urban/rural gaps.

■ Contradictions among the people are much in evidence centered on rising clash of interests, tensions between cadres and the masses, factors of social instability, group disturbances, appeals to higher authorities for intervention in cases, and deteriorating social security in some areas.

Admittedly a certain widening gap in social distribution benefits the mobilizing work enthusiasm of the people. Yet unbridled widening would fuel social polarization, growing social cracks, widening gap, unfair distribution, worsening social fairness and justice, and even intensifying social instability, contradictions and conflicts.

✧ Relative imbalance between economic growth and increased employment. Lack of full employment constitutes a pressing problem in our current economic and social disparity, with job opportunity creation claiming close attention from the party and government leadership. But the employment situation is very stern due to the huge population and the formidable number of farmers.

■ Growing pressure for employment. Of the 1.3 billion population the work force aged between 15 and 64 number 904 million, a huge figure even more than the population of all developed countries combined, with labor supply far surpassing demand. In the period of the Tenth-Five-year Plan (2000-2005), annual increase of new workers amounted to ten million plus another 140 million laid-off workers from state enterprises. The pressure on additional employment comes mainly from migrant surplus rural labor force and urban laid-off workers.

■ Serious unemployment with urban registered unemployment ratio at 4.3% in 2003.

■ Difficulties in the transfer of surplus rural farmers. In 2002, rural labor in China amounted to 490 million people with planting and agriculture absorbing around 100 million, township and village enterprises some 133 million, farmers migrating to cities in search for jobs 99 million and the remaining 150 million surplus rural labor force in need of gradual transfer. Adequate relocation has yet to be arranged for farmers losing their farmland due to state expropriation for industrial use with a total amount of some 24 million mu (six mu = one acre) between 1987 and 2001. As a result, about 34 million farmers who have lost part or all of their land have been reduced to a state of "three-no farmers—no land for farming, no job for employment and no share for subsistence allowances."

■ Rising number of people facing employment difficulties, mostly those over the age of 35, long-time laid-off workers and low-skilled laborers. Such kinds of laid-off people in need of reemployment are mainly concentrated in the middle and western regions of the country, old industrial areas and mining industries depleted of resources.

✧ Relative imbalance between economic growth and comprehensive development of man. Lagging comprehensive development of man constitutes yet another problem in the disparity between economic and social development in China. Better understanding of and closer attention to the comprehensive development of man took place in the process of reform and opening-up and the modernization drive. Still some localities have yet to put sufficient stress on this issue. They fail to raise the quality of psychological and physical health, cultivate ideological and moral standards, enhance cultural/educational levels, protect a safe, stable, and orderly social environment, improve survival environment, elevate the level of material and cultural life and satisfy the needs for all-round development of man. In particular, some individual enterprises even pose severe threats to the security of life and property of their workers. Frequent major production safety accidents occurred there due to lack of necessary labor safety measures or violation of safety rules and regulations in disregard of the security and lives of workers. The causes can be traced to their certain negligence of cultural and ideological progress, ideological and moral education, ideological work, and disregard of cultural and ethnical needs, thus resulting in ideological and moral conditions incompatible with economic growth.

✧ Relative imbalance between economic growth and comprehensive institutional innovation. Incompatibility still exists between rapid economic growth and institutional innovation in China in spite of the historic progress brought to the country by institutional reforms. Indeed it represents a fundamental issue in the socio-economic dichotomy. Economic growth does not necessarily mean all-round social progress. There may exist a great discrepancy between a given aggregate volume of economic growth and the overall condition of social progress. Problems in the process of development should be gradually solved through restructuring, institutional innovations, and orderly, standardized social order so as to promote a comprehensive progress for society and man. Systemic obstacles manifest themselves first and foremost in deep-seated institutional issues left over from the planned economy. Many inconsistencies can also be found in the field of political systems such as imperfect socialist democracy and legal systems in conformity with the objective needs of a socialist market economy. Again, further efforts are needed to improve the system of people's congress so as to ensure that the people are masters of the country. Grass roots democracy and regimes at the basic level await strengthening. The patterns of party leadership and state governance require further reform and improvement. Some party organizations at the grass roots level are lacking in discipline and fighting spirit. Reform and transformations are called for government functions and administrative systems. Imperfect are current systems and mechanisms suited to the accelerated maturing of talented people in answer to the needs of a socialist market economy and relevant existent institutional obstacles have yet to be completely dismantled. Government capability for macro management, social crisis management in particular, is in urgent need of enhancement. Reform in the cadre and personnel management should be intensified. Efforts should be intensified to improve the party's style of work, build a clean government, and combat corruption. A supervisory mechanism over administrative power should be strengthened.

Corruption, violations of law and discipline, rough work style, formalism, and bureaucratism are still in evidence. Strenuous work is still needed to press ahead with the reform of political systems and strengthen the building of political civilization.

Further reform is also needed in the field of cultural systems that lag behind economic restructuring, thus hampering the growth of cultural undertakings. It is a major urgent task to understand how to follow the inherent laws governing the growth of socialist culture and build a socialist cultural mechanism suited to a market economy, favorable for cultural progress and prosperity.

Relative backwardness in social management and slow progress in building a mechanism for effective control over social order merit our close attention—a matter that restrains economic and social development. Now management relationship awaits straightening out. First, there still does not exist a clear separation in functions between the government and enterprises or society. Second, no clear separation also exists in the rights and responsibilities between the central and local governments. Only when their relations are straightened out and rights and responsibilities clearly separated can initiative of both sides be mobilized.

Next, a social control mechanism is yet in place, which meets the needs of a socialist market economy and is consistent with socioeconomic progress and comprehensive development of man. Take health control for example. A new system has yet to be completed, whereas the original cooperative health and medical care system in the rural areas had disappeared in the process of reform. Loopholes also exist in the management of social security. An effective management mechanism is also needed for social undertakings.

Now let us take up the second part of my article.

Second, we need to understand deeply and capture the substance and content of the scientific outlook on development from a height of the world outlook and methodology of the Marxist philosophy so as to achieve an overall, balanced economic and social development.

Different concepts of development will offer different orientations to economic and social development. In fact, some of the current disparities between economic and social development in China can hardly be entirely avoided in the present stage of development. Yet others are closely related to the wrong guiding concept of development in the mind of many leaders. They mistook the saying of Deng Xiaoping that "development is top priority" for "economic growth is top priority," and "development is the Party's top priority in governing and rejuvenating the country" for "economic growth as everything" and "focus on economic growth" for "GDP is the focus." In so doing, they mistook the eventual goal of development for pursuit of sole economic and material targets and development for short-term, temporary economic progress.

Such lop-sided concept of development can be traced to profound theoretical misunderstandings.

Marxist philosophy represents the scientific world outlook and methodology for observing and solving all problems. It provides the philosophical basis for establishing and implementing the scientific outlook on development to guide our balanced economic and social development. Only from the theoretical height of the philosophical world outlook and methodology can we understand the essence of the scientific outlook on development and acquire a scientific knowledge and profound understanding of the need for a harmonious economic and social development.

We should depart from dialectical thinking to understand the substance of the scientific outlook on development and the imperative to strive for an overall, balanced economic and social development.

The tendency toward neglecting coordinated economic and social progress and comprehensive development of man represents a one-sided concept of development. It deviates from materialist dialectics to fall into the long-standing misconception or "area of error" featuring subjectivism and metaphysics, i.e., static, isolated and one-sided approach to things of the world.

The scientific outlook on development is in essence a dialectic concept of development. Materialist dialectics maintains that all things are in movement that is absolute, whereas a standstill is relative. Development stands for a dynamic state of things, but not a dynamic state in general. It signifies a forward, upswing from a lower to higher level of progress by weeding through the old to bring forth the new. Indeed an overall, coordinated, sustainable development reflects a process of dialectic movement of things. Just as it is the case with the development of things, so it is similarly true with social development. What the scientific outlook on development pursues is precisely a dialectic, economic and social development.

Such development is the unity of (economic and social) opposites. Since contradictions represent the root cause for the development of things—the basic law of dialectics, development reflects a process of incessant emergence, growth and solution of contradictions in all things, and therefore dialectic development represents an evolutionary process characterized by the unity of economic and social opposites. In applying dialectics to coordinate economic and social development, we should understand that society develops amid the movement of economic, social, and cultural contradictions, of contradictions among the productive forces, production relations, and the superstructure and among a variety of social contradictions.

As the process of healthy social development indicates precisely the process of solving those above-mentioned contradictions, we should closely follow and understand contradictions existing in our current economic and social life and discover, understand, and solve them with appropriate methods. In the course of guiding the socialist construction of the former Soviet Union, Joseph Stalin committed serous, irremediable blunders. An important lesson was his failure to correctly understand and handle a series of contradictions in the Soviet socialist economic and social development. His biased pursuit of lop-sided progress in economic and social development led to extreme imbalances that accumulated deteriorating and eventual intensified contradictions.

Moreover, dialectic progress also reflects an all-round economic and social development. The development of all things represents a systemic process with systematic, organic components that are inter-related, inter-restraining, and inter-active. It thus constitutes a systematic, integrated development. Similarly, dialectic development should also be a comprehensive one coupled with relatively balanced advances of all inherent factors rather than the thrust of a biased, lop-sided, single factor. As a systems engineer, social development should take into consideration all components with comprehensive advancement of economic, political, and cultural ingredients in mind, only then can social progress be possible as an entirety.

Furthermore, dialectic development also means coordinated economic and social progress. One universal principle of dialectics holds that things are generally interconnected with not a single thing existing in isolation without widespread links to other things. No existence, far less progress could be possible. Therefore, common connections essentially indicate that development of things should be symmetrical, taking account of the progress of other things. If not, it would be a lop-sided development, standstill and even regression. Thus dialectic development emphasizes coordination. Economic growth alone cannot ensure automatic social fairness, justice, harmony, and stability indispensable for realization of a harmonious society. Mere economic growth in disregard of balanced forward movement of other factors would eventually delay its own progress as evidenced by the development journey of many countries across the world.

Still next, dialectic development signifies sustainable economic and social advances. The progress of anything including social development requires the necessary potential, staying power and sustainability.

Judging from the experience of countries world over, sustainability of three resources should be stressed for sustainable development.

- Material resources. It is an issue of development strategy to consider whether natural, environmental, and other material resources can sustain economic and social development.

- Cultural and humanistic resources. Human resources or talented people constitute a key resource. Indispensable are also other cultural and humanistic resources like knowledge, information, thoughts, virtue, and culture. Given insufficient inputs into education, science, technology, culture, and health and not enough attention to cultural and ideological progress, resources in talents, information, culture, and ethics would face depletion and exhaustion with consequences even more terrible than the deficiency in material resources. In the history of world development, some resource-deficient small, poor countries like Singapore and Israel, have gained rapid progress by relying mainly on cultural and humanistic resources.

- Political resources. Healthy political democracy, a sound legal system, political stability, and a resolute leadership are all political resources indispensable for supporting sustainable development. Normal, sustainable development would be impossible for any country suffering political turmoil, chaotic order, and underdeveloped civilization. Just as negligence of material resources would not do, so the same is true with negligence of cultural, humanistic, and political resources.

✧ We should depart from the Marxist conception of history to understand the substance of the scientific outlook on development for guiding an overall, balanced economic and social development.

The Marxist view of history stands for a philosophical interpretation concerning coordinated economic and social development. It serves as the foundation of the view of materialist history for the scientific concept of history, or in essence, the same thing as the concept of development based on the conception of materialist history.

This should be understood from two aspects. First comes historical determinism that maintains that the eventual force propelling social development consists in the production of material goods and material productive forces. In the final analysis, productive forces, economics, and material factors play a decisive role in the march of social history. The key to social development therefore lies in developing productive forces and the economy for continually raising the levels of the material life of the people.

✧ Next, we should also emphasize historical dialectics. We should not consider economics, materials and productive forces as the only factors responsible for social development. We must also pay attention to the role of man, nature, population, law, politics, culture, thoughts, and other social factors. In explaining social development, while stressing the key factors of social development, the Marxist view of history never fails to mention the counteraction of other factors. It emphasizes both the initiative of man and the restraints of nature, both the final decisive factors of materials, economics, productive forces, and the reaction of relations of production, superstructure, politics, culture, and ideology. All in all, it stresses a harmonious development between man and nature, man and society and that among all social factors, all fields and sectors.

Still furthermore, we need to get a deep understanding of the Marxist theory of economic and social forms, a fuller knowledge of the scientific outlook on development for a comprehensive approach to man, economy, and society. A theoretical misconception of taking development as economic growth only regardless of overall social development reflects failure to fully understand the Marxist theory of economic and social forms.

According to this theory, human structure can be divided into two parts, one, social existence or the process of material life; the other, social consciousness or the process of spiritual life. Further division may result in three parts by taking out the middle part or political life that lies in between social existence (material life) and social consciousness (spiritual life). Then from the perspective of human social life, the three parts will be material, political and spiritual life, in other words, economic, political, and cultural life. Still then from the angle of social civilization, they will fall into material. political and spiritual civilizations. Yet still then, from the angle of social structure, there will be productive forces, relations of production, and superstructure. The latter can be further divided into political and ideological superstructure. Finally, from the perspective of social arena, economics, politics, and culture come under consideration.

Social existence, material life, material civilization, economics, productive forces, and economic foundation are determinants respectively of social consciousness, material/spiritual life, politics/culture, production relations, and superstructure. Conversely, the latter play restraining and counteraction roles to all the former. In other words, culture, politics or spiritual/political civilizations restrain and react on economic and material civilizations. None of the three parts is dispensable for social development that results from interaction among various social factors. This theory teaches that economic growth constitutes the foundation and prerequisite, but nevertheless only part of social development as a whole. Thus negligence of fostering political and spiritual civilization and of the progress of social undertakings would end up in a heavy social price.

Yet another theoretical misconception holds wrongly that the Marxist theory of production addresses only material products in disregard of others. Actually, its contents embrace (1) production of consumer goods or material production; (2) production of humankind itself or production of population; (3) spiritual production in the main production of spiritual products such as thoughts, ideas, ideologies, religions, laws, virtue, and theories and finally (4) the production of social relations. From there came families, states, and even more complicated society. All these four aspects of production are connected with and penetrate one another, thus forming the basic content of the Marxist theory of overall production. This theory helps us draw an essential distinction between the Marxist view of history and that of vulgar Marxism that claims economy as the sole determining factor. Then we will understand that comprehensive human production indicates overall development of society including man, culture, society, and spiritual things rather than single material production.

Yet still another relevant theoretical misconception concerns seeing things but not people that pay attention only to economic growth to the neglect of the overall development of man and society. In putting people first for ensuring a harmonious economic and social development, we must make it clear: What is the aim of production? Its moving force? And its main body? An erroneous doctrine asserts that Marxist historical materialism addresses only things, not man where man himself falls vacant. In fact, Marxist historical materialism is such a theory of social development that departs from real man and aims at his development. From such a view of history, Marxism considers man as both the main body and the aim of social development and therefore makes striving for overall development of man as the essential definition for building a future society. Such a theory was put forward on the basis of criticizing capitalist ills.

From the 18th to the 19th centuries, the capitalist societies experienced unprecedented progress, but the increased capitalist material wealth came with the price of sacrificing the all-round development of man. It resulted in a "rule of things over man" that was reduced only to a means for creating material wealth and therefore slaves of things. Accordingly Marxists strongly condemned the inhuman social ills of the capitalist society in the hopes of a new society, which is built on the basic principle of freedom, equality, and full development for everyone. It will be such a future new society, where things no longer rule over man but serve the aim of overall development of man.

The historical experience and lessons of building socialism demonstrates that we must put people first. And take promoting overall development of man as the basic aim of building socialism. In fact, putting people first means treating them as the basis, the nuclei, and the foundation. It also means satisfying the needs of their overall development as the final aim. It further means meeting their natural needs for survival, security, and health and meeting their social needs for democratic rights, for fairness and justice, all-round elevation of quality and realization of their values. We should care for the people, respect, protect, emancipate, liberate, and develop them. All is on the people and for the people. What benefits the all-round development of the people should serve as the point of departure and the final aim that propel our economic and social development.

We should depart from the Marxist theory of knowledge to grasp the substance of the scientific outlook on development to coordinate overall economic and social advances.

The one-sided concept of development can also be traced to the resource of its knowledge. Its essence deviates from the basic principle of seeking truth from facts and of the Marxist theory of knowledge that departs from objective laws. A series of problems that sprang up from our economic and social development are to a considerable extent connected with divorce from reality, subjective surmise, blind pursuit of "political achievements," and acting against the objective law on the part of some people. In fact, the scientific outlook on development is in essence a concept of development that respect objective laws.

The relationship between the objective laws and human subjective initiative constitutes a basic philosophical issue. The subjective initiative of man is subject to the restraints of objective laws. Man can create history only by acting in accordance with objective laws and under certain objective conditions. Needless to say, man is not controlled unconditionally by objective laws to which man can exercise a certain amount of his subjective initiative. But complete denial of the role of objective laws and the belief that man can do whatever he likes to create history is nothing but historical idealism. Conversely, advocacy of man's helplessness before objective laws devoid of any subjective creativeness would be the fallacy of vulgar materialism. Only by respecting, grasping, and acting in accordance with objective laws can man display his initiative and creativeness to the full. Otherwise he would get penalties from objective laws.

The key to establishing and implementing the scientific outlook on development lies in respecting, grasping, and following objective laws. As is well known, social development has its own objective laws of development. For example, we all understand the laws that productive forces should conform to production relations and that superstructure should suit economic base. In addition, there are also laws of economic, cultural, and political development, and the law of coordinated development of economic, political, and cultural civilizations. Violations of them would result in major problems in social development.

✧ We must apply the basic views of Marxism to fully understand the scientific outlook on development.

Integrating Marxist position, viewpoints, and methods with the great practice of China's modernization drive, Chinese communists have come up with a scientific outlook on development, advocating the basic demand for harmonizing economic growth and overall development of society and man, thus clarifying some relevant muddled views.

In fact, neither economic growth nor overall development of man and society is dispensable. In the terminology of the development theory, growth and development are two different terms, with the latter much more rich and complicated in contents. Growth indicates only increase in GDP figures and material wealth. Development instead embraces a comprehensive progressive process that includes economic growth and many other factors like education, science, technology, culture, and politics. In his work, *"Implications of Development,"* British scholar Dudley Seers pointed out that growth and development are two concepts with the former indicating material enlargement. He added that "Growth alone is not enough and actually may even prove to be harmful to society. A country cannot possibly enjoy development unless there is reduced inequality, unemployment, and poverty besides economic growth."

Western advanced capitalist countries have experienced a process from simple economic growth to all-round economic and social development, accompanied by a similar process of concept of economic growth followed up by comprehensive and all-round concepts of development. Conceivably, there existed the reality and rationality for any concept of development at its own time. In the early days of capitalist industrialization, people seemed to believe that a bigger cake derived from economic growth could solve the problems of poverty and development. Therefore, they set economic growth as an important yardstick to assess the development of a country. Then a concept of development took shape that considered growth and development the same thing with a formula of development = economic growth.

This led to rapid economic growth but on the other hand excessive obsession with economic growth to the neglect of overall social progress had also claimed a heavy price for development.

In the development process of modern capitalism, it gradually dawned on the people that economic growth was not the only content of development that represents the comprehensive advances covering life expectancy, education indicators, per capita income, and others. Hence a new composite concept of development came into being with a formula of development = economic growth + social progress. The old concept of a bigger cake has its limitations because unfair distribution would spark devastating negative impact.

Human concept of development has actually undergone a long, long journey of evolution with its great progress as an important fruit of human civilization. By the late twentieth century, people further understood that an overall development of man is the fundamental aim. Solutions cover not only a bigger cake, its fair distribution and even the development of those who eat the cake. In addition to food, there still remains the issue of how to meet the needs of man for an all-round development.

For a long time, the Western capitalist world identified pursuit of maximum material growth and benefits as the goal of development to the negligence of the development of man, thus resulting in grave human alienation.

The new concept of development puts people first, stressing a variety of man's needs for values (material, spiritual, and ecological needs). And a concept of all-round development came into being with a new formula of development = economic growth + social progress + man's overall development. It advocates harmony among man, nature, and society. As a matter of fact, a correct concept of development emphasizes both economic growth and the comprehensive development of society and man.

GDP targets and composite targets for overall development of society and man are both indispensable. Neither excessive lop-sided attention to GDP increase to the neglect of other aspects nor negligence of the positive meaning of its increase is also wrong. Noted U.S. economist Samuelson held that the GDP was one of the great inventions in the 20th century. As a most important universal macroeconomic indicator, it can reflect the economic size, strength, and changes in a country or a region. In normal times, its increase signifies the growth in economic strength and social wealth and serves as the material foundation for economic and social development.

Compared with the pre-reform years when economic growth was neglected under the "leftist line," it signified a progress for our country to adopt the GDP as an important indicator to gauge economic growth. Nevertheless, the GDP also has its glaring defects, such as its inability to reflect the quality of growth, industrial structure, social/humanistic progress, and environmental production. Bigger GDP does not necessarily reflect all-round economic and social progress. This said though, economic and social progress cannot possibly be separated from a rising GDP figure. So we need to gradually improve our GDP check indices and establish a reasonable system of comprehensive check-up indices so as to use the GDP in a scientific manner for offsetting its deficiencies.

Here two tendencies should be guarded against. While focusing on economic construction as our central task, we should not ignore the all-round development of man and society. Different stage of development is confronted with different outstanding problems. Without economic growth, there would be no peace under the heaven. Similarly, without solution of social problems there would also be no long period of peace and stability, and even serious crises may break out.

As a matter of fact, economic growth does not equal social progress. The per capita GDP figure of some Latin American countries exceeded $3,000 and even $5,000 for individual ones, with urbanization rate surpassing 70% at that. Unfortunately, economic and social crises frequently broke out over there due to widening polarization between the rich and the poor, with serious setbacks for development.

At the beginning of reform and opening-up, economic backwardness was the glaring issue in China when most social problems could be traced to the same root cause, so undivided attention should be paid to economic construction. However, along with rapid economic growth in the wake of reform and opening-up, the negative impact of the market economy began to be felt and some deep-seated problems and contradictions surfaced. Therefore, while expanding the economy, we should coordinate an all-round economic and social development. On the one hand, we should not ignore and even negate the approach of focusing on economic construction as the central task under the pretext of the need for overall economic and social progress. On the other hand, we should not oppose the tendency to use economic growth as a replacement for promoting and realizing other social targets.

Third, we need to make overall plans by taking all factors into consideration so as to implement the scientific outlook on development and promote the all-round development of economy, society, and man.

The important thought of "Three Represents"—namely, the Chinese Communist Party represents the development trend of China's advanced productive forces, the orientation of China's advanced culture, and the fundamental interests of the overwhelming majority of the Chinese people—stands as the guidance and theoretical guarantee for guiding the scientific outlook on development and the overall development of economy, society, and man. A correct outlook on life, masses, and political achievements, serves as an ideological guarantee for establishing and implementing the scientific outlook on development and for guiding a harmonious economic and social development. Leading cadres should solve satisfactorily this basic question of outlook on life, foster a correct view of the masses, political achievements, and development. Only then can a real scientific outlook be implemented, overall planning, and all-round consideration be in place.

— The scientific outlook on development is the guideline for comprehensive, balanced economic and social progress.

It is the basic principle to be followed in solving the many problems in our current economic and social development. It is also the guiding policy to be long persisted in realizing all-round development of economy, society, and man.

For this, we must first solve well the concept of development of the leading cadres. They should shift their lop-sided concept of sole stress on economic growth and increased GDP indices to social justice yet to receive sufficient attention. Once economic growth has reached a certain extent, the needs of the people begin to change. They want instead to improve the texture of life as a whole. While pursuing higher income and more plentiful material products, they are demanding better cultural atmosphere, health and medical care conditions, ecological environment, and richer spiritual and cultural life. These are all important signals to assess economic and social development.

Therefore, we must shift from the lop-sided notion of development in pursuit of short-term targets and striking material achievements to the scientific notion of sustainable development with across-board reduction of development cost and price. We should use smaller cost to realize greater development benefits, social cost in particular.

Overall reduction of development cost comes from three aspects. First, we should reduce the cost of ecological environment by resolutely abandoning the practice of seeking development at the expense of destroyed ecological environment. Second, we ought to cut down the cost of resource consumption by resolutely abandoning the practice of sustaining development at the expense of a large amount of natural, cultural, and material resources in disregard of quality and benefits. Third, we must reduce social cost because poverty, unemployment, and income differential would fuel social turmoil and crisis, thus greatly raising the social cost of development. Backwardness in politics, virtue, education, science, technology, culture, and health will equally elevate the social cost of development. So we should definitely abandon the practice of seeking development in disregard of realizing the social goals of justice, fairness, and harmony and in replacement of underestimating the cultivation of political and spiritual civilization, and the scientific concept of emphasizing an all-round development of economy, society, and man. Though undoubtedly an important content in development, economic growth does not represent its whole. Similarly, it only stands for an important interest but not the whole of the people's interests. Lopsided is the concept of development of those who believe that economic growth alone can solve all problems and automatically realize other social goals. Focus on economic construction does not mean that economy alone can represent everything in social development. Indeed it signifies the basic moving force behind social development and represents the material prerequisite to all-round social progress. An appropriate GDP growth is indeed an important propeller of development, but definitely not the entire content of economic and social development that should be a growth in all-round social targets based on economic growth.

Therefore, we should shift our one-sided concept of development away from gluing sole attention on economic growth and putting things first, to the scientific outlook on development by paying equal attention on both economic growth and people-centered all-round development of society and man. By development we mean all-round human advancement based on economic growth. Pursuit of all-round development of man rather than material targets alone represents our ultimate aim.

At the initial stage, people were more concerned with rise in income and plenty of material wealth. So economic growth was then top priority with matters related to all-round development such as education, culture, health, medical treatment, environment, and fostering of social undertakings.

— "Overall planning and all-round consideration" constitutes a scientific method for applying the scientific outlook on development to guide overall, coordinated economic and social development.

In implementing the task we are still in need of a scientific method. Summarizing the lessons of lop-sided development in Soviet socialism and expounding on China's road of socialist construction, Comrade Mao Zedong published his work, *On Ten Major Relations,* in 1956 considering overall planning and all-round consideration a basic method for handling socialist construction and development. He said, "Our policy is one of overall planning and all-round consideration so that everyone is provided for." We should acquire a deep understanding of his thinking in this respect.

It means that we should follow this general policy of departing from the interests of all the Chinese people to "mobilize all the positive factors." He said that "We should depart from the fact of the six billion people in making plans, doing work and considering questions." He added that we should "mobilize all positive factors, unite with all people that can be united and try to transform negative factors as far as possible into positive ones so as to serve the great cause of building socialism." First, departing from the overall situation of the interests of the people of the entire country, we must make unified planning with due consideration for all concerned in light of realistic conditions. Meanwhile, we must also make appropriate arrangements for each to have a role to play, take into consideration both the immediate and long-range interests of the people, as well as their interests in all aspects. Second, we should respect the initiative of the masses; mobilize the enthusiasm of the masses, localities, and all social sectors. The central authorities, the government, the leadership, and the superiors should not take sole charge of everyone and everything. Let the masses and society think of the ways to solve problems.

Overall planning and all-round consideration means also application of dialectics to handling our socialist construction and development. Comrade Mao Zedong taught us how to use the method of dialectics to handle socialist construction and development. He vividly summed up that dialectics deals with two aspects. It uses the approach of two aspects to observe, analyze and solve problems. He said there will be two aspects even after ten thousand years. The future will have its two aspects. The same is true with the present and every individual. In a word, there are two aspects, not one. Seeing only one side of the picture means "know only one aspect of a matter, but be ignorant of the other." In handling major relations and contradictions in socialist construction and development, we should pay attention to two aspects not just one, We should handle well both the principal and non-principal aspects, the dialectics of the key and non-key points in socialist construction and development. We should not pay attention to only one end but have to take into account the interests of the state, the collectives and individuals. Comrade Mao Zedong talked about two aspects with their key points. Overall planning and all-round considerations mean "walking on two legs," "simultaneous development" of various industries, and overall balance." Comrade Mao Zedong put forward a set of "simultaneous development" of various sectors and "walking on two legs" and stressed "overall balance." He emphasized "overall balance" and held that balancing is a fundamental question. With overall balance can mass line only be spoken of. Needless to say, overall balance does not spell requisition without compensation, egalitarianism or taking from the fat to pad the lean. This was "eating from a communal pot," a practice we suffered in the period of planning economy.

Comrade Mao Zedong's method of overall planning and all-round consideration has provided us with a scientific method to implement the scientific outlook on development. Here "overall" signifies macroscopic regulation and control or appropriate intervention at appropriate timing. Planning here means scheming and coordination. As for all-round consideration, it means we should balance various relations and take into account the interests of all sectors. In other words, overall planning and all-round consideration need to pay attention to the overall situation, guidance, intervention, adjustments, balances, and care for other parts and coordination. Needless to say, what Comrade Mao Zedong talked about overall planning and all-round consideration was addressed to coordinating and balancing various relations and contradictions under conditions of planned economy.

The principle of overall planning and all-round consideration put forward at the Third Plenary Session of the Sixteenth National

Congress of the CPC requires instead harmonization of all-round development of economy, society and man under conditions of socialist market economy. We should not lose sight of the many differences between the two. Here we need to combine resource allocation under the market economy and the socialist basic system so as to push economic development by applying market means, which, is also a "double-edged sword." On the one hand, its incentives can mobilize the enthusiasm and creativeness of man for full utilization and tapping of human, natural, and social resources. On the other hand, it has brought about passive, negative impact such as money worship, localism, pleasure seeking, and individualism. Here we need the government to seek overall balance by using the method of coordination of overall planning and all-round consideration to ensure comprehensive, balanced economic and social development. In the 25 years of reform and opening-up, we have developed market economy and obtained tremendous achievements. On the other hand, certain passive impact and negative functions also occurred and relative imbalance sprang up between economic and social development. We should therefore implement the scientific outlook on development, unify planning with due consideration for all concerned in the spirit of the Third Plenary Session of the Sixteen National Congress of the CPC so as to settle well the all-round development of economy, society and man in our country.

We should apply the scientific outlook on development to solve striking problems in disparities between economic and social development.

We should solve well the issue that social undertakings relatively lag behind economic growth according to the Program for Building Socialist Culture by boosting the progress of social undertakings in such fields as education, science, culture, and health. It is an issue involving the overall situation that is related to implementing in full the scientific concept of development. We must strengthen political and ideological work, strengthen ideological and moral cultivation to solve their relative "softness," an important move to promote overall, coordinated economic and social development.

In addition, some glaring problems still remain that reflect current economic and social disharmony.

■   Widening income gap among some social members. Both history and reality
     demonstrate that development may bring about two possible changes. One is
     eventual common prosperity. The other worsening discrepancy between the
     rich and the poor up to social polarization. Naturally, common prosperity is
     inaccessible overnight. We may allow some people and some areas get rich
     first. Then they carry along the late-starters to gradually embark on the
     path of common prosperity. In other words, we allow some people to get rich
     first but do not allow social polarization. We allow the existence of wealth
     differentiation but do not allow excessively widened wealth gap. Then what
     is a comparatively better kind of structure in social wealth distribution? An
     olive-type social structure seems to be favorable for keeping social stability
     because the two small ends represent the small amount of both the affluent
     and the destitute with a bulging number of middle-income social members
     in between. By contrast, a bottle gourd-type social structure with two big
     ends and a narrow middle would inevitably threaten social stability because
     of the sharp confrontation between the rich and the poor in a form of
     polarization with too small a buffer zone in between.

We need to solve this problem of excessively widening the income gap among
some social members by the principle of "efficiency first with due consideration
for fairness." We should actively press ahead with reform in the distribution
system and straighten out distribution relations. We should also intensify
adjustments in distribution and gradually set up an improved, reasonable
second distribution system with the first distribution focusing on efficiency and
the second one more consideration on fairness so as to ensure social justice and
fairness. Here a variety of means like system, mechanism, policy, and taxation
are involved. We need to enlarge the middle-income social members, protect
the low-income members, and make adjustments in taxation among the high-
income members. We need to protect legal incomes according to law, strike
at illegal incomes, investigate, confiscate or rectify unreasonable incomes so
as to establish a fair, orderly distribution order. On the other hand, we need
to set up systems for social safeguards, assistance and insurance centered on
old age, labor, health/medical care insurance, unemployment assistance, and
subsistence allowances. We need also to adopt positive measures to encourage
part of the income members to reach medium richness. It aims to gradually
form an enormous and stable middle-income strata. In sum, a coordination
mechanism is needed where efficiency and fairness are organically unified.

■   Solving urban and rural poverty. In the final analysis, it is an issue of
     gradual elimination of poverty. The productive forces in the country are

relatively backward at the primary stage of socialism. Our modernization will also take up a long duration. These two factors alone predetermine that poverty cannot automatically disappear in a short span of time. The only way out is to deepen the reform, raise productive forces, and foster a variety of social undertakings so as to increase as soon as possible social material and spiritual wealth. Concerted efforts are needed to solve urban poverty through a variety of measures. In the mean time, concentrated efforts are also called for to tackle problems related to agriculture, rural areas, and farmers in order to boost rural economy, increase rural income, and gradually eliminate rural poverty.

■ Solving unemployment. Enlarging employment should be given a still more preeminent place in economic and social development. Economic growth will surely bring about greater employment but not necessarily more job opportunities. In the process of rapid economic growth, for maintaining higher economic benefits and sharpening competition through cutting down labor cost, a certain unemployment is unavoidable. But full employment is also necessary for maintaining social fairness and stability. Here is a dilemma. A rapid GDP growth coupled with declining employment cannot ensure full employment. Nor can this guarantee that all social members share a fair distribution with some people enjoying all the fruit of growth and others denied access and even suffering losses. That will only result in a bad situation characterized by growth without development. Persisting economic growth accompanied by massive unemployment will cast a long shadow over social development in its entirety, cause social turmoil, and restrain economic advances. Capitalist countries suffered heavily from the big unemployed army that nearly buried capitalism itself. It was the same story with ruling parties in the West. We should draw experience and lessons from them. Therefore, full employment should be give equal importance as economic growth in order to promote all-round economic and social development.

Employment may be tackled from three aspects in China today. Economic development is the fundamental way out. Next, the correct policy of "employment through self choice by laborers themselves through market regulation and through government promotion." We should implement a positive employment policy, reform the environment for employment and self job creation, and utilize to the utmost degree employment sources to stimulate employment. Finally, set up a sound system for unemployment rescue and social security for the benefit of all the unemployed.

■ We should deepen institutional reform to remove institutional obstacles that restrain the implement of the scientific outlook on development.

Fundamentally speaking, the task should start from institutional innovation and system building. We should deepen institutional reform to further eliminate institutional obstacles that hamper coordinated economic and social development.

We should press ahead with reforms with priorities step by step so as to further remove obstacles in the economic system that affect harmonious economic and social development, liberate and develop productive forces to the maximum, thus promoting economic development and enriching material wealth of society as a whole. This will then provide a powerful material basis and economic institutional guarantee for raising urban and rural employment, eliminating poverty, and realizing social fairness and justice, and promoting a mechanism for promoting coordinated, sustainable economic and social development.

We should also deepen the reform of management systems to create an institutional guarantee for the all-round development of man and society, improve government functions for social management and public services. We need also to establish a social management system that matches the all-round development of the economy, society, and man. We need to improve the human resources market for fair competition and improve the incentive system for talented people to emerge. So everyone displays his ability to the fullest, thus creating an environment for implementing the strategy of strengthening the country through utilizing our human resources. We also need to reform our education system, build a modern national education system, and a life-long education system, thus forming an education system that suits the needs of economic and social progress. We need also to reform our management system for science and technology to speed up the building of a national system for sci-tech innovations. We still need to establish a culture management system suited to the laws and characteristics of building socialist spiritual civilization and to the needs for building a socialist market economy. It will also be a system that gradually sets up leadership of a party committee, government management, professional self-discipline, and enterprises or undertakings that operate in accordance with the law. We need to strengthen government functions for managing public health and establish a health and medical care system that is suited to the market economy, enhance the service level of public health, and the response ability to public health emergencies.

We further need to press ahead prudently and actively with political restructuring, improve socialist legal system, cultivate socialist political civilization, adhere to and improve the system of the people's congress to ensure that people are the masters of the country. Stick to and improve the multi-party cooperation system under the leadership of the Communist Party of China, enhance grass roots democracy, and strengthen the primary-level government. We need also to reform and improve our decision-making mechanism to ensure democratic and scientific decision-making, deepen the reform of administrative system. We further need to straighten out relations between central and local governments, between governments and enterprises and society, transform functions of the governments, enhance macro-management and public services, thereby gradually setting up clean and a highly-efficient administrative system featuring standardized conduct, harmonious functioning, justice, and transparency. We also need to reform and improve the cadre and personnel system, improve the civil servant system, and establish a sound system for selecting, appointing, managing and supervising personnel. We ought to create a personnel environment featuring openness, equality, competition and selection of the excellent ones, and set up a vigorous cadre management mechanism that practices promotions and demotions, entry, and exit. We further ought to reform and strengthen the party work style and build a clean government, strengthen restraint, and supervision over administrative power. We also ought to reform and improve the supervision system of party discipline, strengthen the socialist legal system, and follow the basic policy of running the country by law. We ought to improve all laws and regulations necessary for market economy development as well as laws and regulations indispensable for all-round development of society and man, reform judicial and law enforcement system and strengthen their supervision. We need also to push forward administration by law and defend judiciary justice so as to establish a legal system favorable for economic, political, and cultural development and all-round social progress.

Our case study of China should point out two things: The first is communication is difficult from many perspectives, but a sense of honor of conscience of purpose can ease a great many problems. The second is that all the world has similar problems that will be made more intense by global competition. You have to look at how to strengthen your nation, but you must now realize that it may require cooperation with others for material benefit more than in the past. Those countries that have the most thoughtful, as opposed to the most emotional, policies will succeed. Thought requires leadership, education, and a society that sees the wisdom of sacrifice. The great issue is how you develop or maintain the individual opportunity and character of the people. Of equal importance is to appreciate the fact that where you presently are on a spectrum is important, but the direction you are headed and the rate of advance are equally as important. China may or may not be able to reach the goals discussed, but if they do, it will have a significant impact on the possible levels of global cooperation. To help them achieve a middle class, a system of law and justice, and a system of human development that promotes education, morality, and conscience makes the opportunity for the development of win/win scenarios more possible. This would lead to a better world for the children of all. But America must undertake its own efforts to develop our social conscience, maintain our character, and preserve our economic competitiveness. Our domestic challenge to continue our social and economic development from the Western perspectives of character, free enterprise, and conscience will be equally difficult for us in a materialistic and fast-paced world as it will be for the Chinese to grow their system. The next 50 years will provide an interesting case study of a developing society facing challenging goals from slightly different perspectives.

Section IV

What Obligations Must We Honor and Teach?

The Concept of Stewardship

In Texas we have long held the concept of stewardship to be one of responsibility and is in a sense the responsibility to the land, to nature, and to principles. Stewardship works with values more than just ideas because it is what you value that you consider passing on. A second concept fits closely with it and is the level and nature of discipline within a society. The broad discipline within a society is how the society operates as a group. Is it fiscally responsible? Is it a society of law rather than men and how is individual dignity respected? The more direct discipline is within society is how the law is directly enforced. Is the discipline to enforce only the written letter of the law or the spirit or intent of the law? Much about the broader discipline is revealed by showing whether peer pressure or power is dominant. Stewardship is recognition that to keep peer pressure the dominant discipline rather than fear of force, you must work to preserve the common values that create that peer pressure. It is the spirit of the law.

We often see that any change in the modern world is particularly difficult because there are such massive numbers of people. We wonder how you can reach that many people to bring about cultural change. With values, the issue is slightly different. In most businesses you produce a great number of final products, but you effectively produce them, hopefully with quality, one product at a time by repeating a process many times. In a sense, that is the same way that values work. They are individualized to people, and therefore you need to look at building systems that let each individual appreciate how that change affects them and how they need to broaden their thoughts to include the importance of the values. It is the system that produces much of the effect and too often we do not appreciate its power. As things continue over time with changes gradually occurring, everyone accepts it because it is what has been in place to a large degree.

You cannot change an existing idea without replacing it with another idea. Similarly, once a new idea has been implanted and is understood, it is almost impossible to remove it. Thus, what becomes the key is having individuals understand the importance of the common good, conscience, and individual responsibility as opposed to a concept where they immediately look to others as the cause and at fault. The perspective they take determines their opinions on issues. Our American culture started with individual responsibility, but it has gradually evolved into victimization.

I was rather amazed when I listened to a presentation on television by the entertainment industry that spoke of their great concern about how both music and film were being downloaded from the Internet through piracy to the extent that theft significantly threatened the business models of the industries. While they were going to try legal action and were going to use technology to protect their situation, they were facing very difficult odds as we moved into the future. To me, this was a very indicative case. Technology is always going to move forward. And it is highly unlikely that you are going to find a satisfactory approach to halt this advance in any field, including legal action, which is expensive and different for small value downloads if the exchange systems are not liable for the content of the downloads.

Therefore it was very odd that the industry did not realize that their greatest protection is really the integrity of the potential audience. They lamented the fact that none of the youth with whom they had visited seemed to have any hesitation about downloading materials. This being wrong or improper to them was very surprising. It is hardly surprising to others or to me when you look at the entertainment industry's efforts in these past years, which often were aimed at creating anti-heroes and an image that downplayed many of the very concepts that are now beginning to haunt them. If we are going to have a society that honors the rights of others, then it is only created by a culture of peer pressure which takes such things to be important and used by the population as a whole to enforce such concepts.

Stewardship is really the maintenance and defense of those values, which have been highly challenged. Honor and stewardship are going to require us to look at how we can build infrastructures that begin to respond to the necessity of showing individuals the importance of integrity— integrity not only in their lives, but also in the creation of the environment that surrounds them and gives the ultimate protection and opportunity to them individually. As we noted in the comments on nations, character must not only be individual but national because your individual interests are determined in part by the success of the groups of which you are a part. So you have distinct responsibility for the common good,

An appreciation of such cultural values is not only the solution to many of the economic problems but is the model that needs to fit for the ultimate potential growth and benefit of a free market system. It is also one that helps define a personal dignity for all, which gives the ability to develop a more feasible world, and it is core to the acceptance of responsibility.

It is also important to understand that such transformational style efforts must occur at two very different levels. The first is the deeper intellectual concept that discusses, refines, and debates the idea that is molded into a consistent set of ideas often by debating options. The second is the popularization of the new idea in a much simpler form that grasps the masses. You need both. Without the depth you have a weak idea, and without the masses you have no power of unity. For all the great minds of the American Revolutionary era, a small book, *Common Sense*, by Thomas Paine captured the spirit and changed the perspective.

Developing a Common Concept

If you seek a perspective of common good and conscience, you need to recognize that change is often difficult. The status quo has its supporters because it suits their interest. Usually only crisis brings the necessity and force for change.

However, it is far from hopeless if you can divide the forces that stand in your way. A perfect example is partisanship in America and how it is politically and socially dividing the country. It primarily suits certain leaders because it gives them enhanced power but does not necessarily bring about the best decisions for the people, and in fact often delays or warps them.

A friend of mine, who had worked with the Texas Legislature and in Washington, lamented how a few changes could make a difference. Washington is divided by an aisle, which separates the two parties. In Texas they sat interspersed so the peer discipline was less and individual decisions easier. The term of the Texas Legislators was only about four months every other year, so a time pressure made people work together and prioritize. While Washington has more business, the constant sessions (except for August recess and a few shorter ones) impose no deadlines. Even so in Washington workweeks are short because fundraising dominates, and members must have time to focus upon it.

Shorter sessions and timelines on legislation would be structural changes that could affect the culture by forcing prioritization. In Texas the ideas worked from the center out. In Washington, partisanship makes them work from the extremes in by how it allocates influence. Usually if you can get just a few of the other party to join you, you can succeed. However, few political people truly want to succeed on issues because in the back of their minds they usually want to preserve the issue to run on and to raise money in the next election. This is frustrating since most people in government would rather be relevant than be an ideologue. But partisan politics doesn't let them work easily with the other side because the focus is on the next election. This is an interesting evolution from the period when candidates "stood for election" based on their past public service and merit rather than today's partisan focus on wedge issues and money. The common good the forum used to reach office has disappeared with the moderate influences to which balance and stability were key factors. Politics creates the equivalent of firewalls to true cooperation for the common good. As my water skier friend noted if he skied on Lake Austin, his waves washed upon the shore and dissipated. If there were a Washington equivalent, it would be a set of cement walls like a canal. The waves would constantly bounce back and forth. Partisanship creates a culture of how it views its approach to business. If we, as a country, value partisanship by being divided by its issues, we will be red and blue states. And we will not look to the critical longer-term issues that must be addressed for our children's sake. We will confuse toughness with what becomes ruthlessness and that creates impenetrable walls for a generation through personal hatred. If we value as a people other issues, politicians will react with change. It is important to note that a great many people caught in the partisanship of government would rather not be there. In the 2003 session of the Texas Legislature several Hispanic leaders with the co-sponsorship of the Speaker of the Texas House and his Democratic predecessor passed a resolution honoring *The Language of Conscience,* and they both allowed me to speak and visit with legislators in a reception following. People noted how rare it was for the two of them to do something together. But both were lifelong friends of mine who had supported these concepts. It was the structure of partisanship and power that brought conflict. If the people demand certain actions by prioritizing their concerns, politicians as well as statesmen take note. The powers in the systems are great but changeable if inertia is overcome since power ultimately belongs to the people. Interestingly, the resolution's uniqueness began a series of visits to show how very diverse Texas think tanks could work jointly with the concept. The issue had become how to get needed good ideas into the process, but where they originated impacted them. Wisdom can be found on both sides of partisanship. Getting the excellence of an idea above the suspicion and envy of origin is a challenge, but can become a manageable one.

In China, the situation is slightly different. There has been significant political change from a controlled economy to a free market-based economy. But the inertia and difficulty is in the transition and its effects on the population as market principles bring significant pressure to old-line industries that have guaranteed a style of life and a social mindset. The creation of a new middle class will be the base of the future China, but it must endure the challenge of change. China's major problem is the disparity of income between the opportunities in the growth areas, mainly on the coasts and the rural areas. Disparity creates the friction a middle class that has much in common solves. So raising the standard of living is a necessity for stability.

America, to keep its middle class from shrinking must begin to address serious imbalances before they become overwhelming in magnitude with the social benefit systems' unfunded deficits being joined by structural government and trade deficits. These are solvable problems, but if addressed before crisis and loss of confidence, solutions are less painful. They may well be problems of the future, but responsible leadership should address them now. No nation is guaranteed future success as history shows. It has its opportunities and when it succeeds and has the benefits of wealth this is when it is often at its greatest challenge. How does it reinvest its wealth—in education and technological competitiveness, in infrastructure, in a vision of a greater future or does it enjoy the benefits of materialism and power that wealth provides? This is the broad issue Enlightened Conservatism calls Discipline in Society. It is how much influence the common good and concerns for the future have on the individual. Is the nation fiscally responsible so that it reinvests its seed corn? Is its educational system realistic and focused on future needs or becoming elitist? What is the quality of education given to the coming generation that must support the existing generations economically? Where is the leadership focused? This influential, broad measure of Discipline in Society is related to the more power oriented direct Discipline in Society of the method of enforcement of law. When peer pressure is the influence, which causes a tightly focused concern on the future for the common good, begins to deteriorate, then the police enforcement power of discipline increases.

As cultural power diminishes, police and legal power increases to fill the vacuum. Great societies seek a balance of harmony and creativity. It is opportunity that is the salvation of the creation of a middle class and that requires a focus on how resources are spent. You must plant seed corn continuously not consume it. Today there are many representations about what nations are doing the exact right things, but the reality is that the laws of competition will make a judgment for history. The creativity necessary to adapt and succeed is fostered by the nature of society, but it must also have the resources to create the opportunity.

In both cases, the United States and China, the people will ultimately be the decision-makers because of their actions or inaction. They can recognize the need for national character and sacrifice (conscience) or avoid it (convenience). They will certainly avoid it if it is not explained in terms where they see the benefit and fairness of their sacrifice.

People today in most of the world want the same things. They value family. They want opportunity. The Mandate of Heaven looks to peace and prosperity, which is the same as the American vision to life, liberty, and the pursuit of happiness. Culturally they may be said differently but the values are very similar because they are of man's nature. Whether we worry about the environment or the self-interest of market economics, we will find the best solutions from working with rather than against each other. One way unifies and grows; the other divides and partitions. Growth is not a zero sum game, so unification has a long-term advantage even if there are short-term difficulties.

Most people want substance in life and are feeling powerless in a very superficial environment. There are natural forces upon which it can rely if understood. Once a man has thought about an idea and fully understood it, it becomes a part of him. The basic idea we all need to comprehend is that the best discipline within any society is not the enforcement of laws, but the conscience of the people.

The question is how to avoid a Tower of Babel with many languages that prevent common efforts. It starts with the definition of a core idea that is enhanced by many others. These are issues that we need to take individually.

The True Nature of Ethics and Conscience

Before discussing the importance of ideas and their creation, it is incumbent to look at what is the most appropriate question. To me, that question is why ethics and by reference, conscience, are less prominent in today's society than they were in times past. If we go back to the case study of my father and the concept of the importance of building a network of uncommon men that create peer pressures among themselves through structures like nonprofit organizations, we need to ask what has changed. My mother was a hospital administrator for a period in her life and her father and all of her uncles were doctors. To them medical ethics were not just about how you handle specialized problems but were obligations you had to the community. One of the reasons for Grandfather Knolle's early death at age 42 could well be traced back to diseases he suffered in leaving to go to help people with fevers in other cities. To him, it was an obligation. The same is true in the practice of law where a profession, which used to embody the wisdom and character that represented justice, has slipped in public perception if you look at modern polls. We need to say little about the business scandals that have taken place in modern times. The professional schools should be teaching ethics, but they are teaching ethics in silos. They are not teaching the broad cultural ethics of conscience, the Golden Rule, and the Common Good. They teach very specialized courses and even those are very relativist in nature by the discussion of case studies.

The problem is that today we do not have strong distinctions on ethical or moral issues within our universities, our media, or in much of society. Our children are taught, far too often, that right and wrong can be judged in a very relative sense depending on how the circumstances are rationalized. And often the concept of victimization rather than individual responsibility works into the rationalization. Violence and discourtesy seem to dominate the entertainment they absorb in youth. Too often ethics as a course is looked upon as less important than the technical training or electives that might fit political correctness or a more specialized course in their major. The reason is often not the fault of ethics. It is not taught well and is confusing when it is made to be relativistic by the professors. We can again apply the observation that you can look at tic tac toe, checkers, and chess as three levels of a very similar game at different levels of comprehension. Ethics itself or just right and wrong are often taught as tic tac toe whereas checkers needs to expand knowledge of the impact that it has on society in which an individual will operate. Chess, on the other hand, is the significant impact on the individual studying it as to his choice of conscience or convenience and what it will eventually do to his perception of personal dignity and responsibility for the common good. This is the essence of the creation of the broad discipline within society. I had received much more lucrative offers before I came back to the bank in Brenham, but I knew that a bank helps build a town. In Dad's day and before him, bankers worked together to build Industrial Parks, municipal efforts at infrastructure, and schools. Their future was the communities' future. To help create was important to me. Today national branches that see the world differently have largely replaced the local banks. But the reality is that the local area is still home. You cannot rely on politicians to build your future. You must create volunteer structures.

When many of us began the Texas Lyceum, we chose that name because Aristotle had been a thinker of both vision and ethics. In *The Language of Conscience* his work *Nichomachean Ethics* was one of the books I recommended for people of conscience. He looked at ethics in a much more natural way. Ethics wasn't a study of a technical set of rules to define the nature of goodness but instead the value it gave you in leading a moral life of fulfillment. It is more a search for wisdom than it is for a process to technically classify knowledge and actions.

Frederic Bastiat, an economist and author, wrote *The Law* in 1850. He focused on liberty and individual dignity. He made a great distinction that law does not give rights but only helps people defend, in an organized manner, the rights they recognize. It is the collective right, which protects the individual right. So ethics is really not a small code that is like a body of law, but it is the unification of cultural values. If they erode, their combination loses its justice, and the population begins to rely on the courts, as the solution after it only becomes a problem. Toleration, an understanding of relativism and other concepts are necessary multicultural vehicles. But at some point civilized society must have core values that not only become the law by combining individual values but that also give it strength.

In Texas our law is based on an old document, the Constitution of 1876. Its Bill of Rights (Article 1, Section 2) states:

> *All political power is inherent in the people and all free governments are founded on their authority, and instituted for their benefit. The faith of the people of Texas stands pledged to the preservation of a republican form of government, and, subject to this limitation only, they have at all times the inalienable right to alter, reform or abolish their government in such matter as they may think expedient.*

That has been the base of Texas law, and regardless of efforts, the old Constitution has not been replaced only modified. Yet with stability, government in Texas has changed drastically to create one of the world's best economic environments. It is in large part because Texas has unique value systems, strong individual responsibility, and limited taxation. I am often told that ethics does not have a strong constituency in politics, but that misses the power of morality and ethics that is present in each election. Negative campaigning showing a lack of ethics works often abusing truth, but it shows the power of ethics and morality in the culture. Ethics' power is basically the Golden Rule, which is the anti-hypocrisy standard. You get the government and laws the culture permits and supports. Individual responsibility to values coordinated into common goals will be critical to the competitive future of many nations in the world. But the process occurs with time as children are taught values. When hate is taught to children in parts of the world to develop the power of vengeance, we had best teach honor for the strength of the power of conscience.

To say that morality is only for the family or the churches to teach misses the point. The entire culture through its peer pressure is what ultimately affects the success or failure of a society. It is the national character we talked about in the failing of democracies of the past. This is the failure to provide opportunity for those that wish to make a better life as Gandhi so aptly described in his weaknesses of society.

The Institutional Creation of Ideas

One of the things most necessary in the world today is a period of enlightenment that to a degree thinks out of the box from the existing frameworks that are focused more on political ideology or economic excess and in some cases potential instability.

The recent interest in Benjamin Franklin, Hamilton, Washington, and other founders of America show a search for the characteristics of free thinkers of common sense. We have few intellectuals that stretch the limits of thought both of the elite and populist masses. Too often the elite look down upon popular thought, and the masses often do not look to the ivory towers above for leadership.

There needs to be a renaissance of thought that links the elite of knowledge with popular common sense wisdom. Both are needed. For one provides a vision from a mountaintop while the other understands the problems of working through the trees in the valley. This is the crucible in which the new thought is slowly developed often in controversy and with limited support of the elite who are challenged or the masses that see no immediate relevance.

They can help set the agenda for a new method of thought or organization of how ideas are processed. They are the thinkers that plow the early ground for the planting and growth of future prioritization. America's cultural focus moved from conservative to more liberal with intellectuals, media, and entertainment pushing to defining the conscience of society on liberal issues. That has reached a point where the pendulum is activated because the more popular masses find elite thought is now relevant to them because of the effects on them. But too often these are defined in wedge issues.

A modern example would be the March 2006 riots in France. Student and labor unions threatened strikes in response to a new law that allows a company to fire a person under the age of 26 within the first two years of being hired without cause. The purpose was to create more employment for youth because companies did not want to take on untried workers for almost lifetime commitments. It made France rethink what socialism should mean. In the minds of many opposed to the law, they look at the history of French Socialism as altruistic and noble in the equality it presents and the rights it grants. To them once they have a job it should not be subject to being taken, they have rights created. But the altruistic part of socialism was the concept of charity or conscience and helping those in need. But with the expansion of the role of government to fill that need, French Socialism has tended to move from the concept of individual responsibility for performance that is critical in the competitive economic world of today. France will have to develop a more enlightened socialism but the riots and the "rights" mentality are the way many people think about the issue. The conscience base of their socialism is not helped by a rigidity that makes them non-competitive and thereby affects the ultimate standard of living of their economy.

The most logical approach to transition in France and elsewhere, to help bring stability would lie in a cultural approach that impacted those two major forces of economics and politics. To do so, you have to have a perspective of ideas that can grow and be developed on a scale of great complexity like the evolution of market economics. There are many things that have to be discovered and learned as well as the formation of a concept that each individual can understand and appreciate its benefit to them. Remembering that people are primarily for themselves, they often do not fully understand any concept, but at the same time they have an instinct as to what might be perceived naturally correct and is in their best interest. They recognize hypocrisy. They recognize superficiality, and if they give an issue thought, they appreciate substance. The problem is that in the modern world, things are highly technical and very specialized. The population generally sees the individual shotgun pellets that do not go very far but have all of the immediate noise. The creation of new sets of ideas and new approaches to problems will not emerge as an immediate revelation. Instead a set of ideas that are developed over time and gradually communicated tends to change society because of their inter-reaction with a series of crises that overcome inertia and gradually push them forward. History has shown that on occasion great acts or great battles make a difference, the battles of Tours and Vienna are examples, but normally the perseverance of ideas gives character and a dedication to a mindset that eventually succeeds. Certain ideas are more successful in times of war and stress as was the concept of legalism in China, but they do not govern well once the stress is relieved. Each individual's personal dignity and ego look at issues of security in one perspective, but after security is more relative, a different mindset takes place. Maslow's Hierarchy of Needs is quite accurate.

Thus, the short-term ideas of ideologies that often play through politics are much more changeable than the more character-based concepts of value systems. Value systems give substance but are much more difficult to create. Unless each individual becomes committed to a concept, they are not that willing to truly sacrifice. And the only way they become that committed is either in personal convenience that it benefits them or with conscience understanding the nobility of the idea and creating the capacity to look beyond themselves to what is truly right. Value systems also provide value judgments on leadership. And if the value system works to build personal dignity with concepts such as the common good, a culture of service, ethics, and the Golden Rule for equality between people, then it sets a high standard for leadership. However, it also sets the base for strong economics through market systems and a more limited government responsibility, both of which are of great assistance to leadership in the longer term.

The great problem of politics is that it is often very short term, and it is very difficult to convince the public of many of these benefits with the nature of the media today. It would be naïve to believe that such a concept can be totally pushed by an individual. On the contrary, a set of ideas needs to be developed thoughtfully over time so that the population is increasing education and sensitivity to what is in their own best interest. These ideas must create the base by which more substance can be argued and create that group of uncommon men and women that understand how the best future can be obtained not only for themselves but for their children. Patience and commitment are necessities. A Thomas Paine simplified style and popular presentation is a necessity. But you need the solid developed core of an idea to simplify.

So the creation and appreciation of a perspective of the more ethical culture we have discussed begins with its study by men of thought. Then ideas can pass to broader groups of people and be ever expanded, much like one man lighting a candle, then ten each light the candle of another ten.

In China during the period of the Hundred Schools, many ideas were put forth to try and correct the problems of society. A few that were the best reasoned emerged to become the basis of the Chinese synthesis. They did not totally agree. In fact the skepticism of Daoism differs from the more positive teachings of Confucius, but the basic issues of morality were a more common base. We have to find those things that we can agree on individually with others, as nations and eventually as cultures, so we can build a positive foundation that lifts all rather than a platform of destruction that lowers all. That foundation requires a unique perspective going into the development of concepts and an absolute appreciation of reality of all of the major forces and powers that will affect the ideas over time. Thus it provides a flexible mechanism to appreciate and identify the critical issues being generated while never forgetting the perspective of conscience with which you begin. It requires people to give respect to the thoughts of others for discussion.

That type of concept is going to be generated only in a limited number of places because it involves many factors that inter-react. It is the very essence of public policy decisions and how they can be coordinated to ultimately affect, over time, the direction of a nation. It can build the character that is necessary to strengthen great democracies by having them recognize the trends that will inevitably weaken them before they get to a crisis. They will hopefully provide an educational base so that people can understand the necessity for sacrifice before points of crisis are met when solutions are extremely limited and success much more questionable.

More than universities, which tend to be theoretical, more specialized in thought, and very technical in approach, the modern day think tanks will in all likelihood be the place of inception.

As I wrote the three books that have combined these concepts, I have used no footnotes, only references to key quotations. They were never intended as an academic approach to these issues to prove a specific point. They are instead a chronicle of experiences of how natural rules shape opportunities. I have never represented that conscience ultimately will win because in history, many cases show that society, as Machiavelli carefully predicted, creates a hostile environment for an honorable man. Sir Thomas More and many others are perfect examples. Yet at the same time, men have joined together and have taken risks to build a greater society because the ultimate goal of man has been to advance civilization. The age old question for each generation is "if change is needed, if not us who, if not now when?"

China is perceived as being a rising power today. And it should never be forgotten that for four thousand years China had one of the world's great cultures and several hundred years or so past, they also had the world's largest economy. The industrial revolution in the West (enlightenment) was not as accepted by the cultural values in China in part because of the rigidity of thought in the system. It is the balance between existing values and enlightenment that is significant. You have to have both to move forward, but the choices and understanding of the issues put forth have to be looked at with more depth than superficial politics if you do not want to err. Any errors may not be immediately apparent but certainly affect the future generations.

The think tanks of today have a benefit over the universities in that they more often have to deal with the reality of power to actually accomplish public policy ends. They are forced to recognize the need to try and blend ideas to have some opportunity for success. There are certainly those that have no purpose other than to be advocates for a particular idea and have no interest in reaching a middle ground. That is how they get their funding and make their living. But I think there are a great number of institutions that have the integrity of purpose to improve society. And they will blend together to try and accomplish positive ends when they are not forced to leave their ultimate principles. That is why we have coined the phrase "The Language of Conscience" because ability for people to cooperate is created in that environment. Most focus their efforts to encourage their fundraising base, but I think there is substantial support today, even in the extremes, for more work to a common ground.

If we can envision three intersecting circles with one being reality, one being the political right, and the other being the political left, we will see that the two circles of the right, and the left may overlap on very few issues. But the circle of reality moves up on the other two to ever-greater size if we have integrity of purpose that does affect reality. If we look at ideas for their wisdom and not their origin, much more good can be accomplished.

Of the institutions that can develop these types of ideals, think tanks are certainly one, but generally work in specialization. They can provide great insight, great knowledge, and great depth, but usually on more individualized issues such as taxes, the environment, and a host of others. Individuals that write and think similarly have areas of expertise but often need to be linked with others to have impact. The universities most certainly play a major part with their research and knowledge of their departments, but often more intently when they create an institute that looks specifically at areas and attempts to bring together the expertise in a much higher level of specialized departments. The ultimate place that ideas need to originate are the more comprehensive public policy think tanks or foundations that look at government from the three major power sources of economics, politics, and culture. They can be the consolidators that try to develop the ultimate strategy of a game of chess. But every strategy needs to have a game plan that is understood by which it can analyze and bring in talent to build a better team. You have to have a top-down vision to appreciate how the parts fit together and what is prioritized. You also have to have a well-broadened perspective that guides how you think.

Much like on every successful sports team, it may not necessarily be the one great player who dominates the action. But it is the teamwork and cooperation of a variety of groups and institutions working together thoughtfully with common purpose that provide the greatest opportunities to contribute to the creation of great ideas. It is not necessarily the most brilliant, but the best suited to the effort that enhances value. Once the strategy is determined, then the relationships of the great think tanks need to be built. Expertise can be assembled and the depth of argument should not be just the opinion of one, but the opinion of several. Then the opinion can be freely debated to find the ultimate truth or most probable approach to success. The primary more global think tanks can be assembled into these arenas, through the specialties of organizations, individuals, secondary think tanks, and universities. Great universities could re-emerge by creating an institute that is coordinated in its resources and in the benefits and reality of the outside world. The point simply is that we need to find new ways to look at issues in a very different world, and it has to include bringing people together more easily and having more open minds beyond controlled environments.

The Critical Communication of an Idea

If messages are so complex that few people understand them, they seldom reach the political power level to develop change. The communication of ideas of value has a power of integrity and trust that are very different from those of just political ideology. The trust can be easily destroyed by hypocrisy. But people are relatively tolerant when they understand the general philosophy. People have to see that it is important to understand why things are being done, not just what is being done, and that requires a different style in the communication of ideas.

The media of today has many of its own problems because more specialized areas of communication are overcoming the major broadcast avenues of the past. That means people may begin to look at ideas in a certain direction or sense that the power of economics may well draw far more supporters to a concept and an idea than in the past. The media at present is dominated by more opinionated players than would normally be admitted. This is true in America both on the right in talk radio and on the left in print and television. Organizations and individuals are being perceived as accurate more on the basis of the natural human desire to be right than necessarily an analysis of the information presented. In America it is very hard to find shows that don't focus on disagreement. There are few that try to concentrate a thirty-minute segment on trying to teach why things occur such as Milton Friedman's tremendous series, *Free to Choose*. The argument that the people would never understand is inaccurate. The right question is how can these thoughts be put forth and the issues simplified. Genius is nothing more than making a very difficult issue simple to understand. The forces of economics and of politics can be harnessed to accomplish these ends.

The development of the Internet and the sophistication of search engines may well make a renaissance of substance more possible as advertising brings popular content rather than more elitist opinions. In some ways, search engines will be the new media. They can add conscience and should to keep the integrity in the Internet necessary for its ultimate use. The European Armies of several past centuries used drums to signal orders in battle not only to get beyond the sound of battle, but to overcome language problems. They found a common medium and a common thought process.

Normally there are only a few percentage points in America between the two parties and these are the undecided. They tend to not commit early because they often try to think about the issues. And they are the place that ideas do make a difference. It will in all likelihood be a time of crisis before enough focus is placed upon those ideas to make a difference. But if someone does not create a positive path that is in place at the time of crisis, then generally only the negative may exist. This negativism offers little for a positive solution.

You must blend this perspective with one of time and patience. One of the most interesting things I have viewed in my travels was the Temple de la Sagrada Familia in Barcelona, Spain. Construction began in 1882 with the vision of architect Antoni Gaudi who worked on it 40 years. He created a style, and the financing came from the people through donations and alms. It is one of the most massive and intricate buildings I have ever seen and well over a century later is still in construction from donations. But the vision was that of a man with a style long before his time of appreciation. His contemporaries often found fault, and the project was looked upon as too massive. But the great changes in the world are often from unpopular or unappreciated contemporary visions that find appreciation with time and possibly crisis. Leaders should remember that most significant efforts show benefit long after they are gone. It is the vision that remains.

Section V

How Successful Are We and How Do We Improve?

Measurement of Cultural Transition

To be truly effective, ethics must not just be a concept but a core value of a culture. Ultimately, culture is the enforcement vehicle to support ethics.

Most people instinctively comprehend the term ethics as "doing the right thing," but the process is often more complicated than that. Much like getting a driver's license, you take the car for granted because you just step into it and hopefully it runs. The system of ethics is really the car itself, how it was designed and built, what makes it function, and how it works—all must be understood if you want to repair it or improve it. To instill ethics as opposed to just teaching it, the culture must aid in developing and appreciating it so that it becomes a natural habit. That natural talent defines character.

The three measurement criteria come at the same point from different perspectives. The discipline within society looks to personal dignity concerns and how the enforcement of law, as well as the strength of the system of law itself functions. The more support of law enforcement the stronger the culture. It is from the perspective of power.

Discipline in Society

What then is law? It is the collective organization of the individual right to a lawful defense. . . . Each of us has a natural right—from God—to defend his person, his liberty, and his property. These are the three basic requirements of life, and the preservation of any one of them is completely dependent upon the preservation of the other two.
— Frederic Bastiat
The Law

Each of us has rights and obligations, as both individuals and part of a group. The balance between individual rights and obligations to protect the group defines the discipline of the society. The creation of laws and the enforcement of those laws define this balance. Enforcement often involves a negative: giving up individual liberties. Is that loss offset by the creation of a positive benefit for the entire group—the body the enforcement is protecting? It all depends on trust of the individual in society's ability to treat all with fairness and integrity under the system of law. The value system is cultural in nature, changing with situations and the times. Ethical fairness of enforcement and the motivation behind the act of enforcement holds the key to trust. It determines the willingness of society to limit its individual rights. Discipline within the society is both on the broader peer pressure of ethical culture at the end of a pendulum and strong power at the other. This pendulum swings one way or the other from the center and also affects the nature of the perception of individual dignity.

Do actions taken out of conscience protect or do they simply show power? These are the questions of cultural value—perceived through each individual's life circumstances. For example, centuries ago the perspective of Thomas Hobbs on the need for security after years of war was different from those of an economically centered, dominant America in the 1960s. Vigilance is necessary—sensitizing society to make logical cultural choices. Vigilance must be used to also ensure that conscience and not convenience drives the enforcement process. Law enforcement, like everyone else, prefers more power to make life simpler, but that power can negatively influence its ultimate power of support.

With the significant changes in the nature of the world due to the rise in terrorism perhaps no issue is more important, or possibly less understood, than the balance of enforcement in society. As a sheriff, my father had a perspective that law enforcement was not so much about putting criminals in jail as it was helping build a support for law enforcement in the community. In guerilla warfare, it is said that a guerilla without the support of the people is like a fish out of water. Similarly, a criminal is at a disadvantage when he is opposed by an active and dedicated citizenry. Just so, an informed citizenry that recognizes and cherishes its rights provides a culture to protect them. Terrorism often looks to criminality for funding and economic support, drugs being an example of how enforcement and positive cultural change go hand in hand. It is critical to remember that the more ethical a society, the more it depends on law enforcement to protect its interests by the honorable enforcement of known law. If people count on each other and enforcement, they do not have to take action in their own hands. If you work to create an environment of trust in society, the rule of law and honorable enforcement are necessary.

But it must always be remembered that the law is but a codification of the rules of the culture. It is the culture that you should measure.

The Texas Peacemaker Award

The Texas Peacemaker Award, given by the Sheriffs' Association of Texas in remembrance of Dad, notes that he had the physical abilities and toughness, but also integrity and appreciation of another's dignity. The reason for my inclusion of "The Life and Times of Jackrabbit Dippel" in the Introduction was to give a sense of the balance he conveyed between these issues.

Trust is a key component of law enforcement since it leads to confidence and support. In a time of instant media when too often the police have become almost militarized with S.W.A.T. teams, these concepts need to be revisited. Dad has been dead over thirty years, but I can never forget the importance of the emphasis he put on personal dignity. It was not just the rights that a man had, not just his safety, but something far more in the all-inclusive concept of dignity. He needed self-respect and should expect the courtesy of respect from others until he made himself undeserving by violating their dignity. But he also understood that dignity had to be gained by accepting responsibility. Rights and respect were not given; they were earned. So he focused on the culture of the community. He also felt the law needs to be enforced not just to punish the guilty but for the perspective of creating an environment and culture that protected the innocent.

There are a number of examples throughout history of the many systems for enforcement of the laws that reflect the basis of a society's culture. At one end is the repressive form like a balloon where the helium molecules are restrained within by the surface. The opposite example is a bar of steel that holds its own shape because the molecules are not separate but are closely bound together. In our example, cultural values make that tie. That is why terrorism and the changes to protect the group will change the balance of individual rights. We see it in airline security with new laws and limitations and also culturally. We have to distinguish between conveniences and basic rights just as we must recognize that the Golden Rule is present here. We give up some conveniences for others just as they give them up for us. If the Golden Rule is not present, and others do not reciprocate, the situation should be questioned.

But the more the police function can be in the form of a "Peacemaker" function rather than a law enforcement function, the more personal dignity will be retained and the more support law enforcement will achieve. There is not a loss of efficiency in being courteous, explaining needs, and building public support for when it is needed. Dad was six foot three, two hundred and forty pounds with tremendous physical abilities and had a gun. It did not take a great deal more than appearance to accomplish ends. But whether that appearance gets respect or fear is the question of measurement, and over time this comes from reputation.

As we enter this new age, we will see this on a more global basis. The West has long had a tradition of law based upon the individual and his rights. The East has had a different history, possibly because they have dense populations and looked not to the individual but to the rights and obligations of the group. Yet, culturally, the East has had much more of an appreciation of individual dignity in its traditions of courtesy. In a global world they will slowly work together as commercial law becomes more critical to commerce.

The image of enforcement becomes a critical issue. I have seen and experienced cases where you could not get law enforcement or prosecuting attorneys to look at mid-six figures case frauds for lack of funds and overwork. But I can see numerous agencies and huge figures of expense when newspapers investigate what would be "questionable" political activities that are minor. I see highly publicized "perpetrators" walk in handcuffs after indictment with attorneys basking in publicity. But to me, indictment is far easier than conviction, and there has been no true defense yet presented. It would be fairer to have such a demonstration after the trial and conviction, so people would know it was not publicity but justice being served.

Do not take this as though I question law enforcement. I am an attorney, was a prosecutor in the Navy, and the son of a sheriff. This having been said, there are different types and approaches to law enforcement. Image and management are issues that matter in law enforcement. It is not publicity but confidence to be sought. Fear and respect are quite different. In an age of terrorism and corruption it is easy to see the values in fear. In many ways it is effective and it accomplishes ends. However, it has problems over the long-term because the support of the people is critical. Juries have opinions based upon what they see personally as fairness. The system is looked upon as politicized not as objective and that hurts law enforcement in the long run because it limits their supporters. As always it is not what you do, or even how professionally you do it, but why people perceive you do it that defines you and ultimately gives you your power. The types of tools and powers allowed depend on the level of trust and perceived ethics. The courts themselves if they become partisan battles lose the aura of ethics. Personal dignity, the perspective of the individual, remains the bottom line. How does he see the nature of enforcement—protective of him or threatening to him?

Over a period of time, due to the terrorism threat, the world will change but in uncertain ways. What characteristics will dominate? The best for society is one that remembers personal dignity and builds trust while allowing substantial police authority to protect the group. That comes from cultural values that make the laws and define the dignities.

The measurement of discipline in society is the most critical one. Does law enforcement overreact or does it have trust? Is the prosecutor seeking justice or glory for another office? That opinion will vary with the level of trust. But thinking out the component parts, explaining actions rather than arrogantly imposing them makes a huge difference. Style has a great deal to do with explaining motivation. The measurement criteria here also give a guideline to what should be good practice if they are developed properly. You can always have actions that aid public security such as surveillance, but the issue is at what cost to law enforcement trust. There is a cost balance that must be found and observed.

The Rule of Law

Although mankind is not perfect, still all hope rests upon
the free voluntary actions of persons with the limits of right;
law or force is to be used for nothing except the administration
of universal justice.
— Frederic Bastiat
The Law

No more important item to ultimate personal dignity or to the effective operation of market economics exceeds the importance of the rule of law. Investment depends on the vision of the future and how well you can protect what money you place in systems. Investment flows to those locations where it is well treated and flees from those where it is not. It is not only corporate investments, but also individual investments, and thus a system of law has to include an ultimate sense of justice. The rights of individuals are tied to the rights of property, and the ultimate financing of great economic systems comes in the creation of secondary markets that allow liquidity to investments. It comes in the perception of future values as to the direction not only the economy, but also the country takes. If you have corruption, foreign investors may try in the beginning to circumvent it. But in the long run if they have limited success and it is a less than favorable environment, they will not want to run the risk and will find other places for their money. Implementing the rule of law is not easy between cultures. Many of my friends in discussing American law, because of the great amount of litigation involved in public companies, see that the rule of law can on occasion appear to be a tyranny of law when it affects the operations of corporations or individuals so that they have a tendency to avoid all risk. So balance aimed at justice and fairness is absolutely essential. Different cultures have different approaches and different histories. On occasion, using cultural approaches blended with a concept of law from other locations can be an interesting approach and can be successful. When Texas became a republic, it added many of the rights of the American Constitution and Declaration of Independence, but it kept much of the Mexican Community Property Law. It has retained much of it through its history. It was a blend that has satisfied Texas well even though it is somewhat different from the majority of other states. The issue is its integrity, its justice, and its enforcement.

The Enforcement of Law

Even though the rule of law is often mentioned as a critical component of any society, the parallel enforcement of the law is equally critical. If infractions of certain individuals are ignored while others are punished, there can be no real sense of law because there is not justice or fairness. The approach to enforcement is critical. In its ultimate form it needs the support of all the people because the juries are composed of them, and they may well elect the justices directly or indirectly. Too often the enforcement of the law is a place where those that wish to impact decisions can focus on convenience.

This convenience is not necessarily just basic corruption, but may well be convenience of action with a belief that conscience requires the actions to destroy the evil. Law enforcement, like the military, is on the front line and sees the worst. They see injustices in the system, and it exerts a pressure to react in a way that affects style, perception, and eventually effectiveness. But it is easy for just a wrong step to become a journey in the wrong direction.

The question for good law enforcement is the distinction between being feared and being respected. A good example is the level of professionalism versus the level of effectiveness. An officer can give a failure to wear a seatbelt ticket to Christmas shoppers entering a discount store and be very professional and rigid in doing so with lights on and a sense of show. Did the driver deserve the ticket? Yes and probably will think twice about wearing the seatbelt the next time as the public policy intended. But was it effective law enforcement if the driver took away the impression that this was a poor way to allocate time with other serious traffic problems during the holidays, not to mention targeting Christmas shoppers, and the style of the officer's arrest. You can say very professional words and have a sense of bearing, but if the driver feels less guilt at his own actions, but resentment for the circumstance of the level of fairness, you have made him fear and lose respect for law enforcement as a friend. You want the public to think of you as positive for helping, not employing a "gotcha" mentality. No one likes to get tickets; there is always some resentment and disgust at the situation. A parallel exists to bureaucracies of government that have pseudo police power by inspections or granting permits.

With prosecution it is often the same. Are all cases treated equally? The critical point, as Dad made throughout his life, was that the integrity of the law has to be supplemented by the integrity of the enforcement process. We dealt with much of this in *The Language of Conscience* in the discussion of the Texas Peacemaker Award, but it is most certainly a point that can never be overlooked.

Whether it is in the police power of enforcement or the administrative power of the legal system, its internal cultural ethics must be the focus. For example, the Bar in my home state sends out reminders encouraging pro bono legal work for the poor. However, a few years back the form wanted you to report hours and encouraged giving money to certain groups if you did not. But the only way you received credit was if you did actual legal work. The fact that I spent a significant amount of time and money on two children's charities for the homeless and those in medical need was meaningless unless it was legal work. As I explained, the charities wanted me to raise money and prepare strategic plans as the best and most valuable use of my time for them. I felt it was counter productive to make a distinction between service to others when you do so at their request. But it is very typical of professional, self-governing organizations that operate in silos of thought.

Ethics is very similar. Legal ethics is defined meticulously, but I think it has lost its sense of justice. The law allows great latitude in pleadings so the equivalent of libel is allowed and people, such as corporate Boards of Directors, can be sued individually with little risk if they are even tangentially involved. The abuses I have seen in recent years astound me, and I feel border on legal extortion in some cases. Yes, defendants have a right to a day in court, but at what expense and how do you reclaim honor or damage? The legal system does not subject itself to much liability. It is not changing the law that should be the focus here, but instead a strict code of ethics to protect the public from abuses. If the professional organizations cannot fulfill this necessity, then outside forces will necessarily have to do so to bring a recognition of fairness to the process. The courts and judges have become too much of a political football in recent years as politics has been in gridlock. The answer is not more Republicans or Democrats. It is a return to the essence of fairness in the law that is best accomplished by strict codes of ethics with certain and significant penalties for attorneys who abuse the system. The plaintiff and lawyers should find sufficient facts, or use the system to do so, before abusing others needlessly. Laws here are hard; ethics is not. It is not a question of partisan or nonpartisan judges or of elective versus life appointment judges. It is a question of exactly what approach to administrating the law they take. That is the issue of institutional culture and its ethical enforcement regardless. American legal systems have lost focus on that issue by being myopic. When I was in the Naval JAG, the military justice was focused on a core of ethics supported by honor. You accused very carefully because honor and dignity were closely related. Facts were critical early, not to be found true or false after accusations had done damage.

A Culture of Ethics
The Importance of a System of Measurement

There is a balance between the rule of law and the culture of ethics, which are both based upon accepting individual responsibility. If the legal system becomes so driven by victimization that liability is placed on anyone who accepts any responsibility, you reach a point where you discourage individual responsibility and replace it with the convenience of rationalization. How do you seek and measure that balance?

There are many different criteria for judging levels of culture. The simplest is whether the culture is moving from our interest in virtues to our interest in vices. Some people look to the level of rights that are given to women. Others look to the level of economic development through statistics, others the sophistication of education, and still others the levels of tolerance. The difficulty in judging levels of ethics in a society is the classic question that you often find in universities, by whose values are you going to judge. While morality serves as the basis of religion, in order to bring about enough of a consensus to enhance the level of ethics and morality (which is man's relationship to fellow man) the more fundamental and basic approach has to be taken. With all of the tests being given to children, it would be interesting to see how they would respond to questionnaires at different levels about how they would react to certain ethically questionable circumstances. Interestingly, if teachers have a test for which they have some responsibility, they often end up teaching toward it. We have many character-based programs in our schools presently; the question is their effectiveness. These are the places that universities could be of tremendous benefit in helping design thoughtful ways to educate and in testing the perspectives that have been taught.

Technology can both aid and hurt this movement toward a culture of ethics. The ability of criminals to use the Internet for fraud, particularly sophisticated fake websites, will do much to hinder the development of public trust. But it balances by increasing the value of trust and personal reputation. We can now "Google" our potential partners such that their past follows them and serves as a natural pressure on them to preserve their reputation as an asset.

This century we will be much more sensitized to ethical issues because they will become even more personal. The 1800s were the age of chemistry, the 1900s the age of physics, but the 2000s will be the age of biology and thereby biomedicine. Knowledge of DNA and its implications for cloning and research will make social decisions, on a global scale, much more important to each of us. We have to re-examine our perspectives of life, as we have known it. This itself will be controversial.

As the new sciences increasingly find "intelligent design" in complicated areas such as DNA, it will bring much more focus to the question of the nature of creation as science and religion continue their frictions at a new level, putting Darwin's evolution of creation against the concept of a more direct creation through the concept of intelligent design.

In the commercial sector, there could well be a far greater emphasis in each of the professions by which they could self regulate and report on their activities to give a bite to their actions. And the adoption of stronger corporate culture programs that are truly effective as described by many of the writings of the Ethics Officer Association and enforced by the penalties of the federal sentencing guidelines would be a great movement forward. Stricter compliance with SEC and state securities laws, as well as a monitoring of the level of enforcement, and the integrity of enforcement would move toward the concept of keeping men upright while you are attempting to make them upright. It is not good business to make profit crossing the ethical edge. It is greed, and it seriously deserves the punishment of society.

Defining ethics or its enforcing laws are not that difficult. Such laws often are a blend of approaches toward a common set of ideals that in a sense mellow each other. Conscience, which often rests on the Golden Rule of Christ or the Silver Rule of Confucius, does not vary that much when we have to place ourselves in someone else's shoes. It is amazing the level of fairness and understanding that occurs when that position is adopted. Whenever a product has to be divided evenly, there is no better approach than to let the other man choose which half he wants. These approaches have a power that is associated with natural law. The great difficulty is that they have not been contemplated in many of these ways, and the simplicity of their value is lost in the complexity of the times. It is for this reason that study, structure, and expansion could be most effective in shaping and understanding what are in effect the common basic rules of societies by which they could work together.

The simplest ideas are often the most correct, but they have to be sorted out from the complex arguments in which they are often obscured.

Keeping Men Upright—Governance and Laws

Our criminal laws, our securities laws in economics, and our series of regulations are all meant to define conduct and provide penalties when they are not followed. They are in effect legislating basic morality between men, much as the Chinese concept of "Legalism" tried to shape men by rewards and punishments. With the Sarbanes Oxley legislation after the recent corporate scandals, you saw a much more strenuous corporate effort because of the debilitating effects of corruption on not only the free market system, but on the confidence that is absolutely essential to it from investors. The ethics within a culture has to have some guidelines and reasonable enforcement. People need to know the rules so they can plan and act accordingly, and enforcement has to be reasonable in that it is not suddenly undertaken after years of being ignored.

Some of the best means of keeping men and companies upright are not just in public sector laws but are also in private sector institutions such as the Better Business Bureau and credit rating agencies. They are the competitive private sector approach that does a tremendous amount of good because they provide a constant pressure on behalf of ethics.

The Better Business Bureaus simply collect the complaints of companies and individuals about other companies and give them an opportunity at dispute resolution between the private parties involved. If their efforts are ignored, it normally reflects poorly upon an offending company that has many complaints. However, this requires a broad involvement of a number of people using the service, and it requires the support of the nonprofit association by the private sector. Similarly, organizations such as the Ethics Officer Association that we covered in more detail with several others in *The Language of Conscience* gives a great deal of support as to how corporations can build a culture of conscience within the organization. It does not matter how many rules you have implemented in the corporate ethics policy. It depends instead on how effectively people at various levels understand senior management's intent so they act in an ethical fashion. Are there toll free numbers for them to call and report problems? Have they had meetings both with their supervisors, and independently, that explain in training what is expected of them should they face certain problems? Is there an ethics officer in the organization that has real power? These are the types of rules that law enforcement and the federal courts look to in the sentencing guidelines to determine how effectively senior management has built an appropriate culture. If there were only a few bad apples in an infraction that could become very clear. On the other hand, if the culture of the institution was such that the tree was diseased that can become very clear also after a set of interviews at various levels with employees. I have included a bit more information on the Better Business Bureaus as an example of methods that can enhance ethics through competition for credibility because it is a fine case study of why corporate reputation and brands are values to be protected, so positive views are good business. Developing countries with corruption problems can learn much from the growth of this concept.

Men Being Upright—The Power of Culture

We have discussed in detail previously the critical component parts of having an atmosphere or an environment of culture in which men work that requires each of them to be more biased toward conscience than convenience. Perhaps nothing is more important in the creation of this environment than the system itself showing its desire to enhance conscience. In many organizations there are close talent levels between people to be promoted. However, if it becomes known that one of the key consideration factors is going to be the level of ethics of the people involved, it can change the very nature of any organization. When you have a culture of convenience, each person fights as diligently as possible to get every advantage and almost all of the key personnel tend to be ambitious. They look to how to get to the next step. The younger they are in life, the more that ambition tends to be driven as a part of their personal dignity. However, if they know that the next step forward is not necessarily best achieved by ruthlessness but instead the ability to work constructively with others in partnership, then you begin to change attitudes very early in life. This however needs training and needs understanding, but the ability to promote can have tremendous impact upon the formation of future cultures. What is valued is what is measured and vice versa.

A Case Study of the Better Business Bureaus

The Council of Better Business Bureaus (CBBB), located in Arlington, Virginia, is the umbrella organization for the local Better Business Bureaus in the U.S., which are supported by 240,000 local business members. Through the national memberships of more than 300 leading-edge companies and the network of member BBBs, the Council provides programs and services on behalf of the Better Business Bureau system. The CBBB also monitors and investigates complaints about national advertising, issues reports on national charitable organizations and administers the BBB alternative dispute resolution programs.

Perhaps no better description of its services over many years and the often unrecognized part it has played as an ethical catalyst in American business could be presented than by giving remarks of a half century of American presidents. In them you see the evolution of the organization to the areas of focus in a changing technical world:

From President John F. Kennedy:

By serving the public as a clearinghouse of factual information about business practices affecting the consumer, the Better Business Bureaus throughout the country effectively express the business community's sense of responsibility for high ethical standards and integrity in trade practices and business-consumer relations. Their work on both the local and national levels helps to build and strengthen public understanding and confidence in our competitive enterprise system, the mainspring of our economic progress.

From President Richard Nixon:

With effective education and protection programs, the Better Business Bureaus have made a real contribution over the years to better consumer relations and higher ethical standards in business. The consumer needs to understand how modern business operates, and the business community—for its own long-range interest as well as the consumer's immediate interest—needs to maintain high ethical standards in advertising and selling its products. The Better Business Bureaus are a splendid example of both enlightened self-discipline and distinguished public service.

From President Jimmy Carter:

The Better Business Bureaus have worked for sixty-five years to assure fair play in the marketplace. Long before the existence of an organized consumer movement, they acted as advocates for consumers and, in the process, raised the level of business credibility in our country. Your activities grow increasingly important as complexities of distribution widen the gap between producers and consumers and as more sophisticated technology makes products and services less comprehensible to the public.

In a videotape message to attendees of the 1987 Annual Assembly of the Council of Better Business Bureaus, the 75th Anniversary, President Ronald Reagan voiced his support:

Few organizations have the rich heritage of service that distinguishes the history of the Better Business Bureaus. Fewer still can point with pride to years of selfless sacrifice, yet that is the hallmark of the Bureaus activities . . . Down through the years the Better Business Bureaus have resolutely stayed the course, in the '20s they squashed swindlers on Wall Street and restored American confidence in that vital institution. By World War II, wartime savings were being protected by the Bureaus.... Today the Bureaus remain proud protectors of American consumers. As educators and mediators the men and women who serve the Better Business Bureaus continue to be champions of honesty and fairness. Businesses accept the Bureaus' informed impartiality. Consumers have confidence that the Bureaus will go the extra mile to get complaints resolved and see that justice is done. In some respects the Better Business Bureaus have come a long way. But in at least one respect you remain the same. Your name remains synonymous with integrity, honesty, and reliability. Your legacy is as proud as your future is bright. . . .

In a message to delegates at the 1990 Annual Assembly of the Council of Better Business Bureaus, President George Bush stated:

One of the greatest strengths of our free enterprise system lies in the willingness of American businessmen and women to respect the rights of consumers while advancing their companies' interest. Over the years, Better Business Bureaus have effectively promoted truth and fairness in the marketplace and, in so doing, have earned the confidence and gratitude of the American public. By encouraging high standards of quality in the goods and services offered by United States business and industry, you make ours a healthier, stronger economy. At the same time, you also demonstrate how effectively local, business-supported, nonprofit organizations can serve the public without requiring the use of taxpayers' hard-earned dollars. On behalf of a grateful nation, I salute you.

In a message written for BBB *Solutions* magazine, May 1994, President Bill Clinton stated:

In today's increasingly competitive global economy, Americans must strive to make every dollar count. The volunteer mediators and arbitrators of the Alternative Dispute Resolution Division in the Better Business Bureau are helping us meet this important challenge, saving many Americans' valuable time and money. Through hard work and dedication, these volunteers settle conflicts for countless businesses and consumers, letting the wheels of our economy continue to run smoothly.

As America recognizes the tremendous potential of alternative forms of dispute resolution, I encourage businesses and consumers to seek assistance when necessary. By relying on effective, efficient methods of overcoming disagreements, all those involved can get back to the business of improving the quality of American products and strengthening our national economy.

I commend the staff of the BBB and their outstanding volunteers for distinguished service to our country.

In the future preserving ones "brand" will be critical because of the value given to integrity, so understanding this nonprofit system of mediation and reporting is a valuable insight on how to affect the culture.

The Common Good Through A Culture of Service

As I mentioned before, what you do is important. How well you do it is significant. But why you do it is critical. Knowledge is understanding what to do. Wisdom is in understanding why you do it. But the real virtue is in completing the effort by doing it.

Perhaps the most critical area in judging conscience within a society is the level of development of its nonprofit institutions because it tells you a lot about how society views the common good. If they appreciate the need to help others, they understand the inter-relationship of men. By the Golden Rule, they would expect the same. It is not compassion alone but also a sense of obligation. A culture of service strengthens conscience by linking its parts. Does the government have to undertake almost all charitable and social efforts? Or is there a considerable amount of activity done by a structure of nonprofit organizations, and how much support do these nonprofit institutions have both financially and in the social capital of volunteerism from society? While government can do an effective job in many areas, what builds the actual concern for other people is recognition of obligations between people. If society decides that only the government should take on responsibilities, there are not that many cross-relationships that build the other benefits of conscience. This is not to say that different societies do not have other mechanisms for doing so.

In Latin America and in Asia the family structure is much more extended and takes a far more significant and detailed approach to these issues. In the West we deal historically with nonprofit organizations such as the American Red Cross, the Boy Scouts, the churches, the Salvation Army, the Better Business Bureaus, the nonprofit hospitals and insurance companies, and a variety of other institutions. The extended families undertake some of the same responsibilities. However, as an economy evolves with free enterprise markets, it becomes increasingly important to have a moral component within it. And often that moral component is developed by the nonprofit sector of the economy because it is how people self-regulate themselves through associations such as the medical societies, the legal Bars, and other professional associations. The groups like the Better Business Bureau take the concept of face and help quantify and record unfavorable actions as well as helping people solve problems between themselves.

The use of private foundations and public foundations where money is left in a pool to support many of these efforts that are in keeping with the wishes of the benefactors serve as a very major strength to the nonprofit arena and allows it to undertake the advancement of ever-wider areas and levels of service.

There is a significant amount of measurement in some ways present in some societies by the evaluation of charities and their effectiveness, particularly in the cost of their fundraising However, it has not been done on the basis of the effectiveness of the institutions or a very careful study of the types and prominence of institutions and the trends in the inception of new nonprofits. My fear is that in America, rather than institutions aimed at conscience being formed, there is increasingly a cottage industry of institutions created for political purposes or for the benefit of founders because they see the revenues that can be generated on controversial issues. A thoughtful system of measurement that understands the level of impact that nonprofit organizations have within the culture and how they could be enhanced from the perspective of service would be both interesting and of great benefit. Just as academia always asks, "teach whose values?" society should often ask charities and nonprofits, "service to whom?" The perspectives should be from the common good, well defined.

Nonprofit Institutions

As we have learned, the method of production and the cultural system are very much entwined. While the strength of one may influence the other depending on the society, they generally have to work in tandem. Since free markets do best with limited government regulation, taxation, and size, the needs of society that are not filled by government have to be supplied by the private sector through some means. Part of this is in the acceptance of individual responsibility by the population, which reduces their potential needs from others. But a large part of what needs to be done is charity, and public service has to rest on a series of nonprofit organizations that are dedicated to filling these needs. While some nonprofit organizations such as the Boy Scouts, the Girl Scouts, church affiliated groups, and others work on the basic concept of developing conscience in the society, others are focused upon solving specific needs. The Red Cross, the Salvation Army, Covenant House, and a host of service organizations from Rotary Clubs, Kiwanis, and Lions International provide networks that pull together people to jointly support projects. Many of the individual service clubs may not do work directly, but they do a great amount to instill the concept of service, which is often then found in other organizations.

When people tend to bind together for a common purpose, it lets them learn to take leadership positions, it lets them understand that there are other qualities in life beyond materialism, and it provides a network of associates that builds their confidence to take on more difficult projects. There are innumerable organizations that fill these needs. To me they are the representation of the power of conscience. If men are inherently evil, then such institutions would not grow and flourish for they represent the charity of man and the strength of his inner-conscience. They are perhaps one of the best reflections of man's understanding of the power of the common good in that we all have relationships to each other and have a distinct benefit in certain types of societies that provide us opportunity and an appropriate personal dignity. Personal dignity is a very important consideration in the nonprofit structure because doing things for others generally gives us a higher esteem of ourselves and does much to create peer pressure to do more good. The Golden Rule (individual) and the Common Good (group) are the base of the law (ultimately the base of the relationship of the individual and the group).

Quite often in the nonprofit sector, as it advances, you have those people that are most interested in the project because of what it accomplishes, and you have those that wish for their own sense of self to be recognized for what they did. It is thus often worthwhile to realize that many times you can succeed best by letting others take the credit. Ultimately people know who was the driving force. Strong nonprofit leaders know that strength and success generally come from combined efforts and from the fellowship that ensues. Nonprofit leaders teach others and are inspired themselves. And because of the recognition they have to eventually find successors to their positions as they move on to higher levels of involvement.

In effect, the leaders of nonprofits recognize that they owe an obligation to society and that getting involved is a way they pay their dues. The growth of this nonprofit structure is often internal. You develop a sense of uncommon men and women that we have discussed by letting them interact with others that have similar ideals. The structure is encouraged to take on problems that exist on local levels, because oftentimes it is not just the resources that are important but the social capital and talents of people that realize problems on a first hand basis that can be the easiest and best solutions. Normally the government only gives money and the spending of the bureaucracy administering the money may well make it inefficient. If the private sector is involved, oftentimes it is on a volunteer basis, and it is that concern and care that matter most. In rural areas where problems are often unique and local popular involvement is crucial, this is an especially effective approach.

When I served on the Covenant House Board in Houston, we worked with homeless kids. It was very clear to me that what was important if they went to a ballgame was not the fact that they saw the ballgame and someone gave them the money for a ticket, but was instead the fact that someone went with them and cared enough about them to give them a sense of worth and being. If you were willing to get up early and cook pancakes for them, they realized somebody went beyond the expected and truly cared. This is the ultimate strength of the nonprofits. It is the heart. Nonprofits can operate through charities or oftentimes through service organizations. Perhaps the most significant structure in the United States was the evolution of the Blue Cross Blue Shield system originally as a non-investor owned organization that provided health insurance and sought to accomplish a needed public end effectively. It was not just the insurance that they provided, but the insight they often gave to how problems should be solved. They support charities like the Caring for Children Foundations, which often address specific needs and helps provide efficient systems to be understood and copied by government.

Government can play a tremendous part in encouraging the development of nonprofit systems to assume many types of responsibilities. But it has to be aware that many of its regulations and strings make it difficult for people on a volunteer basis to integrate with governmental systems. What government can do, as it has in the West, is subsidize the concept through tax policy that brings about willingness of the private sector to give the funds to accomplish these ends. Government can also impede the growth of non-investor owned institutions by their policies. Non-investor owned companies cannot issue stock to compete. They must grow capital or merge. Too often State Attorneys General see them as a cow to be milked and not the workhorses they actually are. Shortsighted policies that do not allow competitive growth can ultimately destroy the common good purposes they are supposed to protect. But the best charities are those that give opportunity for independence not just financial assistance.

Philanthropy and Foundations

The foundations created by the wealthy, often providing the opportunities for individuals giving small amounts, have done a great deal to fund the nonprofit sector. Foundations can be of many types. In *The*

Language of Conscience we talked about the need for a clarity of purpose and an absolute credibility and transparency if it was going to be a public foundation. Private foundations that are normally sponsored by the wealthy are more an individualistic category. Andrew Carnegie perhaps started the modern trend of foundations with his philanthropy and his very targeted giving. In recent years the Bill and Melinda Gates Foundation has been one that has shown thoughtful research to leverage its gifts. The Meadows Foundation of Dallas has been one of those that has most strongly leveraged giving by targeting the needs of nonprofits themselves in administration and support services. The Houston Endowment has been an excellent example of visionary force on critical issues on a regular basis. Some of the best-spent money is that which researches a problem to learn the fundamental questions that need to be addressed before attempting to fund answers. Quite often the most sophisticated foundations have addressed this point and look very carefully where their funds should be committed. One of the greatest benefits in building a nonprofit system is to look at how to strengthen society by finding the places where it is weakest.

Raising Funds

There is perhaps no effort more key to the nonprofit sector than the fundraising capacity. If tax laws and governmental support allow for a structure of nonprofits, and if there has been some work among major foundations to help build a support structure to provide guidance in administration and operations, then the key effort for any new project is to define it very carefully. Who will be involved, how it will accomplish its ends, and how it will be financed? It is the same in business strategic planning. What product will be sold to what group of people, and how will the sale be executed?

In *The Language of Conscience*, we gave examples of how documents can be written to explain to people what purpose is to be undertaken and how it will be addressed. Giving people a clear vision is absolutely essential. It is hard to ask for money if you have not prepared a clear understanding of what the final product will entail and achieve. Additionally, the need for absolute discretion and transparency in handling funding services and the expenditure of money is essential. Credibility is the most important value that a charity has and if it is ever tarnished it is almost irredeemable. Thus, great care needs to be taken to build systems that accomplish these ends even if they are not required simply because they build the foundation for future fundraising.

In seeking money, the qualification of donors is absolutely essential. To go to a man that could give a hundred thousand dollars and ask for ten thousand is as bad as going to a man that could give ten thousand and asking for a hundred thousand dollars. In the latter the request is unrealistic. In the former he might well be insulted or think you had not done your homework properly because he would be playing a minor part where he was used to playing a major part. Thus, building a database of givers and knowing the levels of qualification is critically important. There are many fundraising books and experts that can give ideas that help fit with each society. Seminars on fundraising and on grant writing are common in the West and an expertise is relatively easy to build through thoughtful programs. The key is to start with explaining to a potential giver why you came specifically to him and why his interests brought you there as much as his money and reputation for support.

Websites can provide information. But because it is a method by which the younger generation can become much more actively involved, much of what has to be focused upon in instilling values is involving levels of leadership over transcending generations and training them through this process. Nonprofit service is really mentoring both in knowledge of how to raise and spend funds, but also in the wisdom of why to make choices. Blogging may be the new form of open expression. But to be of substance, it has to be organized in thought and must build wisdom upon the foundation of knowledge provided. It is not effective just to have daily exchanges. Each day's effort needs to be an addition that adds to a base of thought and wisdom. An institution's fundraising is the same. It builds on an ever-growing base if it is to have permanence. So you must constantly go back to givers, thank them, and explain why their money has been well spent. An existing dedicated giver is worth a number of new ones. Use Rabam's approach to charity to explain what their money is accomplishing.

The Use of the Website

The website, thelanguageofconscience.com, will provide an opportunity for many people to better refine a process that uses these general concepts and helps bring the type of enlightenment and balance of thought that needs to be injected into thoughtful consideration. Its web links will hopefully be a resource and catalyst of contacts to further these goals. At the core the triangles are a graphic summary of the most critical items discussed placed into a process of thought.

History is filled with seemingly unimportant items of great impact. The Comanche dominated Texas against all others for centuries because of their fierce nature and horsemanship, which gave them mobility. The Texas Rangers finally matched them in ability but could not dominate until they found the perfect weapon in the Colt repeating pistol, which had been rejected by most military at the time. Several pistols per Ranger changed the dynamics of close fighting because you did not have reloading delay.

Attila had dominated the Romans in part because he had been sent as a child to the Roman Court of Honorius upon his Father's death and therefore had the advantage of understanding the Romans and their tactics. However, when he met the Romans under Aetius near Chalons, he lost badly. Aeitus had been the Roman youth sent in exchange to learn from the Huns as a boy and understood them, an unanticipated dynamic at the time.

Technology combined with knowledge often surprises expected winners. Perhaps the best example might be the battle of Vienna, which stopped the Ottoman Turks from entering Europe. One has to wonder how the Turkish cavalry felt as it lined up opposite the Polish Husaria, their heavy cavalry. The Poles dressed uniquely with tall wings with many feathers fastened to the saddlebacks or backplate and with an animal skin draped over their armor. This was a most distinct look for the time, which probably caused some amusement. But when they charged, the feathers blew wide in the wind and created a sound that gradually built into one resembling a freight train. The opposing men did not fear them, but the horses they rode did. The horses thought they faced thousands of birds of prey descending upon them with a horrible sound, and they did not wish to charge into such an image. This created a significant disadvantage for the Turks.

The point of these observations is simply that the Internet is greatly under appreciated for what it can do to distribute and refine ideas. Our era of time can be spent seeking physical entertainment of ever more base content and violence that follows the circuses of Rome or we can value thought and a quest for excellence. At one time that was more of an individual effort because a few broadcast media dominated thought. Now each individual has a chance to spend his or her time in ways that they choose. But if they want to be a small part of the conscience of man and broaden it, they have a vehicle to do it as never before. The powers that be in all societies underestimate the power of ideas. But the shaping of ideas, the motivation of ideas, and the ultimate power of ideas come from working with others so efforts can be leveraged. Neils Bohr, the great physicist, made the *Copenhagen Observation* that each man's mind is but a model of the world based on his personal knowledge and experience. If you combine a number of minds, you have a model that better approximates the reality of the world. Similarly, the thoughts above are only an approach to generating thought, and each person or group may well incorporate it to their own circumstances.

Perhaps no project is more interesting to me than Google's effort to bring knowledge together by working with several great libraries and making the knowledge available on the Internet. Once knowledge is available, and it gradually will be from many sources, how will wisdom be achieved in categorizing and prioritizing it to a perspective? That is what the triangles fundamentally try to do. They go more broadly than Google's "do no evil" in that they are an effort at the positive creation of conscience by creating peer pressure. In life you must view all things, both absolutely and relatively. In business your size and balance sheet are both absolute in total dollars, but they are also relative in size to your competitors. That determines much of your possible strategy. The Internet changes absolutes and relativity to the possible advantage of conscience. Convenience has greed and ambition that help it in the absolute world. Conscience has more absolute principles, but can gain an advantage relative to convenience if it can bind together uncommon men in an effort more easily. It simply speeds up knowledge and wisdom.

In the history of health, nothing has been more important in stopping disease than the knowledge of germs and what it was that man faced. Before that knowledge, intelligent men looked to shooting cannons to frighten bad spirits and looked upon bloodletting to cleanse the blood of disease as a key treatment. Once man recognized his enemy, public health could attach the means of transmission with great effect.

Corruption, the example of convenience, is very similar. You have to address its root causes which are natural to man and society. Unlike germs, you have, not a physical enemy, but a metaphysical one of an idea. As we have said, ideas can only be replaced by other ideas, so a school of thought must be developed that looks upon corruption not unlike a disease of society and looks to its transmission and prevention, which primarily entails education and cultural awareness for success. Major educational and policy institutions play a key part. Every culture is different, so it is significant that they work together between cultures to find ideas and best practices. However, each culture will have its own ethical system that can be strengthened from within. The medicine of the West is high technology and often focused first on treating symptoms because of the patient's immediate desire for relief. The medicine of the East looks more to patients and treating the ultimate cause. Societies approach problems in different ways culturally and that fact cannot be overlooked. However, it is best when you combine both. The Internet will eventually be a weighing machine of values because search engines will create a prioritization of the most significant interests of the population as they refine their advertising sales strategies. At present there are few competitors from the conscience arena to compete with entertainment. But time may well show a new cycle, and the new technology will be available to help it rise more quickly. The issue for the conscience sites will be trust and how you generate it? But that is also the problem of the Internet and the giants of technology, so you may find future support where it is unexpected.

Perhaps it is said best by Dr. Kai-Fu Lee, the eminent computer scientist who is President of Google Greater China, in his book, *Be Your Personal Best,* when he quoted a section from *The Language of Conscience* and crystallized the concept, summarily:

Conscience is the foundation of the internet age. What Mr. Dippel wrote in his book, The Language of Conscience, tells us that conscience is critical to our second information age, The Internet Age. This new age not only covers knowledge, but also conscience. What Mr. Dippel is saying is that exposure to a much larger scale with the internet has changed the whole world. Anyone may offer information or services to anyone. In this internet world, credibility is more critical. Without credibility, a person who has a problem in conscience will have no way to live or hide.

Section VI

The Battle of Conscience over Convenience is Constant, but have We Created a New Paradigm in our Children?

In *The Language of Conscience* I talked of an effort in Texas called Texans for Quality Education, Inc. The organization studied a number of the recent education reforms in Texas in the early 1980s through the eyes of polls with all of the various educational partners. If there was one impression that I retained from the effort, it was that it is extremely difficult to teach anything because of the various complexities in the educational system. Education often becomes focused on many issues such as division of resources, control, methods of instruction, testing, etc. It is easy in the forest to lose the mountaintop observation that you are training the next generation in global competition to preserve your standard of life and your core values. As one educator explained to me, education years ago focused on a more scientific management approach. Like the assembly line, each effort was specialized and improved, but what was lacking was the effort to watch how the parts all fit together. It is the final product that matters. It is not how well made it is that gives its value, but it is utility and scarcity and those change with time.

But a second equally important point was that what you taught was not nearly as significant as what the child actually learned. While the education issue often focuses on the theoretical intricacies of education, the ultimate goal is the model of the world formed in children's minds that is enhanced as they grow older. It is enhanced not only by what they are taught in schools and universities, but what they perceive from their parents, the institutions of society, and other people. This is a model within the mind that is instilled because it comes from many sources including personal experience, which has a tendency to give it a much more serious impact on the model. Much of this is shaped, even from an earlier age, by the natural human desire to be correct. We form early opinions, and we have a tendency because of the nature of how society is being polarized, to accept opinions that confirm our beliefs and select sources that parallel them. Our personal dignity is a key component of our level of satisfaction and what we feel to be success. It may be success only if we have more material wealth than others, if we have more power than others, or to some, if we can take a satisfaction in making a better world. Nearly always there are some combinations of these factors because each of us is different.

We are all of different ages, which change our experience levels and our perspectives. We come from different backgrounds of history and geography. We come additionally from different levels of financial success. All of these factors shape our thoughts throughout life. The one constant that can help shape and return us to a perspective is that of how we work with each other. What is the level of morality that we have in treating our fellow men? If we treat them with the respect of the Golden Rule, we build a society that has a habit of more courtesy and more open thought because we are willing to listen to the ideas of others. It is this consciousness of conscience that helps build the environment that instills the best of models. It is what gives nations their character, and it is what gives economic systems their greatest levels of opportunity.

The thoughts given in the series of the three books, including *The New Legacy* and *The Language of Conscience,* are not based on academic approaches. They are based instead on a synthesis of what history has shown within societies of repeating trends and how they tend to not only affect each other, but also on some occasions, balance each other. The democracies of the past that did the most to enhance personal dignity always had disagreements. All societies will have disagreements within themselves. The question is how those disagreements are solved and how intelligently the governing structure looks to public policy on a longer-term basis. Unity is a critical part of power, a concept often forgotten.

Few changes take place abruptly. Nearly all take place over longer periods of time that require perseverance. This generally requires a willingness to sacrifice in almost any society, and you sacrifice best for values that you hold. Again, you pass forward to your children those things that you value the most. And you probably have your greatest satisfaction when you can join with others, usually in a nonprofit effort of voluntary good will, to achieve improvements in civilization together. There is never a total movement in any direction with civilization. Only marginal changes can have significant impact because they create the peer pressure in which we live. And they focus on the values and approaches of whether man is pushed to be inherently evil and thereby affected by fear or corruption. Or whether he can be developed and sensitized into being inherently good through conscience, which brings the recognition of his individual responsibilities for himself and to help others.

The battle for the nature of man is ongoing; it is never won or lost on earth among men. The two teams that fight to control the era both have successes and losses on a daily basis. Conscience and convenience are evenly matched, but the main players of convenience—greed, fear, arrogance, and their teammates are big, strong, emotions. The team of conscience—love, honor, courage, humility, and their teammates succeed when they play together as a team, not individually one on one. So the game is often decided by how well coached conscience is and how deep the motivation. As in any team, tradition and training are the critical factors. But once the players are on the field, the game is in their hands and they are constantly rotating. That is why the traditional system that teaches and motivates matters so much. You need the coaches and you need the traditions. It doesn't take a lot of coaches, just some good ones with a system and tradition of honor. If you chose to read this book, you are a coach that can address the principles to your individual circumstance and use the advice of Mark Twain, which I followed, in writing it:

The secret of getting ahead is getting started.
The secret of getting things started is breaking your complex
overwhelming tasks into small manageable tasks, and then
starting on the first one.

But as this book has hopefully shown, that is best served by a shared motivation of why you wish to do it and an acceptance of individual responsibility on your part and others to sacrifice to complete it. It is easy to do something that benefits oneself; it requires uncommon men to be dedicated to others.

You cannot be naïve and believe that the world will change absolutely from your efforts. At best you make a change in relativity that affects not only the present but also the future.

Section VII

Creating a Composite Review Matrix

The Rosetta Stone of Cultures:
Understanding the Relationships of Power and Influence
To Drive Analysis and Focus Decisions

*Power forces others to do your will. Influence persuades others
to shape their decision. When you are concerned with personal
dignity, influence recognizes it where power may diminish it.
Convenience often uses power because it is effective and easy.
Conscience usually involves influence
because it must work upon the inner values of others.*
— Tieman H. Dippel, Jr.
www.thelanguageofconscience.com

*In the modern world communication provides us innumerable
opinions to influences us. The power to act requires significant
unity or there is gridlock, so the creation of unity is the starting
point of the creation of power. The creation of unity is the
recognition of common interest, which is a catalyst.*
— Tieman H. Dippel, Jr.
www.thelanguageofconscience.com

Understanding Enlightened Conservatism
To Drive Analysis and Focus Decisions

The primary section of the book defined the general thoughts and presented required information. The previous speeches and materials consolidated the thought. This addendum largely reviews the triangles more technically and is repetitive since its purpose is a summary of the concepts previously presented with the exception of the works of Maslow and Rambam. It is useful as a review if desired. Perhaps the most difficult issue in life is to gain and maintain a perspective that gives an objective evaluation of how to succeed while, at the same time, allowing us to be satisfied and happy with the time that we spend on earth. As we realize that the earth is but a speck in the size of the universe and that the very limited life span each of us enjoys is but a second in the eras of time, we gain an appreciation of the vastness of the world and the natural physical laws that regulate our existence. Simultaneously, we have an appreciation that in the last 5,000 years of well-recorded history of man, though incredibly small in the eons of the universe's existence, we have made tremendous strides to conquer physical barriers and to move the concept of civilization forward.

Our greatest challenge of the future will not be the growth of knowledge. It compounds quickly. But wisdom, the ability to use that knowledge constructively, may be in increasingly short supply. The very complexity of new technology lends incredible levels of complication to understanding issues and seeing the derivative relationships that eventually occur. The convenience of instant information reduces the need for patterned thought to aid memory. This tremendously impacts the time-developed cultures that have been a codification of how civilization has advanced. While people often seek the right answers, even understanding the right questions has become extremely difficult. As we noted René Descartes began the equivalent of a scientific method through breaking down ideas into components.

In the construction of the triangles the same logic is at least partially used but is applied to forces or powers as opposed to ideas. There are some fundamental forces but there are other forces that are combinations, and it is helpful to break them down. The problem in doing so is that understanding society is not just lateral relationships but often three dimensional because of the complexity of modern times, which are constantly changing society. The selection of character and individual responsibility to represent the perspective of conscience is far more key than is appreciated because it gives a common and grounded perspective that is more absolute. Relativism would not be designed the same way. The same forces could be used for organizing power for convenience but would need to use other books of gaining and maintaining power to develop the measurements of success and the methods of approach. If you do not care about generational costs of programs for example, convenience would suggest that you ignore them in the present arguments.

The primary forces can be looked upon in two groups: (1) enlightenment or change force (often represented by technological advances and education) and (2) cultural structure or inertia force (cultural values, traditional economics, and historical interests). They constantly interact, occasionally positively, but often with friction. The nature of the balance between them affects the stability of society. The ultimate goal needs to be a balance, but what should be the fulcrum of the scale? If you use individual responsibility and the desire for man to be satisfied with himself and undertake the necessary obligations to society as well as receive its ultimate benefits, this needs to be personal dignity. It is also the definition of stability and harmony in the society. Although not a necessary fundamental, the primary forces or powers are economics, politics, and cultural values. They play a part in the frictions within the fundamental forces. But like Descartes' concept of clear ideas that could be distinguished from others, they are better understood in these contexts. So at a second level of analysis you need to look upon their impacts. The other forces are often a combination of the fundamental powers of economics, politics, and culture. Healthcare, the environment, tax policy, and many major issues are complex ideas that involve all of these forces. If a philosopher would follow Descartes' logic, he would then break down the complex issues into the simpler ones to better understand and explain them. That is effectively what the triangles attempt to do with the next stages giving tools of analysis, trend theory, and measurement. The last section deals with the three most critical measurement criteria for the goals of conscience within a society allowing judgment of process and understanding.

The technology of science brings the world much closer together and gives us the power to build an atom bomb. However, the question is whether we have the wisdom to know how to use that same power constructively and how we, as the six billion residents of a common planet, find ways to understand each other and define the common denominators by which civilization can advance.

When I first wrote *The New Legacy*, the set of thoughts that were included was termed "Enlightened Conservatism" by Tim Richardson, the editor of the *Quorum Report*. Fifteen years later as *The Language of Conscience* and *The New Legacy* were being translated into Chinese that phrase became increasingly important because of the need to identify a process of thought in dealing with a concept. The romance languages, such as French, Italian, Spanish, and English have a Latin derivation and thereby are easily translated word for word. The languages of the East, however, use a different set of symbols that translate concepts rather than words. To accurately translate presented concepts you have to understand much more about the individual writing and much more about the ideas, as a whole.

It is very difficult to take just pieces of thought and convey them without having an overview, a perspective of what I was trying to achieve and how the process fits together. Such a process needs to be named to be understood and codified. So I went back to the concept of enlightened conservatism. Originally, it was chosen because it perhaps defined a perspective of political philosophy based on individual responsibility. But in the more modern presentation it represents the balance between two competing forces—enlightenment, which reflects not only the tremendous increase in education, opportunity, and technology within the world, but also the impacts of globalization and inter-reaction—and the second concept of culture, which represents the traditional values that have been codified often with good reasons over generations and are often supported by an economic and political structure that protect them. Ultimately it focused on how to unify people divided by this friction. It is often said that the problem with balancing a budget or the government contract with a society rests with the fact that one man's waste is another man's revenue. Each has a significant momentum of its own, and it is inevitable that they clash when the speed of technology and growth create such uncertainty in the world that it pulls people in different directions.

You can analyze a situation from two directions. You can look from the bottom up or you can look from the top down. If you have analyzed it properly you should end up with the same answer just as this approach in math can be used to prove an answer. The codification of the values and beliefs focusing on family in *The New Legacy* are really expanded in significant detail in *The Language of Conscience,* as it looks more at the relationships between different areas of life. Perspective depends on where you stand in life. Maslow's Hierarchy of Needs can provide a number of differing perspectives depending on where one is positioned in the hierarchy. At higher levels the concept of the natural human desire to be right, combined with a sense of personal dignity, is probably the strategic driver, but that leaves the question of being right about what? And, what are the drivers of your "personal dignity"? The material benefits of success have a great magnetism. But does an extra two houses or a bigger yacht replace the satisfaction that can come from spending time with family, helping homeless kids or appreciating life? It all depends on one's perspective. You can organize your life toward many different ends. How happy and satisfied you tend to be depends on that perspective of life. When you reach a certain level of affluence, what really adds to the quality of life and defines "personal dignity" is the balance of enlightenment and wisdom.

The Chinese philosopher Lao-tzu saw many of the evils of highly intense competition centuries ago. In the corporate scandals of today where greed has replaced self-interest we see them greatly exemplified. I seriously question whether a life totally dedicated to little but political acclaim or vast wealth is as satisfying as one that has the time to appreciate life, unless the success is used to accomplish more than personal ends. My father was always concerned with not how many people knew his name, but more with what the people who did know his name thought of it. This is not to say that ambition of achievement is at all wrong, but the key is the motivation behind your efforts. Are they for you alone or are they for the good of society? If you begin with that perspective from youth, work your way through life, and keep true to the choice, then when you reach the final stages, there is satisfaction with a life well lived. This was a concept of Aristotle and of Christ. It was a concept of Confucius and many others. If you have been driven by convenience you may have acquired much. But often the satisfaction is never present because you are driven to still acquire more. Only a few ever reach the number one level in anything competitive. To understand the concept of personal dignity that is the balancing force, we need to review the work of two past philosophers, Maslow and Rambam. In thinking about this work, it is worthwhile to also consider that men are equal in the concept of personal dignity. And equity among them, in the sense of the rights to dignity and opportunity, are issues of equity that must be preserved. But this must be balanced against the fact that ideas are not equal. Some are far more important than others to outcomes and unintended consequences. So excellence is sought in ideas to select the best for the common good. Free trade versus protectionism is an example—individual unfairness but normally more competition and a better standard of living as a whole. Thinking through these balances in different societies, from different cultures, economic position, legal systems and other factors do not always get the same answers, and should not. In some advanced economies resources will go to great universities, (ten different books in one great library for excellence) in others to a much broader need (the same book to ten libraries for equity). The method of thought to find that balance ought to be similar, and in that, much common ground can be covered to help the greater good.

Our triangles need to recognize these basic observations as they balance policy and action consideration between the forces. Reality is a necessity, but similarly, when man has achieved a level where thought is given, other decisions can be more intelligent and strategic. Understanding the importance of opportunity becomes critical.

Maslow's Hierarchy of Needs
As supplemented by Rambam's (Maimonide) Eight Levels of Charity

Anticipate charity by preventing poverty; assist the reduced
fellow man, either by a considerable gift, or a sum of money, or
by teaching him a trade, or by putting him in the way of business
so that he may earn an honest livelihood and not be forced to the
dreadful alternative of holding out his hand for charity.
This is the highest step and summit of charity's golden ladder.
— Maimonides

The concept of personal dignity is very much affected by human motivation. Abraham Maslow in his 1943 paper, *A Theory of Human Motivations,* synthesized these human needs based on two groupings, deficiency needs and growth needs, which often are portrayed as a pyramid with four "deficiency needs" and a top "being need."

The deficiency needs had to be met before you could move to higher levels. They included physiological concerns such as hunger and thirst, then moved to safety and security, then the concept of belonging and love or an affiliation with others that lets one be accepted, and finally esteem, which gains approval and recognition both of others and self. In moving to growth needs there are important concepts such as cognitive understanding, then aesthetic concerns of symmetry such as symmetry and beauty, and finally the concept of self-actualization, which is the finding of self-fulfillment and recognition of potential that very closely parallels Enlightened Conservatism's concept of personal dignity. Maslow's final concept of self-transcendence, which connects beyond the ego, automatically includes helping others find fulfillment and realize their potential. To Maslow, human beings were motivated by unsatisfied needs, and there was an order of needs. While his approach has its critics, it has a substance of reality. You can only maximize potential when you have a stable environment.

Maimonides (also known as Moses Ben Maimonides, or the Jewish acronym Rambam) was born in 1135 to a family of scholars in Moorish Spain. His older brother David, a pearl merchant, supported him until his loss at sea. Maimonides then became a physician of great reputation in large part due to his emphasis on preventive medicine. He arose to become the court physician to the Sultan Saladin, as well as an acknowledged religious leader of his own Egyptian Jewish community. Although not a complete devotee of Aristotle, he did a great amount of work to bridge the works of Aristotle and science. He sought to harmonize it and adopted the

Aristotelian Four Faculties of the Soul, which noted that two perfections dwell in the soul, moral and intellectual. To them the source of virtue or vice lies in the capacity of thought and desire. Much of his work influenced later thinkers such as Saint Thomas Aquinas whose writings did much to blend Christianity with the works of Aristotle.

But to me, some of Maimonides' finest work was done in the arena of Maslow's final level of need where man looked to helping other men. How that was done tells a great deal about the individual, and a great deal more about the society in which he exists. Charity is positive however it is accomplished, but if a part of charity is focused upon self-benefit and aggrandizement, public relations, or the obligations of "society," then is it the same charity as one which is more private and intended for no reason other than the doing of good anonymously?

Maimonides was a unique person because he demonstrates taking Jewish history and teachings and blending them with Islam's concern of charity for the poor and produces writings that help explain the wisdom of philosophers such as Aristotle both to Judaism and later as a base for understanding its relationship to Christianity. These are basic thoughts that are often not as appreciated in the modern world as they should be. He understood however, that each new era has to be adapted to a different set of times. But the rules he placed for showing the different values of charity are very appropriate today and tell us a lot about the type of culture that we need to seek. They compare closely with many of the quotations we have studied.

Rambam's Eight Levels of Charity

The highest level of charity is giving a fellow Jew a gift, a loan, or a job so that he can become financially independent.

Giving to the poor in such a way that the benefactor does not know the identity of the recipient, nor the recipient of that benefactor.

The benefactor knows the identity of the recipient, but the recipient does not know the benefactor.

The recipient knows the benefactor, but the benefactor does not know the recipient.

Giving money directly to a poor person before he asks.

Giving after the poor person asks.

Giving less than the proper sum, but cheerfully.

Giving begrudgingly is the lowest level.

Two lessons are very obvious from the highest two methods of giving. The first is that the gift of opportunity can often exceed the gift of money because it lets a man acquire personal dignity. The second is how money is given, just like my Grandfather's story of cutting sacks of flour and cracking eggs, defines the giver.

These two concepts hopefully set a stage for the ideas presented within the triangles. There is necessitated a certain level of needs being satisfied before they become fully operational. But those needs are addressed in the economics, politics, and culture that set the stage for the standard of living and its rate of increase within a society. Once those needs are achieved, the concept of personal dignity and how it impacts the balances within individuals and within society are critically important. When you reach a certain level of affluence, great amounts of additional money usually add only a temporary benefit to your self-esteem and your sense of dignity. At some point, to be truly effective, you lose interest in yourself. At that point you are free to accomplish a great deal more for when you do not care what others think about you, you are free of many constraints. You can rent happiness by the success of your actions, but it is very difficult to buy because it always requires a bigger "fix" to provide satisfaction.

The Origin of the Triangles of Enlightened Conservatism
A Method of Summary of Critical Ideas

In my freshman year of law school, my tort law professor made an observation that has always remained with me. "How you think about an issue often determines what you think about the issue." An example might be a pot placed on a balcony that a stiff wind blows down hitting a passerby. The tort concept of duty would examine what obligation the owner had to the passerby for his safety, how the wind should be judged, and what duty existed. But if you thought of the issue from a perspective not of duty but of compensation for injury, the question would be who should pay for the injury as a perspective, and you get a different answer. Your perspective often determines your answer. Half full or half empty is an example. Public issues are very similar. The issues of equity and excellence are both critical in education, but division of resources between them depend on where you stand. Do you want ten books in one great library of excellence or do you need the same book in ten libraries? The point is that you have to have balance because you need both in society. You need a balance that gives you the common good of group obligations and you need the respect for personal dignity of the individual.

In today's modern American world, partisanship, media sound bites, and political correctness dominate the powers of politics, economics, and culture in such a way the forces of enlightenment (mainly technology and education) clash with the existing structure (mainly cultural values and establishment entrenchment) with unperceived consequences. Only as you reach crisis do you really focus on the best future choices. The concept of enlightened conservatism is simply a cultural approach to understanding the forces of enlightenment and the interaction with existing structure and values. It begins with a perspective that individual responsibility is required in a society that must both have a high regard for personal dignity but understand that while people are equal, ideas are not. Some have more impact for the future than others, and you must seek excellence in ideas to survive in a very competitive world. The ways you develop thought and the knowledge you must have of the powers of economics, politics, and culture and their inter-relationships are critical. But if you begin with a perspective of developing a society on a thought process of conscience over convenience you think very differently about what the ultimate society should be.

You have three cultures that let you judge your success. The first is the Discipline in Society that is the level of the rule of law, which is the basic set of rules required of the group. The second is the Culture of Ethics or morality where, because of the Golden Rule, many expect more of others out of common obligation, and finally the Culture of Service, usually for nonprofit organizations that represent where a man does more than others expect of him because he has taken his concept of personal dignity to a high level of compassion. What is not understood is that you need a balance between all three. The Triangles of Enlightened Conservatism were created nothing more than an icon of thought that helped visualize a number of relationships keeping focus while remembering other factors. Life is not divisible into silos, it interacts and actions have reactions. What the triangles represent however is that how you think is important, and what eventual culture you want for your children has a lot to do with your actions. It is not what you teach them at home alone for the world may corrupt them or make their beliefs a burden. It is the culture that matters, but the culture is shaped by the politics and the economics. How you think determines what you think, and how you think does a great deal to define you and your values.

As we continued to develop concepts, we found the triangles useful at different levels. As we have discussed, you have three levels of increasing complexity of options and strategy—tic tac toe, checkers, and chess. The triangles are similar. The simplest use is an explanation of the general concepts. The "checkers" or middle complexity is the preparation of argument or policy considerations involving related issues. The chess is when each component is understood so well that you can anticipate effects. This latter use would be exemplified by the fact that policy control may well shift from government control to *natural law*. Taking some of our previous examples, as with any complex system, it reaches a point that is unsustainable and change occurs. The aging demographics, and the pressure they put on government retirement and healthcare systems occurring in the context of trade deficits and government deficits, will at some stage reach a point of crisis and confidence that changes have to take place. Much of the force will come from the investment markets where the issue of liquidity is different from net worth of retirement systems. How the market force will react is as much a social issue as a political or economic one. We can reduce cost of living adjustments, which will pressure the unprepared. We can means test to show compassion, but what is the morality in punishing those who have sacrificed, saved, and prepared? How does that reward individual responsibility? The point is the triangles become a good way to assess even natural forces because they focus on the drivers and the motivations behind the drivers, so that logical and confidence-building approaches can be explained more clearly.

In working with the triangles, I looked at many of the trends and patterns that futurists tend to follow as issues that would impact civilization in the future. Nearly all fall fairly logically and automatically into the categories if they are looked upon broadly. The judiciary certainly falls into politics, etc. A few trends were not directly related to the logic path by separate categories but were important. A good example would be the environment that will increasingly become a critical future trend worldwide. It is less a driver of actions than a recipient of the impact of actions. It has implications in economics. The preservation of nature certainly fits in cultural values as almost a basic. It could fit in conscience, and it is certainly political. Those types of forces and trends usually have a specialized issue that emerges at a particular time or a combination thereof. The triangles focus on strategic drivers. Education is a similar issue that is critical but is a component of many of the critical issues. But it is driven by policy more than driving policy—usually politics versus economics. They simply have to be analyzed as a part of the forces within the triangles. The triangles were designed as simply a way to categorize major issues from a certain perspective. They show how to group information looking to see what levels of expertise are available if global think tanks focus on the development of more comprehensive ideas. They are a checklist to make sure you have thought of most considerations and also that you have not forgotten the perspective from which you began. They allow a general overview with the option that any larger macro area can then be studied at a micro approach with relativity to the whole.

The great arenas of power, economics, politics, and media/culture are self-explanatory because they affect society by different inter-relationships and different places in time. They are very interconnected. As we pointed out previously, the method of production or the system of economics has direct impact on the culture of society and on politics because it affects the development of ideas. The next level looked at how you analyzed, measured, and viewed trends in the information that you placed together. All three are critically important.

The triangles themselves are not as significant as what can be done to enhance the ideas over study and time. They simply suggest a process that logically ties together the natural laws that affect the nature of man, the ultimate balance necessary between change and tradition, the forces of power within the world in economics, politics, and media/culture, the tools of understanding that are aimed not just at knowledge but wisdom in analysis, measurement, trends, and ultimately the goals that define what history has shown us to be the strongest of societies and the most powerful way for a great civilization to bring out its best characteristics. (Only ideas change the world over the scope of long periods of time because each of us individually contributes our part and has some impact of varying degrees while we live.) But what they do is serve as a reminder of what is important if you use them by habit. On the Texas cattle drives the cook had the responsibility of turning the wagon tongue toward the North Star each night. The next morning, when the Star was not there and activity was hectic, you still had the benefit of its guidance to make decisions. The use of the triangles is similar. Conscience is injected into thought.

The pyramids were built as great monuments to death in a civilization that focused less upon life. They were physical structures that endured through time. The metaphysical structures, the pyramids of ideas, have proceeded through history in their development. The great question is going to be whether man has the wisdom to find solutions to a very challenging and threatening era or where another cycle like the Dark Ages will re-emerge. Terrorism and corruption are but symbolic of the challenges that will be faced. And unless there are greater ideas that can unify the broad base of mankind, we will face an environment, and leave one for our children, that is far inferior than could be created.

The Rosetta Stone of Cultures

I have often tried to learn the way great men thought not just from their writings but the environment in which they lived that shaped them. It helped separate what was absolute or long lasting principles in their writings and what was relative to their times. To do that, I often visited their homes or place of burial where materials often gave more depth. One such visit was to the home of Nostradamus (Michel de Nostradame) in Salon-de-Provence, France. A Frenchman of the Sixteenth Century his future predictions have been debated for five hundred years. He was a noted doctor of this time and interestingly, medicine then combined not just the use of herbs and experience, but a combination with it of astrology.

Doctors also prepared readings on a patient that took his zodiac sign and the movement of the planets to see the effect on the weaknesses of this body. Nostradamus became a great astronomer from this and moved to predictions of events and weather in his almanacs. But he was also a great student of history and the writings of philosophers and historians. He took the great moments and changes of history, put them with the regular movements of the universe, and in his quatrains predicted beyond the year 3000. While difficult to understand since he wrote with fear of the Inquisitions of the time he has had a place in history ever since.

While I do not try to understand the stars or even Nostradamus, I have been fascinated by his use of the regularity of the universe juxtaposed with history because history does tend to repeat in cycles. To me it is not the stars that control man, but man's failure to gain perspective of history and great trends and cycles. The reason is that our lives are often but a part of a cycle, but it can tell us much of how we should order our society if we care for our children. I remember a tour guide telling me once that wise men seemed to live longer. I have always felt the opposite was true— the older you lived, the more wisdom you achieved because your base of knowledge and cycles grew.

The triangles above are simply a base to enhance the organization of that growing knowledge so it can be more easily remembered as a part of a matrix. Just like any filing system, having a known procedure lets habit and the subconscious file knowledge away. It then lets discussions also be with others on a more common basis. Differing parties, if they both try to use conscience, will have something in common that helps respect and discussion.

Conclusion

As Always, How You Think Determines
What You Think

Not long ago, I was asked in an interview about my most tense moments in life. The interviewer had just questioned me about the seminar at the Central Party School in September of 2004 where I had six of the finest Chinese minds questioning me in Chinese on a book I had not reviewed in a year and a half. She suggested it might well have been such a moment.

However, I chose another one as the most tense, which on the surface might seem odd, but probably helps conclude a lot of our thought in a more crystallized fashion. It was the moment that I was presenting my daughter Beth at the Washington Thanksgiving Debutante Ball and Cotillion in the Capitol a few years past.

In a sense, it was not a unique event because I have participated in a number of social functions in my life, and with two daughters I have made presentations at a number of debutante balls. However, certain points in life become crystallizations and bring a focus to thought at a different level. That event was a very unique one for a number of reasons and very different from how it might normally be perceived. A little bit of history perhaps sets the stage.

As I mentioned earlier, in Brenham, Texas, there is an event called the Brenham Maifest in which the youth participate in a Junior Maifest, and the older high school teenagers in a Senior Maifest. The younger Maifest is built on a theme with numbers of costumes; the Senior Maifest may be elaborate costumes or tuxedos. But for over a hundred years it has been a focus of what brought a smaller community together—an appreciation of family. All the community concentrated on the kids. The parents were there, the grandparents were there, and the carnival and festivities that surrounded it added an atmosphere of gaiety. This event took place on Mother's Day and brought everyone that had been from the community back, if possible. My son Tee and my daughter Meg had both been king and queen of the Maifest in earlier years, but my daughter Beth had not been. And in the old family tradition of equality, an equalizing event is always needed to keep the kids "balanced." Since Meg and Beth had both done debutante balls in Galveston, Tyler, and Nacogdoches, those were equal. This unique opportunity appeared when a good friend of mine, a former Army Ranger, saw a picture of Beth and me on the cover of *Texas Business Magazine* for a Father's Day issue, which carried an article I had written. He sent the magazine to the founder of the Washington Debutante Ball and Cotillion, Ms. Mary-Stuart Montague Price, who had for over fifty years put together a very unique event. We had over the years been offered opportunities to go to New York for balls, but he sent me information on the Washington Debutante Ball and Cotillion that was very interesting. All of the military academies and many of the other military related colleges and institutions were represented by contingents in uniform who played a significant part in the event. While a number of the sponsors were Ambassadors and Congressmen, many others involved had a military background so the event had a sense of "honor." Thanks to his efforts we had received an invitation, and Beth was excited because the family would have time in Washington to also see the sights.

The event was an extremely well orchestrated one over several days with large receptions. At one of the first receptions, I had the opportunity to visit with a number of the younger cadets in uniform and tell them a bit of my military experience. And I suggested there were certain organizations they should join simply to network and meet people. At the close of one of these conversations a reporter from the *The Washington Post* approached me. She was doing a story on the Debutante Ball for her newspaper and was conducting a series of interviews with different participants. She found it interesting that with a number of debutantes around, so many of the younger men had been visiting with me and wondered why. I explained in part, and we started talking about the event and a number of the different impressions that people had of it both from within and from without.

To some people, particularly those not a part of it, it seemed to be an event of "class" with wealthy people paying a significant amount to be a part of society. Some perceived it to be an event where you put on a very significant show as was the case of many society functions.

I explained that from my perspective it was really very different. I had grown up in a small garage apartment and our family had worked hard to accomplish what it achieved. But we had not necessarily ever felt we were inferior to or above anyone else. Personal dignity was found in many places, and it was as an issue of equality not status.

I explained that how you looked at this event defined you more than the event defined you. This was a rare opportunity for my daughter to be particularly happy. She loves to dance, and she had the chance to dance two nights with a number of outstanding young men. The songs played by all the military forces at the conclusion were symbolic to us. Beth's grandparents were in the audience, as well as her siblings and their families and some friends. The picture that we took of all of us together was a picture of the best of us at a time when we were all happy for her. It was not the money spent on this event that was that significant. Instead it was the crystallization of family not just in pictures but also in sentiment. The reporter found my approach interesting and reported it as a perspective.

On the final night she was taking a number of pictures and noticed that I was with Beth and seemed particularly nervous. She was an excellent reporter and laughed and said that she really did not expect me to be nervous about going out on stage. I noted to her that this was not going out on stage. The girls from each area had their own way of bowing—the Ohio girls made an "O," and the Texas girls usually did what was called the "Dallas or Texas Dip," a swan-like magnificent bow if gracefully done. However, if she slipped, she would fall flat on her face. A significant part of how well she performed depended on how well the father held his hand absolutely rigid through the entire event for balance and how he did his part of the coordination. That bothered me a lot more than most other things that I had done because my daughter would never forgive me if she fell flat on her face in front of an audience in these circumstances that night. My absolute hero was the other Texan who had twin daughters and was going to have to use both hands in a greatly underappreciated feat.

The reporter was also intrigued about the difference in cultures and did part of the article focusing upon it taking a picture that included Beth called "Networking in a Ball Gown." As we went out that night it was a rather interesting event because you looked out at a very large audience with my son behind as an escort along with Beth's military escort, and my daughter and I as she was introduced. As she bowed, what struck me at that moment, was not that situation, but almost a chilling effect of recognition and remembrance of my mother who had died long before, but who loved culture and would have been inherently proud of Beth at that moment as were her grandparents, the Wrights, who looked at her from a table not too distant. My father would have very much sensed and liked the honor, the sense of responsibility and substance that filled the room. It was not so much an event of society as he would have perceived it, or Mother would have perceived it, as it was a time that life came to a crystallization of understanding that was important. It was not that we were there in the Capitol at a significant event showing off our daughter. It was that our daughter was having the best night of her life, in her opinion, and had already received invitations to the West Point and Annapolis Balls. Money was not the issue. Most of the young men there in uniform saw the military as their chance for a great future and they were people of character with whom you enjoyed visiting. It was a time that all of the family realized how important we were to each other and took joy in the fact that God had given us the opportunity to reach this point in life and reach a unity that came from a strength of values that had been taught. It was not arrogance but the humility of appreciation that dominated that evening.

It was as if that night Mother and Dad, though long gone, sat in judgment on how I had lived my life and what was important to me. The way they taught me to think, and thus would have thought about the situation, had nothing to do with society, money, privilege, or class. It had everything to do with family, happiness, and an appreciation of honor, dignity, and life for the right reasons. Had I spent my life doing a number of other things, we probably would not have been there that night with the family's orientation to its approach to its event. How our kids looked at the event and perceived it, measured Kitty and my efforts to raise them.

As I had told the interviewer who had asked of the difficult moment, knowing self is more difficult than knowing others. And the event in Washington gave me a better understanding of myself and a satisfaction of acceptance than the event in China she had mentioned previously. But the event in China is just as indicative of how you think about things determines what you think about things. As we began that meeting, what I already knew is that the Chinese had published the book and only did so by consensus. So we had a common perspective even if a different language. One of their great philosophy professors did the first analysis and pointed out clearly that there was not a total agreement with many of the points in my book. But the core that made it of value was that it understood dignity, honor, and the importance of culture to life and that understanding can be built on those principles and relationships. He was quick to note it was not the normal work of a scholar that was footnoted and steeped in sources, but instead more original thought of a synthesis that was more applicable to modern times. The Chinese had distinctions between the approaches of scholars and sages that included appreciating the development of ways of thought, and in these modern times both original thought and adaptability are important. Both cases, incredibly diverse as they are, make the point that how you look at life depends a great amount on what you think of life and how you proceed. The values you hold dear and the intensity with which you understand and value them sets your perspective and is the core of your personal dignity. Whether it is in Texas or China, cutting brush on a ranch or at a debutante ball, that dignity should not change to the circumstance but should adapt the circumstance to you.

Summary - Key Thoughts from the Heart

(Continued from The Heart of the Book without the Nutshell)

In my freshman year of law school, my tort law professor made an observation that has always remained with me. "How you think about an issue often determines what you think about the issue." An example might be a pot placed on a balcony that a stiff wind blows down hitting a passerby. The tort concept of duty would examine what obligation the owner had to the passerby for his safety, how the wind should be judged, and what duty existed. But if you thought of the issue from a perspective not of duty but of compensation for injury, the question would be who should pay for the injury as a perspective, and you get a different answer. The wind cannot pay, only the individual. Your perspective often determines your answer.

In today's modern world, partisanship, media sound bites, and political correctness dominate the powers of politics, economics, and culture in such a way the forces of enlightenment (mainly technology and education) clash with the existing structure (mainly cultural values and establishment entrenchment) with unperceived consequences. Only as you reach crisis do you really focus on the best future choices. The concept of enlightened conservatism is simply a cultural approach to understanding the forces of enlightenment and the interaction with existing structure and values. It begins with a perspective that individual responsibility is required in a society that must both have a high regard for personal dignity but understand that while people are equal, ideas are not. Some have more impact for the future than others, and you must seek excellence in ideas to survive in a very competitive world. The ways you develop thought and the knowledge you must have of the powers of economics, politics, and culture and their interrelationships are critical. But if you begin with a perspective of developing a society on a thought process of conscience over convenience, you think very differently about what the ultimate society should be. The law does not create the culture, but the culture decides what individual laws and rights it will enforce.

So while the law is more obvious, the culture is the true point of focus for change.

You have three cultures that let you judge your success. The first is the Discipline in Society that is the level of the rule of law, which is the basic set of rules required of the group and how strongly it is enforced. The second is the Culture of Ethics or morality where, because of the Golden Rule, many expect more of others out of common obligation, and finally the Culture of Service, usually for nonprofit organizations that represent where a man does more than others expect of him because he has taken his concept of personal dignity to a high level of compassion. What is not understood is that you need a balance between all three. The Triangles of Enlightened Conservatism were created nothing more than an icon of thought that helped visualize a number of relationships, keeping focus while remembering other factors. Life is not divisible into silos; it interacts and actions have reactions. What the triangles represent however is that how you think is important, and what eventual culture you want for your children has a lot to do with your actions. It is not what you teach them at home alone for the world may corrupt them or make their beliefs a burden. It is the culture that matters, but the culture is shaped by the politics and the economics. How you think determines what you think, and how you think does a great deal to define you and your values.

Tieman H. Dippel, Jr.
www.thelanguageofconscience.com

In the Next Decade

How you think becomes critically important when the pace of technology and communication make knowledge obsolete quickly. No longer are theories permanent or strategies long lasting for situations change and wisdom evolves. Technology will be important, but it is not creativity. It will be the creative use of technology that will be one of the great drivers of the future. But most important of all will be a framework of knowledge in which perspective can be gained so there is a structure of thought to be molded. Education must not just teach facts and technology for the future, but it must develop a structured mind with a base of values for an anchor, a realistic perspective of the world as a map of options, and a system of creative thought that takes the wisdom of the first two and applies it to the changed environment. You need all three parts, and the problem with modern education is that it specializes in each rather than seeking the combination. If you have such an education, materialism is less critical and more easily recognized, so satisfaction with one's personal dignity is more easily achieved. You can go into a store for drinking glasses and find the finest crystal or the cheapest plastic. We all look to build our dignity by having the best we can and choose the best we can afford. But what really is important is what we drink from it. Our focus ought to be on the substance we drink, not the vehicle be it a job, position, house or car. Education is more than just creativity and just knowledge. It has to provide wisdom for thought to be at a level of excellence. That requires a foundation that only education over time can provide and a perspective of life that is appropriate for it to be received.

Tieman H. Dippel, Jr.
www.thelanguageofconscience.com

The relationship between China and the United States will be the pivotal driver of the next decade. This will be a transition decade that establishes relationships and balances that will reach far into the future. Will there be two competing superpowers or a symbiotic relationship that creates the environment of the next century? Presently, the two are linked by economics not only in the production of goods and consumption, but also increasingly by financial considerations as China invests heavily in American debt adding critical marginal funding to the American economy. But this will create imbalances. How the risks are monitored and addressed has a great impact on the world's economic growth. To me, the critical issue may well not be the economics or the politics, but the perspective of thought that is driven by the people of both nations. They determine the politics and they react to the economics. But their perspective is set not just by the information they hold but also by the sense of the intent of their leadership and the confidence within it. The future challenges are going to require a type of leadership that instills confidence and comes from a cultural perspective of how people view themselves—a personal dignity and character forged both from history and a concern for their family's future as well as the immediate.

When I am asked my thoughts on China, I describe it as similar to my experience during the Vietnam Era when I was in the Navy. Even though I was a lawyer in the Judge Advocate General's Corps, we were also trained for leadership in fire control and some training in navigation. Perhaps nothing gave me more of an understanding of the complexity of guiding a great ship than the training in the BZ Trainer at Newport, Rhode Island. In a simulated convoy, all of us were in teams to direct a large ship on the screen and keep it in position. You quickly learned that small boats reacted more quickly, that big ones were very complex, and that you had to start movements early with a significant respect for the time, speed, and power of other obstacles. It was easy to crash without careful thought and experience. China is like that great ship. The United States is as well. The media has its stories of individual instances that give many different impressions of each because we focus on the short term in media. But in reality, both countries will have groups that differ internally. The key is where the trend is determined that sets the course for the longer term like that ship. How long are the timeframes allowing decision? How experienced is the Captain for uncharted water? How much power does the ship possess to keep a course? What big obstacles must be anticipated? For the United States, partisanship clouds the answer to many of these questions because it deprives the power to unify behind a decision. Also the financial imbalances are big obstacles, but America has a history of being resilient and unified in a crisis. But what made that resiliency is a dedication to character and values that allowed sacrifice. Its retention of its culture of values is essential.

China is different in that it is much more centrally controlled and uses the benefits of that consolidation of power for growth. It also is in uncharted waters as it broadens its market economy at an uncertain time in the world that is in part caused by its growth and investment decisions. But China is not as opaque or confusing as most would make it. The Communist Party controls the government, the military, and has a great impact on the culture. It understands the power of culture because of its history, and it often uses culture to accomplish its ends. For that reason you need look at the ideological think tank of the Communist Party to see the ideas being generated for consideration of the leadership Captains. The location is on the grounds of the Summer Palace where these future leaders are trained. It is called the Central Party School in China, often referred to as the Cadre School abroad. It is their finest minds focused, in part, on how to run that ship in the BZ Trainer. China understands the importance of time and thinks in generations in making moves. It understands obstacles by focusing on fighting corruption as a necessity for building the economic system to bring balance to growth areas and rural areas. And it understands that the long history of culture in China is a tremendous power to unify its people to keep stability during economic turmoil. It also understands the problems China will face with the environment, the necessity of future growth, and the host of problems all large nations have when governments must make choices.

The school's research will increasingly become a part of their vision of a "Harmonious Society" that gives insight on how China looks at the future. It may be a trial balloon for discussion, but it is discussion at the highest levels.

China usually does what is in its best interest, as its leadership understands it. So the interaction of East and West is best served by building bridges so that a more complete understanding of implications of mutual actions can be appreciated. That is difficult to do in economics or in politics, but culture is the unifying force. The School has begun to build its bridges thoughtfully and knowledgably on that base. They are focusing on cultural values, morality, and ethics as cultural components that hopefully will form a significant base in their "harmonious society" with the Eastern appreciation of personal dignity and "face." If there is a cleavage point on the diamond of understanding China and in many ways the future world, it will be what is in the concept of a "harmonious society" and how well the leadership of China embraces its core and the world seeks to understand it. As the great Chinese philosopher Lao-tzu noted, "Wisdom is knowing others, enlightenment is knowing self." Be it China or the United States, it is important where you are currently positioned, but that is now historic. The real issue of change is in what direction you are headed, how committed you are, and how fast is the rate of change. This is what can be affected, but it must be studied and understood. What is the direction of America, of China, of the rest of the world and how does it interplay?

To me the future is brighter than many people think because the world will face crisis, but crisis brings a desire for wisdom. And leadership is becoming more prepared and thoughtful than is probably perceived by our reading of the media. Values will be seen to matter because sacrifice toward a solution necessitates a vision of the future and a willingness to care beyond self. The battle of cultures will ultimately be, not between cultures, but within cultures for what visions of the future take hold and what values are chosen. Those cultures with character's determination and dedication have the balance of history on their side. It is not the strongest that survive, and it is not the most intelligent. It is the most adaptable and that requires the cultural ability of unification of common values. The world will always have crises. The problem is that those of the future may have more serious disruptions because of the leverage of size. The individual problems may not be as much of a necessary focus as the method by which we address them cooperatively. How we think about them and the process we use to solve them may be more critical to the future than individual problems themselves. The Golden Rule has always been a good beginning until man or government leaves conscience to seek personal convenience. Ultimately, with time, the results came from what each succeeding generation retains or builds in its values. Instilling these values in many ways follow an old Chinese proverb that applies to children and in building cultural bridges.

> *Tell me; I forget,*
> *Show me; I remember,*
> *Involve me; I understand.*

> Tieman H. Dippel, Jr.
> *Instilling Values in Transcending*
> *Generations*

Addendum

Refinement of Critical Thoughts
Presented in the Previous Text and the Triangles

What Relationships Must We Recognize?

Assembling the Knowledge Gained into a Framework for Discussion

As I assembled information for this book, these were chapters that refined thought and perspective but tended to pull attention from the book's thought line. As I described the Bible Study, "Four Hours Through the Old Testament," which took each chapter with a quick summary that built an understanding of how the books of the Old Testament built up to and then from David. It showed why David was a particular focus and his critical relationship with God put devotion into context as a focus point. The Bible Study had a straight line of the critical books making this point and the books that dropped out of the primary line, which talked of special people that made specific points. They were not in the primary line because you lost focus on the main story. But they were important in refining it once you had the main story in perspective.

Over the years on the website, www.thelanguageofconscience.com, I have collected essays and articles that I have been asked to write or speak on these various subjects. They were practical as a base of thought because most had been requested for specific and practical purposes. Many of these were too detailed for the primary book but cover a refinement of thought.

I first started looking at a number of former speeches on many of those different subjects and trying to place them in a very logical outline that would not be repetitive and that would make an eventual point. This was after I first tried to combine the material into several summary chapters. The difficulty is that they do not make a good linear outline because many of the points are indirectly connected to others. It was much more like connecting a series of very different dots. Just like the pictures that used to be on the mall walls that were thousands of individual dots presenting no picture until you changed your perspective to a more distant one. Then all of sudden a third dimensional picture emerged surprisingly in great detail. Here the goal is to get a perspective that lets you look at a concept. Since much of this material will be translated into other languages, it is also far easier to convey a concept if you have a number of reference points. For that reason repetition is not a detriment but a benefit. With my apologies to English language readers, I have taken the approach of including them given on very specialized approaches to these concepts that add a series of dimensions both about the strength of society, the nature of fear, love, power, and culture, and how many of these factors work with each other. They provide a background of a common mind with which we can begin to look at the triangles and organize our perspective for life and the decisions that are made in life both as an individual and as a nation. Then we can set the measurement criteria by which we will judge where not only our society, but others' may stand, and what are the important characteristics to help move toward the ultimate perspective of character. The repetition is often in quotations of philosophers. Look at them as cornerstones of ideas and for the content more than the source.

One thing that is fundamental to our understanding is that love and honor are the drivers of conscience. Fear and greed are the drivers of convenience. A perspective of conscience or convenience sets the method of influence for a culture. The next section gives a sense of these basic issues and how they balance each other and affect each other. You often cannot truly experience joy without knowing despair, but avoidance of despair causes action. Overindulgence of joy on occasion also causes despair. We have covered the many issues affecting society, this addendum assembles them into larger issues. This section refines and consolidates key thoughts so that the final section, the graphics of the triangles, serves as a tool for individual thought that helps marshal the risks, relationships, and approach to addressing problems from a perspective of character. It embodies the wisdom that history presents only to the degree it is fully understood. This section's purpose is to deepen that understanding since what has been presented is broad. Because much of the background necessary to set the discussion for distinction is repetitive, some speeches have been abridged and modified. These complete speeches and others are found in the archive of www.thelanguageofconscience.com.

On Absolutism and Relativity

In understanding the supplement as well as the main text, it is critical to create a perspective of how theory and reality relate. They are not polar opposites but interact. An absolute for a ship's navigator is that the shortest distance between points is a straight line. But if there are islands or shoals, the shortest relative course adjusts to them. The problem is that you often make so many adjustments you forget where you are going or decide it is not worth getting there. Conscience can seem naïve as a perspective when you often see convenience dominate; it requires a longer view than the immediate.

One of the best approaches is to not only read biographies to understand men and women but to visit their homes or burial places. The more detailed information there puts their thought process in perspective just as visiting the sites on which battles turned gives you a sense of history. The farmhouse at Waterloo, Pickett's charge at Gettysburg or General Bee dying at Manassas encouraged Jackson to rally and stand like a "Stonewall." The moment of decision is clearer in battles than in the art of politics. I have visited Monticello many times to stand by Jefferson's grave and note what he wished on his tombstone was not his achievements but the ideas he helped create. At Washington's Mount Vernon, Jackson's Hermitage, the Adams home outside Boston, Henry Clay's mansion or a host of others you see that current periods for them were always controversial but history sorted them out. At the Roman Forum you can see how small the Senate Building actually was and how close to the prison of St. Peter and St. Paul, the Rostrum where Mark Anthony spoke and the monument of Julius Caesar and the Arch of Constantine. History was constantly in flux, and the relativity changed many paths in a civilization built in part by the power of conquest.

But a favorite place of mine as a bridge to modern time is Florence, Italy, the Capitol of the Western Renaissance. While the Plaza of the Duomo is impressive, I spent time at the home of Dante Alighieri who was their great poet and an originator not only of the Italian language, but an early writer of the concepts of conscience and convenience, of assembling knowledge into wisdom. My favorite place is the Basilica of Santa Croce (Holy Cross) where Dante's statue stands with respect at a church that is the burial place of many of Florence's great leaders, thinkers, and artists. Michelangelo Buonarroti, a great artist rests near

Niccolo Machiavelli, the author of *The Prince*, with others such as Galilio Galilei, Medici family members, and monuments to the memory of many such—Dante, Leonardo da Vinci, and Raphael. I wanted to better understand Machiavelli. He understood the best way to keep power was a satisfied people and played a significant part in the Florentine Republic. But when relativity overcame principle and dictatorial power was the reality, *The Prince* guided dictatorial ambitions and worked more to the concept of ends justifying means and that appearing to do good might be more important than doing good. It is the best study of convenience and realism in life and looks at man as inherently evil. But Machiavelli's life was far more complex and broader than that. *The Prince* was written at a unique time and for a unique purpose. He was a brilliant man that understood much, but the circumstances of the times set the stage for the analysis. The culture of that period was of convenience. What he could have done in a different culture today has always been of interest to me because *The Prince* reflected his observations of Cesare Borgia's life. He was willing to see a leader set aside ethical values for the stability of the state. I believe in the strength of the opposing theory, that strength of character with force behind principle can accomplish more, but we are in a different time period and culture. The good must understand evil; the evil pretend to be good. Life has not changed except in technology. But that microcosm that was Florence of his day, all the same powers— economics, politics, and culture interacted as today.

If you go to the Uffizi Gallery walkway, you see the same men in statue and you reach at the Plaza Vecchio, the political center of Florence since 1294. There is a figure on horseback, the first of the Medici, Cosmo I, who built power through the economics of banking and trade and whose family became a great benefactor of culture. Nearby is a replica of Michelangelo's "David." The original stood there for many years before being protected in a museum nearby. Most people looked at "David" as an artwork, but I was focused upon what the guide told us. The Medicis ruled in different periods with a Republic in between. In the interim Republic "David" was said to symbolize freedom. With the restoration of the Medicis to power it was redefined to symbolize power and intelligence (the defeat of Goliath). "David" was art, but it was a symbol of cultural value and was understood as such. "Freedom" was a description of personal dignity in its ultimate sense. Machiavelli was a leader in the Republican period and wrote *The Prince* to redeem himself to serve his state and its future dedicated it to a Medici. But the point is that "David" could represent both "Freedom" of idealism and "Power and Intelligence" of reality. They do not have to be in opposition if the culture values conscience.

What I learned in Florence out of that microcosm was the same premise on which this book is based. There is a different style and outcome to whether you use a tactic of conscience or convenience. Machiavelli may have been a Republican at heart and his Discourses on statecraft were very intelligent, but in *The Prince* he effectively did one thing that was significant. He separated statecraft and ethics. His style was to look at how you most effectively accomplished ends. His purpose was to find a way to unify his part of Italy, but in doing so you have a very different style of leadership. The leadership of convenience can lie to the opposition under a white flag and succeed with treachery, but probably only once because it will be a lot harder the next time to have people talk. You lead by fear and intimidation. To me these are effective tools similar to terrorism, but I do not see how they effectively are unification tools in the long run. The Divine Right of Kings, the Mandate of Heaven, and the American Constitution all have looked to honor as a tool of unification. Granted, you can fool by perception for a period by appearing good, but ultimately the people judging their happiness through their personal dignity will act. Legalism in China was a similar approach that could be effective in war but difficult as a system to govern when not threatened. Enlightened Conservatism, as the concept is presented, looks to an ultimate unification of people on conscience as its purpose. That requires that ethics be in statesmanship because you lead not by intimidation but by example and service to the people. Yes, it requires toughness but for what purpose.

Today is a different time, and I think Machiavelli might have had a different approach in this culture, but if not, a leader needs to understand that the choice of method has very significant consequences to how he chooses friends and tactics and how he ultimately succeeds. If it is unification over time, ethics is necessary for personal dignity that gives stability. But to preserve the culture that allows that type of leadership to have any chance to succeed, then the people need to have the personal responsibility to recognize their obligations to the common good. It is not the leader that is the ultimate decision maker, but the people by their values, which are what their parents have handed down to them and what they have experienced in their lives. Does the culture separate true ethics from statecraft or government? Reality often overcomes hope, but to the skeptics of attempting conscience, I would only ask is convenience what you wish? If not, do not criticize unless you have a better solution, which you put forward, and if you are not putting it forward, who will do so when?

This book is dedicated to those men who have and will endeavor to this end. Many have not succeeded in their time, but left building blocks for us today. Our challenge is to use them well and not let the relative shoals we face make us lose sight of the more absolute straight line of our ultimate goal. These following observations are specialized and can seem more theoretical than realistic. But when you chart courses, you need as accurate a map as possible, and they fill in how relationships in the triangles have to be viewed. Entertainment, sports, reality shows, and a host of options catch our attention. But ultimately the most important of issues is our happiness and that of our family. So the time spent on enhancing our personal dignity, and the freedom it gives, has a value that defines us. We spend our time as we wish; we define our conscience or convenience quotient by that ultimate reality of life.

On Fear, Love, Power, and Culture

For the laws of nature (as justice, equity, modesty, mercy, and, in sum, doing to others as we would be done to), of themselves, without the terror of some power to cause them to be observed, are contrary to our natural passions, that carry us to partiality, pride, revenge, and the like.
—Thomas Hobbes
Leviathan

Kindness in words creates confidence, kindness in thinking creates profoundness, and kindness in giving creates love.
— Lao-tzu

Machiavelli felt it was better to be feared than loved, and, as noted, I have the greatest of respect for Niccolo Machiavelli as an observer of the nature of man. He saw man as inherently evil, and thereby you had to focus on his nature, which was dominated by convenience over conscience. Perhaps the greatest force to affect that personal convenience was personal fear. However, to be fair to Machiavelli, his observations were set in a time period with a surrounding culture. Machiavelli would in all likelihood have preferred things to be different, but even Hobbs looked at man as being inherently evil because of the culture of Hobbs' times. You may look to other periods, such as the inception of America and those that bound together in sacrifice for its Declaration of Independence. Or you may look to the efforts of what many see as the greatest generation after World War II, when they not only brought freedom, but moved to create a better world with the Marshall Plan. Then you see the most powerful component was not fear, but was instead conscience, and the greatest driver of conscience is love. Fear drives convenience to dominate while love drives conscience to dominate. A sense of honor usually supplements love; a sense of greed usually aligns with fear. Which is dominant in any period depends on the culture, what it values, and what it teaches its children. Conscience must be sensitized to reach the level where love overcomes fear. Good character where conscience overcomes convenience is much easier on an individual level because there is a better appreciation of the Golden Rule and the common good. Convenience dominates in the levels of power because convenience finds many allies in ambition, greed, hubris, and their cousins. Conscience reaches power when the culture of the society appreciates conscience as a value and the powers of it being convenient are thus pulled to its side. History shows us that there have been periods where man's evil dominated. Other periods showed great charity. They occur in different societies simultaneously because each of us has the forces fighting within us. God gave us free choice to choose our nature, but the nature of the culture influences.

Growing up in Texas, part of your education was simple stories. Some were a bit dated such as the advice "not to squat while you are wearing spurs." Others are longer lasting such as the fact that "you should not complain about having no boots when you realize that other people have no feet." And a few get a bit more complicated. One is the old story of the little boy who went into a café and sat at one of the few tables. The waitress came up and asked what he wanted, and he asked her how much an ice cream sundae cost. Seeing that he tied up one of her few tables, she said fifty-cents rather abruptly. He slowly got his money out and counted it in one hand and then asked her how much for just a bowl of ice cream. Becoming increasingly frustrated as more people waited she answered, "thirty-five cents." He said he would take the ice cream. She served it. He finished it, paid for it and went on his way. When she returned to clean the table she saw two nickels and five pennies stacked neatly beside the bowl as her tip. Obviously, he could have had what he wanted, but he cared more about seeing that he was fair to her for he understood obligation.

That simple story can help each of us define ourselves. Was the boy naïve in not getting what he wished and should he have conveniently just gotten the sundae? Was his concern for her such that it embarrassed her for having taken him so lightly when he was thinking more about her than himself, or should she have just "realistically" realized that the fifteen cents was a rather minor benefit for tying up a table? Even more important, what was the attitude of the surrounding people who watched and understood? They were the ones that would form the culture of the times. Did they admire the boy and the values that he showed? Or did they themselves feel imposed upon because he was a small customer, and they were going to buy more and were delayed? Did they become irritated with the waitress for treating him poorly, and in keeping with the times, feel that he should have sued her for discrimination? Or, did they simply not care? Did they wonder what their child would have done in a similar situation?

The last question has to become a concern if we are going to have a society that moves forward. Even before we can decide what we want to teach, we have to recognize the need that it be taught. And we have to make it our personal responsibility to do so. Machiavelli was totally right in his observation that half of life is fate, the other half you can control. Our family has always felt that if you took actions in God's favor on those you could control, you could ask God's favor on those that you did not. You normally receive in life as a result of what you give. The issue is the culture of the times and the power over whether the child that succeeds is one who lives for convenience or one who lives by conscience. It is not an issue of just what we teach our children. It is instead an issue of how actively we shape our society. Fear and love drive power, which drives culture. It all depends on which is stronger. But they are not opposite tactics even though they may define different drivers of philosophy. Fear of the future can drive good causes while fear to control can be negative to them. Separating the tactic and its motivation is essential. Even if you do not assume that man is inherently evil, the tactics and insight of works like *The Prince* are essential to understanding strategy.

On Critical Issues

The following articles are chosen to give a perspective much as loading data into a computer. The software that we will use to analyze it will be in the triangles of enlightened conservatism, but there is a basic understanding of inner-relationships that is essential to understanding that level of thought. It is also important to address many of the negatives that the world holds for conscience. There is a belief that it is a weakness not a strength, which is inaccurate. There is a thought that it is naïve and that the true levels of higher politics and diplomacy make it insignificant. That is only true if you do not understand how to use it most effectively. Everything is in the perspective of how these issues are viewed.

The first speech, "Our Warring States, The Divine Right of Kings, and the Mandate of Heaven," is one that was written for one of the major Texas think tanks. Many universities have a tendency to have less interest in value-based discussions because of concerns for academic freedom and the age-old conflict of science and religion. Think tanks, however, have to deal with power, which ultimately shapes the society. This particular piece talks much of ancient Chinese history and how societies can begin to divide and then give thought to how to come back together. It is on the evolution of societies and how thinkers can make a big difference by generating ideas into the process that defines the questions before answering them.

The second speech, "Understanding the Power of Character," also looks at societies, but at how the strength of character is what preserves them. The third, "Veritas Non Nobis Nati Solum," takes many of the same themes but puts them in an historical perspective. The fourth was one presented on the significance of ethics and how they set the stage for philosophy, which will have a tendency to pull together the first three. The fifth gives a perspective on the issue from leadership both from the normal perspective and also from the perspective of the culture of service since it is that nonprofit environment where society comes together to help others in the place of government that has such significant impact. The next articles, "Economics from a Mountaintop," "On Enforcement, the Golden Rule," and "Obligations, Great Universities and Cultural Values" pick some individual items that need to be emphasized in the process. The final articles, "Distinguishing Between Values and Ideological Based Systems" and "On Developing a Catalyst for Global Integrity" will be more easily understood after reading the rest. The material should be more easily assimilated with these points being made. Let me again emphasize a concentration on the content of the quotation more than the source. We previously looked at the significance of the authors. In different context the content of some quotations may be relevant in different ways. It is not so much a core of repetition of thoughts as differing levels of understanding the thought.

On the Healing of Divisions Within Societies
Our Warring States, The Divine Right of Kings,
and The Mandate of Heaven
Texas Institute for Health Policy Research
April 23, 2004

Our greatest glory is not in never falling,
but in rising every time we fall.
— Confucius

George Washington is looked upon as the Father of the United States not just for what he accomplished as a General and President, but perhaps more, for what he did not do. With his personal popularity and leadership he was easily in the position to assume a kingship of the United States and begin a monarchy which others suggested. Instead, he chose the concept of the ideas in the American Constitution based on the Declaration of Independence. He forcefully argued for the dignity of man in his letter to the Touro Synagogue in Newport, Rhode Island in support of the Bill of Rights which, to me, captured his belief in the importance of the dignity of every person. The monarchies of Europe may have been fresh upon his mind and most certainly the Western concept of the Divine Right of Kings. The monarchies had looked to a concept that the kings received their power from a divine right given to their ancestors by God, and therefore they could do no wrong. This concept perhaps reached its zenith with James I of England but fell rather quickly with the execution of Charles I. It ascended to a peak with Louis XIV in France but had a fateful encounter of reality with the French Revolution. Washington may well have realized the frailty and unfairness of such a system in making his judgment, but I wonder also if with his knowledge of history he pondered the actions of a man who had lived thousands of years before who found himself in a similar situation.

Around 1000 years BC, the Zhou people rebelled against one of the first Chinese Dynasties, the Shang. The King of the Zhou was a boy, but his uncle was the true power behind the throne and is remembered in history by the name the Duke of Zhou. He could have taken power but was instead, like Washington, a leader of virtue and was the key advisor to his nephew. As such, he became the symbol of the gentleman of honor. He also probably played a very significant part in the evolution of a moral rationale for power called the "Mandate of Heaven." While the Chinese "Heaven" is different from the West and much more like a tao, or "natural order" of the world in the place of a divinity, the Mandate of Heaven was a concept of how life ought to exist and the responsibility of leadership. It is the proper relationship between the leader and the governed that brings balance allowing both peace and prosperity. When a leader no longer is worthy of the Mandate of Heaven, he can be conquered by another and that is the presumed reason that he lost. Thus, the actions of the ruler are important for the concept of the Mandate of Heaven gives him power and authority, but also obligations to maintain the positive natural order. It gave a legitimacy that could be descended, but it brings focus to the obligations of power in relation to the people.

It is a concept not at all different from the basics of the American Constitution, which looked to the best interests of the people. The common theme of concern of the culture should be the personal dignity of the individual, that economically he has prosperity, that politically the government works in his behalf, and culturally that he has the right to pursue happiness, which can only be found when he has the dignity of man that is supported by the concept of civilization. That culture of dignity cannot emerge unless the nature of man has been refined to appreciate conscience and a concern for others rather than the convenience of total self-interest or greed. Convenience often dominates the realms of power, and conscience is only found in power when it is convenient for leaders to possess it because that is what the culture, or civilization, values. If not, the cultural system can disintegrate with pride becoming arrogance, with self-interest becoming greed then corruption, and with personal dignity declining from the character of individual responsibility to the political correctness of victimhood. The great Zhou culture declined over a period of time and went through the Spring and Autumn Period to the era known as that of the Warring States. Central authority became regionalized with hundreds of kings and principalities, and with it many of the concepts of prosperity and peace that were favored by the Mandate of Heaven were lost.

Within that period was an era of the time of the Hundred Schools in which thought, particularly about the significance of the culture of civilization, affected China. With so many rulers there emerged a class of advisors to the rulers both in military affairs and in the bureaucracy of government. More than bureaucrats, they became an influential power of their own. They began to give considerable thought as to what had happened to the great concepts of the Zhou Dynasty and how they had fallen into such times of peril. There were perceived answers to the problems. Powerful were the thoughts of

Confucius with his doctrine of relationships and obligations or reciprocity. To him, it was a lack of order and people honoring responsibilities that was the ultimate cause of the decline. Lao-tzu in his concepts of the "Way" and Daoism added skepticism, but at the same time reinforced some of the positive visions of the nature of man. It was a time when men realized that if you do not hold together the basic framework of civilization by looking to the obligations of men to each other, which is the development and maintenance of a system of honor and conscience, then society as a whole does lose the benefits of "the Mandate of Heaven."

Other parts of Chinese history have shown that concepts such as the Elements of Legalism with the Qin might bring unification because of the power of reward and punishments. But long-term success lies in the values that transcend generations. In the West the same could be seen from Athens' loss in the Peloponnesian Wars after Pericles died of the plague and his successors no longer had the Athenian vision.

Today, we find ourselves again in a slightly similar position of Warring States. American pundits look to our elections in terms of the red states (conservative) and the blue states (liberal), and then with some distinction, the battleground states where the elections and power will be determined. They talk of the concentration on soccer moms or on NASCAR dads. They look at the fact we have cultural divides within those states that are significant with the coasts having one set of dominant majorities and Central America having another. They split us politically as big government versus small government. They split us economically as rich versus poor. You have little discussion of the true concepts of American values or the Mandate of Heaven in the sense of how men should work together. But you increasingly seem to see a resurgence of the modern concept of the Divine Right of Kings, or the growth of the arrogance of power. Elections are based on the funding by vested interests with negativism aimed at personal convenience, the ultimate strategy. Another good example is:

Rome in the third century A.D. had a similar situation in that the legions had loyalty to their commanders not the state, and a series of wars and infighting weakened the nation.

The divisions have become so far apart that they no longer communicate. They are not debates, but shouting matches. There is not discussion, but interruption. We are a nation divided and are becoming more divided. We need to ask how did we get here and how do we proceed positively for our children's sake?

How we have reached this point could well be a synthesis of many opinions. Primary among them are certain basic concepts:

First is one of the most powerful components of the nature of man. Even beyond self-interest, the natural human desire to be correct is incredibly strong. People look at the information they receive from the perspective of how they wish to see it. The same set of facts may be half empty to one person or half full to another. The more we have begun to assimilate with groups similar to ourselves and with similar perspectives, the more we reinforce this method of how to assess information or even where we get information. We see in it those things that support our views, but we dismiss those things that do not support them. Our minds become increasingly closed because we are bombarded with information and choose what we process. Much of it is superficial. This may happen culturally. It happens geographically by how we live in various suburbs and enclaves. It happens because the elite of society put forth a political correctness that shapes many of these perceptions that are often enhanced not only by news media and the universities, but cultural establishments such as Hollywood. It has gradually happened politically because of redistricting that has increasingly made representatives' districts more partisan so that the more extreme position at either party dominate and few elections are settled in the General Election where middle ground discussion used to take place.

In economics we have created enclaves of different levels of wealth as families have moved for issues such as better school districts or taxes. In nation building, diversity is important because the personal dignity of which I spoke earlier is essential to any society. When individuals do not receive proper respect, they go into groups in order to gain that respect as a group. That is logical and positive. But that is the beginning of the process, not the end. The ultimate goal is to have respect for all people based on certain characteristics, not keep them divided in separate groups that are easily polarized by policies. Martin Luther King probably expressed this best when he received the Nobel Peace Prize. He talked of men of good intent and men of not good intent, or to me, men of conscience and men of convenience. In his famous "I Have a Dream" speech he wished that his children would be judged by their character.

. . . When Confucius noted that the cause of the Chinese decline rested in a lack of reciprocity of relationships, he developed a very ritualistic system. This system has evolved into much of modern courtesy and protocol of how men should greet each other and how they should indicate their respect for each other. It set a tone of how disputes should be settled. It was not a concept of weakness, but a concept of strength. It was a concept of Washington and a concept of the Duke of Zhou.

An additional synthesis of what has caused our problem has been the issues of time and speed. Our world today, because of technology, is extremely fast-paced, and we have to process tremendous amounts of information. In times past, speed was limited to a sailing vessel going between coasts or a stagecoach, later a train, and only in this last century the tremendous expansion of speed through a series of advances forward with jets, communication and the Internet. That has dramatically changed the balance between the two concepts of knowledge and wisdom. Knowledge expands like a penny (two cents, four cents, eight cents, sixteen cents, thirty-two cents, sixty-four cents, one hundred twenty-eight cents). Knowledge builds upon itself to explode in size and will require much more specialized focus for expertise and works against a broadened perspective. It naturally has us looking at individual trees in the forest rather than having the mountaintop perspective.

Wisdom is quite different. When people had time to think about the information that they received and to process it, they made more thoughtful decisions rather than more emotional ones that were driven by time. They built a process or perspective that created a model in their minds of how the world functions. Today that is very difficult to do with depth. We all know more about the solar system than Copernicus because of the evolution of technology and our education, but we probably have less wisdom than Solomon because few of us have spent the time thinking of such process.

. . . Each generation only knows what it is taught, and what it is taught is what it values. The change within society is particularly important because no matter what we teach our children, they are going to experience a culture of one nature or another. If we teach them conscience and it is a culture of convenience, they will either be at a disadvantage in maintaining their values or they will be corrupted. The issue is not only training our children, but looking at generational cultural ethics to plant in them the values that we wish them to teach their children. The issue becomes how do we separate out fundamental values of the nature of man by which we can develop his sense of conscience . . . It is the cultural difference between an individualized perspective of the Devine Right of Kings or the Mandate of Heaven.

There is a battle within each society, within each nation, as to which prevails. It is not an easy question of good versus evil. Conscience versus convenience is a very interim concept that constantly fights in each of us. . . . But if we allow such a culture of convenience to dominate, it only leads to a further downward spiral. Just as Athens found itself in the Peloponnesian Wars with evermore ruthlessness beginning to occur, you must recognize that it is not what you do or even how well you do it, but why you do it that ultimately matters. That is the only time that conscience begins to dominate the culture. Ethics is the operating system of basic morality, and it is the touchstone by which you can judge the strength of conscience in a society. But the ultimate issue is cultural ethics—what you teach to the next generation not the specialized courses of the professions or academia. There is a fundamental ethics that is the base for legal, medical, business, and other specialized teachings. It is the foundation of ethics for society as a whole. Group acceptance is more critical than just individual because that is what gives the power to the concept to shape the culture. Power is the ultimate issue, and it lives by accumulation and expansion and use to reach higher levels. Therefore the direction that power takes, for conscience or convenience, sets the trend for society through the culture of how men interact . . . Convenience uses anger and fear as effective political tools. Unless the next generation understands how to control them, convenience will be successful.

A third issue of synthesis in this age of complexity is to find leadership that is transformational be it individual or institutional. To have the power to make change, it will, in all likelihood, need to be on the value-based systems of culture rather than the ideology-based systems of economics and politics. More likely history has shown the evolution of new systems that unify us often come from the chaos of decline rather than inspiration. Even so, it is important that systems of thought be developed so that they are in place in the times needed. The thoughtful advisors of the Chinese Warring States did much to set the structure of future Chinese culture that was able to even envelop its conquerors over many of the next centuries. Just so the thinkers of today must find systems that can unify by looking at the power of ideas and how they can be transmitted to future generations . . .

The thoughtful advisors of today are much more likely to be found in individuals and in think tanks that look to practical experience. While the think tanks of today are as divided as much of the rest of the country in their advocacy of certain positions, they have the advantage that they understand the levers of power because they work with it in trying to bring change. The question for the think tanks lies in how to unite in a language of conscience to find at least the fundamental issues to be debated. Finding the right questions performs a great service. Oftentimes the solutions may differ on perspective, but facts can perhaps be more sensibly assembled and stipulated. Once you can agree on the basis of the question, you have a far greater opportunity to discuss the issue rather than debate it. . . . The best of education is that it often allows you to be comfortable in your own beliefs while not having to express anger in dealing with others. The battle is to create a culture that values logical discussion and leadership. Today, transformational issues are at extremes of politics not at the wisdom of discussion. They will not reach a more ideal balance until power shifts reality. It is not as naïve or futile as many would suggest. The power of ideals (ideas of values) cuts across other divides and is a powerful force. How it is articulated and by whom matters. Hypocrisy and negative campaigning limit the political arenas. The battle will be in the other institutions of society.

One great problem with today's partisanship is the inability to make a decision because of gridlock. If anything is done becomes the focus more than what was done. It is said that a parallel is a talking dog. The big issue is that he spoke, not what he said. All effort is on reaching a political decision, but the long-term consequences are lost to the short-term bargaining. This will eventually have severe results in our social programs. Our technology makes negative campaigning ever toxic because any failing, or alleged failing, is repeated many times. It is not different from the change in Congress when the media began to focus on publicity. Every congressional committee developed sub committees so more members could be chairmen and gain control of a sector affecting special interests. It brought contributions and fame through added power. Today ethics has become a tool to eliminate people if they have any involvement and knowledge of a subject rather than a focus on the person's character. All this builds the need for a different vision that has to create organizations of enough credibility that can stand the pressure to debunk the improper. The media used to be such a force, but it has moved to sensationalism, entertainment, and lessened ethics. The first step to change the culture has to be understanding the causes and problems the trends bring. The second is the development of positive alternatives on a broad scale with different perspective but unified by a concern for the common good and our children's future. There will be many alternatives pondered as dissatisfaction grows. An example could be the Louisiana State election system that lets you run as a Republican or a Democrat but all on the same ballot. That pulls power back to discussion of the whole electorate as opposed to present redistricting. It is a problem not just in America.

While there will possibly be a hundred schools of thought or more in our age as the global world tries to find bridges to build with each other, there is the need for something that is the equivalent of the Rosetta Stone. This equivalent would allow differing parties to coordinate their thoughts in categorized areas so they may discuss them with greater clarity and more process. For those focusing on conscience there needs to be a base of perspectives so you do not have a "Tower of Babel" weakness. Ideas have to start somewhere, so they can be refined by better thought at higher levels. Thought must also include the relativity of power in its various forms to eventually have any real impact. There must be a system of measurement for success so strategic drivers can be discussed and quantified. Much of the work in the website (www.thelanguageofconscience.com) rests upon a series of triangles that look toward this process from a perspective of conscience and how to develop an understanding of the forces that impact society. . . . This century will test the power of civilization to unify by conscience against terror and the corruption of convenience. Convenience is natural, but who will develop and empower the ideals of conscience that are diminishing in a culture of gratification?

On Understanding The Power of Character

Nations have no permanent allies, only permanent interests.
— Lord Palmerston

Power corrupts, and absolute power corrupts absolutely.
— Lord Acton

Those who are victorious plan effectively and change decisively. They are like a great river that maintains its course, but adjusts it flow. . . . They have form but are formless. They are skilled in both planning and adapting and need not fear the result of a thousand battles; for they win in advance, defeating those that have already lost.
— Sun-tzu

All of the thoughts above are truisms of history for they expose the reality of the world as it exists and has existed. What is unique is how the rise of terrorism on a global scale requires one to look at the first two comments from the reference point of Sun-tzu's theory of strategy that leaders must be able to change to meet the challenge of the times. Change in perspective is easy when a country is in chaos and is driven by crisis. Any solution usually looks better than what exists. Yet true leadership is particularly difficult at the time that individuals or nations are at a peak of power for it is often in that unique state of semi hubris that the greatest opportunities to exert power wisely exist and the greatest mistakes are made.

Lord Acton's observation is not always correct. George Washington could have had a third term or been considered royalty yet chose to decline and set a direction that built a great nation. Marcus Aurelius dominated the world as it was known for well over fifteen years, yet kept to a stoic belief that looked to the good of the people. Perhaps no better parallel can exist than the examples of Athens in its battle with Sparta and Athens' final decline in the Peloponnesian Wars. Athens began the war at a peak with one of its most thoughtful leaders, Pericles, in charge. As a leader he understood the realities, economic, political, and cultural, that kept a people together. After his death from the plague, there was movement toward ever more political and ruthless leaders that did not hesitate to change and match the culture of the times with increasing savagery and a far longer and more vicious style of war. Issues that often had been decided by short-term engagements were transformed by hatred into an almost three-decade cancerous effort. Such brought the end of Athens as it was known and the principles that had built it as one of the first great democracies.

I have often wondered how Pericles would have viewed the times that followed his death, but I feel certain he would have appreciated the importance of the later comments of Lord Acton and Lord Palmerston. Because eventually it was an alliance of the Spartans with the Persians combined with the arrogance and, in cases, ignorance of Athenian leaders that set the stage for loss. But the people had changed themselves following the sequence depicted by the Scottish historian, Sir Alex Fraser Tyler:

> *From Bondage to Spiritual Faith*
> *From Spiritual Faith to Great Courage*
> *From Courage to Liberty*
> *From Liberty to Abundance*
> *From Abundance to Selfishness*
> *From Selfishness to Complacency*
> *From Complacency to Apathy*
> *From Apathy to Dependence*
> *From Dependence back to Bondage.*

He noted that the average age of the world's greatest civilization had been 200 years and followed a sequence. To me the categories are measurements of the society's cultural minds. Two of the most memorable observations in American history came from different eras, but keep the same theme that morality supports strength of character of a nation:

Of all the habits that lead to political prosperity,
Religion and Morality are indispensable supports.
— President George Washington
(In his Farewell Address)

At such a time in history, we who are free must proclaim anew our
faith. This faith is the abiding creed of our fathers. It is our faith in the
deathless dignity of man, governed by eternal natural and moral laws.
— President Dwight D. Eisenhower
(In his 1953 Inaugural Address)

In the modern day, Athens serves as a reminder of the importance of critical leadership not just militarily through the power of politics. But it also is a reminder of the critical understanding of the economic impact of actions and the necessity of keeping the culture of support that creates the confidence from the people. . . .

Just as a football player moves from high school, to college, to the professional arena, there is an ever-faster stronger game that requires a concentration on the game and less concentration on other factors. Because of the reality of those considerations, the best thing to do is not just to try to affect the individual who has to work in that environment. But instead, structure the characteristics of that environment so that the leaders react to it. That is why the culture of the people sets the stage for the level of leadership. The only way to thus get conscience into power is to make it convenient for leaders to have conscience. And you do that by affecting the culture as to how it judges their actions. It matters little if we raise our children to have good character if the environment that they face, is one that does not hold those same values. Inevitably they will have disadvantages against those of convenience or they will be corrupted by the system. So on an individual basis Sun-tzu's concept of the necessity of adaptation to the times to win a battle means that we increasingly must look toward the concept of changing the culture to maintain and regain strength within it based on character. If not, we continue a transition where politics alone and the convenience of what can be promised at the moment will weaken the nation such that all future leaders increasingly move toward those considerations to stay in power.

Lord Palmerston had an observation of nations not having permanent allies, but permanent interests have to be evaluated in the terms of the times.

Nationally, the last centuries of history have had nations aligned with each other on the basis of geography, history, economic interests, and a series of changing paradigms. But just as the Greeks may have disagreed among themselves, they had before united against the Persians. For Athens, the enhancement of the division shifted the tone of the time at the end of the Peloponnesian War when the unity of the Greeks was no more.

Respect is often met with respect and brutality with brutality. The globalization of the world, its interconnection, and the threat of terrorism require a different appraisal of how those interests have to be judged. No longer can they be just on the individual basis of the immediate needs of the times. Perhaps more important for the future is how you will have nations that can cooperate with each other on very common themes that develop an international culture of concern for life and the future. In every nation there are men of conscience and there are men of convenience. The sooner we recognize the point that there is a basic need to address the nature of man as being not inherently evil, but redeemable, and look toward trying to develop that end even though it may take generations, the better the world will eventually be. It is not naïve to believe that concepts like the Golden Rule and the common good can have success. It requires an appreciation of them as it has throughout history. This is a level of commonality at the morality of how man treats each other in respecting life. It often cannot be taken to the concept of religions where each man has a different idea of how he wishes to meet his maker. However, working to constantly encourage how bridges can be built culturally and to do those things possible within the realms of safety and economics to move toward that end provides some of the best potential solutions to long-term problems of mistrust.

There will always be terrorism. There will always be despots. Just as every man and every nation will on occasion choose convenience over conscience even though they are well intended. It is the nature of choice that has been given us. Our goal is to establish society such that it holds together our own nation and provides the best foot forward for its relationship with others. That does not take a context of avoiding force if necessary, but better defines in what cases force should be used. And it draws attention to the critical issue of positive long-term cultural bridges that are often ignored in the short-term alliances of economics and politics.

Consistency of purpose creates principle and principle is what others appreciate over time. Others align with those of conscience not because they are necessarily for you or against you, but they are for themselves and appreciate the benefits it gives to them. Sun-tzu gave strategy two key points: planning and adapting. It is critical today that we realize that the ideologies of politics and economics that have driven the world for the last centuries may need to adapt to the powers of value-based culture. And it is also critical that we realize that where common interests can be found in all civilizations that we emphasize the importance of life, the necessity of considering the common good, and the ultimate validity of the Golden Rule. Concern for others through a culture of character is not naïve in weakness but the source of ultimate strength.

Gandhi looked at strength of character and defined it by listing Society's Seven Deadly Sins:

> *Politics without principle*
> *Wealth without work*
> *Commerce without morality*
> *Pleasure without conscience*
> *Science without humanity*
> *Work without sacrifice*
> *Education without character*

Benjamin Franklin spoke to this when he said:

> *Those who can give up essential liberty to purchase a little temporary safety, deserve neither liberty nor safety.*

However, the best description of the interplay within society came from Senator Daniel Patrick Moynihan who observed:

> *The central conservative truth is that it is culture, not politics that determines the success of a society. The central liberal truth is that politics can change a culture and save it from itself.*

On the Cultural Impact of Individual Life

Veritas: Non Nobis Nati Solum

The ultimate "truth" of not only an individual life, but also the culture that controls it, was best expressed by the motto of the earliest American Chamber of Commerce. That motto translated from the Latin is "truth: not for ourselves alone." Within society civilized people have to work together to achieve the greater good that benefits each individual. An accurate comparison would be a freshman high school band compared to a quality orchestra. The number of musicians might be close to the same, the instruments very similar, the physical cause of sound exact, but the difference—the net result—is dramatic. It is not just the expertise that is enhanced with each individual player's experience, but it is also the understanding of the importance of how you combine with others to reach a final goal of excellence. But only if you have heard the orchestra play, do you fully appreciate the differences between the two groups.

Society is not unlike that comparison. We are only one generation of teaching away from a significant loss of refinement and diminished search for excellence. And the culture of the times emphasizes the values to go forward. If the orchestra is never heard, it is very easy to accept the freshman band as great music. The wisdom of the past can be diminished by the fascination of advancing knowledge alone and by the tyranny of time of the present.

The three drivers of power are economics, politics, and media/culture, and while we concentrate on them, we often forget how inter-related the three are. Each is shaped by the concept of the nature of man. Perhaps Thomas Paine in *The Rights of Man* written in 1792 said it most effectively:

> *The more perfect civilization is, the less occasion*
> *has it for government, because the more does it regulate its own*
> *affairs, and govern itself . . . all the great laws of society*
> *are laws of nature.*

His point is well taken. Politics, often the argument of smaller versus larger government, of individual responsibility versus victimhood, and of right versus left usually concentrates on appealing to our individual interests of convenience. Thereby, it diminishes the defense of the common good. A small tax on each of us for a specific interest may not be felt, but eventually the combined effect of governmental burden changes the relationship of men and their government. In economics, it often becomes defined as a battle of the rich versus the poor and increasingly can become an issue of how the economic pie is split. Do people work together to expand it for a greater share for each or divisively argue about the size of their slice? This decision makes a huge difference in the future. Culture is increasingly growing to dominate media because of the economic impact it has. Due to the change from broadcast to narrow cast distribution, culture is beginning to be appreciated. The ultimate war of society over the nature of man and how he interacts will eventually be fought even though very significant battles culturally with economics and politics are being affected.

For each of us there is a continuing battle between fairly simplistic factors. We have, on the one hand, a natural desire to make life easier and to achieve things that we wish as early as possible (convenience). And, on the other hand, we have a value system (conscience) that sets the limits with a variety of parameters on our actions. Throughout history these two have battled each other to define the nature of man. The cycle of domination of a period's culture often moves between them. The realists, Machiavelli and Hobbs, saw man as being inherently evil, as did the original author of *The Science of the Thick and the Black.* They may not have wished such, but it was certainly the case of their times. Thus, to be able to direct and control him, one appeals to his self-interest or his convenience. You can manipulate him by helping him to obtain the things he desired, which could easily lead to corruption. His focus is primarily his existence.

The opposing view, the idealists, Christ, Aristotle, and Confucius, looked at man as more redeemable. And the key to that redemption was the understanding that his conscience developed a concern for others. In almost all the great religions, this concern takes place in the form of the concept of the Golden Rule of Christ, the Silver Rule of Confucius, and the appreciation of the common good. *The Language of Conscience,* as a concept of character as a bridge, recognizes an appreciation of the honest interest of being an adversary of principle not convenience. It is not hard for people to have true convictions on opposite sides of issues. However honest, respectful discussion can do far more long term good in finding a policy worthy of sacrifice and implementation as opposed to one at either extreme that leaves instability or that freezes action and inertia to any change. You can govern from the concept of the common good or you can battle from the extremes of positions.

The great difficulty in the idealist perspective lies in the nature of the operation of society, which is driven by the concept of power. Conscience works best at an individual level, but convenience almost dominates the higher levels of power because of the nature of power and the corrupting forces that surround it. A man of convenience always has a great advantage over an individual man of character or conscience because he has lesser restrictions on actions and lesser concerns for the implications. So the only way that men of conscience eventually win are to combine together for ideals *not for themselves alone.* They form relationships that promote these ideas and the combined force of their efforts dominate over the individual man of convenience who may have short-term allies but few long-term trusted allies. At many times in history both these two forces compete against each other. Man has shown himself to be inherently evil with much of his barbarism and terror. Man has also shown himself to be inherently good in his innumerable acts of charity and concern for others. The question is which characteristic dominates. The culture is never going to be purely driven one way or another. It is much more determined by a preponderance of force determined by the culture of the time. The ultimate power is with people by their action or inaction and the culture determines what motivates them. Fear may dominate and cause acceptance or disgust, and repression may incite the passion for change.

The key characteristic to be remembered is that conscience dominates at an individual level, but convenience dominates in power. And the only way to put conscience into power is to make it convenient by having the culture value it at a high level. The question thus becomes how do we put forth the concept of cultural ethics, teaching conscience to the next generation in such a way that it sets the stage for a more positive future.

Far too often people feel that society can be changed by great acts. Certainly history has shown the effect of battles such as Tours or Vienna and acts like Cromwell's dismissal of the Rogue Parliament or the unique efforts like that of Emile Zola, the French novelist as he wrote *J'accuse,* in the French Dryfuss affair. But far more often true change comes from perseverance through education and cultural change. Power is the force to make or resist change, and can be positive or negative. The strategy of power is simple: the first goal is to establish strength; the second is to use strength to accomplish goals, usually greater power. But the establishment and use require critical components. In the short term they may be physical, but in the longer term they may be metaphysical. Perhaps as astute an observer of power as Machiavelli was John Maynard Keynes who well described the origin of true power:

> *The ideas of economists and political philosophers, both*
> *when they are right and when they are wrong, are more powerful*
> *than is commonly understood. Indeed the world is ruled by*
> *little else. I am sure that the power of vested interests is vastly*
> *exaggerated compared to the gradual encroachment of ideas.*

The challenge of that concept is that it takes an understanding of values and a sense of place for any society to really move forward. Russia in recent years quickly changed systems but did not have a concept of free enterprise. China has been more successful with gradual liberalization that allows people to understand capitalism's value. . . .The old saying that people are not for or against you, but are for themselves has merit. But people have to be educated as to why it affects them.

The same type of work and thought needs to be placed now not on politics, not on economics, but on the concept of culture and how we not only work together internally with our diversity but with the rest of the world. Economics and politics have great power implications on a personal basis. Culture is more a combination of society's views that can be more difficult to affect because they are personal. In each society there are those that believe in conscience, and there are those that are driven by convenience. We often make our national alliances in politics by nationalistic interests. Lord Palmerston noted that nations do not have permanent allies only permanent interests. The deeper question is how those interests are defined. Out of convenience they are often short term to accomplish specific ends, but in conscience it is a longer-term concern to bring about common basic values. In history the former dominated. With terrorism now setting the stage, eventually, the latter will be fully appreciated as a necessity. This appreciation of the necessity of a culture of individual responsibility requires that you have a strong and building middle class.

Yes, there must be the free market drivers as Adam Smith discussed in *The Wealth of Nations.* But we should not forget that his primary book during his life was *The Theory of Moral Sentiment,* which talked about the relationship between all of these internal drives. There is a difference between self-interest and greed, the source of corruption that corrodes the system. There is an importance to the keeping of fairness and morality within markets. Competition is seriously diminished in any market that is not honest and transparent. The values of all assets economically depend on the vision of the future and the present expectation of that future dominated by the negatives does little to advance society in the long run.

. . . Society as a whole is going to have to build a culture on a much broader plain that demands leadership to look at fundamental values that are transformational more than necessarily just transactional in doing legislative business. The discontent with much of our political system rests with the failure to address this concern. People no longer feel that the common good is what is being sought but instead that the special benefits will eventually weaken the system for all.

If individual responsibility is to be taught it has to also exist in a culture. If parents teach their children to be honest—and the culture in which they are sent is not one of that nature—then either their children are corrupted as will be their grandchildren or they fail because they are not willing to do those things that they feel improper. Thus, it becomes incumbent that the culture keeps its strength by demanding this devotion to conscience. It is significant that this cuts across political lines. It is not an issue that is right versus left, Democrat versus Republican, rich versus poor. The character of an individual and the values that he holds are quite separate from many of those characteristics. That is the difficulty with society today. People feel separated into boxes that don't necessarily fit their overall set of values and their concern with the future. When I wrote *The New Legacy,* the uniqueness of the endorsements that I received was not only that they were from both parties but from diverse organizations. The same has been true, even more so, with the publication of *The Language of Conscience.* What it indicates is that people of conscience do value it at a much higher level than is appreciated by the media or even the polls. People do ask about these issues and increasingly when they are asked, the polls show great concerns about the fabric of society and how it is evolving. If there is a purpose to which a number of organizations could devote a part, it is building this concept into their own activities and their own efforts such that it is taught to the next generation and is brought into discussion. While people would say this is the work of great philosophers and university professors, I would note that too often their efforts are academic, and these needs are very practical and real.

I would point out that these are not new issues. The expanse of knowledge may change, but wisdom often remains the same. Aristotle thought the earth was the center of the universe. However, time has enlightened his view of the necessity of a moral life that is much more metaphysical than physical and transcends generations. It is with history that we need to begin to understand our present circumstance. Much of the concept of enlightened conservatism is based upon a comment attributed to Abraham Lincoln which some question may have been the work of his biographer. But I think it captured Lincoln and the concept of life as effectively as anything else I have seen:

> *You cannot bring about prosperity by discouraging thrift. You cannot strengthen the weak by weakening the strong. You cannot help the wage earner by downing the wage payer. You cannot further the brotherhood of man by encouraging class hatred. You cannot help the poor by destroying the rich. You cannot establish sound security on borrowed money. You cannot keep*

out of trouble by spending more than you earn. You cannot build
character and courage by taking away a man's initiative and
independence. You cannot help men permanently by doing for
them what they could and should do for themselves.

Similarly, the world operates through leadership or through crisis. And visionary leadership requires a special culture and places a strong reliance upon values. You have value systems and you have ideological systems. The ideological systems are much more political and change much more quickly. Socialism, communism, and capitalism would be examples. Values systems are much more related to cultural aspects such as Christianity, Judaism, Confucianism, Islam, and many others. Value systems have more substance over time. Ideological systems exist because they normally have the support of the culture and change to its pressure more easily. Perhaps the best way to point out the need to shift focus to a true understanding of culture as the critical component of the future would be to look at some of the quotations of history. Then to look at some of the similarities of the most powerful modern cultures to see that there are bridges possible can be achieved through common conscience and not the convenience of alliance and misinterpretation. The age of terrorism brings in the great concern that intimidation can wear down a society. The strength of the culture is the ultimate issue; history makes that clear. It is equally clear that great value systems have much in common to unite them if we build bridges on similarities of concern for the future of our families. There is no doubt that strength is necessary to oppose evil, but that strength only comes from longer term goals worthy of sacrifice as opposed to short term interests. That sacrifice comes from a devotion to values. And when they are hollowed out of a society, its wealth may continue for several generations because of the inertia and mass of its arenas of power. Eventually it will decline if it does not revitalize its character. This has been expressed in great civilizations in many ways but with a common understanding:

I fully subscribe to the judgment of those writers who maintain
that of all the differences between man and the lower animals,
the moral sense of conscience is by far the most important. . . . It
is the most noble of all of the attributes of man.
— Charles (Robert) Darwin
The Descent of Man 1871, Chapter 4

This is the seal of the absolute and sublime destiny of man—that he knows what is good and what is evil; that his destiny is his very ability to will either good or evil.
— George Wilhelm Friedrich Hegel
The Philosophy of History

Always treat others as you would like them to treat you. This is the teaching of the laws of Moses in a nutshell.
— Jesus Christ
The Sermon on the Mount
(Matthew 7:12)
Living Bible Paraphrase by Tyndale

Tsze-Kung asked, saying "Is there one word which may serve as the rule of practice for all on one's life?" The Master said, "Is not reciprocity such a word? What you do not want done to yourself, do not do to others."
— Confucius
(BK X, v, 23)

He who wishes to secure the good of others has already secured his own
— Confucius

When the people of the world all know beauty as beauty, there arises the recognition of ugliness. When they all know the good as good, there arises the recognition of evil.
— Lao-tzu
The Way of Lao-tzu I

The people's good is the highest law.
— Marcus Tullius Cicero
De Legibus, III

*This is the noble Eightfold way: Namely right view, right
intention, right speech, right action, self livelihood, right
effort, right mindfulness, right concentration. This, monks, is a
Middle Path, of which the Taghagata (the Buddha) has gained
enlightenment, which provides insight and knowledge, and tends
to calm, to higher knowledge, enlightenment, Nirvana.*
— Buddha (Siddhartha Butama)
The Sermon at Benares

*Wealth and children are the adornment of this present life, but good
works, which are lasting are better in the sight of thy Lord as to
recompense, and better as to hope.*
— The Koran (18:46)

*I do not understand how someone can elevate himself by
suppressing or denigrating another.*
— Gandhi

Probably the ultimate responsibility of a person or of a society is
to have the character or individual responsibility to act at the critical
times that a tipping point of conscience as morality exists in a life or
a civilization. It is at those times that leadership is most valuable and
is most tested. Perhaps the most appropriate sentiment is one that has
often been found throughout the thinkers of history. They recognize
these critical issues that I have seen attributed to in similar form from
Dante to Martin Luther King, Jr., that hold the conceptual thought that
*the hottest fires in hell should be reserved for those who shirk their
responsibility at a time of moral crisis.*

On the Nature of Man, Morality, Ethics, and Choice
Blinn College/Better Business Bureau Seminar
Bryan, Texas — March 2004

Being the first speaker and at an early hour, the best way to begin a
fairly heavy and lengthy discussion is to gain a perspective for us to use
during the day. To explain that perspective in involving ethics, I want to
tell an old story about the two young boys, John and Jim, who at eight and
ten, had developed a bad ethical problem. They were kleptomaniacs. They

simply took what they wanted each time they were in a store. Their parents were quite upset with their behavior and both lectured and punished them often explaining why it was wrong. Finally, in frustration, they realized that since the family was quite religious, the Minister might be of some help and went to him seeking advice. He listened and gave this advice. "Why don't you take John back to your home and leave Jim with me since he is the older brother. They are both good kids and when I explain to him that God is watching all of their bad acts and sees what they are doing even when no one else is around, then I think he will stop these activities and help influence his younger brother." They all agreed to that plan and left Jim, taking John home with them. The Minister began by saying, "Jim, I understand that you and your brother have been stealing a number of things that were not yours. Your parents have told you that this is wrong, but you have not stopped. Now I need to ask you one very important question. Where is God?" Jim looked at him with big eyes, and the Minister emphasized again, "Jim, tell me where is God?" Suddenly Jim jumped up, ran out the door, went to his house, found his brother and pulled him into hiding in a dark closet. His brother John asked, "Jim, what happened?" Jim looked at him and said, "Boy, are we in trouble now. God is missing and everyone thinks we have taken Him." The point is we can be talking about the same thing. But we need to be very certain that we are looking from the same perspective and that we have not necessarily just found the right answers but have identified the right questions.

As we begin today's program looking at ethics, I think several quotations I noted earlier, point out that the issue of ethics is part of a much bigger picture, and it has been with us forever since man has free choice. We would like this morning to talk about the fundamental nature of man, the concept of morality as a relationship between people separated from religion, the operating system of that morality which is ethics, and the individual choices that men must make in the current culture and environment.

To develop the theme of how our three speeches fit together, I think the best illustration would be a reference to an apple. You have a set of roots that are not visible but that provide most of the tree's strength from its nutrients and moisture. You have a trunk that gives it stability and the position from which the branches with their leaves can grow to reach what sunlight is available. And you have fruit that is produced. Individual cases of improper or questionable conduct dominate the media, and we focus upon them just as we do upon bad apples. The real question is whether the problem is a few bad apples or a diseased and failing tree. And if it is the latter, what are its causes.

By the tree analogy, we understand that the nature of man or his character, which involves his choosing conscience over convenience, is really the root system that supplies the strength to the rest of the tree above the sight line. The trunk is the morality of man, not necessarily to the level of religion but how man operates with his fellow men. Does he use the Golden Rule? Is he concerned for the common good? Does he care about the future where he is willing to sacrifice for a better world? The branches are the ethics systems, the operating systems of these concepts of morality that exist within the culture of the day. Just like the sunlight that shapes the branches so the leaves are properly positioned, the culture of the time—what it values—makes a huge difference in the perception of the ethics systems. Then finally, we have the apples themselves. Like individuals making choices, are they simply attacked by insects that affect them? Do they not produce because of the disease of the tree? Or is it a few individual apples that are bad and the tree itself still strong?

I am going to cover the roots and the trunk, the nature of man, and the concept of morality of how men work with each other. Bill is going to talk about the limbs of ethics and the surrounding culture that identifies and influences the personal behavior of the culture. Charlie will talk about the individual apples through decisions on business ethics on a more focused approach. . . .

Conscience generally operates when you have the Golden Rule, the common good, and a vision for a greater future for all as its determinant points. Convenience has the forces of ambition, greed as opposed to self-interest, and the intensity of competition are among the factors that drive it forward. Generally, conscience works most easily on an individual level where people work with each other in a less intense environment. On the other hand, convenience almost always dominates the realms of power that have a pressure environment. The only true way to get conscience into power is to make it convenient by having the culture of the times value and reward it. So the nature of man at any particular point is determined, in part, by the culture of the day. If the society values conscience and ethics, then it promotes conscience and ethics because it is the system by which you judge your peers. If the system has little value for conscience and is dominated by convenience, it does not matter what rules are written or what perceptions are put forward, the nature of the system can easily corrupt the ethics. So the roots of the tree, the nature of the conscience of man, are what are at the source of almost all systems of ethics. This is greatly influenced by what is taught at the family level, what is reinforced in the institutions, and what is recognized and valued by society as a whole. You sacrifice for, and you pass on, those values you cherish. Each generation's education strengthens or lessens the cultural values.

To completely understand the nature of man and the culture that affects it, you need to understand several component parts that intersect in the different confluence at any time. There are three great sectors of power: economics, politics, and media/culture. These power centers are present in each part of society. Our modern politics has moved from a century ago where contributions to campaigns were more the charity of interested people to become today much more of a high dollar competition of vested financial interests. Our economics similarly have progressed from the time of Adam Smith. During his lifetime, the principal book that he taught was his *The Theory of Moral Sentiments* in which he found self-interest to be the most powerful influence, and this led to the writing of *The Wealth Of Nations*. However, there is a significant difference in economics from self-interest to greed.

Many of our modern problems came in areas of confluence of new sophisticated financing techniques, incentive pay innovations, and short-term focus. People focused on narrow knowledge not broader wisdom for perspective. As a system, markets work through the functioning of competition. The higher the level of competition, the more effective the market and the greater benefit derived. However, that assumes moral markets in which there is no corruption or favoritism. Once the latter enters markets through a culture of convenience, the markets are ineffective. The value of any asset looks to the potential of the future and discounts backward. So the strength of the culture and the rule of law that it supports is critically important in present valuations. The level of political government regulation and morality of markets thus affect economics and vice versa. Culture and media, in part, fit together because when you have a broadcast media of a few sources, it dominates and affects the culture. However, when you have a circumstance where there are many sources of information, the culture drives the economics of the media and becomes more dominant as we have seen with the rise of the Internet and many other sources of entertainment and information.

Within these three areas of power, you have the effect of what I call enlightenment and cultural values. Enlightenment is education, technology, opportunity, and all of the driving forces of modernism that push for change. Cultural values are the lessons learned over a much longer period and inscribed into the society. They change much more slowly and set the tone for many of the rules of society. These two are often in conflict and do a great deal to shape the culture over time.

Perhaps the best example would be the fact that the last century was dominated by ideologies or mainly political ideas of how a society should operate. Capitalism, Communism, Fascism, Socialism, all had different approaches to the relationship of government and men. Value systems such as Christianity, Judaism, Buddhism, Hinduism, and others all looked at the relationship of men from a more spiritual and cultural perspective. Islam is to a degree a combination of the two, in that it looks to both religion and politics. Ideological systems often react more rapidly to the effects of change because political ideas can adjust more easily. Value systems are much more driven by the cultural values that they instill. The Golden Rule and the common good tend to be much slower to change. Confucianism, with some of the later teachings of Lao-tzu, forms the basic culture of much of Asia. Though not a religion, it was a value-based system of loyalty, integrity, and courtesy with a core philosophy of reciprocity or Confucius' Silver Rule. While it diminished in the Cultural Revolution, its principles are now re-emerging as a cultural force in China as the country searches for a refinement of cultural ethics. In the West, Rome in its conquered lands made people citizens or slaves but normally adopted their Gods as part of an ideological system to unify the Empire. It is interesting to note that many of their wars are with a small tribe of Jews who had a value system that believed you could only honor one God.

The reason for covering this past perspective of history is that in the world today we tend to focus far too much on smaller items to truly understand the bigger picture that needs to be understood to build a support for a concept of ethics.

That is our difference with ethics here. We look at it as a paragraph or put ethics in "professional silos." One set of rules that fit law, another for medicine, and some for business. We have learned to look at issues legally, not ethically. We look technically rather that subjectively with substance.

We don't look at it in the sense of cultural ethics. What our kids learn at a young age matters greatly because the family is the greatest single influence in their lives. But what our institutions teach in the concept of conscience versus convenience, the Golden Rule and the common good is equally important, and it is often not being taught. The values that a society keeps are those that it teaches its young because it values them. Conscience is driven by individual responsibility. Its acceptance means that you take responsibility for your actions in regard to others. Too often today our culture begins to look at victimization. We use lawsuits or we want subsidies from government. We want other people to solve problems and give us rights that perhaps we have not earned.

...A nation's competitiveness and standard of living ultimately depends upon the character of the nation and how willing it is to work, to learn, and to cooperate. Victimization is not a concept of strength. As Thomas Paine pointed out in his quotation, culture is your best guide to limited government because what people tend to do for themselves the government does not need to do. We must maintain and support a middle class with these values but that requires us to keep character within the society and to rely on leadership rather than ultimate crisis to solve problems.

Culture, whether it supports conscience or convenience, tends to re-enforce itself. One of the groups that have been most supportive of *The Language of Conscience* has been the Ethics Officer Association, which represents many of the Fortune 500 companies. From them I learned the importance of a corporate culture. In the Federal sentencing standards for corporate crime, whether or not you have a compliance system including an ethics officer, often determines the level of punishment of a company. If it is only a single bad apple that has caused the problem and the culture of the company is strong with integrity, then normally sentencing takes this into account. At the same time, if the company as a whole does not have an effective system and is based on convenience, it comes forth as well. Normally, you don't find this information by talking to the Chief Executive Officer or to other high-ranking officials although they are the ones that set the tone for the culture. Several days' investigation with different levels of staff, asking them how they have been trained and how they handle situations, tells you much more about the company because it defines the operating culture. So image can be very deceiving, and the reality is that the corporate culture is what ultimately shapes corporate destiny.

However, our concern is not just the ethics of a company but also the ethics of our society and global ethics as well. Regardless of what we teach our children in the sense of integrity, conscience, and ethics, if they go into an environment that is dominated by convenience and corruption, then inevitably they will either fail or they will be corrupted. The competitive reality of life is that the man who has no principles on average has much wider latitude and advantages than a person who self-imposes principles. Conscience limits you because you do care about the effects on others. However, you have the distinct advantage that you are able to align with others of similar principle in close association. This gives you an advantage over the individual who believes only in the convenience of his own affairs and may have temporary alliances but very few true allies because he is less trustworthy.

That is why America has been so unique in its concept of nonprofit institutions. Very few other places in the world have the structures that have been so dramatic, and they have been the pillars of accepting responsibility through social capitalism. The Chambers of Commerce, Better Business Bureaus, the American Red Cross, the Boy Scouts, churches, foundations, and service clubs are the places where people of conscience come together to change society for the better. They assume individual responsibility collectively. They are what demonstrate, in their strength or in their weakness, whether the culture is one that is dominated by conscience or convenience and thus its character. . . .

The concern that I often have had is that America is not unlike Athens at the beginning of the Peloponnesian Wars. Pericles understood that Athens was near its peak. But after his death of the plague, several decades of war and brutality hollowed out one of the great advances of civilization.

Similarly, when we look at ourselves today and seek a perspective, we need to wonder whether the institutions that we have are but a handshake and a smile of image. Do they truly have the heart and mind that is necessary to maintain an advance of civilization that requires a strength of purpose. Nations can exist for long periods when they have accumulated wealth because like a checking account that has a surplus, you can keep writing checks without adding to it for a period of time. But at some stage reality enters.

The website on which this speech will be placed, as well as a number of other writings and information on the concepts I presented, can be found at www.thelangugeofconscience.com. If you have an interest in broadening the perspectives, there's a set of relationship graphs in the form of triangles that carry these concepts to a number of more substantive levels. However, when you look at enlightenment and cultural values and the balance that oftentimes needs to be found between them, you go to a question of the nature of leadership of a society. The society tells you a great deal about itself about what it values, its rewards, and how they are granted. It tells you a lot about itself in the nature of the leadership that it selects. Is the leadership transactional and simply barters between different groups or is it transformational and able to change the nature of society by unifying people to its principles? Is it a society that values not just the civil rights of its people by the rule of law, but more importantly the cultural concepts of courtesy and personal dignity? Is it a culture that enforces the discipline within society by peer pressure that people place on each other or one that has to rely increasingly on courts and government? All of those considerations impact the concept of ethics within society by not simply learning the rules of what might be proper etiquette but also the heartfelt understanding of where the lines of proper conduct within a society are drawn. It is not a case of what you do or even how well you do it as much as it is a case of why you do it.

The point is we all shape the culture. And it is not how we raise our kids, but how we take aggressive actions to show what we value. If we value conscience enough, then the roots and the trunk of that tree are going to be particularly healthy. And even though the ethics systems may change to a degree in the culture of the times, the strength of their principles will withstand a lot of winds and even drought. If the foundations are not secure, then the tree topples in wind and in drought because the roots are too shallow.

The fact you are here this morning probably approximates the old advice that you don't have memory loss if you are worrying about having it. If you worry about ethics, then that may well not be your problem. So the comments I have made will helpfully help you convert others to the importance of ethics. The battle between conscience and convenience is never won, only temporarily influenced. But in our small time of existence let each of us ask God to favor us on the half of life that fate determines and live the half that we do control in such a way that we deserve His favor.

On The Nature of Leadership
Speech, Texas Lyceum Association
May 3, 2003

Niccolo Machiavelli noted that half of life is controlled by fate, the other half you can control. If you carried his thought further to leverage your controlled half to its fullest extent, you need to combine with the efforts of others. To see that it is most effectively directed to your goals, you must lead with a focused purpose.

Leadership has been examined and defined in many ways throughout history. However, a synthesis of the most appropriate approaches probably would look at its two clear divisions—tactical leadership (what you do and how well you do it), and value-based leadership (why you do it). Tactical leadership is really more effective organization. The style of approach of Sun-tzu and Von Clauswitz would best be described as to organize tactics and systemic organization. The military is a good comparison. It emphasizes teaching officers to take responsibility for making a decision. So decisions are made, but made strategically. It is said that chess was invented by a general to teach his officers patience with strategy. In 1986

Congress changed the structure of the American military from a chain of command that moved from the Defense Secretary to the Joint Chiefs of Staff and down to their individual organizations, to the Head of the Central Command. These commands had members of all of the forces working jointly, not independently. This culture of easy interaction made it far more effective than the old structure. This type of leadership is a lot like the physical sciences with natural rules of building power. It can often be accomplished in a variety of ways for totally different purposes, and that is where value-based leadership comes in. A Hitler or a Stalin could be looked upon as a strong leader under tactical leadership alone because they achieved power and control. How they would be viewed in value-based leadership would be quite different.

I would divide the true groups of thought in a tactical, value-based leadership combination into the realists and the idealists. Machiavelli in his book, *The Prince,* looked at men as being inherently evil. Thomas Hobbs had a similar perspective. Both understood the more Republican principles and goals and contributed to their development, but they both saw the weakness in men and often reflected this recognition in their tactical strategy. To them you had to understand evil even to do good. In the East, *The Science of the Thick and the Black* (thick skin—black heart) shows that the concept is universal. This is the group that I would call the realists who look at and use the weakness of men. The other group, the idealists, would include Christ and Aristotle in the West, Confucius and Lao-tzu in the East. They believed that men could become enlightened and sought to bring out the best in men. They looked to developing man's strength. So their leadership was more value-based.

It is important to understand that leadership's two parts—(1) what you do and how well you do it, and (2) why you do it—are quite connected. Chess is much like basic checkers except there are different pieces with more moves. Adding the value-based component to tactical leadership is much the same. Sun-tzu looked upon the level of commitment of his men and the opponent as a major part of his "the Way," which was one of the most critical aspects of strategy. Unity is power. America's troops in Iraq have been often characterized by the media as successful because of technology and resources. I would venture that those familiar with military culture would give a far higher component to the value of the commitment of the forces. While Sun-tzu wrote *The Art of War* in the East, Alexander was the West's first unique strategist. He was tutored by Aristotle and looked beyond battle tactics to the time of year, the supplies of the land and the broad aspects of supply in a war. There were refined tactics, but he also gave men a vision of why the battle was important, not to him, but according to what they valued.

The problem is that value-based leadership can have two types of values—conscience (a concern for others) and convenience (the concern for self or a limited few). Leaders of conscience usually look to taking actions for the benefit of others; they tend to be willing to sacrifice for a greater good. Convenience is driven by ambition, self-interest, vanity, and similar desires. Some leaders of conscience certainly use convenience, but dominant style usually takes you one direction or the other. All leaders always have these factors battling within them. The practicality of staying leaders usually bends the best of men on occasion. To not be a hypocrite and to be truly successful in being a decisive leader, usually one style dominates. Those that choose tactical convenience often use Machiavelli's very effective principles or look to its organizational equivalent, Saul Alinsky's *Rules for Radicals*. (*The Prince* tells the rich how to stay in power while the *Rules for Radicals* tells the poor how to take power.) They both look carefully at the nature of men and how they make decisions. The leaders of convenience have an advantage on leaders of conscience in that the latter have self-imposed restrictions on their actions because they seek a different longer-term goal beyond short-term gratification. Good character is the choice of conscience over convenience and is implemented by personal responsibility. Leaders of conscience look to ideas, usually value-based systems of principles, more than ideologies that change more easily. That does not mean they should not learn the tactical principles of convenience to fully understand their use and approach. Their strength comes from their ability to make alliances on their principles and leverage their joint strength. Men of convenience often lose allies as a result of their shorter-term tactics. Leaders of conscience have an advantage of a stronger "way" or commitment if they can organize it properly. The disadvantage is that it requires people to have perseverance.

The key to which dominates in a time period is found in the culture of that time. Conscience often dominates on an individual level; convenience almost always dominates at the higher levels of power due to ambition, competition, self-interest, and similar factors. The only way for conscience to get into power is for it to be convenient because the nature of the culture values conscience. Then the power of convenience is aligned with conscience and is its tool.

There is the risk that men of conscience take when they too freely use the power tools of convenience. They create a culture where convenience brings success and power, not necessarily conscience. It is the culture of the nation that lets it be free. The government should do only those things that people do not settle among themselves. If they have a value-based culture, it lets the Golden Rule and the common good settle most problems by the people working together eventually in nonprofit organizations. That is where conscience-based leadership is often developed and provides the strength of the middle class both economically and morally. You have to develop leaders that recognize these issues and understand the lessons of history.

Conscience versus convenience is not a battle of angels and devils, but of small acts that are more easily rationalized. A leader for conscience needs to realize he seeks to build a culture of character to provide him the ultimate environment in which to operate. If the environment is a culture of convenience, then he often must change to survive. If his goal is the future and concern for family, for others, and for the positive advancement of civilization, then he must lead with a vision recognizing that people are seldom for or against you, but are for themselves. If you show that the common good and the Golden Rule are most protective of them and their most valued all inclusive asset, their personal dignity, then you will find the most powerful "way" to lead, not by appealing to their weakness but their strength.

It should not be forgotten that leadership is often more effective when it concentrates on uniting people of similar thought as opposed to attempting to unify people that are in disagreement. Quite often there is a difference between being a chairman of a committee and only a moderator. Being a chairman requires an affirmative action of pushing through an agenda and making change. A moderator often focuses more on discussion. The chairman tends to be more focused on the prioritization of ideas while a moderator more on the equality of including all within the group. The more difficult the challenge and need to be accomplished, the more important it is to concentrate on the affirmative side of unification.

On the Interaction of Economics and Culture

In a media environment filled with detailed, short-term information, it is easy to feel as if one is lost in a forest of data. In such a case, you need to get out of the valley and up a mountaintop to get perspective of where you are generally and the direction to move.

The stock market moves on a short-term information of occurrence and sentiment. An interest rate cut, uncertainty or a disaster can affect it, but the real issue is the trend, where will it or a company be two-years hence or ten-years hence?

To find an even higher mountaintop would be to understand the long-term interplay of economics, politics, and culture. Karl Marx viewed history as simply being economics in action. It was the key mover. Adam Smith saw all of the interaction of internal values in his *The Theory of Moral Sentiment,* but broke out self-interest as the most powerful of his "invisible hand" on which *The Wealth of Nations* was based.

Of the three arenas of power, economics, politics, and media/culture, economics does the most to set the environment for the other two. Quite often the moralities of the culture or the emotionalism of the politics are used to hide or shield what may well be core economic goals. Whether it be Gandhi's 1930 "salt march" to protest the British monopoly on salt production, Martin Luther King, Jr.'s boycotts or similar actions, economics is inevitably related to political and cultural issues.

However, that environment normally is controlled by the mindset, values, and economic status of the people as a whole.

It is often determined by whether the society is dominated by or moving toward a strong middle class. The alternative involves varying degrees of discrepancy between rich and poor. There is usually an economic equilibrium in society. It has a lot to do with peoples' impressions of the future and their own level of opportunity. They envy the rich less if they or their children have a chance to be one. If they perceive their future is a hopeless struggle, they challenge the system.

Since wealth has a tendency to accumulate or concentrate because of the economic advantage it gives if well used, the question of redistribution replays throughout the ages.

Sometimes revolution redistributes, other times politics enters with policies toward that end or changes in governmental form.

Sometimes the economic system is such that it happens naturally. Many families go from "shirtsleeves to shirtsleeves" through generations because wealth is passed, but not the wealth creation values. Other times the currency is debased to help debtors or inflation/deflation serve as a vehicle of transfer. (Although inflation generally helps the wealthy who have hard assets.)

The politics and culture do intervene with this process. You effectively have two major systems of approach—socialism and free market capitalism. Socialistic approaches have given way to the free market in modern times because they have been less efficient in a fast paced, consumer driven environment and often had problems of bureaucratic corruption and ineffective central control. Capitalism, unchecked, has its own history of greed and excess but even with its problems lends more of a productive bias to the system because it rewards value creation. Markets work, but to be most efficient, they need optimum competition, which comes from a moral, honest market. That requires ethics in the culture and some oversight for fairness from politics. It has a distinct bias toward liberty and freedom of choice, and gives a concept of higher market value to certain skills rather than others. Where socialism looks to equality of individuals, markets must look to equality of opportunity.

To me, the market system with enforced and natural cultural ethics, complimented by a strong middle class, given opportunity at education and capital is the goal to be sought. It naturally provides a movement between the stratas of society depending on one's ability. The issue of charity for the truly needy is a separate cultural issue.

If the system provides opportunity and it should if talent is fully valued, then the rich are not resented as much as copied, and movement in the stratas of society takes place.

We often view the present American system as being set, with little movement between stratas, but that is not the case. Age makes a difference regardless of race, religion, or beginning economic class. When young you have less assets, often college debts, at retirement you usually have higher income and assets. Some born wealthy cannot manage wealth and fail. Education is a big contributor as is access to capital. Debt can help greatly or hurt as in the case of leveraged debt in a downturn. The point is, if the opportunity for movement in the stratas exists, it dramatically changes the perspective of the masses as to the need and degree for change in the system. The old Chinese proverb that it is better to teach a man to fish than to give a man a fish is on point. If government policies focus on redistribution for political gain and not on creation of opportunity, you eventually change the system such that opportunity is diminished.

What a family should want is not a structure that redistributes their money, but the opportunity to build wealth that transcends generations. That is usually a wealth creation set of values that is a great part of the family's values. Usually this value set learns that greed, over time, causes mistaken judgment and alienates potential long-term partners. While many hit "home runs" by being in the right place or having a very talented rare skill, on average, families become wealthy over time through work and each generation preparing a nest egg for the next and teaching them the skills or getting them the education. They stairstep the family. If a man cares only about three houses he might enjoy he may take risks; if he cares about building a solid inheritance, he may be more conservative.

But what he must consider is that if the system in which he operates loses equilibrium in politics, economics or cultural values, it may diminish or take all he has or would leave. So he must care far beyond politics and his self-interest to the vision of a system that carries forward stability.

On the Obligations of Great Universities

Historically, the ancient friction between the church and science has never been fully bridged. St. Thomas Aquinas synthesized to a great degree the concepts of the science of Aristotle and Christian teachings. However, the academic freedom of ideas and the university have always had a heightened sensitivity to not only religion, but also the teaching of values with the question always being asked whose values unless the institution was established for a certain purpose. In the modern day these distinctions are often not quite as obvious, but while they are more sublime, they are increasingly important as civilization struggles to maintain its fabric of social structure.

The goal of great universities is to have a worldwide recognition that today is primarily driven by its expansion of knowledge through research and the peer ratings that it carries among other universities. Increasingly the focus of the ratings is on the quality of students and on the quality of faculty. The faculty reacts to the pressure of its peers nationally and internationally primarily by devoting time to research and to writings that are respected in the field. While money is certainly a resource deemed important, the true currency of such scholars is their recognition by others and their advancement in their fields. This has increasingly made research funding and research strategies a dominant part of great universities. In many cases they achieved to create a genius in mathematics or physics but not necessarily a person most dedicated to the advancement of mankind. The focus is often entirely upon his work and its quality and quantity.

There is thus a necessity for each university, that wishes to be a great university, to have a position of involvement or as it is called, "a seat at the table" with its peers. There is thus a natural momentum to begin to define great universities in the terms of their research and their faculty, as well as their students, that becomes increasingly predominant in the ratings of major magazines and services. Those rating criteria become more the focus of what the university tries to achieve as it is perceived to be measured by outsiders and the publicity affecting its reputation internally and within its region. Students and parents look to these ratings as well, but perhaps we should step back and look at the consequences. Comparisons of privately endowed to public ones are deceptive. Class size, a critical component of ratings, will always favor private institutions since public ones must work to address political involvement. Comparisons of public universities that are tiered, such as California where students' abilities place them at different levels of universities and community colleges, are different from more general admission public universities such as those in Texas which has four major systems. The question is what purpose should a university serve for its constituents' support? Excellence should always be a goal, but the question is excellence in what, and that requires looking not just presently but to the future.

Another audience, the people in the form of the state or government that often supports public universities, as well as the parents who entrust their children to the university for a finishing enlightenment for life, may have necessarily very different interests than those of the "peers at the table." They may be much more interested in concepts of leadership and ethics and helping them gain a broad perspective to shape their lives and future. To them the issue may not necessarily be whether the university is the greatest research university, but whether it fulfills a value, rather than an ideological purpose, of advancing civilization through the promotion of wisdom as well as knowledge. Wisdom is the necessary component that tells us how to use the knowledge that we find. In a globalized world filled with cultural conflicts this becomes extremely important. We may not today have the wisdom of Solomon. Neils Bohr in his Copenhagen Observation observed much beyond physics in that every man's mind is but a model of the world. And only by bringing in the experiences of others and their knowledge can you have a more realistic model of the world that will not fail. Scientists need ethics as much as anyone or tests are suspect and the convenience drawn by fame creates the culture.

But this focuses upon the point of obligation of a university, particularly a public one, to advance civilization by having man have concern for other men. The issue is one of the nature of man and how it needs to be refined. If man is inherently evil, then you appeal to his weaknesses and particularly his nature of convenience by which he cares only for himself. This is how you succeed to manipulate him. If that becomes the cultural environment of the times, then it adopts a life all its own because to not use convenience as the dominant strategy puts you at a disadvantage. If man is redeemable he could be enlightened to where his chief goal was to be concerned with others beyond himself. This only occurs when man is rallied to a concept of principles, values, and ideals that have him not look to himself or even in a sense to others, but to a higher calling in a better world. This sense of the battle between teaching conscience versus convenience is in the essence the advancement of civilization. If a university is not to enlighten, if it is not to teach students the concern they should have for others on a more organized value-based approach such as the common good, the Golden Rule, and the importance that culture has in creating and maintaining that value-based system, then what ultimate purpose does a university have?

The support for funds for great universities constantly is a battle between the concepts of equity and excellence. Should you have ten different books in one great library that has excellence or should funds be expended for the same one book in ten different libraries for equity that gives a breadth of knowledge at a lower level? Another example is that one of the deciding criteria of excellence is peer comparisons in the number of students in a class. That is fine for excellence, but it is the opposite of productivity that would focus on providing a greater number of well-educated students to help America compete in a world where your ability to innovate will keep your standard of living. It is not just the quality of your engineers but the quantity that keeps a nation competitive. These are battles usually decided in different ways by the political perspectives of the times. However, the best solution is one by which you have a balance, and that requires a sacrifice on behalf of excellence; and people sacrifice only for those reasons that they deem to be truly of value to them. Therefore if universities are going to look at their criteria for judgment of greatness in this century, I hope that it will go beyond just the peer pressures of the advancement of knowledge. I hope it will go to the advancement of wisdom by looking into how they can coordinate their efforts to again address the problems that we face globally—having people learn that civilization is truly the effort to understand each other and the principle of the Golden Rule. This will require structured changes in universities that are built like individual silos through departments focusing intently on research and publication. There must be more university coordination that has to be supported by the administration and more outside influences must be added to inject realism and promote relevance in the greater whole of society.

To accomplish this, we need to do more than promote ethics on a broad based effort, which is increasingly done in a very minimal shotgun pellet style fashion, and we must realize why the classics were so important in the evolution of society. The Greeks built their temples and theaters on mountaintops such that the wind helped the acoustics in blowing back the words. They gave us the great tragedies that became the arts. However, the cultural values of the society were what those tragedies taught, that if you committed adultery you lost your wife, if you lied to your friend you lost your friend, and that life's happiness rested on many things beyond just the acquisition of wealth. We now promote with great fanfare the cultural arts, we have, however, lost the depth to conceive the importance of the cultural values. We as a people need to show what we value by asking our universities to at least address at a basic level the concepts of conscience.

Parents understand that it is not just what they teach their children, but it is the environment in which they will work that matters. If you have an environment that they must enter that is controlled by corruption, then the values that they teach their children are lost because they are either corrupted by the system or unsuccessful within it because their integrity becomes a detriment. It is the creation of this environment that the university, as the highest level of learning, has an obligation to address. Most importantly the great universities of the twenty-first century may not necessarily be the ones that have the highest scores in mathematics or science, but may be the ones that build the great systems of ethical values. For the ultimate seal of a university ought not to be just that it has great scholars, but also that the handshake of a person from that university has the meaning of integrity. Greatness is a concept usually associated with the taking of risk. Great universities are going to have to define themselves in ways beyond their peers so that they do not follow after others but lead the curve. The ultimate issue of the twenty-first century will be the teaching of wisdom through the building of civilization through advancement of a culture of ethics, as well as advancing scientific knowledge. Balance is required.

Intellectual diversity must become as critical an issue as racial diversity if many great universities are to be relevant. Think tanks take public policy positions from given perspectives, but the job of great universities is to educate and provide a balance of thought. To teach how to think, is a sacred responsibility that in many instances is warped in the name of "academic freedom." Too often the fundamental values of man are avoided out of fear of controversy or are the victim of political correctness. That has a great cost in the influence of universities, and more importantly, is a threat to the concept of wisdom. Often liberal academia takes pride in the dominance they hold in major university thought. But the dominance is at great cost to their ultimate influence. The diversity of student bodies usually enhances the atmosphere of creative thought and exchange of ideas. But if this diversity does not also apply to political beliefs, students are deprived of the balance of thought which is the way of gaining wisdom. This results in academia not being as influential as it was in the past, the 1960s for example, in affecting the broader society as well as bringing practical relevance back to the universities. The focus of academia is often now on smaller, politically correct issues rather than the big issues where thought is increasingly critical.

Universities would do well to address the problems on their own in an effort to preserve their own influence. They need to stimulate intellectual competition using the same system of checks and balances they insist on for diversity of student bodies in the protection of the diversity of ideas. Rather than taking pride in legal cases that attempt to bar military recruiters from campuses because of the military "don't ask, don't tell policy on homosexuality," universities ought to embody their own arguments. There is little chance of changing a culture if you attempt to punish it rather than engage it intellectually. Wisdom comes from trying to find solutions, and that requires honest discussion, which cannot occur in climates where the intensity of opposition simply alienates the other party. Liberal societies must have some basic concepts of shared values that are not just in its laws but in a shared moral code. This has to include items that are critical to personal dignity such as free expression of ideas, equality of all men, and tolerance. When universities lose relevance and remove themselves from the discussion, wisdom loses a balancing factor.

On Distinguishing Between Value and Ideologically Based Systems

While values will fall within the category of ideas and ideas often describe values, the accumulation of patterns of ideas set a philosophy and often take on the concept of an ideological system or a value system, and sometimes both in combination. The distinctions between them often depend upon whether it is a set of ideas that describe what to do and how to do it or why you do it. Both systems tell you what to do and often how to go about it. But an ideological system, in the reality of its operation, usually focuses more on operational concepts where value-based systems tend to focus more on the morality or the "why you do what you do" concept. They tend to be much more conscience-based. An example would be the ideologies of the last century, which include capitalism, communism, fascism, and others. Value-based systems in contrast could be Christianity, Judaism, Confucianism, Islam, Buddhism, and a number of other combinations of religious or moral concepts. In some cases such as an Islamic theocracy, you have a direct combination of the two.

When you look at the strategic drivers of the environment within a society, normally you have both systems present, but one may predominate more than others and set the culture or the environment for the society. It may not always be particularly obvious, but it can have a significant impact. People have always noted that there is a difference between the state of California and the state of Texas. California tends to have a great number of ideas generated on many fronts (often initiatives or referendums). Texas, on the other hand, is a more value-based state that while changing still operates with a hand of history from its frontier days where it established a set of values and limited the legislature to a short term every two years.

Today you see an evolution of systems that are moving in different directions. The Communism of China is evolving not only into free markets but to regenerate and understand the great cultural history of China that evolves from Confucianism that is a value-based system of integrity. It forms a necessary component of market capitalism since markets are most effective when they have the most effective competition, and effective competition only emerges from an integrity in markets that are not fixed. Value-based systems in other parts of the world have tended to be lost in the modern technology of communication and entertainment, but also in some cases are re-emerging. The Middle East is a key example of fundamentalism opposing modernity.

The key point is that most true value systems change very little or change very slowly because they are a concept of an individual way of life based upon a great deal of historical evolution and testing. Ideological systems are important because they fit to the times and synthesize the ideas that exist in part with the new technology or enlightenment. As we talk of enlightened conservatism being the creation of an ethical environment that looks to three forces, the distinction between these systems become important. The first is enlightenment, which often involves technology, markets, and opportunity to let people increase their standard of living and operate in a modern world. Second, we look at cultural values that really are the maintenance of value systems that are more slow to change but set the pattern and structure, the skeleton of a society in which people have certain rules where they work with others. In most value systems the concern is for helping others through conscience rather than the convenience that can take place within ideological systems as a method of operation, primarily through nongovernmental nonprofit organizations.

The third and ultimate force is the perception of personal dignity of each individual. That dignity requires the respect of others and the concern for each individual. But it also requires a standard of living that allows one to go beyond the basic of "Maslow's Hierarchy of Needs." The combination of these two concepts, ideological systems and value systems, will be one of the very significant issues of the next century. Ideological systems will remain significantly important because basically they are the operating systems of the modern politics and economics. We have to learn to work with each other both within society and globally as to the value systems of how we view each other, how we treat each other, and how we decide to settle our issues. These value systems are going to tell through the strength of our culture whether we trust totally the ideological systems to settle it through government and the courts. Or they will tell whether they will reveal that we have cultures because of the peer pressure of the beliefs of the values systems are ones that settle issues at the lower common denominator looking at the dignity of man, the Golden Rule, and the common good. An understanding of these more powerful forces within society help in analyzing where ideas originate and what their consequences may be. They also provide alternatives to the emerging viciousness of politics and greed of economics. Modern man constantly is driven to choose on issues of conscience or convenience. He is not ever going to be perfect, and the credibility of a society is not based on his moral perfection but more upon his character to accept responsibility for his actions and his failings. This moral consequence of society is not developed in an ideology but in respect for a value system that transcends generations.

This is increasingly lost in modern America as well-intentioned cultural advocates of differing views no longer look to the issues but personify them in the political parties and the Presidency. Be it President Clinton or President Bush, there is a growing tendency to fan hate because it suits extreme political purpose. The greatest risk to our society is this development of ignorant hate. We can learn to disagree on cultural issues and argue on them. But once we lose perspective from thought to emotion, we lose control of the process of enlightenment. Our greatest enemy is not the opposition, but the loss of our internal value systems that are our compass. For without them, emotion manipulates us easily to others' will.

It is not so much that we disagree that is crucial as it is how we disagree and whether there is a process of discussion.

On Understanding the Systems of Cooperative Capitalism

In *The Language of Conscience* we devoted much of the book to the creation of a culture of service. One of the final measurement criteria of the triangles of enlightened conservatism is how effective this nonprofit effort succeeds within a society because it reflects how much people are willing to do for each other rather than depend upon the government or others to serve them. It is a core test of the acceptance of individual responsibility, and it tells a great deal about how developed the economic system has become. *The Language of Conscience* provides a great amount of insight as to how charitable organizations such as the Red Cross, the Salvation Army, Covenant House, and many other organizations benefit society by taking the human capital in volunteerism as well as contributions, and working with those in need. It is important because the best of charity is where you give of yourself rather than simply giving material goods. It is that giving and concern that builds personal dignity within the giver and often, because of the sincerity of the act, the receiver. It allows a different economic and political structure because with people helping each other, individual responsibility replaces a concept of victimization where the legal tort system, the government or other groups are assessed the responsibility to take care of the issue. It is what gives strength to a society in all other formats. Too often a concern for others is looked upon as a weakness in that you do not perceive what could be your greatest benefit personally. But in reality it is an ultimate show of strength because of your interest and understanding of the ultimate nature of life and the way it works.

While we discussed the importance of these nonprofit structures, how they are developed, and the logic in explaining them to build the leadership behind them in *The Language of Conscience*, we need to increasingly focus on the necessity of those ten or fifteen percent of the people that are the uncommon people who take time to get involved in this type structure. The part they play in building family strength is covered in *The New Legacy*. You will never have all of society participate actively although you need all to have the culture appreciated because that is what enhances the peoples' involvement. If you have a culture in which the leaders are attuned to this type of voluntary public service, you make it something of significant value. And the political leadership appreciates the peer pressure that is created and brings conscience more to the forefront because of the power of its morality. It allows for less government because people solve problems among themselves and by themselves. What was not discussed in greater detail in *The Language of Conscience* was the relationship between the nonprofit sector and the for-profit sector of the economy and how the nonprofit sector on a much larger economic scale has considerable impact. This was a question often posed to me both in America and in China.

Since many of the world's economies are moving from the centralized government or oligopoly approaches that are more common in developing economies moving to market economies, this becomes an increasingly important issue because it gives options and an insight into structural issues. Increasing technology, global growth, and simply the expansion of populations put many of the existing systems under great pressure because centralized planning has the ability to work in certain arenas. But the more complex systems become, the more necessary it is to turn control over to natural forces that have a better ability to react to the fundamental nature and pricing of markets and make automatic corrections that do not waste resources.

The difficulty with pure market economy is that it is often harsh on some segments of the population because of the nature of change it quickly makes due to competition and because the market only is efficient when you have true competition. If this environment is carried a step further, it leads to the problems of corruption because of the significant benefits involved. Markets are efficient, but the natural law that makes them so, creates harshness because of the directness that results. The more you cushion the effect by intervening in the market, the more you lose effectiveness. Regulation and bureaucracy are perfect examples of this.

That is why, within a market economy, the nonprofit sector fills two very important needs. The first is that it helps create a culture that maintains a sense of integrity of caring for others that tempers the drive toward self-interest of a market economy by giving a broadened perspective, and secondarily it provides balance through major large nonprofit organizations to enhance competition in certain fields while focusing also on addressing problems in society.

As countries develop more privatized systems it becomes important for them to understand the range of nonprofit institutions that may be a bridge between pure privatization and the current situation. Russia showed the great havoc that can occur when you have an immediate transference to private ownership when the concepts are not well understood. We increasingly do not appreciate our nonprofit institutions and the parts that they play within the economy. There is very limited appreciation given to the unique nature of how morality plays a tremendous part in the free enterprise system to create balance. This is not done just on an individual or small volunteer basis, but by larger institutions that approach issues from a culture of nonpublic ownership.

Perhaps the best way to divide the market economy in the United States is to look at two divisions of the types of companies. The first is investor-owned companies. These can fall in the category of privately owned companies and the publicly owned companies that are traded on the stock exchange. The second group is non-investor owned companies such as nonprofits, mutuals, charities or similar charters. They do not get the same amount of publicity in that many people are not investors in them. What is not appreciated is the significant size of what would be called the non-investor owned companies. These are three very distinct categories—mutual companies, nonprofits, and charities—that are often confused. These are three very distinct categories that are often confused.

Basically, the investor-owned category is one that rents their capital from their shareholders and owners. They pay dividends to them. They accumulate earnings for them, and the stockholders are not the same people as the customers that are served. Thus, the goal of the company is to benefit the shareholders that put money into the company not necessarily those that buy its products.

Non-investor owned insurers get their capital from retained earnings not from stock offerings. In mutual companies the policy owners, or the service receivers, actually own the company. In other words, using mutual insurance companies as perhaps one of the major examples, the policy owners actually own the capital that is built up by the company. If a mutual is ever liquidated, the benefit goes to those people that have had services from the company and have supported it. Nearly all of the earnings stay in the company on their behalf, and the interest of the users of the company is the focus of the governance of the company. The non-investor owned companies would still have boards of directors and many of the same considerations that are in normal competitive companies. In fact, they often have to compete head to head with existing for-profit companies. Not-for-profit companies and charity institutions are two very distinct other categories. Often not-for-profit corporations are created for special purposes to provide services to customers and generally look at retaining less profit and putting more benefits (lower costs, advanced consumer technology) back to the people that they serve. Charities have a different approach in that their entire goal is to provide for others the monies that they receive or spend the money for services they provide.

There are many different variations of all different sizes of these three types of approaches. But they provide vehicles that fit into certain circumstances more appropriately than other forms. Healthcare is a perfect example of more involvement of charities, nonprofits, and mutuals. The reason is that not only an economic set of considerations is involved, but also a moral set of responsibilities. These sectors in particular are ones that use the non-investor owned system to ease the burden of pure market economics. This assists the government in using the private sector to accomplish ends that have some moral balance. Thus they subsidize them often by tax considerations, but they also temper the nature of the market. Quite often it is difficult for a for-profit health insurer to raise prices in a state with a strong not-for-profit Blue Cross Plan that approaches the nonprofit approach as one in which it should lower prices when it has covered its risk levels because it is a service provider. These larger mutual and particularly nonprofit companies significantly provide ceilings by focusing differently on their goals. They also provide floors in their willingness to take less profitable business for the common good.

An appreciation of these companies needs to be enhanced in America because they help to shore up the nature of our economic system. They are also particularly valuable tools if understood to fit into certain circumstances in privatization efforts in developing countries. Too often in developing countries, privatization entails selling the entire company at an auction with investment bankers guiding the process. Many times the culture within the country does not understand the nature of shares if they are given to them and they easily lose the benefit. Additionally, often if you privatize in developing countries, the privatization sells off a monopoly that is public to a private monopoly. The private monopoly has significant benefits that do not necessarily help the economy grow by building in the competition that is necessary. Only a few countries have taken systems that privatized by dividing companies and selling them so there would be competition within the markets. Thereby they were insuring, to the degree possible, that not only the government got the best price for the company for its coffers, but also more importantly the ultimate savings to the country's economy would be significant with more efficient markets.

In some cases the non-investor-owned approach is a possible transition from government ownership to private ownership to eventual demutualization. Oftentimes this is not the favored approach for the executives of corporations and others who prefer to buy them at great discounts—as occurred in Russia. But nearly always in demutualizations, management does very well. The point is that there are different vehicles by which conceptual approaches can be taken that ultimately protect the interests of the people. Mutualization shifts the ownership from the general public to the users of the product. But they are ultimately the ones that have to pay the price and have the greatest sensitivity to the operation of the company. So as eventual owners they may be more demanding than the general public as a whole.

The differences in operations between investor-owned and nonprofit owned are significant but not that great. Capital expenditures for operations are mostly "pay as you go." Both investor-owned and nonprofit owned have disciplined use of cost benefit analyses. They both cannot outspend the bottom line with the investor-owned capitalizing slightly more and with non-investor-owned tending to expense for tax reasons. The major difference is the capital expenditure for acquisitions. Investor-owned can make big bids for other companies and can acquire large blocks of business by going to the market for capital to allow their expansion. They use equity capital as a currency. The non-investor-owned generally have to work with other non-investor-owned companies if they merge. They cannot normally make large bids unless they have retained capital sufficient to do so. However, they can acquire bigger blocks of business by merger with other similar companies from retained earnings.

The access to capital is one of the more significant issues, but it often has less impact than is advertised. Non-investor-owned companies can use retained earnings, bank debt, bond issuance, and oftentimes in some industries like insurance, surplus notes. These are all available to the investor-owned, but they have the ability to secure equity. The existence of the equity is what tends to change the focus of the nature of the company.

It is important to understand that mutual and not-for-profit operations are not *for-loss* operations and they are not charities. The key is they are not beholden to equity expectations, which means they do not have to be fixated on each quarter's results. They also can take a longer-term view because stockholder analysts on a regular basis do not necessarily scrutinize them. Nonetheless, they have not historically been inefficient managers but relatively good managers. They are not without overseers in that they have boards of directors that often subject themselves to the same rules as the major for-profit corporations. If they are of any size, they also have a reality check by the rating agencies' analysis of their operations and problems on a fairly regular basis. The concept of the mutuals put a clear focus on what is best for members. It lets a focus be on longer-term issues such as product lines and pricing. They are often closer to their customers and the alignment of interest changes a focus beyond just profitability. Whereas an investor-owned has an obligation to maximize shareholder value, and that often means meeting Wall Street quarterly earnings targets. The accountability to shareholders requires board members to reflect shareholder interest. Thus, an investor-owned plan basically provides a service in order to make a profit.

A non-investor owned plan generally makes a profit to provide a service. It maximizes customer value and sustains services for the long-term. The policyholders, providers, and owners are all involved in the process and the board members reflect a variety of interests that are served.

While this is a very summarized explanation of the inter-reaction of non-investor owned and investor-owned companies, it should give an understanding that a great part of what brings balance to the American economic system is a sense of conscience that is reflected not in charity but in a hybrid system of organizations that can serve as checks and balances to bring out the best in the system. If you have a pure market system without conscience, corruption becomes rampant because the culture is affected by the economics. Thus, if you want to build a balance into the system, the competitive nature of nonprofit institutions for a different set of goals becomes extremely important. But it only works if you have a strong understanding of and devotion to the concept of nonprofits helping others. Far too often, the part of the system to which people look for nonprofits are the charitable institutions or the service clubs such as the Rotary, Lions, Kiwanis, and others. In reality, the system—particularly in the provision of services—has many nonprofit players. In the financial industry there are many life insurance and health insurance companies that are mutuals. Credit unions are another example of companies that work on a consumer basis. In healthcare, many of your hospitals are nonprofit in nature. The focus is often on investor-owned companies because they get the publicity. Maintaining the strength of the non-investor owned segment is important to America and is important to developing countries because they help create the culture of service by providing a balance that keeps self-interest from becoming greed both by the morality of their purpose as charities and the honorable and focused competition from the people's interest as a balancing factor to absolute free markets.

On the Nature of the Game
Tic Tac Toe – Checkers – Chess?
Presented to the Texas Institute for Health Policy Research
November 5, 2004
Austin, Texas

Ladies and Gentlemen,

It is truly a pleasure to have an opportunity to visit with you about your Shared Vision Project for the State of Texas healthcare and bringing together the strategic players. I am honored that your staff has previously distributed copies of the book, *The Language of Conscience,* to you and a presentation piece that sets part of the background for a concept that I think is not only important in healthcare but in how society begins to unify principles of character and conscience. What you are attempting to do is extremely important because this is a strategic driver of the future. The greatest future challenges to the United States will be the economic impact of an aging population that will require substantially more healthcare funding at a time when resources become increasingly limited because of the competitive position of the United States and much of the rest of the world. Those that understand political budgets realize that budgets are a contract with the people. And when you have a state constitution that requires a balanced budget as Texas does, this leads to many questions in what that budget can provide. Nationally the Social Security and Medicare system, as well as many other health support projects, are going to be the greatest challenges to fiscal responsibility that we will face as demographics move with very negative impacts on funding. They will be the place that crisis will eventually emerge. If they are not answered, they will have a fiscal impact that creates significant deficits and a loss of confidence in the American economy. That would, in turn, create a loss of confidence in the dollar, and thereby a significant impact on the well-being and standard of living of Americans. Because America is the main consuming society, a large portion of the world will be negatively affected as well.

These are issues in which all have a significant part, and they are complex and difficult. I have had the opportunity over the last years to serve as Chairman of the Finance Committee, and now the Strategic Planning Committee of Health Care Services Corporation, which is the parent of Blue Cross Blue Shield of Texas, Illinois, and New Mexico. It looks at healthcare from the perspective of one of the largest non-investor-owned insurers. In watching this issue, I have seen much of the work that you have assembled. But I also see a number of perspectives that dramatically cloud the issue of the solution to healthcare. For that reason, what I would like to talk about today is not necessarily the healthcare project itself, but a much broader context of how not only you and I, but much of the rest of the world, is going to have to reinvent our approaches to how society works with each other. We talked of a healthcare system, but I perceive it more as a series of groups, each focusing on its own self-interest maximization. It is not consumer-centric but will have to become so in order to bring market discipline. Your project helps the individual parties move toward this end, but the problem goes far beyond healthcare. The issue is the difference between knowledge and wisdom, and it is a significant one. We are growing massively in knowledge. The costs of healthcare are not just healthcare inflation, but the quality of healthcare that we have now as compared to the year 2000, accounts for a significant amount of this increase. Healthcare is both an economic and a moral issue and that makes it much more complex than a discussion of just economic self-interest. The pieces of the puzzle will not fit together until each party is willing to shape their part to a common vision. This will require sacrifice and a process of fairness.

The best way to make my point in the time allowed today is to talk about three games: (1) tic tac toe, which really is two sets of parallel lines where you attempt to win by having a straight line of X's or O's as you play against an opponent; (2) checkers where you have a much bigger board of a number of colored squares where each side has different colored players that move according to certain rules that limit the types and direction of movement (but therefore is much more complicated than tic tac toe); and finally (3) chess in which you have a similar board to that of checkers, but players that can move in different ways because of their status which makes for a very complicated game of strategy. In effect, you have three games and three levels of thinking. They are similar in basic concept, but they vary in the levels of complexity and knowledge required to succeed and win. You can be a great checkers player and truly understand that game but perhaps are not mentally into chess. Or you can be a tic tac toe player that just enjoys the game and doesn't care very much about learning the complexity of the others.

These have significant parallels to life. I think an example might be a baseball player. When you are in Little League you are only interested in hitting the ball. Tic tac toe in watching baseball is just seeing a hitter try to hit the ball that the pitcher throws. Checkers might be a bit different. It is a more refined understanding that hitting is not just how to swing the bat and make contact with the ball. But can you see the spin on the ball to give you an idea of what type ball is coming at what location to position the bat? How well can you judge the arm movement of the pitcher to get an idea of where you might best position your swing? Chess takes all of those talents, the ability to swing the bat of tic tac toe, understanding the physical characteristics of the pitcher (and hopefully the seams on the ball if you have good enough eyesight), and adds a dimension for chess of the mental game. What do you know of his history, what are his major pitches, and more importantly when does he use them? How do most pitchers pitch to you so that you cover your weaknesses, while at the same time anticipating based on historical knowledge of how he will strategize pitching the ball to you?

Each of these is at different levels of understanding. They involve different characteristics. An average person watching a ballgame views it from the perspective of tic tac toe, a very simple, "does he hit the ball?" The more knowledgeable people appreciate the increasing levels even to the point of fully understanding the significance of statistics in the sport. It is to this point the difference between just knowledge and wisdom, which is the use of that knowledge that I would like for us to discuss today. Your project can be the tic tac toe of providing information on healthcare and options in Texas or it can be the checkers of bringing together with a true shared vision all of the players within healthcare of how different parties can work with each other. Perhaps you can find the best solution that both continues the growth in excellence in medical care, while at the same time having rules for equity that allow its broader usage. Or you can look one step further, to the chess of the ultimate issue, how can we use this issue to explain to society the necessity of building a culture of conscience as opposed to convenience in order that we may work together to accomplish ends that are best for society with civility? This last issue is important because it involves the concept of power. We can have all of the right answers to the health issues, all of the right compromises with shared vision partners, but unless there is the power, the ultimate will, to do what is best for society in the common good, then it matters little because it will fail. Government reacts to pressure as well as vision and it plays a huge part in this issue. The nature of our society is that we often look more to the creation of words and ideas and feel good about attempting to do the right thing. The issue is instead *doing the right thing* because if we do not begin to address these problems, we will inevitably, as a nation, weaken and divide.

The big issue is whether there is a will strong enough to seek change. This issue is a strategic one not just for its importance but the inefficiencies of many parts of the system that can be corrected to produce funds to smooth change. *The Language of Conscience* was a book that I wrote primarily for several character groups in the United States and as a bridge with the Confucian Museum with whom I had worked on a sister state project in China. It was never intended to have the responses given to it that have occurred, but the responses give insight as to the interest in bridging together. Your staff has been kind enough to distribute the Resolution from the Texas Legislature that had the leaders of both parties commend the book and the concept we have worked with over the last thirty years to unify people. As we all know, this was one of the most difficult sessions of the Texas Legislature. But at the same time the effort for the Resolution revealed that there are a number of people that do not wish the bitterness of partisanship but would like to find ways and methods by which a middle ground can be found. The nature of political partisanship does not allow people to work with each other as easily as in the past. So there have to be third parties that can provide an honest broker's approach to ideas and thought. It was this Resolution and perspective of the process that has united our effort.

You have a world in which there is opportunity to have power affected by conscience. The nature of power is such that it is often driven by conscience at a lower level of personal relationship because of the Golden Rule. But in higher levels of power, almost always, convenience tends to dominate unless the culture of the people is such that conscience is appreciated. Whether we look to Machiavelli's concept of man being inherently evil or Aristotle, Christ, and Confucius' belief that he was redeemable, it is the nature of the culture and predominance of the values that shape the era. So today, what you do, if you wish to go to the levels of chess with a shared vision project, is to look beyond just healthcare. How can this project be used as an example not just of how you bring the healthcare industry together but how you unify society to make decisions for the right reasons? That is not something that you can do alone. There have to be many people that begin to understand this concept, and it may take many years for true change to take place. But an idea is the only way that you replace other ideas, and once ideas are understood they cannot be removed from the mind. You rely not on a leader alone because the nature of politics may well destroy him or her. And you rely not on institutions. You rely on your internal dedication knowing that your purpose has to be based on the history of honor in which you have lived your life that has been taught to you by your ancestors and on your concern for the future of your children.

There are many groups of conscience that will be addressing these issues in different ways, but your project may be one of the most significant tasks in showing how it can work. You have already brought the major think tanks of the state, from diverse sides, together to see how at least the preliminary knowledge can be gained. You have searched to bring together all of the different parties with interest throughout the state in order that all could be represented, but you have chosen carefully to find the character of those people to be ones that believe in principle and follow the language of conscience of true belief with a respect for those on the other side who are true believers in their principles. The method of discussion that you have attempted to assemble is very noteworthy and is recognized by people on all sides. You have contacted much of the leadership of the state to get their input and their ideas as well as to make them aware of the consequences of actions. You have in Camille Miller perhaps one of the most knowledgeable people in the history of budgets within the state from her work with Lieutenant Governor Bob Bullock and Lieutenant Governor Bill Hobby. There is no more serious a mind at understanding the impact of public policy to broad issues. But more importantly she has brought to your project a heart that cares about unifying people and that is, in this case, even more significant. It is wisdom combined with knowledge. You have additionally assembled a great number of talented, knowledgeable people in the field with substantial research bases of information. So the preliminaries of how a project should be undertaken have been well conceived. And it is noteworthy that many of the state's finest foundations have understood your ultimate goal and approach and responded to funding your purpose.

However, the ultimate strategy of our chess game has to be that people understand the method or process by which we come to our conclusions and why we do it. There will inevitably be disagreements and in all likelihood you should present options with the consequences of each defined. When we formed the Texas Lyceum twenty-five years ago, it was dedicated to these ideals, vision, and integrity as taught by Aristotle in the Lyceum, which was a grove of trees. It will have its twenty-fifth anniversary next April and has done a great deal to unify much of the leadership of this state, both Republican and Democratic, in the concept that you can work together. It has had a history of bringing together conferences to bring forth ideas. But what is missing today is the key point with which the Lyceum began. Ideas matter greatly. It is not a case of just debating them. It is a case of explaining their importance. What good does it do for all of the major think tanks to spend great amounts of money and provide research if they are only focused on partisan sides that do not really help find the solutions to issues within the center? Texas has been a state of values.

The *Economist Magazine* several years ago looked to us as having a method of approach that brought people together and as such might be a solution for the future. With the animosity of redistricting much of that has been lost and it needs to be regained. Texas is a value-based state that looks to individual responsibility, character, the Golden Rule, and the common good. Many other parts of the country have become more ideological and just have ideas that tend to change more with the times. There is thus a battle between a basic moral concept of how men should work with each other and an issue of relativity that values can vary depending on the circumstances, and you can easily rationalize taking actions in a different context. It is understanding this change in the nature of our culture, and identifying it, that is the ultimate solution to how the game of chess can be played. The people within society have obligations to each other and only by understanding these obligations do we find the integrity of purpose by which we can have final solutions that are not just in our interests but in the common good as a whole. The final book in this series is one now being finished that deals very much with these points. It is called *Instilling Values in Transcending Generations* because the future of society rests on what we are going to teach our children and what examples we show them. Healthcare is a critical issue, and it is one of the areas of focus. You can hire a carpenter because he has a saw and can use it. Or you can hire a carpenter because he has a vision far greater of how to build a house. You are one of the few groups that have sought to look at the greater picture.

Part of that greater picture is bringing together the various component parts that you have. I would suggest that you could symbolize what you and they value, by coming together to give awards to those members of the legislature and government that truly have embodied this concept. There are many awards given with great publicity often for those who have helped them. But there are few awards given for those that have truly cared about people and the nature of society and have spoken a *language of conscience* that was awarded not on what people have done or even how well they have done it. Instead it should be based on why they have acted that brings a focus that defines them, and also defines you because of what you have valued. It would well be the lighting of a candle that might light many others because of the nature and uniqueness of this effort. In our legislature the Democrats and Republicans still sit amidst each other, not on separate sides of a division. It is symbolic and appropriate, but is becoming less appreciated unless the people, by their actions, show resolve to demand the focus not on partisanship but the common good.

I would leave you with a final story that I might put in a little different form because it will give some insight to some critical points as you move through this legislative session and understand the nature of government.

One time I was asked why I had been successful in writing the background issues for the Arts and Humanities Commission to get a 200% increase in the Proposition 13 session of the legislature, or with the work of the development of the Texas Economic Development Commission, or in many cases the building of many of the research and character groups that we have formed over the years. My response was that coming from a small town I have a great appreciation of natural law. More than all of the sophistication of great bodies of knowledge, you can learn great lessons from simple things. We have great complex central planning systems that have all been replaced by markets because no man is so smart that he knows all of the answers. And natural forces have to have impact. But in dealing with men and the personal dignity of each individual and how he looks at the natural desire to be right as he focuses his perspectives, then you have to understand the viewpoints of those in power, and the background that provides their limits of knowledge. As Sun-tzu noted in *The Art of War,* pick your battles and know your opponent as well as yourself.

The best way that I can explain this natural law rests in my relationship with my wife Kitty. We have been married thirty-three years, have three wonderful children and have been quite happy even though we are, for all practical purposes, significant opposites. She likes the temperature at 83 degrees; I prefer it at 65 degrees. Having been to Sweetbrier, studied at the Sorbonne in Paris, and having developed superb taste, her personality was shaped by culture. My background was shaped to a great degree by my father who was a sheriff and by a background in law, banking, and the military. Nonetheless, my goal in life has always been to please her, and she discovered years ago the benefits of well run spas and clinics. So whenever we vacation, I try to make certain there is an excellent spa nearby that she can enjoy. This has led to a unique set of experiences that give real insight into politics and the ways the world naturally works.

A typical example was one recent vacation when we were in Mexico. She attended the spas near where we were staying, and someone recommended to her a very special spa about fifteen miles away. As usual, I did not want her to go on her own, so we took a taxi outside the hotel, and I planned to return after I saw that she was happy there. On the way the cab driver managed to indicate that he had five kids, had been in line a long time and unfortunately he did not get but $10 (I had asked) for taking us all this long distance because of a zone system. If he had taken us just across town he would have gotten $6 and been back in line. The more I got to know him the more I liked him, and he seemed to be a sincere person who really cared about his family. When we arrived, the spa was very obvious in location, and I let Kitty out. However, the man greeting me insisted that I get out even though I kept explaining that this was my driver for security and that he was going to take me back. I did not see any other cabs available so I really did not want to wait and felt that I owed the driver the payment for the trip back to make up for his inconvenience. This was a good intent on my part, but possibly not well explained with the language barriers. In any case, the attendant finally put up his hands and told the driver to take me back, and I assumed that I had done a good thing for him out of fairness and was somewhat pleased with myself. As we were driving back, he was obviously very nervous and crossed himself in a religious fashion constantly. I then asked him why he seemed concerned because he would be getting twice the fee, and a tip, and he deserved it. He then somewhat explained to me (through a language barrier) that we had crossed a state line driving to the spa, and he was a cab driver in the wrong state taking somebody back to his state. By the local rules, he would have a $200 fine and a lot of problems if he was stopped, and he was not sure what would happen to me for insisting that he take me back. This, of course, was an explanation I had wished someone had given more clearly, but my logical approach was to take a nap on the floorboard until we reached the state line. There are several lessons for politics from this story. The first is that even though you may try to do what you think is right, it is wise to have a skepticism about unintended consequences in advance. Confucianism is a very positive set of relationships for affirmative actions in Chinese culture. However, it is tempered by the Daoism of Lao-tzu who also wanted the right consequences but had skepticism of unintended consequences. The second lesson is that even though there may be logical and well-intentioned actions, these are often easily overcome by economic considerations. In the logical situation of my taking that taxi cab, the real problem was a set of rules based on economic considerations of what taxi drivers should benefit in what circumstances. Economics often trumps intelligent responses; watch the money involved to understand the existing or proposed system.

The other set of lessons came from a spa in Central America. I took Kitty to one she particularly liked because it had the European approach and was much more medicinal. While I usually don't join her at spas, she was rather insistent that it might be a good idea for me to take one of their programs for weight loss. This came after a recent trip to China for the announcement of the publication of *The Language of Conscience,* and one of my friends that I had met as part of a former delegation to the United States greeted me and made a comment that "I was growing in the nature of Buddha." I, of course, thanked him thinking that he liked the references in the book, and how I had included many of the similarities of various religions. My other friend, who understood Chinese, whispered in my ear that the translation wasn't quite right. What he is saying is that you have gained a lot of weight and are beginning to look like Buddha. This, of course, brought forth my humility and the idea that perhaps the spa concept was not half bad.

As part of the treatment you had a variety of circulatory massages with Dead Sea salts, you had heat treatments, steam, and various other approaches, but mainly were not supposed to eat a great deal. I was actually having some success until about the last day when someone noticed on my arm this inch and a half perfectly round bruise with two red punctures that looked like fang marks about a quarter of an inch apart in a white center. This was of great concern to the attendants who thought I should immediately go to a clinic, which is where they would go if it had happened to them. Since I was a foreigner with a very bad bite, I felt it and said there was no pain there. And they said that was even worse because it was probably deadened. That was not the answer I wanted to hear, and the more I looked at it, the more it appeared to resemble a bite from a Diamondback Rattler (or a very big mean insect). My question was how I could have gotten bitten because I had only been working on the book at the hotel, eating supper at restaurants, walking back and forth to the hotel, at the clinic, and I never remembered anything happening Then they pointed out that bugs often get in couches. And I remembered that I had slept (65 degrees where possible) while watching television on a couch. I also remembered at our ranch how one time I had had a number of small snakes get into a couch to get off the cold ground. Thus, I was now convinced I must have been bitten by some terrible insect while lying on the couch at the hotel. The question was what did I do now.

The first option logically was to go home to Brenham and have it treated there. That brought to mind my previous experience of when I was bitten by a brown recluse spider that had gotten into my pants while I was wearing a swimsuit taking the kids on a fishing experience to an island off Central America. (This taught me not only to watch for scorpions in my boots, but also to particularly watch for spiders in my pants.) The brown recluse is a bad bite that makes a big chunk of meat fall out, and there is not much you can do about it. The doctor at the local hospital recognized it because of experience in dealing with horses in Central America, but managed to show it to all of the staff and in the end wanted to take pictures. Because of its location high up on the back of my leg, I did not feel this was a very helpful solution. Then I remembered another trip to Latin America where I had been bitten by something and had a fever for two weeks even though we sent blood samples to the best hospitals trying to figure out what it was. It finally went away, but there were not many solutions medically. That led me to think about treatment. I started thinking about taking antibiotics quickly and remembered my experience in China where I had taken a preventive antibiotic in anticipation of problems, but had gotten very sick at the end. The Chinese had been extremely careful to see that everything was washed before I ate it so they were confused as to why I was sick. In trying to look at whether I could take more antibiotics, I read the instructions in more detail and found that you were not supposed to drink alcohol or be in direct sunlight with the antibiotic or it would have a photochemical reaction. In other words, in trying to prevent a problem I had made myself sick by not being as informed as I should have been. So maybe taking antibiotics was not the best of ideas not knowing what the circumstances were.

So, at this point, the question was did I go to a local clinic as the three staff people recommended and trust that level of medicine having a more direct knowledge of Central American insects. Or, since they thought it was so serious, did I try to find the best insect man in Latin America by calling my partner who was a consultant in Mexico City and had such ties. I did not really feel bad before. But as they said, it took time for venoms to have effect. And I have to admit about then I was not feeling nearly as good as I had before. About this time, the head of the spa and clinic walked in because one of the staff had told her about my bite. After looking at it closely and putting it in the sunlight, she said, "I am very sorry." I, of course, immediately asked how serious she thought it was. She replied, "It is nothing, it is a spa bruise from the Dead Sea salts. Sometimes they don't dissolve and cut like that. It may look like a bite, but it is not one. It will go away in a couple of days." Getting my glasses and looking more closely in the light, you could see that rather than two puncture marks, they were little cuts in the skin that probably had stopped the circulation to make the white spot, and the other bruise was not really that bad.

The point for politics is thus: In the Chinese experience I had tried to prevent problems that were not necessarily certain to occur. I had not checked just how carefully people would be worrying about taking care of these consequences on their own. And I managed to take actions in anticipation of problems that because the consequences were not fully understood created the problems themselves. This is not greatly different from our taxi example, except there I was trying to do a good act. Here I was trying to take a preventive action and did not fully understand the range of consequences. On the bite, I would probably not have believed it to be as big a problem had it not been that the local people, who I considered experts in the field, all made it to be a bigger problem because that is how they saw it. And that is how they led to a train of thought that let all of the other consequences be put logically in an order. It is very important to understand that how a train of thought in a certain direction begins is of extreme consequence. Because the nature of the mind is such that if you have a preconception of how you look at information, the information itself all begins to logically fit together. It is one of the most powerful aspects of politics in the natural human desire to be correct and thus all information is viewed from the prism with which you see issues.

The fact that my past experience had all been negative, put in the back of my mind consequences that might not have all been relevant here, but because it was the only experience that I had, it played a major part in the decision and thought process through which I moved forward. The fact that after another perspective had been given, I was able to look carefully at the circumstances of a different perception and have some degree of confidence was critically important because I could confirm one of the concepts more easily. That would have been far easier to do in the beginning if both concepts had been presented.

The point for telling these stories is very simple. It is to tell you who you are in the situation of this overall debate. In every circumstance, there is a relationship or a position that has to be defined. The Lord's Prayer begins with "Our Father" not "Our Judge," so it gives a perception of how to look at the information that follows. You, on this issue of health, can be the people looking at individual issues such as the bite and give your most honest opinion that you believe is what it is. But I think it is far more important that you be the spa director to look at the overall situation and recognize not at the tic tac toe level, not at the checkers level, but at the chess of power how you enter to bring reason to a process. It involves not just knowing about bites, not just knowing about options, but it involves knowing the consequence of all actions taking place. The legislature has its own history of experience that shapes its perspective and drives its actions. Understand these before you present. You must get the true perspective.

That is not an easy undertaking because understanding all of the powers and all of the motivations that have to work in a system are particularly difficult. To assist you, the other handout that has been given to you is a set of inverted triangles that are called "The Triangles of Enlightened Conservatism." They are a tool that may be of help to you in evaluating consequences. They can be used at the level of tic tac toe, checkers or chess because they have been devised to create thought at different levels. They involve the major forces of economics, politics, and culture (including media and entertainment). They look at the goals of where different things balance each other, such as enlightenment and existing cultural values and why personal dignity, which is the balance on which you build sacrifice, is the critical point because it can provide stability. They look at the methods by which you can analyze, discern trends, and make measurements. This helps you in realizing whether you are simply by debt pushing the problem off to another generation or morally addressing it now. They look at the environments that you need to create to have a culture of conscience because the entire triangles are built upon a concept of individual responsibility and character. If you become familiar with them they are simple ways to review all issues and train yourself to think with a bit more depth. What is the economics of the taxi driver that may overcome the effort of conscience? What are the broad ranges of things that need to be looked at in understanding an issue in the case of the bite? Most importantly, can we find examples to create and reward those that move forward to find the common good, obey the Golden Rule, and to bring out the best in society?

May I commend you for your efforts not only to find the right answers in healthcare, but also to do it in a way that sets an example to show why things should be done.

On the Evolution of Conscience
From Morality to Religion

The fourth President of the United States, James Madison was the dominant force in the creation of the Constitution of the United States, and recognized how intertwined public values were with the private values, he noted:

We have staked the whole of our political institutions upon the capacity of mankind for self-government, upon the capacity of each and all of us to govern ourselves, to control ourselves, to sustain ourselves according to the Ten Commandments of God.

Perhaps the most surprising set of observations that I received in regard to *The Language of Conscience* involved my discussion of the ultimate nature of man when I noted that Machiavelli and *The Science of the Thick and the Black* looked upon man as being inherently evil while Confucius, Aristotle, and Christ looked upon him as being redeemable. One friend said to me that by including Christ, I would lose a number of academics and liberals because I was bringing in theology. Another friend noted that I would lose a great number of Christians because I included Christ on the same level as Aristotle and Confucius without making a distinction. In China one of the questions posed to me was whether my concept of conscience was one of the moralities of man or was the result of my religion. To discuss the issue of morality, religion, and conscience is often inviting the flames and jaws of controversy. But it is perhaps the most important point to be drawn in understanding what is necessary for the advancement of civilization. Of the three strategic drivers of civilization, politics and economics are driven by competition whereas culture is the binding power and its strength to keep stability is essential. The battle between conscience and convenience is won or lost in the peer pressure of that part of culture where man imposes rules upon himself. Religions have a great impact upon this so they excite passion in both directions. Understanding the evolution of conscience or the ability to inherently recognize good and evil makes issues less controversial.

In effect, conscience is an evolution. It has both capacity, which I would relate with religion, and content, which I would relate more with morality and the Golden Rule. The easiest way to make this distinction would be to look at the Ten Commandments of the Old Testament. A part of them relate to man's relationship with man, and, for our purposes, we shall define that as morality.

- Honor thy father and thy mother.
- Thou shall not kill.
- Thou shall not commit adultery.
- Thou shall not steal.
- Thou shall not bear false witness against thy neighbor.
- Thou shall not covet thy neighbor's house, thou shall not covet thy neighbor's wife, nor his manservant, nor his maidservant, nor his ox, nor his ass, nor anything that is thy neighbor's.

These with the Golden Rule are rules of how men should operate in their relationship with other men. They are the beginning of a civil society and are philosophy not unlike Aristotle, Confucius or many of the other worldly philosophers. They are the basics of conduct between men and are the place that a culture is established that provides guidelines morally and ethically as to how we treat each other. They are common to many religions in principle.

Religions often evolve a refinement of those guidelines. The other portions of the Ten Commandments relate to men's relation with God.

- Thou shalt have no other gods before me.
- Thou shalt not make unto thee any graven image, or any likeness of anything that is in heaven above, or that is in the earth beneath. . . .
- Thou shall not take the name of the Lord thy God in vain. . . .
- Remember the Sabbath day and keep it holy. . . .

These are covenants made with God that were then superseded by the covenant of Christ.

The critical point is that there are relations between men, and there are relations that every man has with his Maker as he defines his Maker. It is thus important to make a distinction between morality and religion in this sense. Because morality should not be opposed solely because some disagree with religion, nor should it be opposed in those areas where it is good solely because it does not have the perfection of one's religion. It is an issue that was well put forth by John Fletcher Moulton (or Lord Moulton) who divided actions into the three divisions that were effectively the law that had to be obeyed, free choice, and the domain he called "The Domain of Obedience to the Unenforceable." It is the place that man internally sets his own law where he acknowledges his responsibilities and his personal moral commitments.

It is in this area of "morality" as opposed to the legal dictates of society and the realm of free choice that the world will now engage definition. The realm of conscience versus convenience is discussed in both *The Language of Conscience* and the preceding pages. The concept of a tipping point that was brought forth in Malcolm Gladwell's *The Tipping Point* where a change in perception finally reaches a critical mass and brings about a new reality is very much on point. In this case it may be a slower revolution that is taking place that strengthens morality to the point that peer pressure of culture changes the nature of society positively even with the change of technology or it can be that the deterioration of morality reaches a critical mass where convenience makes it extremely difficult to re-establish the bonds of morality to the levels they previously existed. The world, as well as individual nations, is at a point of flux that is moving to definitions.

The critical point is much like the arguments about the failure of Rome. Some have argued that the economic decline brought the moral decline; others have argued that the moral decline led to the economic decline. To me, the significant issue was that the economic and the moral decline seemed to feed upon each other. Here, we have a society where many with religion demand almost that it be the law. And those who oppose religion normally support law but wish it to be certain to exclude religion. In effect, both sides minimize the importance of the fact that they both should care greatly about this third realm of morality and find ways to work together to make it succeed. For those that fear the influence of religion and prefer secular law alone, they should realize that law and justice are two very different things. There is a broader realm beyond just the law between men that matter—a culture of morality that fulfills the justice within the law by keeping the peer pressure of the common good and the Golden Rule in place. Similarly, those who look to religion must understand that unless you create an environment of morality that people can begin to understand, become educated, and evolve to higher levels of knowledge, you never succeed in converting them truly to any religion. Religions involve the evolution of man between thinking of how he works with others, which is knowledge to the sense of enlightenment of self-understanding of which Lao-tzu spoke. Each man develops his own relationship with the concept of God as he defines it. The refinement of conscience from the levels of morality between men often guides man to his relationship with the higher being. In Christianity, God gave us free choice and with it the responsibility for our actions. This causes me to try to live a life and to promote the values of a relationship with Him. But it does not cause me to believe that I can force others to believe other than by my example. Conversions at the point of force are not consistent with the relationship that I believe God seeks. I am reminded in the New Testament of the story of Christ when he was in Samaria and asked a Samaritan woman to allow him to use her bucket and receive a drink. He talked of the difference between physical water and the values of the soul. He made a very interesting point, "You worship what you do not know; we worship what we know, . . ."

Each of us has a perspective of religion that is usually gained from our parents but is influenced a great deal by history, geography, and our culture. When we were young we accepted in faith. As we grow older and have the experiences of life we challenge it, and either it fades in importance or it becomes a far more critical part of our being. But the very evolution of most religions depends in part on the strong moral structure that precedes them. They define how we treat others as a prerequisite to a relationship with a higher being. In Christianity, sin is the sense of separation from God, but the very cause of that separation is placing materialism and selfishness as false gods because convenience has overcome the conscience of morality. If conscience is developed in morality, with a strong culture, it provides the base upon which men can enlighten themselves to a true relationship with their God. There are those that oppose religion as "the opiate of the masses." But to me an inner commitment of enlightenment beyond self is the ultimate goal of a civilization. Life is a journey of learning, and each man evolves differently.

Christianity is similar to many religions. Men to gain emphasis have added theology, and structure, and often liberties are taken in this emphasis. The cause of conflict within religions and between them often falls into the category of whether the relationship with God is direct or through a structured intermediary. That intermediary always has a vested interest, and it can be of conscience or convenience as history shows. I am reminded of sitting in the Sistine Chapel of the Vatican and someone noting to me the differences from symbolism of a loving God's relationship with man on the ceiling to a more vengeful God with the depictions in later years. These paintings occurred over a long period, the latter of which saw the rise of Luther's Protestantism, which affected perspective. The Sale of Indulgences where you could pay for relief of sin, the nature of The Inquisition, and other historical examples show structural changes in religion over time. The interpretation of Buddhism has changed in ways depending on its geographic location. Even non-religious philosophical teachings like Confucianism are interpreted differently both in time and geography. The Koran does not have an ultimate interpreter, so the various wordings have been adopted in many ways, some fundamentalist and some broadened. So the question to me has always been what was the essence of what Jesus taught? It was effectively the concept of character. He did not teach structure, but denounced the Pharisees and their rules as hypocrites who loved their positions. I have always seen Jesus as teaching that character required certain key beliefs but the issue of consequence was eternal to each man. Much like the Greek Stoics that believed no man could injure you unless you allowed it, the outer world has only the character we give it by our own thought whether we recognize that fact or not. Our thoughts, and the values they carry, mold us. That is why character, or the morality we seek, is so critical within a society. Its greater appreciation leads to the conscience of higher thought and relationship. Perhaps the best description of God I have seen is found in The Doctrine Covenants of The Church of Jesus Christ Latter-Day Saints 93:36: "The glory of God is intelligence or in other words light and truth." It captures the concept of almost all religions.

So the preservation and development of that culture of morality, in a positive evolution of civilization is absolutely critical to the growth of religion. At the same time, a world that is ruled only by laws and not by the morality of the ethics and justice that keep the enforcement of law with integrity, can hardly be the goal of those who would suppress morality in order to avoid embracing religion. Often the materialism that hurts society is not just the possessions of worldly goods but is the possession of intellectual pride, self-satisfaction, and social prestige. The first key to building a consensus often lies in recognizing the concepts that we do not embrace and determining the method by which we will discuss them. This is particularly difficult in circumstances of religion because it is a matter of faith that conveys the obligation. The same is true in matters of secular principle of the division of law and religion. The point to be made is that fundamental morality, as opposed to religion which is often far more specific on issues, is an area that can have a great deal of joint agreement if both sides tend to look at the benefits it provides as opposed to the emotions that it generates.

It is quite possible to be a servant of Christ and a friend of Confucius and Aristotle. My parents baptized me into the Christian faith as a Methodist before I could reason. But as life proceeded, even as I learned the intricacies of science, I have never seen it inconsistent with the concept of a Creator. There is much that I do not know, but I do not worship that. But what I do know is that the God I follow is best defined in the Lord's Prayer as Our Father and looks upon a life that should be based on love rather than hate, upon the support of the family as a core to values, and one that brings enlightenment by causing me to think of these issues in relation to others. I am one who recognizes men's failings because I take some comfort that the Old Testament centered on David in that everything before David focused on the path to him, and everything after David focused from him. David was far from a perfect man, but he gave absolute devotion to God. So even if I cannot achieve perfection, I believe God will consider my motivations and efforts. Each religion has its own approach to finding God. To some it is but recognition of nature. But the essence is the understanding that we have been given the capacity for free choice in how we live our lives. Outside forces will affect us physically, but we control and define our internal commitment and character. How men need react in the area of morality and religion are quite different. In religion, commitment by free choice is what God seeks so the effort should be enlightenment of others as to the quality of that relationship with God by example and commitment, but not by force. Engagement in morality is a different circumstance. The nature of man and how we live with each other is not between man and God but is instead between a culture and us as men as a society. We use our political system to write the laws that we must follow. We use our economic system to enhance our standard of life. But we use our cultural system to effectively set our quality of life because it addresses our perception of our self-worth and individual dignity. The concept of moral values does matter because it is the basis of character and destiny. They are necessary to be preserved for those who both wish their secular values and those who wish their religion to be expanded. There is common ground for the advancement of civilization, but only if issues become defined in the paradigm of the continuum of the evolution of conscience.

On Developing a Catalyst for Global Integrity
Understanding the Importance of the Constituency for Ethics
And the Nature of Ethics as Power
Presented to The Integrity Task Force FIDIC
September 7, 2005
Beijing, China

Thank you both for your kind invitation to join you at your meetings today and most importantly for the work that you have done on developing a Corporate Integrity System with a concept to global business. When I wrote *The Language of Conscience,* your work and that of the Ethics Officer Association in America were two of the case examples that were critically important because they dealt not just with ethics but also with the realities of life.

In our limited time this morning I would like to speak to a much more significant issue which is how systems such as these can effectively be placed into operation in a global environment far too often dominated by corruption. I have had the opportunity to work with many people and to get the insights of very diverse parties as to how to structure a perspective on these issues. You quickly see that first and foremost integrity is a cultural power more then an economic or political power and that is very important in refining a strategy on how to enhance it. . . . The reason good ideas of the mind often do not work is a lack of understanding the function of the powers of reality that both support and hinder them. As engineering consultants facing this daily, you understand the reality of the interaction of which I speak. . . .

As we globally expand business and become more closely entwined, the individual cultural values seem to shrink into smaller groups even within societies for preservation and are not necessarily being as broadened, as logic would expect. It shows that cultural values are more important than is perceived. This means that we are increasingly going to have to find a method by which to blend cultures that come from within ourselves and thereby provide common values that unify us rather than separate us.

In the East, it is expressed as bringing harmony to cultures and between cultures. Within each culture there is a battle over character. This battle is between conscience and convenience. Conscience has two parts—obligation and compassion. In the realms of power, convenience often dominates at higher levels because of the nature of ambition, greed, vanity, and simply the nature of competition. Conscience does much better in other arenas where the Golden Rule sets the stage for integrity. The secret is that to get conscience into power we must make it convenient in its own right. And the way that we do that is to have it appreciated by the culture as a whole so that people strive to demonstrate it in order to advance. So the battle for integrity is cultural, not directly economic or political. Marcus Aurelius noted that men should be upright, not be kept upright. This shows the two forces for integrity. One is the law if it is obeyed. The other is cultural morality, which sets peer pressure. But because it also supports the law, it is the basic power to be expanded.

That means we need to understand two significant factors of conscience. The first is what is its constituency, and the second is how to look upon it as a cultural power. Ethics is but a thought definition of the terms of what society looks upon as being proper behavior in the morality or obligation between men. Integrity is its functional counterpart in the sense of putting ethics into actions. If we think of both as a codification of the basics of morality, it is what men owe each other beyond the legal requirements of law. The law is the codification of the minimum that we owe each other within society as determined by culture. The culture determines the law, not the law the culture. The enforcement of the law is also the tool of the culture because it directly affects the politics that drive it. So the power of ethics, of conscience, of integrity, depends a great deal on how it is perceived and used, and it is a tremendous power. It is used as the reason for dislodging politicians or people in economic positions. It is used in negative politics often improperly, but to show that people did not do things, as they should. It is used in the prosecution and allegation of corruption for many purposes. The point that I would make is that the concept of ethics and integrity is an extremely powerful one, but like many of the concepts of thought in history, it is a power that can be distorted, abused or rationalized away.

The discussion of ethics and integrity or character (when you choose conscience over convenience) suffers on occasion in the modern world because they are often looked upon as the values that they are. They require an established set of acceptable rules of behavior. And as you try to combine cultures, one of the forces that is most prominent is that of toleration which presses the force of relativity as opposed to the force of morality with its more defined limits. What this often does is diminish, rationalize, and make ineffective the power of true ethics because of the loss of respect. People ask whose values should we follow and thereby diminish the fact that there are fundamental values. To me the fundamental values are the Golden Rule, the common good, and the goal of the enlightenment of man that he may understand conscience and both its parts of obligation and compassion. It is in effect the search for the judgment criteria by which each individual values his personal dignity. The problem that the current environment provides is that the ethics groups with which we work and of which we are a part are often but individualized shotgun pellets. They go in more diverse directions with noise, but do not travel any distance. Therefore they are not effective in hitting a much more distant target of creating a true power for integrity. Only if we find catalysts both in ideas and in the realism of combining the efforts of organizations can we truly be like a rifle bullet that has the intelligence to look at the target that we need to strike. The goal must be the capacity to have integrity as a vehicle that helps eliminate corruption and terrorism to allow a better world and an advancement of civilization.

Where many of these thoughts may be noble, clear thoughts of the mind, the problem is how we implement them in the reality of the complex ideas in the realms of the powers of economics, politics, and culture. To focus on the fact that culture is the ultimate goal because it is the peer pressure of the culture that brings about change is a necessary fundamental understanding. It is why rather than studying the highly technical aspects of ethics choices and theory, which may be irrelevant to the reality of where the world is headed, we must study the very nature of man and try to impact the values that our children hold so that each generation can come closer together on common values from their own cultures. Studying the rules of physics of atoms in quantum mechanics is totally different from studying the rules of relativity when you need to address questions of the universe. Many times our study of ethics looks on small issues when we must focus on the big picture. This is a critical point that is increasingly lost in our educational institutions. The future is not so much a battle between cultures as it is going to be determined by a battle within cultures. You are a group of people most knowledgeable in these problems because as the premier consulting engineers of the world you deal globally, and you understand the nature of these forces. It is why your efforts to develop concepts that change the nature of culture within corporations by changing the peer pressure between corporations can have such impact globally over time if it is understood and introduced. I know that often there is a frustration that the constituency of integrity and ethics seems to have little power within the mercenary global economic system. But the age of culture is now evolving. The '60s and '70s not only changed the dynamics of economics in the '80s and '90s, but the next twenty years and beyond. Because of these changes and the emergence of terrorism and corruption, it will increasingly be the battleground of the intellectual thought. You do not fight bad ideas with a vacuum of ideas; you must develop constructive ones to compete. The outcome will depend not upon the power of ethics, but whose judgment of values is truly implemented. So there has to be a constituency that demands that the Golden Rule, the anti-hypocrisy rule as I often refer to it, is at the fundamental core of thought.

We now are in some of the final stages of an era where economic corruption in all nations is emerging as a serious problem. It is in different forms, but it is the nature of the evolution of current business. Political terrorism feeds upon that corruption and has many similar cultural causes. The question will be in this cultural era whether conscience or convenience dominates. It's not within singular organizations or with one set of parents teaching their kids the proper values. For every corporation works in a global marketplace and every child has to work in combination within a culture of its business or within society. It is going to be a choice between each of us as parents and as individuals how we unify a set of concepts to provide the basic dignity of man and the sense of honor that must be at his core, and then instill these actions in our children, not only by what we teach but also by our actions. We should not try to tell others what to do, but lead them by the example of our own enlightenment and the benefits provided. Enough peer pressure creates the law and enforcement that has power because of the support.

I use the word honor differently than I do the thoughts of integrity and ethics and even conscience. They are to me ideas of the mind that are more pure. The world is much more affected by the word honor than integrity because it is ultimately an action term of warriors. Honor is a term that connotes not only believing in certain fundamental concepts but also more importantly being a person of action to implement them not only out of self-respect but also of obligation. It is a cultural term of reality.

This is a distinction that I make because we are emerging in a battle to be fought between forces that I would call honor and the forces of corruption, which are to me dishonor. We must think not terms of law, but terms that unify cultures. The Chinese culture was built in large part from a history of the Duke of Zhou and his sense of honor. My father was a man of absolute honor, and it mattered far more to him than material gain. It was not a product of formal education as much as life experience. The stability of societies and the support for their political thought will increasingly be impacted by these values. And what we need, being a group of dedicated believers is a concept that unifies a set of ideas that can help these concepts move forward. We need an intellectual foundation that is not based upon relativism or absolute toleration but is instead founded upon a set of concepts of the dignity of man involving obligations of men to each other and to a concept of honor to enforce it beyond just law and legalism. That is the core of the essence of *The Language of Conscience*.

It is far more greatly broadened by the new book *Instilling Values in Transcending Generations*. I am distributing a set of triangles, both in English and in Chinese, that will give you some insight as to the thought process that has been developed to try and move forward on some of these concepts. Some people call it the Rosetta Stone of Cultures, but others look upon it more appropriately as a perspective for enhancing conscience. What has been important in this effort is that it did not start as an effort to teach people ethics. The first books were written primarily to help explain character to three groups with whom I most actively worked in Texas. In the modern times I felt they were forgetting that it is not what you do, or even how well you do it, but why you do it that is the critical issue. That process has gradually involved a number of people. With Dr. Felipe Ochoa, your Chairman, I have gone over the years to witness the ethics compacts drawn by organizations in Latin

America on the principles for which you have stood. You are a sterling example of trying to do something for the right reasons. The Ethics Officer Association in the United States, which has many of the Fortune 500 ethics officers, has done much of the same work to try and define cultures within corporations. But my point has been that each of these is but a pellet in the shotgun blast lessening the ability to have an impact. That is why I was extremely happy to see *The Language of Conscience* and the summary of your work published by the Press of the Central Party School of the Communist Party. Their action in publishing it as the first Western book with their Press insignia says much about their interest in fighting corruption. Yesterday several of us, including your Chairman, had the opportunity to visit with the School at a seminar on how to teach leadership for a culture of ethics and service, and we learned of their concepts for a Harmonious Society which included many of our common values. We are beginning to form a nucleus of a catalyst for the power of honor beyond just the thoughts of integrity and ethics. The Central Party School is one of the most powerful think tanks in the world because of its impact upon China. Because of Chinese culture they understand the power of culture itself and what it ultimately means to a civilization. While only time will determine whether any efforts are successful, the ability for you, them, and other ethics organizations to build relationships and work together is absolutely critical because it gives a power to the ideas of integrity which are defended through the warrior sense of honor. These books are but ideas that I have tried to compile to give insights from history that could be studied and better developed within differing civilizations. They help to define the issue of cultural ethics, the fundamental values of the Golden Rule, the common good, the rule of law and the right to property, and the promotion of conscience that are necessary to civilization. They have to be taught to the next generation. That requires a new leadership and engagement because now our battle is often to define ethics, often by what values, and to battle for the promotion of ethics. The engagement must be beyond these issues, and the discussion not just of fundamental values, but the responsibilities of educational institutions globally to recognize and teach the obligations of men within society.

The ultimate goal, if I had one, was to help initiate with you and many others a unification of groups that cared about developing these concepts enough not only to study them, but to teach them, and in teaching them, to put them into the realm of world competition for ideas. The values of the concept of integrity to the individual are no different than the power of competition to benefit the individual, which was a fundamental driver of the emergence of market economic systems. It takes years to have effect, but thoughts must be planted to grow. These are not my ideas or any of yours individually; they are the ideas cumulatively of the positive movement of civilization that will need rediscovering for their importance. We individually are insignificant, but cumulatively we can do a great deal to develop them not only through these organizations but also through universities in our home countries. How you think determines what you think if you want a society of integrity, and values should determine how you think. That is the essence of those triangles. It is the essence of the critical decisions that will determine much of the future world's relationships between cultures, and I think it is why you are here today. You would not be spending your time in Beijing at an Integrity Task Force meeting if it did not matter deeply to you.

Thank you again for your contributions and allowing me to use them. I hope that these books and the cross–introductions to other organizations they provide will be of benefit to you in your efforts.

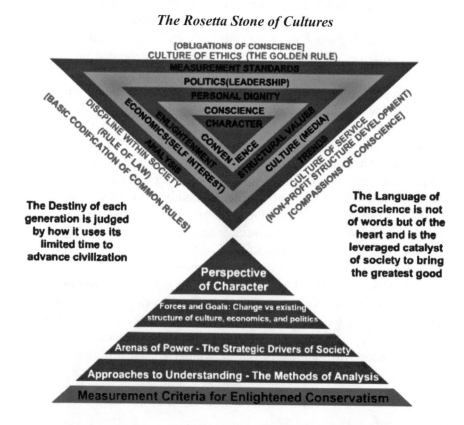

The Rosetta Stone of Cultures

Or said in another way:

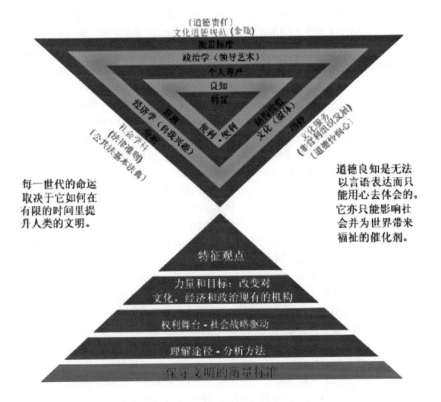

On Helpful Insights to
The Triangles of Enlightened Conservatism

Conscience is the root of all true courage,
if a man would be brave let him obey his conscience.
— James Freeman Clark

The Ultimate Three Areas of Measurement

In choosing the three methods to measure achievement in a society under enlightened conservatism, it was appropriate to look at three cultures as representative of critical levels of development. They are related but independent in many ways. They reflect the development of a sense of commitment to fellow men, a sense of obligation to fellow men, and a sense of caring or love toward other men.

The first is the level of discipline in society that is represented by the rule of law, which is the common basis of commitment. Its level of development toward justice and method of enforcement give a good insight to how society as a whole views common relationships. The second goes beyond obligation to the concept of respect, which is more personal, but builds peer pressure. We may call it ethics as put forth by the Golden Rule or the Silver Rule, but it really is a definition of our peer respect for another's personal dignity. It goes beyond the strict rule of law to the levels of courtesy and personal respect. It is the moral obligation we feel to others and accept from them. The final measurement is the culture of service that is shown both individually and as a group through peer pressure. It is the culture of service where we demonstrate our concern and our compassion for others through our service on behalf of others and not just ourselves. It is best judged by nonprofit obligations or undertakings promoted by the common good when society begins to solve its own problems beyond government by taking more responsibility. Each level has both personal or group considerations, but the evolution of a method of thought grows as you move from obligation to respect and then to compassion. Since all three support each other, you cannot concentrate on one without looking at the support of the others or you lose balance. All these tie back to the sense of individual responsibility or character, which is the perspective at the start. It is a bottom-up and top-down consistency that helps originate thought on the decision in the critical areas in the center.

The Best Use of the Triangles

The most strategic way to think through problems is to divide them into smaller parts and find what is relevant and of the greatest priority. Using the triangles as a tool to train our minds not to forget how other critical parts may enter into the equation uses it as a checklist of reminders. Beyond that it is a good vehicle for response to opposing argument to be sure you not only have arranged your arguments properly but also have seen the implications beyond the debate of opposing arguments. It also keeps you focused. It is very easy to get misled in arguments of intensity if you do not have something that brings you back to focus. They are simple training tools or vehicles for the division of thought at depth, but in either case they symbolize not just a concept but also a process of thought.

The triangles were never intended to be a highly sophisticated or complex decision matrix. What the two parts were designed to do is simply take the vast majority of ideas that we have talked about in other segments of the books and put them in manageable categories. It is much like taking society and comparing it to an art museum. In one part you have the delicate classic art of Rembrandt and Franz Hals, in another the modern art of Picasso, and in another the impressionism of Monet. Society, like art, tends to be such that though the styles coexist, certain ones dominate in different eras of time. Economics, politics, and media/culture, as we have seen, are strategic drivers of society. While they are totally inter-related, each can be one that has significant impact or dominance at a particular period. So it becomes important to take ideas and place them in the proper parts of the museum and then to understand how the different parts of the museum fit together. The impressionism of Monet, for example, came as a distinct trend, different from the fine detail that preceded it. For what Monet concentrated on were not the individual items in great detail, but instead was the scene—the impact that the weather, such as the ice and the wind or the sunlight, conveyed upon the scene as a whole. The items were much more generic, but the power of the painting came from the creation of the impact of the environment.

Such is about to be the case of the power of culture. There are times when economic and political institutions stand alone and are the defined view, but in certain times of turmoil and change, the power of external forces dominate the moment.

One of America's great problems is maintaining its competitiveness. We are falling behind in our technical infrastructure, not because of our market system and its competitiveness but because of our restriction of it by politics. We have learned to use political influence and legal practice to build structural impasses to change because of entrenched economic interests. This failure of adaptability, which can be enhanced by protectionism, is going to be America's greatest challenge. Partisanship only enhances this hardening of structure and greatly reduces the needed adaptability for competitiveness. Similarly, our culture increasingly values entertainment for its vision of success—being a great hip-hop artist or basketball star is far more glamorous than being an engineer or scientist. Law that is more conducive to reorganizing wealth than its creation is looked at as a way to wealth as well. But lawyers study what went wrong in business by studying case law of the problems. They often see law and legislation that they help create from the position of protection, which is important. But they seldom look to the other consequences in the longer term of the nation's competitive position. That did not matter so much in the past when we had a great margin of capital, but in the future competitive world it is critical.

What will bring change is the eventual dissatisfaction of people as a whole when their personal dignity or concern with their own and their children's future takes effect and demands change. The question is how such a change will take place when the political parties are so entrenched, and it takes such huge sums to bring an idea forward in an environment where negative politics, individualized candidates, and party structure dominate. I think there will be an evolution of the Internet. Already, many are moving to it for shopping, entertainment, and an ever-increasing array of information. Blogging is in its infancy; both parties and candidates will have to pay more attention to it as the population becomes familiar with it. But more importantly, everyone does not have to be on the Internet. For the Internet can equally be an excellent vehicle for the development and conveyance of ideas of change. The problem is that much information presently is biased, superficial, and specific. What is needed are a few strong centers of thought on an organized pattern that provide a strong foundation for adaptability to problems and a common way to begin to address them. This can either be from an individual's personal convenience needs or from the conscience perspective of character that we have discussed. Both types of sites will originate and become influential. The triangles are no more than a beginning attempt to find a common method of analysis. Eventually ideas will change the current structure. The key will be which ideas get the most exposure for what reasons. But the Internet gives thinkers a greater opportunity than they have in the current structure to bring forth new ideas and creativity. They can be synthesizers of many different thoughts, but they will need a common pattern of thought just as they need a common language, which can be translated and has to have a structure. The language of conscience concept does nothing more than try to advance that format from the perspective of character.

Powerful emerging nations like China and India will have the same considerations, only in different formats. Eventually, it will be perceived that the world is often different than it appears. The largest living organism is supposedly a grove of trees that was always perceived to be a collection of separate trees, which instead were connected and had simply been an expansion. Humanity is not a lot unlike that grove of trees. We look upon ourselves as separate, in different groups, but with communication and transportation, a medical virus or a computer virus can effect us all. Environmental problems, terrorism or corruption can spread easily. Change will take place, and the issue will be whether we can find a more acceptable method to discuss it, a more binding conscience with the

Golden Rule to accept sacrifice, and a more positive way to think about solving problems by addressing them and not blaming others. Networks and blogging will allow the people to affect the structure as enlightenment evolves to its next stage. The issue is what will drive the thought of the culture they try to put into place both nationally and globally.

When we talk of a culture of conscience being necessary, it is important to understand that it would be naïve to believe that you could ever accomplish total conscience or anything near it. The very nature of man, the nature of competition, and the nature of power will always make it fortunate for the culture to be one that is generally one of conscience. Therefore the peer pressure exerted by the culture for conscience and ethics is such that it makes the culture a powerful part of putting conscience into power. The issue is not one of morality alone. It is almost completely an issue of the power of morality and how to develop and use that power in order to exert a peer pressure and a structure that rewards integrity and punishes corruption.

The triangles do no more than start by focusing on the absolutely essential perspective of character that has to be recognized and understood by many different institutions as a common goal. In setting the goals, you need to categorize related ideas into the forces of enlightenment, the forces of cultural values. How you balance them to an acceptable consequence of personal dignity is essential for men to truly have the prosperity of life. There are certain basic rights and freedoms including the benefits of individual work and appropriate opportunity that must be present and improving. Oftentimes a society cannot provide all these things at once and immediately, but it is the trend and direction upon which it is headed that can be the point of the most significant focus. America may have a high standard of living, but it may grow slowly. Developing nations may have a low standard but feel a significant rise. It is not the absolute but the dejection and intensity that often affect satisfaction. Concepts such as these factor into understanding the use of the triangles. But perhaps the most significant use is keeping focused on the message. In media interviews there are only a half dozen or so structures of questions an interviewer can ask. The experts teach you how to recognize them and usually answer with something that bridges back to your core message, so you talk about it on the air rather than the controversial issues. The triangles, with conscience as a core and a framework in which to categorize the core of a question, are an ideal bridge to discuss conscience.

Using the Triangles as a Catalyst

A good example of how the triangles can be used in analyzing issues would be the critical issue of retirement planning and how demographics become complicated. As we discussed, analysis and trends give a fairly clear understanding of the fact that traditional sources of retirement are going to be challenged as private pensions and government assistance are heavily pressured by the demographic change. When we go to economics, we see the hard choices shown if the government maintains support in taxes and cuts spending or the dangers of borrowing. So the belief is that benefits will have to be reduced. However, if you look at the political part of the triangle, you realize that older people vote and younger people often do not vote. The same demographics are going to have them increasing much faster in numbers with time to be very organized and focused upon their same interest. So while it appears that economical benefits have to be reduced, the politics may make it difficult or unlikely. If over 30% of the people are over 65 and less than 10% are under thirty then it will have politicians' attention. That issue alone could change the nature of government because it has such a huge impact upon its finances. It is the type of issue that needs to be addressed early with time to allow enough supplemental income saved that visionary wisdom of the common good, not personal desperation and emotion, drive national policies and thereby save national strength and principles.

One of the best uses for the triangles has been to pull together arguments in a strategic manner. I have often used the examples of a shotgun blast with many pellets going in different directions with a lot of noise compared to a carefully aimed rifle bullet at a defined target.

The triangles are an excellent way to combine all the pellets into the bullet. In *The Language of Conscience* we had many examples of public policy studies. The Texas Arts Plans in particular used the concept of a leveraged catalyst. Here you found an approach, which looked to accomplishing what you were undertaking with minimal cost—we created arts councils with the funding that put on events, which generated sales tax for the state that effectively returned the original funding and commissioned economic studies to show that the amount generated was more than the cost making the benefit free. How money is spent matters, and anticipating other benefits and potential costs are equally necessary in packaging an argument for politics or evaluating the feasibility economically. America must remain competitive so it must remain creative and public policy encourages or discourages that environment by taxes and regulatory burden. A culture of individual responsibility requires a culture of opportunity.

All the triangles do is provide the checklist of concerns so that you can find your strongest argument and tie the other parts together. It simply lets you take a number of smaller points and package them together in a more thoughtful and supportive manner. As I have noted, people are seldom for or against you but for themselves, and the arguments that most affect them should be found in the broader categories presented in the sections of the triangles.

Enlightenment

Enlightenment is really an evolution of civilization aided by the concepts of education and opportunity with technology as a driving tool. I connect them because education without opportunity has limited impact. But the two concepts together spread a concept of enlightenment because they allow growth economically and culturally. One of the people from whom I learned a great deal in life was Dr. George Kosmetsky who founded many companies, but the IC2 (Institute for Constructive Capitalism) was most on point. Enlightenment as a goal embodies new technology, and he probably said it best in singling out what has the greatest economic impact:

Today's generation must understand that its legacy is to chart its own course. This generation must understand and accept that there is no existing road map for its future—and embrace the responsibility to develop its own. The generational resource is science and technology, which needs to be nurtured and better understood. Effective science and technology commercialization is the key to political and economic power—and to individual quality of life. How this generation manages and utilizes this resource will determine the degree to which it is possible to achieve shared prosperity at home and abroad.

The Chinese have a proverb: The hundred rivers converge at the sea, which recognizes that peoples of different virtues and talents flow together to make up the whole of a society. If the common principles are positive ones, it is a better society. So the values of which we speak in culture are the unifying ones that tend to bring out the best in us through recognizing our obligation to each other. If not, the dirty and impure waters can dominate the nature of the combined waters.

If individual character is lost, the individual looks to others—principally government—to solve his needs more easily. That leads us to the internal destruction of democracies such as Athens as described by the Scottish philosopher and historian Professor Alexander (circa 1787) who noted:

> *A democracy cannot exist as a permanent form of government.*
> *It can exist only until the voters discover that they can vote*
> *themselves largesse from the public treasury. From that moment*
> *on the majority always votes for the candidates promising the*
> *most benefits from the public treasury, with the result that a*
> *democracy always collapses over loose fiscal policy, (which is)*
> *always followed by a dictatorship.*

Through eras and different societies, the same natural truths determine fate over time but are often ignored in the short-term when convenience controls power. For a democracy to survive or be created, the individual responsibility must be maintained from generation to generation. It is not a form of government as much as a value system.

Through eras and different societies, the same natural truths determine fate over time but are often ignored in the short-term when convenience controls power. For a democracy to survive or be created, the individual responsibility must be maintained from generation to generation. It is not a form of government as much as a value system.

Economics

Economics is now dominated by the market economy in the world although there are rising questions as to its effectiveness in areas where it is not properly administered. Personally, I believe that market systems provide the mechanism that does the most good for the most people in the long run. Economic freedom requires and is judged by issues such as the rule of law, the protection of property, the ability to contract effectively, low taxes, free trade, limited regulation, an independent monetary system, and the related disciplines required for effectiveness including business ethics to reduce corruption. These enhance the performance of the economy and increase the common standard of living, but they form a business culture together and are not individual functions. It is important because it affects not only growth, but also private investment, which is critical. Markets must have a concern for morality. Markets only succeed when they have efficient competition, and the level of that competition is determined by the moral nature of the market free of inside information, corruption or other inefficiencies. The growth of a society comes from the creation of wealth not its distribution. As Winston Churchill noted, "We contend that for a nation to try to tax itself into prosperity is like a man standing in a bucket and trying to lift himself by the handle."

Similarly, markets work very closely with politics. Government sets the stage for the degree of opportunity within the system by its regulatory effect on competition. Regulation favors big business over free enterprise—small business. Imbalances within economics, such as no strong middle class, have tremendous impact upon the nature of politics, particularly if you have a democracy. If you have a great disparity in wealth, you set the stage in politics for change. There is a place for government regulation to avoid fraud, inspire fairness, and guarantee the opportunity but not the result. Taxation raises money for the government budget, which is the contract between the people and the government. Its size matters, its philosophy matters, and how revenues are raised matters. These are key in every civilization. In Latin America, also at the Zocolo or Main Square in Mexico City, the Temple Mayor site of their civilization is worthy of study. The Eagle and Jaguar, warriors who collect taxes, saw some prosperous villages monthly and poor ones annually. The point being that natural laws not government edicts dominate in the end.

Unity Under a Rule of Law

Secondly, you need to look at trends over time, not snapshots at any one time. The influence of a culture is gradual as the people learn to value the changes. The reason that study is important is that it keeps focus on critical points. Corporate governance, for example, can be affected more quickly, but children learning character look to transcending generations.

The rule of law gives a fairness that protects investment, which encourages the growth of capital essential to the system. It is the reduced risk that spurs the capital investment, which increases the standard of living through new technology. Each of us has an individual interest in maintaining fairness in society. So we must make an affirmative effort for the principle even if the individual issue does not affect us. Perhaps no one said it better than Sir Thomas More when he noted, "What are we to do if those chasing after devils decide to chase after us?" Everyone's rights and dignity depend on the support and the values of others.

If you are not ruled by a set of principles, you are ruled by men or a man. This rule can often evolve to a form of tyranny because of the nature of convenience. Values are what give laws not only their justice, but also their legitimacy.

A culture of ethics is essential because it keeps self-interest from becoming greed. It supports middle-class opportunity rather than class division and is in effect the test of the Golden Rule. It also grows a middle class, which people have a vested interest in the stability of society.

Compassion

In understanding this highest culture you also validate the other components of the triangles. To reach the culture you must encourage individual responsibility and conscience. Once the culture is achieved it then helps maintain political order and stability as well as aid growth of commerce. In economics free markets require that integrity exist for their best performance by competition. This gives the ultimate opportunity to achieve in the tradition of Rambam and is necessary for the ultimate personal dignity. Because of the nature of the world, there will never be perfection and the parts will always have frictions, but the power of culture and ideas that are its force help seek harmony and balance. The more that is done by each generation to move the world to the appreciation of this conscience, the more it will be attained. Some may do it in the name of religion, others in the name of philosophy, and others because it is not only right but the source of great power. But each, in his own way, sees harmony in society through the lens of conscience as opposed to convenience and will ultimately realize that beyond obligation to the group of fellow men, compassion is the ultimate goal. However, it also is seen that you can never lose sight of the fact that obligation and the nature of the power of the building blocks of society are critical to the creation and maintenance of this culture of service and compassion. It does not arise as a Utopia on its own, but requires that we shape the building blocks that are the support of its pyramid.

Such is the logic and purpose of the triangles. They help you see your ultimate goal of compassion, but also help you understand that compassion does not exist alone, but is a final product of forces. You must both engineer back from the goal, and at the same time build back from the bottom. The goal of the triangles is to give a perspective from the top down as well as the bottom up so policies and logic can be coordinated. In life the weak are often ruled by the strong, and the strong are directed by the intelligent. The secret is for the intelligent to have the wisdom of the value of conscience and not the knowledge of the power of convenience. All any man can do is his best doing what he can for the right reasons, which includes maximizing his effect by increasing his knowledge and perspective. Then he must enter teamwork with others to accomplish a common end. Teams are not groups of great individual talents but are groupings of coordinated participants focused on a common goal. The triangles become the common game plan of discussion to help build a unity of understanding. Teamwork, and leadership within it, is basically a culture based on trust, and it leverages the individual effort dramatically. Unity is power.

Acknowledgements

There are innumerable people and organizations to whom I owe substantial gratitude for their assistance in not only formulating, editing, and producing this book and its predecessors, but also most importantly for giving the support and dedication for its completion. Mrs. Sylvia Odenwald, the editor and chief, and her assistants, Mrs. Carol Austin and Ms. Edonna Dunavan, spent innumerable hours in the process. I need to especially thank my assistants for the book, Mrs. Judy Stockton and Mrs. Sharon Jasinski, for their significant efforts and George and Robyn Pond and Usman Ghani for their help. Grateful appreciation goes to my family and the Hopkins, Schreiner, Lockart, Tredennick, Windham, Shivers, Teeple, Roan, and other families, who gave not only ideas but also efforts such as the YO Gatherings that brought our generations together to help set our values.

Special thanks to the Lee Family, particularly Vivian Lee and her Foundation, CHARC, who with Ted Li helped to serve as the bridge with the Chinese section of the book. And her sister, Vicky Lee, has supported *The Language of Conscience* project from its inception. Thanks also to Mr. Mike Masson, Mr. Roger Ream, Congressman Phil Crane, and The Fund for American Studies for their support. Mr. Sherm Wolfe contributed significantly to the thoughts on non-investor owned economic options. A special thanks to Mr. Paul Koether and his wife, Natalie (now deceased), for their efforts to teach me the intricacies of financial markets.

The conversion of the concepts of the book into a reality could only occur with the support of two organizations that have begun collaboration to build a bridge between cultures based on ethics. The Texas Lyceum, with its Chairman Walter Tomlinson, President Jordan Cowman, and Vice Presidents Dougal Cameron and David Spencer, has served as a base of American interest. But the ideas within belong to a generation of Texans, primarily the Lyceum's founding directors and those that have carried on concepts and have helped develop them at significant sacrifice ever since. While I may have chronicled concepts, it is the observations, criticisms, and ideas of others that have matured the thoughts.

The Central Party School of the Communist Party of China has been a key to the book's completion, not just in its interest in the ideals and contribution of materials but the sincere interest of its scholars to examine them. In a time that ideas of substance have limited exposure to study, the opportunity to discuss them was a driving force. A special thanks is due to Dr. Wang Weiguang for his leadership and allowing his works to be included, to Mr. Li Yuanchao, the Director of the Press of the Central Party School, and the Press itself for allowing its previous works to be used, to Mr. Zheng Bijiang for allowing abridgment and inclusion of his writings on China's Peaceful Rise, to Professor Jia for her contribution, and to Mr. Chen Guoji and Mr. Lao Zhongyi for their efforts in the Collaboration Agreement with the Texas Lyceum. Books are about ideas, but ideas take people to express them and distribute them. It is not the people, but the ideas and values they represent, that truly affect history. The framework of each generation pushes them forth. These are the uncommon men I described in transcending generations. Many organizations of character have supported this effort and to them I give my thanks as well as to the men of history whose thoughts I could synthesize.

In Memoriam

On February 9, 2005, Spc. Clinton R. Gertson was killed by sniper fire in the city of Mosul, Iraq while serving with the Army's 24th Infantry Regiment. He was a Purple Heart recipient who had been wounded in a suicide bombing that killed twenty-two people at an army mess hall in Mosul the previous year. After 9/11 happened, he felt that he needed to join the military to make a difference. He could have returned home in January from his original two-year tour of duty, but he re-enlisted. He returned not just to the Infantry, but to the elite Stryker 24th Brigade, which was on the point of taking battle to the adversary. His father Gayle noted that January 30th was one of Clint's most special days in his short life. (He turned 26 that day, which was the same day they held the elections in Iraq.) His perspective of the war, as he discussed with his father, focused neither on the political debate of justifications nor on the administration of the war. Instead he talked to his father about the little kids who were no different than kids anywhere else in the world. He felt they really needed help to have the type of life and dignity that we often take for granted. As his father mentioned, one of his last conversations emphasized the fact that because of his unit's losses, Clint well noted, *"freedom was not free."*

This book talks about the concept of power in many different forms—political (with its military extension), economic, and, most importantly, cultural power. The core of the book is that it is not what you do or even how well you do it that ultimately is as critical as why you do it. This defines you on the scale of conscience versus convenience both in the eyes of man and your God. Clint may have been a much decorated and highly respected soldier, but in reality he was an all American boy from down the road at Eagle Lake, Texas, who loved to hunt and fish, farm rice, and run cattle. He did what he did in Iraq not just because he was told to, for he volunteered. Instead it was because he recognized the importance of helping a people that did not understand him. He perceived the point that his goal was to let them, as well as their wives and children, have a choice or vote for their future against those who had threatened to kill them if they used that power to gain their dignity of freedom.

Issues become very complicated as they are discussed in the politics of governments, in the high realms of power, and in academic citadels. However, the reality of life is that civilizations move forward to a better world more often by the individual lives of a Clint Gertson who recognizes the ultimate purpose in life is to make a better world for the next generation. Clint was the first-cousin of my daughter-in-law, Tee's wife, Sunny Gertson Dippel. He certainly kept true to the values of a life well lived, even though regrettably short.

About the Author

In 1953, philosopher and intellectual historian Isaiah Berlin wrote in his essay, "The Hedgehog and the Fox," "the Fox knows many things while the Hedgehog knows but one big thing."

Journalists like to identify political leaders as being one or the other. Ronald Reagan was a Hedgehog whose organizing principle was the "big thing" called anti-communism. Bill Clinton was frequently depicted as a man who knew so much that he pursued too much.

The author of this book, my friend of decades, Skipper Dippel (Tieman to those who don't know him) is that most rare of creatures: one who combines the best of the Hedgehog and the Fox. Skipper knows one big thing: conscience must be paramount for a civil society. But he also knows many other things and pursues many ends, often unrelated, but somehow never contradictory.

Skipper is a scholar, a businessman, a lawyer, an activist for many worthy causes, a philanthropist, a politician, a family man, and above all and in the highest sense of the word a "citizen."

One big thing Skipper knows is that everyone has a philosophy whether they know it or not. They may be a Christian or a Moslem, a Republican or a Democrat, a Crip or a Blood, but they have and act on a philosophy. The fundamental question is whether their philosophy is grounded in conscience or "convenience." Does a man or woman seek to discern right and stand by it or do they do what is most convenient no matter the cost to others and their own diminished conscience.

Brenham, Texas, Skipper's lifelong residence, is a small idyllic town on the lush coastal plains of Texas midway between Austin and Houston. When Texans lived mostly in small towns, places like Brenham and Decatur (my home) could produce political powerhouses. Now that most Texans live in four metropolitan areas, with their vaults of political money and media reach, movers and shakers are rarely found in the small towns of Texas. Skipper is an exception.

It is true he has the resources to write big checks and occasionally does. He can also raise a few bucks. But Skipper Dippel has not been a mover in Texas political and civic affairs for a quarter century because of fund raising prowess. He attained and maintained that status because it is widely known and accepted that Skipper acts only on conscience.

He is a true moral force, and I have always been amazed at the power of moral force in a state where might is mightily respected. The late Texas Lt. Gov. Bob Bullock, a man who understood political might better than most, once told me that he found himself perplexed over a piece of legislation that was of no real interest to him, but was critical to many of his friends who were evenly divided for and against. When he heard Skipper opposed the bill he decided to oppose it too (although the two never discussed it personally). Why? Because he assumed it was the "right" thing to do.

To the astonishment of those who knew him in college, Skipper has never run for public office. Nor has he ever really proclaimed a party allegiance. Instead he has worked through a plethora of networks, some formal some not. These have included religious, political, academic, civic, professional, arts, and business organizations. Some he founded, some he led, some he helped lead, some he simply helped shape as a member or even as just an outside friend.

Why? Why not run for office? Why not leave Brenham, strike out for Austin or Houston? Why run a small bank when none doubt he could have run a major bank? Why spend a lifetime enmeshed in organizations and networks that must literally number over 100? First, because he believes this is how and where a free people can be truly effective. He believes it is where conscience can at least have its day in court.

Second, he believes in the power of history and culture. His history and his culture are the history and culture of Texas. The Texas into which he and I were born is largely vanished. Oil and cattle don't matter much more than Brenham or Decatur. And if nations are fading in importance states like Texas surely are too. But there is still a culture and a history that lives on, there is still a Texas way, and Skipper, the quintessential Texan is determined to see that the best of what that was survives him.

His books are intended as handbooks for those who would lead on the "big thing" of conscience, and on the "many things" that include history, culture, responsibility, accountability, and activism within all of the venues a free society provides. And it is about seeing that the best of Texas survives.

— Scott Bennett, former Public Affairs Editor and Director for *Texas Business* magazine and former editorial writer and nationally distributed columnist for *The Dallas Morning News*, is currently a management and marketing consultant in Dallas.

For more information on this book and
others in the Language of Conscience Series
and additional related information, go to
www.thelanguageofconscience.com